GENERAL (NOW MARSHAL) PÉTAIN

Pétain commanded during the long critical period of the seige of Verdun.

III.

THE LITERARY DIGEST
History of the World War

Compiled from Original and Contemporary Sources: American, British, French, German, and Others

BY

FRANCIS WHITING HALSEY

Author of "The Old New York Frontier," Editor of "Great Epochs in
American History," "Seeing Europe with Famous Authors,"
"Balfour, Viviani, and Joffre, Their Speeches
in America," etc.

IN TEN VOLUMES—ILLUSTRATED

VOLUME III

THE AUTUMN ALLIED OFFENSIVE—THE ASSAULT ON VERDUN—
OPERATIONS ON THE NORTHERN FRONT—THE BATTLE OF
THE SOMME—THE GERMAN RETREAT AND THE
ARRAS AND AISNE BATTLES

July 12, 1915—May 24, 1917

FUNK & WAGNALLS COMPANY
NEW YORK AND LONDON
1919

CONTENTS—VOLUME THREE

ON THE WESTERN FRONT—*Continued*

PAGE

PART VII. THE AUTUMN ALLIED OFFENSIVE

I. BEFORE THE REAL OFFENSIVE BEGAN (July 1, 1915—September 18, 1915) 3

II. THE OFFENSIVE IN THE CHAMPAGNE COUNTRY (September 25, 1915—December 25, 1915) 12

III. THE OFFENSIVE IN ARTOIS AROUND ARRAS, GIVENCHY, LOOS, AND LENS (September 25, 1915—December 15, 1915) . . 25

IV. THE HOHENZOLLERN REDOUBT AND GEN. SIR JOHN FRENCH'S RETIREMENT (October 13, 1915—December 15, 1915) . . 43

V. AIRCRAFT IN THE AUTUMN OFFENSIVE—THE COMING OF THE FOKKER (September 25, 1915—December 15, 1915) . . 59

PART VIII. THE GREAT GERMAN ASSAULT ON VERDUN

I. THE FIRST PHASE: DOUAUMONT AND VAUX AND FORTS WEST OF THE MEUSE—THE COMING OF RUSSIANS TO FRANCE (January 24, 1916—April 30, 1916) 71

II. THE SECOND PHASE: HILL 304, DOUAUMONT AGAIN, AND THE FALL OF FORT VAUX (May 3, 1916—August 30, 1916) . 115

III. THE LATER PHASE: DOUAUMONT AND VAUX RECOVERED—JOFFRE A MARSHAL—AS TO NIVELLE AND PÉTAIN (October 29, 1916 —December 18, 1916) 141

PART IX. ALLIED OPERATIONS IN THE NORTH BEFORE THE SOMME BATTLE BEGAN

I. MONTHS OF WAITING WITH MINOR ENGAGEMENTS—THE INSUR-RECTION IN IRELAND (December 19, 1915—August 10, 1916) 157

II. THE THIRD BATTLE OF YPRES—CANADIAN VALOR AND KITCH-ENER'S DEATH (April 27, 1916—June 29, 1916) . . . 172

CONTENTS—VOLUME THREE

PART X. THE ALLIED DRIVE ON THE SOMME

PAGE

I. The Preparations and the First Fortnight's Fighting (July 1, 1916—July 14, 1916) 191

II. Five Memorable Weeks with Péronne and Bapaume as Objectives—Hindenburg Succeeds Falkenhayn (July 14, 1916—August 22, 1916) 221

III. Guillemont, Combles, and Thiepval—The ''Tank's'' Arrival (September 2, 1916—September 27, 1916) . . . 254

IV. Further Progress Toward Bapaume and Péronne—The Battle for the Ancre Valley (October 1, 1916—January 17, 1917) 288

PART XI. THE GERMAN RETREAT IN THE WEST AND THE NEW ARRAS AND AISNE BATTLES

I. Bapaume, Noyon, and Péronne Abandoned—A Land of Utter Desolation (February 1, 1917—March 21, 1917) . . 317

II. The Battle of Arras, with Vimy Ridge and Lens as the First Phase—Clancy and Genet (April 7, 1917—April 26, 1917) 344

III. Germans, Under Fire, Abandon the Aisne Country—The Battle for Moronvilliers Heights (March, 1917—May 6, 1917) 374

IV. The Battle of Arras, with Fresnoy and Bullecourt as the Second Phase (May 1, 1917—May 29, 1917) 393

ILLUSTRATIONS—VOLUME THREE

FULL PAGES

PAGE

GENERAL (NOW MARSHAL) PÉTAIN . . . *Frontispiece*

AN ALLIED COUNCIL OF WAR AT FRENCH HEADQUARTERS . 2

THE SO-CALLED "TOWER BRIDGE" AT LOOS 31

AFTER THE EXPLOSION OF A MINE . . . . *facing page* 48

VERDUN BEFORE THE WAR 70

BATTERED CASEMATES NEAR FORT VAUX 117

VERDUN AT THE END OF THE WAR 137

GENERAL NIVELLE . . . . *facing page* 144

MARSHAL JOFFRE IN FULL UNIFORM . . . *facing page* 152

IN VERDUN—FIGHTING FIRES CAUSED BY GERMAN SHELLS . 154

HAIG, JOFFRE, AND LLOYD GEORGE AT THE FRONT . . . 156

A BRITISH GUN IN THE SOMME BATTLE 190

BRITISH SOLDIERS HOISTING A SHELL INTO A 15-IN. HOWITZER
facing page 208

A FRENCH ATTACK ON GERMAN TRENCHES ON THE SOMME
facing page 264

A TANK AND ITS PROGENITOR 283

BRITISH SOLDIERS EQUIPPED WITH NEW HELMETS *facing page* 288

THE DESTROYED CASTLE OF COUCY 316

AFTER VIMY RIDGE WAS TAKEN 351

GERMAN PRISONERS CAPTURED ON THE WESTERN FRONT
facing page 360

TEXT ILLUSTRATIONS

A FRENCH SOLDIER WHO WAS HIT BY NINE BULLETS . . 6

GOOSE-STEP AT THE FRONT 9

PROTECTED SHELTERS FOR AMBULANCE WORK 13

A CONCEALED 155-MM. FRENCH GUN 17

A FRENCH GUN CONCEALED FROM THE ENEMY . . . 21

FRENCH TROOPS IN A COMMUNICATING TRENCH 24

A PROTECTED FRENCH TRENCH 27

A BRITISH SOLDIER IN A GAS-MASK 35

ILLUSTRATIONS—VOLUME THREE

PAGE

Emilienne Moreau 36

Ruins of the Hotel de Ville at Arras 37

The Ruins of Arras Cathedral 39

Canadians in British Helmets 45

The Ruined Church of Ablaire-Saint-Nazaire . . 49

French Dog Kennels Behind the Front 52

A Machine-Gun Nest 58

Adolph Pégoud's Monument 63

A German Fokker 67

The Rusting Skeleton of a Burned Zeppelin . . 68

French Shells at Verdun 75

French Reservists on the Way to Verdun . . . 79

A Surgical Dressing-Station 87

French Dugouts Before Verdun 91

Effects of Shell-Fire in Verdun 99

A Ruined Street in Verdun 103

Around Verdun, Near Douaumont 109

Russian Soldiers Arriving at Marseilles 111

A French Cemetery Near the Verdun Battlefield . . 121

Madam Raynal Being Decorated at the Invalides . . 123

General Charles Mangin 128

Mass in a Vault at Fort Douaumont 131

A French Officer's Quarters on the Moselle . . 133

Barbed Wire in a Lorraine Wood 140

French Anti-Barbed-Wire Gun 143

A Protected Ammunition Magazine Behind French Lines 147

A French Officer's Shelter on the Eastern Front . 149

French Trenches on the Meuse 153

British Shells Accumulated in a Storehouse . . 159

A French Trench with a Metal Roof 163

Liberty Hall in Dublin After the Insurrection . . 166

Ruined Buildings in Sackville Street, Dublin . . 167

Post-Office in Dublin After the Insurrection . . 169

Sir Roger Casement 170

Removing Wounded from Vimy Ridge 175

What Remained of Fricourt Village 177

Veterans Among Canadian Troops 179

ILLUSTRATIONS—VOLUME THREE

PAGE

British Troops Moving in a Sunken Road 181

Field-Marshal (Viscount) Kitchener 187

Infantry Resting En Route to the Front 193

British Naval Guns in Land Operations 195

Sighting a British Gun for Action 197

East Indians in Prayer on the Western Front . . 199

Starting French Balloons at the Front 203

A French Soixante-Quinze, or "75" 205

French Dispatch-Bearer's Car 211

Shelters on the Somme 213

A Devastated Town in the Somme Region . . . 217

One of the Largest of French Guns 219

Tractor Hauling an American Gun in France . . 223

Flooded Country on the Somme, Near Péronne . . 225

What Was Left of Chaulnes 229

Hindo-Chinese Labor in France 235

Devastation in Northern France 241

Scene in a Village After it Was Retaken . . . 245

General Eric von Falkenhayn 250

Field-Marshal von Hindenburg 251

A German Trench After Being Bombarded . . . 257

German Huts Near the Meuse 261

A Fire-proof Church in Northern France . . . 265

Parisians Watching a German "Taube" 267

Loos in a Quarter Where a Church Once Stood . . 273

A French 80-mm. Gun 275

A Zeppelin That Fell into a French Forest . . 279

Tanks Going into Action 285

Failure of a Tank to Cross a Trench 287

Captured German Cannon at the Invalides . . . 291

A Shattered German Trench in Northern France . 295

King George in a Devastated Field 299

Giant Searchlight Used in the Defense of Paris . 301

Frontier Trenches in Winter 305

General Count Sixt von Arnim 309

French Motor Battery Going to the Front . . . 312

Respiration-Drill at the Front 313

vii

ILLUSTRATIONS—VOLUME THREE

PAGE

Péronne After the Evacuation by the Germans . . . 325

A Street in Noyon Flooded by the Germans 327

After the Blight of War Had Passed 339

Edith Wharton 341

General Maud'huy in a First-Line Trench 345

Captured British Tank Shown in Berlin 355

Distributing Cigarets at the Front 357

German Dugouts 30 Feet Deep . ., ... 362

German Trenches Under Shell-fire 363

Ruins of a Village in Artois 369

Gun-Screen Behind an Undergrowth 375

On the Yser 378

A French Chapel in a Cellar at Reims 380

A Lookout East of Reims 385

"The Dragon's Cave" 391

A French Scout in a Shell-torn Area 392

A Zeppelin Descending When on Fire 400

MAPS

Champagne and Argonne . . . . . *facing page* 8

A French Offensive in the Autumn of 1915 *facing page* 16

The Battle of Loos 42

Before Verdun Was Attacked 73

The Field of Battle at Verdun 81

Eastern France Around Verdun . . . . *facing page* 88

The Third Battle of Ypres 171

The Anglo-French Offensive on the Somme . *facing page* 200

The Somme Gains and the German Retreat . . . 331

The British Offensive Around Arras in April, 1917

facing page 368

The Fight for Moronvilliers Heights East of Reims—
Germans Trench System Shown . . . *facing page* 392

ON THE WESTERN FRONT

Part VII

THE AUTUMN ALLIED OFFENSIVE

AN ALLIED COUNCIL OF WAR AT FRENCH HEADQUARTERS

BEFORE THE REAL OFFENSIVE BEGAN

July 1, 1915—September 18, 1915

TO a superficial observer Germany's arms, at the end of June, had been everywhere crowned with success. It was true that her original scheme had failed, and that she had been compelled to adopt a plan for which she had small liking. But with patience she had made the change, and the new policy thus far had won success. She had held the Allies in the West with a minimum of men by virtue of an artillery machine to which they could not show an equal, and with fortifications of a strength hitherto unknown. Applying her main force in the East she had won a great battle on the Dunajec river, had driven back Russia, now short of munitions because of negligence and treachery in her own household, had won back Galicia, penetrated into Poland, and had in her grip great fortresses whose cession meant for Russia not only a crushing loss in guns, but an indefinite further retreat—an astonishing retreat it became in August and September. She held tracts of enemy-soil in Poland, Belgium, and France, and had a completely unified command, so that all their strength could be applied to accomplish the purposes of her General Staff. At the same time, Turkey had held back the Allied advance in Gallipoli, and was soon to bring it to a standstill.

Against these successes the Allies had to show the conquest of German colonies, a few miles gained in Italy, the occupation of the end of Gallipoli, a Turkish peninsula, some advances on the Tigris, activities in Egypt, and one or two costly failures on the Western Front. All the military results of the first year of the war ending on August 1 showed in the west in the main German successes. All but a small western fraction of Belgium was still a captive and in process of

3

Germanization. Lille and all northeastern France, between the Oise and the Meuse, were occupied by German troops who had battered down Lille, driven a wedge across the upper Meuse, and had the Woëvre in their hands. Their furthermost battle-front was only thirty miles from Paris. They held their western conquests with a line of trenches through which the Allies in vain had sought to break.

Germany's early disasters in East Prussia had been atoned for at Tannenburg, and Hindenburg, after several failures, with Mackenzen's notable help, had finally secured all western Poland. Austria had blundered at the start, losing the better part of Galicia, but since the opening of the New Year her failures had been redeemed. East Prussia was now inviolate and German armies were hammering at the gates of Riga. With Galicia won back Russian armies had been driven inside their own frontier. The Warsaw triangle had been assailed and Warsaw seemed doomed, so that it looked as if all Poland would soon be in German hands, as indeed it soon was. If Germany had been granted no Sedan in the East, she had at least completely broken the Russian offensive. One sentence could describe the naval position. It was wholly in favor of the Allies. From all known seas German merchantmen and German ships of war had disappeared.

Ever since May, when the Germans at the Dunajec began to roll back the Russians in the East, there had been talk in the press of London, Paris, and Berlin, of a strong Allied aggressive in Flanders and northern France. There was much speculation as to which army would take the initiative. Experts declared that neither ally could hope to gain any permanent victory, because of the perfect network of German trenches that extended for miles back from the front. All through May, June, and July, the Allies waited, while making occasional infantry attacks, or counter-attacks, under cover of artillery fire, in order to test the resistance. No serious attempt was made in those months to put into execution the great lesson learned by the British at Neuve Chapelle, altho early in June there had been some fighting around Souchez and later attacks and counter-attacks were made for possession of the Château Hooge. Trenches, from thirty to two hundred yards apart, now represented the first lines of the opposing armies. Behind the British were second and third lines, with further positions at intervals in the rear. The Germans had as many as these, and something more. The ramifications were endless. Great redoubts, almost flush with the ground, consisting of a labyrinth of trenches and machine-gun stations, studded their front. In natural defensive areas, such as the mining districts of the Pas de Calais, every acre contained a fort. In the fullest sense of the word the German lines in the west were a fortress.

The number of the Allies could only be given approximately. In September French commanded a force little short of a million men out of which from half a million to 600,000 men were combatants. The French line was manned by some two million troops, and there were considerable reserves preparing in the depots. Such numbers gave the Allies a superiority over the enemy, but every atom of that superiority was needed for a successful attack.

Early September saw perfect weather, with the clear, cool days that an east wind brings in northern France. In the evening smoke from little fires of field refuse cloaked the country like a sea-fog. When, early in the month, a general bombardment began along the whole Allied front its purpose was to serve as a screen behind which preparations for an attack could be made. It was violent alike in Lorraine, Champagne, Artois, and again around Ypres. It naturally drew a counter-bombardment. But it was a demonstration rather than an attack. Before the summer ended there had been fighting in which close observers believed they saw the beginnings of a larger offensive. On July 12 French official reports had admitted the loss of the Souchez cemetery, after a furious attack, but at other times spoke of the repulse of the Germans. A German official statement mentioned operations in the St. Mihiel region and French statements referred to violent artillery actions north of the Oise, near Quennevières, and in the Argonne. At Combres, and in the forest of Ailly, on the heights of the Meuse, in the Woëvre region, the French penetrated German lines. Fighting also continued in the Vosges and in Upper

Alsace. Northwest of Altkirch the Germans made a surprize attack and captured one position over a width of 500 yards.

There had been fighting at Hooge at the end of July and the beginning of August, but it had no strategic significance, being only an incident in a struggle with small losses and small gains to which the policy of holding the Ypres salient had committed the British. The Germans had held the château and the Bellewaarde Lake since May. On July 30 the Germans delivered a violent attack, sapped up close to the line, and launched a torrent of liquid fire pumped from machines and ignited in its passage. The combination of artillery bombardment, liquid fire, trench-mortars, and bombs was irresistible. Two companies were nearly blotted out. Germans carried the first line and won the crater. The British fell back to the second line, which ran northwest from the corner of the Zouave Wood. Thereupon the Germans began to attack with shell the region behind the British front, and turned the Zouave Wood into a death-trap.

© AMERICAN PRESS ASSOCIATION.

A FRENCH SOLDIER WHO HAD BEEN HIT BY NINE BULLETS

A counter-attack was set for August 9. Over a horrible no-man's-land, strewn with barbed wire-entanglements and the bodies of unburied dead, British infantry swept up to the fringe of their own shell-fire. The gunners then lengthened their range, men poured into the German trenches, and with bayonet and bomb cleared out the Germans. Two hundred ensconced in a pit of death died to a man. The attack then swept beyond the crater, and carried the ruins of stables. Throughout that long day the bombardment continued, the British losses increasing till they reached before nightfall a total of nearly 2,000. Presently the fighting died away, and the opposing lines returned to their normal condition of intermittent artillery fire. The British had restored the Hooge part of this front, which had been left in a precarious state by the German success of July 30, to as good condition as possible. The new army had won its spurs, but at heavy cost.

During August an offensive occurred in Alsace. Operations southwest of Münster were carried out with definite plan. They were directed on the approaches to Sondernach and Metzeral, and thence on the villages themselves. Münster is the meeting-point of two valleys, one running toward the Schulcht, the other toward Metzeral. The Fecht Valley and the Kleinthal meet in the town and pass through it. The Fecht then continues its course to the northwest. The railway from Münster to Colmar follows it closely for six miles, and then turning to the right, reaches Colmar. If, on leaving Münster, instead of following the Fecht Valley, one turned to the left, after a steep climb through pine woods, he would reach the forest of Kubelberg. East of it were the Baren Kopf and the Linge Kopf. On these spurs during August there was hard fighting, the Bavarian losses being heavy.

In this district artillery duels for a long time were continuous. French 6-inch and German 8-inch guns were fired with great regularity. On August 4 and 6 some 40,000 shells of all calibers fell on French trenches and on shelters and communication trenches, almost entirely destroying them. The losses were considerable, and included stretcher-bearers and telephonists as well as fighting units. On August 17 the French resumed their progress. Their first attack made them masters of a part of the Schratzmaennele, the summit of which they occupied on August 22. After a month of hard fighting the objective at which they aimed was attained. The Germans, who had opposed to them no less than seven brigades, had for the moment ceased to dispute the ground. From the summit of the Schratzmaennele Chasseurs could look down on the valley of Münster and the plain of Alsace.

German troops early in the season gained possession in eastern France of La Fille Morte [1] and the Allies had left in their hands 64 officers and more than 3,400 men, 2 mountain- and 2 revolver-cannon, 34 machine-guns, 51 mine-throwers, 5 bronze mortars, and a large amount of ammunition, weapons, and tools. German reports said that 2,000 dead Frenchmen covered the battlefield and were buried by German troops the next day. In Argonne battles, from June 20 to July 13, prisoners taken by the Germans numbered 116 officers and over 7,000 men. More than 4,000 dead were counted, and the number of wounded was estimated at from 5,000 to 6,000. The total French losses in this period were said by the Germans to amount to from 16,000 to 17,000. [2]

Early in September the German Crown Prince, after fifteen days of Allied artillery fire, made an attempt to break through the French lines in the Argonne. In a drive which aimed to loosen the French salient around Verdun, Berlin claimed that the Germans took trenches over a front of one and one-quarter miles, and to a depth of from 300 to 500 meters, captured 2,000 prisoners, 48 machine-guns, and 64 mine-throwers. The attack was supported by artillery. After guns had prepared the way, infantry charged. Among the works taken was the important position of Marie Thérèse. Paris said the Germans renewed their attacks with ferocity, but that, with the exception of a trench section east of Laon de Binarille, the French lines held. This was the second effort of the Kaiser's heir to win a victory in this region within three months and, altho on each occasion he gained ground, he was apparently as far from his objective as he was on previous occasions. His offensive movement did not modify the situation in the Argonne.

The Crown Prince's army, after the whole season's several attempts to break through the Allied lines, lost up-

---

[1] Local name for a hillock, the highest point of the Haute Chevauchée.

[2] German Great Headquarters report as printed in the *Nord Deutsche Allgemeine Zeitung*.

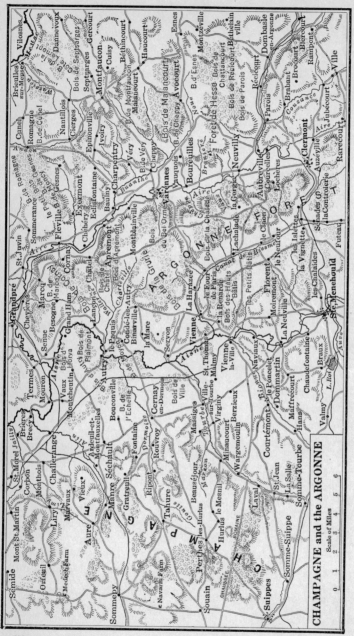

CHAMPAGNE and the ARGONNE

Scale of Miles

0 1 2 3 4 5 6

ward of 100,000 men, one corps alone losing 40,000 from the ranks in September—obviously an exaggeration. A dispatch to the Central News from northern France at the same time gave a sensational report, said to be from a German source, *via* Rotterdam, that the Crown Prince was suffering from mental aberration, the result of the worries of the campaign. The Crown Prince was known not to have spared himself in his attempts to strike a decisive blow. Prisoners

GOOSE-STEP AT THE FRONT
In the doorway are the German Crown Prince and the King of Saxony

said he did not sleep for three days during the September offensive.

The only major action during the midsummer months was this assault of the Crown Prince in the Argonne, a resolute offensive movement, tho unsuccessful. The heir of the Hohenzollerns had been blamed for much that happened at the Battle of the Marne, and his reputation in his own country had suffered. For more than eight months, with a small army, he had been stationed in the Argonne, engaged in forest warfare barren of results. The rival trenches in this region had stood at the end of May not very far from where they stood at the beginning of October, 1914. It was necessary to do something in Napoleon's phrase, *pour chauffer la Gloire,* for the discredited military position of the heir-apparent was repugnant to German ideas of successful statecraft. Accordingly he had received reinforcements. He had had the Sixteenth Corps of Lorraine, and now received from von Strantz's army of Metz several divisions of the Württemberg Landwehr. In all, perhaps he had 50,000 men.

The Crown Prince's attacks had begun on June 20. Between then and July 2 four attacks were delivered against the angle formed by the French lines and the Vienna-Binarville road. Much use was made of asphyxiating shells, but the results were inconsiderable, the total gain being a few hundred yards. On July 7 he flung his main strength against the French right in the neighborhood of the eastern ridge, called the Haute Chevauchée. After a violent artillery bombardment, two divisions of the Sixteenth Corps were hurled against the French between Fontaine Madame and the highest point of the Haute Chevauchée. This position was carried, and the Germans advanced their center and left behind a space of nearly a mile. On the 14th the French counter-attacked at the other side of the forest, where they gained some ground both in the wood of La Gruie and beyond it to the west toward the village of Servon. After that the fighting languished. The Crown Prince was pushed back from the Haute Chevauchée or La Fille Morte. The total result of a month's struggle was a German gain of an average of 400 yards on their Argonne front. The casualties on both sides were probably much the same. Last of the news items from the front before the great offensive began was one of September 18, saying French artillery had severed at St. Mihiel the "great bridge" across the Meuse, besides a bridge of boats and three foot-bridges. The German forces at this salient had thus lost a large part of their means of communication with the district on the western bank of the Meuse where they had held a foothold since September 26, 1914.

The unremitting French artillery attack that occurred in the September Champagne drive had been made possible by equally unremitting French efforts in the production of projectiles in factories transformed by an equipment of American machine-tools and which had been working regularly twenty-four hours a day. One of these great establishments near Paris made more than 5,000 shells every day, not to mention a number of aeroplane motors. Before the war these works had produced annually 600 automobiles. After the Battle of the Marne, when France realized the real nature of the war and her lack of shells and heavy guns, she set to work at once to supply her deficiencies. Every factory which could be turned to the purpose was utilized. Every scrap of talent in the nation was called upon. Local committees were formed everywhere to organize the effort. The result was that, early in the New Year, France had multiplied her material by six, and was in the way to multiply it by nine.[3]

[3] Principal Sources: "Nelson's History of the War," by John Buchan; The *Times*, London; The *Times*, The *Sun*, The *World*, New York; *The Outlook;* Associated Press dispatches; The *Tribune*, New York; The *Morning Post*, London.

II

THE OFFENSIVE IN THE CHAMPAGNE COUNTRY

September 25 1915—December 25, 1915

THAT the Allies had actually taken the offensive in vigorous manner was the unmistakable meaning of the fierce drives and gains made on September 25—the French operating in Champagne, the British in Artois. To realize what they accomplished, it was necessary to remember the conditions against which they contended. An advance through German lines could have been made only after an artillery attack so furious that it practically blasted the defenders off the face of the earth. Wire-entanglements had to be swept away by shell-fire, trenches made untenable by high-explosive shells and shrapnel, and artillery overpowered by superior fire. For the French to gain under such conditions a strip of hostile territory fifteen miles in length and from one to two miles in width had been a herculean task. Those who expected any extended and immediate retirement of the German line in France as a result of the operations were doomed to disappointment. Such drives as were made entailed an amount of preparation in the matter of supplies and information as could hardly have been overestimated. The range of each hostile fortification had to be determined and the position also of the German reserves. The object of such drives was, not to force back the entire line, but to cut through at points where the attack would endanger, if not sever, the German line of communications. In the Champagne the offensive was in the hands of Castelnau, who was now famous throughout France for his leadership at the Grand Couronné in 1914.

At this stage of the war one rule governed advances. The ground had to be prepared thoroughly by artillery before infantry could advance, and this had to be done for each advance. In the first battle near Arras, in October, 1914, the artillery parks were nothing like so formidable as they were in September, 1915, when French guns fired as many as 500,000 rounds in fifty-two hours. A significant feature of the September advance was the activity of the air-fleet in damaging railway communications at vital spots behind the lines. This handicapped German movements seriously, the more so as the aviators kept it up, and practically made daily raids. In this way the Germans were hampered in rushing strong reinforcements from one part of their line to another.

When the main bombardment began in Champagne on Sep-

PROTECTED SHELTERS FOR AMBULANCE WORK IN CHAMPAGNE

tember 25 hell was literally let loose from thousands of places. Everywhere at that time stress and expectancy had prevailed. Commanders knew only the orders given for their men, but every one expected a great event while every mind spoke in whispers. About midnight every gun was speaking. From thirty miles off they sounded like the roll of giant drums, with no cessation. Sometimes the noise rose to a crescendo, when it had the volume of thunder near at hand. In the misty night nothing was visible but flashes from guns or the bursting of shells. As the pandemonium went on troops moved into communication trenches. Great masses just behind the front began to percolate into a labyrinth of narrow ways which led to the first line while between them and the sky was a canopy of flying projectiles. Whenever they raised their heads, they saw the darkness of the night lightened up with splashes of fire. Suddenly at dawn the guns ceased and gunners shifted ranges and lengthened fuses. Infantry were getting over parapets. In preparation for this attack, besides ordinary equipment the men were armed with trench knives for that desperate close-quarter fighting of which a summer's work at the "labyrinth" had warned them. As the French moved forward in their new horizon-blue coats and steel helmets anticipation grew. Huge Creusot howitzers, christened "Les Vainqueurs," were speaking.

At dawn, as men drank coffee, they looked on a gray and dismal world. A light rain was falling. Wet chalk stuck to shoes and clothes. It was the weather of Valmy, that battle in the same month, one hundred and thirteen years before, on those same sodden downs where peasants and mechanics with the ardor and the guns of the French Revolution turned homeward the most seasoned and famous troops in Europe. On September 25 and 26, the French claimed to have driven the Germans back for two and a half miles along a front of fifteen. The number of un-wounded German prisoners reported taken was 20,000. On September 29 the French War Office estimated the total German losses at 120,000 in killed, wounded or captured. Figures for the French losses did not come to hand, but they were large. The gains caused rejoicing and exultation among the Allies, as proof that long, weary months of waiting for succor were apparently over; that men and munitions were now ready.

Nothing like this action in Allied aggressiveness had been reported since the battle of the Marne. The only engagements in any way comparable were the far less extended and less general attacks on Neuve Chapelle and Hill No. 60 in the spring. But the moral effect in encouragement and hopefulness was probably greater than the military. The armies under Castelnau in this territory were in the center of a great rampart reared against the Germans. What that rampart was could be realized only by those who saw it, who spent days in the trenches, which were its ultimate expression, who studied an intricate and vast mechanism which kept it fed and supplied, who visited the caverns in which men were sheltered, explored concealed machine-gun emplacements, wandered through acre upon acre of communication trenches, trampled over miles of corduroy roads, stumbled on sandbag cities, and wandered in new homes underneath the ruins of old in cellars, drains, and graveyards. Nothing so stupendous, painstaking, and ingenious had been seen in the history of war.

The field of battle was that of Atilla, or a little north of the region where historians have looked in vain for the exact spot where the great Hun made his last stand a thousand and five hundred years ago. Even in time of peace this region is a desolate land with an ungrateful soil of chalk, the roads few and the villages scarce. Nearly all the villages lie on the banks of small streams which have cut for themselves beds in chalk hills. Here the front had been transformed by German engineers into complicated and elaborate trenches, the ground split up into more or less regular rectangles, each armed with an abundance of machine-guns, and capable of standing a siege, or delaying the advance of an enemy, or becoming a center of resistance and a rallying point for counter-attack.

The portion of the line attacked by the French consisted of two main positions separated by two or more miles. First-line defenses consisted of a complicated net-work of defense- and communication-trenches formed by at least three, and in some places by five, parallel trench-lines facing the French, and cut up into compartments by lateral defense-lines, the trench-line some 400 yards in depth. Between each two trenches were large fields of barbed wire-entanglements some sixty or seventy yards in depth. The second line consisted of a single trench with here and there a support trench, constructed on the unseen side of a hill-crest, only the upper slopes of which were under observation by the French and held only by machine-gun sections and artillery spotters, whose advance posts were linked up by tunnels with trenches behind them. The whole two miles separating the two positions were fortified and netted with transversal, diagonal, and lateral works and communication trenches, which, protected by barbed wire and armed with mitrailleuses, became a by-system of fortifications capable of putting up another fight after hostile infantry had swept over other positions.

The combined offensive, French and British, was made at several points on a two-hundred-mile line reaching first from Verdun past Reims to Soissons (the nearest point to Paris) and turning northward through Arras, La Bassée, Ypres, and thence to the North Sea, the British part, north of Arras, being dealt with in the next chapter. For days before the actual attack, there had been a terrific bombardment by Allied guns all along the line, so that the Germans, who knew that an attack was imminent, could not locate the real points on which a later formidable attack would be concentrated. West and south of Verdun the French made their strongest attack and their greatest gains. A counter-attack from the Germans followed, but in the main the French appeared to hold their advance. In the Argonne the French also accomplished something of value.

But the main struggle was on a grayish-white chalk plateau stretching northward, capped here and there by dirty white German blockhouses and fortresses constructed out of sand-bags and chalk-boulders. Fir-woods, planted in the hope of utilizing an otherwise sterile ground, abounded, but these now disappeared under the ravages of shell-fire, or remained only as bearded stubble. Away to the left, the fighting took place on richly wooded slopes over which runs an old Roman road to Reims. On the right, like a thunder-cloud on the horizon, lay the misty bulk of the Argonne ridge. First in importance and results was the attack made on a seventeen-mile front between Auberive and Ville-sur-Tourbe. Here the German line was penetrated to a depth varying from one to four kilometers, the French being able to consolidate the positions they gained, and withstand strong counter-attacks. Nothing was so remarkable as the rapidity with which the first line was carried over tremendous obstacles which met the infantry once they swept over the trenches. In some points all semblance of resistance was obliterated by the bombardment; but in others a little nest

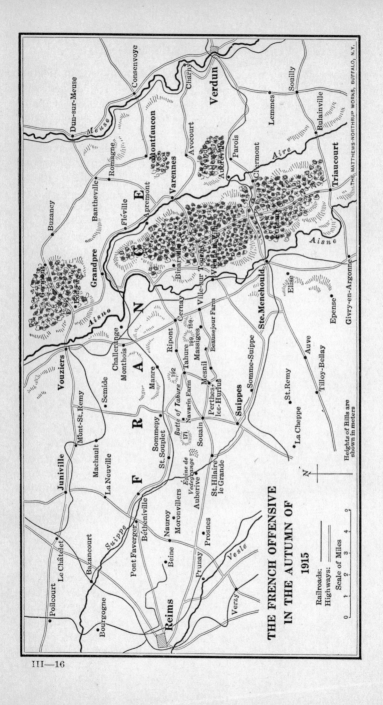

THE FRENCH OFFENSIVE
IN THE AUTUMN OF
1915

Railroads:
Highways:
Scale of Miles
0 1 2 3 4 5

Heights of Hills are
shown in meters

N

THE MATTHEWS-NORTHRUP WORKS, BUFFALO, N.Y.

of machine-guns, untouched by artillery fire, delayed the advance for hours.

The first men who dashed out of the trenches had about 250 yards to cover before they could reach the first German lines. Practically the whole front of the first line was taken before noon the first day, altho at several points resistance was maintained. The Germans formed a number of re-sistance-centers, separated each from another by weaker

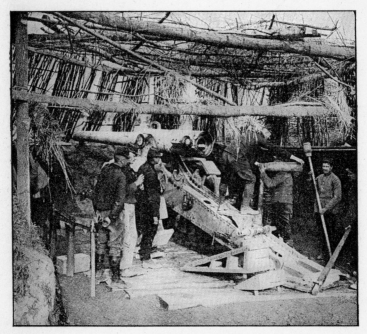

A CONCEALED 155 MM. FRENCH GUN

trench fortifications under protection of bastions. The French struck boldly for the weaker line, meanwhile getting their teeth into strong positions, bombing and firing while their comrades got round to the flanks of the bastions and forced a surrender or retreat. The assault at the two ends of the line around Auberive and Servon failed to carry the positions, but under converging artillery fire and counter-attacks men fought on, pinned two wings down, and thus facilitated work upon the center. In the Souvain section it was not until September 28 that the French got into real contact with the second German positions. The capture of the Main de Massiges and an advance made toward Tahure, on the north, threatened Tahure and the ridge behind it and also menaced the Mesnil Ridge, which had been turned into a regular fortress salient. Roads here were practically non-existent, or had been rapidly and roughly constructed over a pitted district which had been subjected to a downpour of French shells. There were no communication-trenches for the relief and revictualing of men with food and ammunition. In addition to natural difficulties, the Germans, in an endeavor to upset the French, flooded the countryside with gas-shells.

The points against which the French attack was directed more particularly were the Ridge of Tahure, the village of that name, and the "Tooth-brush" Wood. To the east, fighting raged around the Navarin Farm. On these points French artillery-fire was concentrated. The attack upon Tahure Ridge started from trenches parallel to German positions, which were dug under German fire by an obstinate Normandy regiment. The dash on Tahure Ridge facilitated the work of the French south of Tahure. The whole position was carried by a flank attack west, and a frontal attack south, of the village, in the "Tooth-brush" Wood. Here, between the first German trench and the village of Tahure—a distance of about two miles—the Germans had seven parallel lines of trenches, all of which were rendered practically useless by the success of Picardy troops in getting through to Tahure Ridge.

By the time the French guns had reduced the "Tooth-brush" Wood to a scraggy heap of splinters, the resistance of the Germans had practically been overcome. With the fall of the Ridge and "Tooth-brush" Wood, the position of the defenders of the village of Tahure, which lies in a sharp fold of the ground between two heights, became futile, and the French entered the village without much difficulty. According to one of the prisoners, the bombardment had created a panic in the village, many of whose defenders fled. The

French swept on about 600 yards beyond the eastern out-skirts of the village.

The position of Tahure was of such importance to the Germans that a few days later they made a determined effort to retake it, pouring out from heavy artillery a cloud of 8.4-inch and 6-inch suffocating gas-shells. For twenty minutes this drum-fire was kept up and a great cloud, spotted here and there black and white, shrouded the whole position. The infantry assault melted away before French artillery fire. William Philip Simms [4] wrote from Paris afterward that, in the middle of the battle, his first impression was that "Judgment Day had come"; that he had been left behind to roam the disrupted earth alone:

"As far as the eye could see undulated one vast, pitted waste of chalk, with snags of annihilated forests sticking up, gaunt and white and covered with dust, against the skyline, and with arms and legs and other fragments of dead men lying stinking like common garbage on a titanic dump. This was the work of the French artillery. Here the Germans had been. Here they were still, but rotting. Hell's furies seemed to have been forestalled and outdone. For three days I was permitted to wander over the ground won by the French. I had talked previously with many officers and men concerning the efficacy of the French shell-fire, but even thus prepared and despite what I had hitherto observed personally, I was totally surprized by what I saw. Over ten square miles practically no vegetation was left. Even the rabbits and rats had not escaped. Almost 3,000,000 shells were hurled into this area in three days, digging pits from five to seventy-five feet deep, the latter 130 to 150 feet across. As a result of concentrated fire the whole country was covered with a white powder."

E. Alexander Powell [5] shared all that Mr. Simms felt. "Hell," he said, "holds no horrors for one who has seen the battlefield of Champagne." Could Dante have been beside him during three of those days he "would never have written the *Inferno,* because the Hell of his imagination would have seemed colorless and tame." A stretch of rolling moorland, five miles wide and fifteen long, had been converted into a slaughter-house, a cesspool, and a garbage-

[4] Correspondent of United Press.
[5] Correspondent of The New York *World.*

dump combined—such was the battlefield of Champagne. Barring the Marne, he thought it "the greatest battle ever fought and the bloodiest." Approximately a million and a half Frenchmen and Germans took part. Europe there lost more men in killed and wounded than had fought at Gettysburg. The thing that imprest him most was the enormous amount of preparatory work that had been done by the French before a gun was fired. Close to 3,000 field-guns were concentrated along those fifteen miles of battle-front, and behind each were stacked 2,000 shells. In order to bring up ammunition and supplies, the French had built across that rolling plain a macadamized highway forty feet wide and nine miles long. In order that infantry might reach their stations without being annihilated by German shell-fire, they had dug ten miles of communication trenches eight feet deep and wide enough for four men to walk abreast in.

Castelnau said before beginning this offensive that he wanted the bombardment to be so terrific that his men might go to the opposing trench lines "with their rifles at the shoulder." Never before had such a whirlwind of shell and chemicals been unloosed upon the earth. Unfinished letters found on prisoners bore eloquent testimony to the horror of the bombardment. One of the most graphic accounts was furnished by a German writer named Wegener: [6]

"It is Friday morning. During the night we have been hearing the sound of distant gun-fire which in volume and duration had exceeded anything we have experienced since we have been here. Yesterday evening the bombardment was exceptionally lively; it then died down toward midnight. But at about 4 o'clock it started afresh, with unprecedented intensity—a typical big-scale bombardment, with shot following shot in an unbroken rumbling of thunder, like the roll of drums. One hour, two hours, four hours—and still no end to it! The thunder of distant guns can be heard better on the hills than down in the valley. I went to the top of a hill which rises outside the town, and have just returned. The guns are still thundering. On the top of the hill the whole atmosphere was in a state of dull vibration; it seemed as if one perceived the sound not only with the ear, but as if one had the physical sensation of being shaken by the air-waves. It

[6] Printed in The Cologne *Gazette*.

was if the sound came up from the unknown depths of the earth. Indeed, more than anything it was like the uncanny underground rumble of a distant volcano in eruption, shaking—as I have repeatedly experienced it in Java and in Martinique—the earth's crust for miles around and making it tremble like a man in a fit of ague. It was the most remarkable and exciting sensation imaginable. All around, as far as the eye could reach, the countryside lay bathed in a gracious peace, and through the clear, sunlit air, from beyond the sky-line, came those awe-inspiring sounds. It seemed to come straight from the south, or perhaps from south-southwest, and therefore from Champagne.''

The French, because of artillery, which had abolished the

A FRENCH GUN CONCEALED FROM THE ENEMY

German first-line defenses, had won a local triumph, measured by prisoners and cannon captured. They had advanced from one to three miles on a front of ten, and had got within effective range of the railroad they aimed for, but they had not pierced the German third line. Nor did they actually reach the railroad, and late in October had to fight desperately to hold their gains. The results of all this heroism, of this straining and toiling in the factories of France, of the vast work of staff preparations which had gone on without a break for five months, were, however, important. The victory in the Champagne, altho from the military point of view tactical, was almost the first definite notification to the world that the initiative along the Western Front had passed from the Germans to the Allies. By the end of October the Germans organized counter-attacks in Champagne along a front of five miles and on both occasions were subjected to a serious check. At one time they reached the summit of Butte-de-Tahure, but French artillery- and infantry-fire forced them to retreat. Large numbers of their dead bodies were left on the field. The German infantry engaged in the assault were chiefly troops recently transferred from the Russian front.

Altho comparatively small attention was directed to the Aisne district, Allied progress in these weeks was made there. Roughly, there were fifty miles of front in this sector, calculating it from Ribecourt to Berry-au-Bac. For the most part, it had constituted for over a year the unshakable backbone of the German line in France. At the same time, if the German positions had proved invulnerable, so had the French, because in both cases natural defenses existed in quarries and rugged hillside-walls on both sides of the river. Probably the Germans would have established their first line on the south side of the river had they had time to complete their preparations; but the haste with which their right wing fled after the battle of the Marne had compelled them to take the position already prepared on the north side.

Progress from Berry-au-Bac was shown along the valley of La Miette River. From Berry-au-Bac the plain of Reims was further threatened by strong French positions down the Aisne-Marne Canal, where at Sapifneul (the lock-keeper's house) and La Neuville they 'd bridgeheads. The French had a large number of heavy uns in the Aisne sector, and the bombardment was maintained at extraordinary pressure, proving that the Allies had good supplies of ammunition. Further east, where the rocky hills begin and vast subterranean quarries abound, it was much harder to make an impression on the main German position than in the chalky soil of Champagne. Soissons itself was clear of Germans, but the Germans were just across the river, within shot of high French positions.

THE AUTUMN ALLIED OFFENSIVE

At Hartmannsweilerkopf in Alsace French troops in the third week of December made a capture of 1,300 prisoners and a line of German trenches. This was a sample of other battlefields which in these late months of the year stood out on the eastern frontier. For nearly a year possession of this summit, dominating the approach to Mülhausen, had been contested in many engagements. The total of troops engaged there during this period and of the losses endured, if concentrated into a day or a week, would have made the place memorable as the scene of one of the world's great battles, but spread out over eleven months, the fighting hardly approached the idea of a battle. It more resembled a duel than a battle, or a siege. Again and again battalions met on that sanguinary hill to exchange shots, with the monotonous persistence of antagonists on duelling-ground. Each suffered and inflicted suffering on his opponent. Each refused to abandon his possession and each called for new pistols after every exchange. The duel indeed was forced upon the Germans by the French, for to abandon these mountain trenches would have amounted to opening the way for a French advance on Mülhausen.

Guns here thundered away remorselessly on December 24, but Alsatians paid little attention to the bombardment, being concerned with something they regarded as more important —the weather, for it rained heavily and it was Christmas eve, and in every house, poor and rich alike there was a Christmas-tree. The general commanding had relaxed the severity of martial law, so that roads and streets were open to every one all night long. The windows of little shops were gay with Christmas trees. The general himself was present at a Christmas-tree party, given by the inhabitants and attended the midnight mass held in the church. In one of the hotels was a tree decked with candles, oranges, and simple toys that reached to the roof. Christmas and war were thus strangely mingled. Around one huge tree, ablaze with lights, were gathered soldiers in uniform, and girls and children in the beautiful Alsatian costume. Just before midnight the whole party went through the rain to midnight mass. Any one who listened could have heard the distant boom of guns that night, for men were fighting only a mile or two away.

But the church was filled to overflowing with women from farms and villages, and men in uniforms of every shade of blue. In the front seats were three generals, one of them the commander of the whole district.[7]

[7] Principal Sources: The *Times,* London; The London *Times'* "History of the War"; "Nelson's History of the War," by John Buchan; The Cologne *Gazette;* The *World,* The *Times,* The *Sun,* New York; The *Morning Post,* London; Associated Press and United Press dispatches.

FRENCH OFFICIAL PHOTO.

FRENCH TROOPS IN A COMMUNICATING TRENCH

III

THE OFFENSIVE IN ARTOIS, AROUND ARRAS, GIVENCHY, LOOS, AND LENS

September 25, 1915—December 15, 1915

PROBABLY the most notable center of fighting in this autumn offensive was not in Champagne but in Artois—that is, in the central part of the opposing trenches which ran south from Ostend to Soissons. In a military sense, however, the attack in the north was subsidiary to the battle in Champagne. By the third week of September, because of reinforcements from England, the British army had been able to extend its right wing to Grenay, opposite Loos and Lens, taking over a section from the French and consolidating and enlarging trenches which ran southward from the Béthune-La Bassée Canal to the ridge and plateau of Notre-Dame de Lorette. The British in numbers were believed to be sufficient now for an offensive, but it was not with numbers alone that they had been strengthened. The troops sent to France had arrived properly equipped with a due proportion of artillery, in which were a large number of howitzers, furnished with material which fulfilled expectations, and ready to play their part in destroying broad belts of barbed wire which covered the German line. No troops, however gallant, could hope to penetrate these obstacles so long as troops in the trenches behind them could bring to bear on the assailants a concentrated fire from machine-guns and rifles.

The region north of Arras had perhaps been more formidably fortified by the Germans than any other portion of their front. It was an extremely thickly populated neighborhood and a *terrain* full of difficulties and it was not to be expected that an advance here would be as rapid as one in Champagne. The distance between British and German trenches varied from 100 to 500 yards. In one region following an almost imperceptible rise to the southwest trenches ran parallel. Here were long grass and other self-grown crops, and cabbage in patches on chalky soil in which dull gray sand-bag parapets marked the presence of German trenches, before which were barbed wire entanglements. The first line was well west of Loos, the second, running in a slight depression, covered part of the town and then turned abruptly east and ran through the middle of Loos. Behind Loos was a third line. A power-station furnished trenches and dugouts with electric light, and an elaborate telephone system enabled German commanders to support any point with infantry and gun-fire. Observation posts, constructed of reinforced concrete topped by steel cupolas, machine-gun emplacements encased in concrete and iron rails, and dugouts from fifteen to thirty feet deep abounded. A typical dugout went down to a depth of twenty feet, the shaft being boarded in. By means of a pulley a machine-gun could be lifted or lowered in this shaft as occasion required. By a ladder occupants descended to a room six feet or so high, also boarded, and furnished with table, chairs, and four sleeping-bunks. Out of it a staircase led into another trench. Some of these subterranean bedrooms had whitewashed walls and were lit by lamps and decorated with pictures.

Arras as it lay already in ruins was sometimes said to be more impressive than Ypres, tho it was not so large a place. While it was not easy to find a house in Ypres which still had glass in all its windows, or the front of which was not more or less pitted with rifle and shrapnel bullets, there were whole streets in Arras still structurally intact, much as parts of Antwerp were on the last day of the bombardment, when the houses all stood, but the streets were littered with glass and splinters of stone and brick, and quite empty of human beings. The worst of the ruin in Arras was concentrated in three or four points, the most notable of which were in the Place de la Gare, and the Petite Place, with the ruins of the beautiful Hotel de Ville, and others in the neighborhood of the cathedral. Each of these points had served as a constant mark for German gunners. The station building had become a skeleton of twisted iron and stone, with shell-holes and heaps of rubbish blocking the platforms. Here was desolation itself, hardly a building having anything approaching an intact front, and facing you, hanging ridiculously across the space where once was a hotel, still clinging by its two ends to the standing walls of buildings on either side, was a large sign reading, "Chambres pour Voyageurs!" The Petite Place was a heartbreaking sight, with ruins of the beautiful sixteenth century Hotel de Ville, one of the finest in France. Three only of seven Gothic arches still stood, and even those were chipped and battered. There were still inhabitants in Arras. Three women kept open a little shop for the sale of postcards and souvenirs for visitors, sleeping

A PROTECTED FRENCH TRENCH

at night in cellars underground. More pitiful perhaps than the Hotel de Ville was what was left of the Cathedral of St. Vaast. It was not old—barely a century—but it was massive. Hardly in Rome itself could one see ruin on a more complete scale.

Not alone were French and Belgian men, women, and children in this war zone made homeless when war swept over their country; there were thousands of homeless dogs as well. These animals, who had been in great favor among the people as draft animals and pets, were not cared for by any Belgian Relief Fund, but had to shift for themselves, and poor shifting they made of it at first. After a time they had recourse for aid to a source denied to their two-legged companions-in-despair; they found friends in soldiers. Many were taken into trenches on both sides. Along British lines they found a warm welcome with food, and a comfortable, if somewhat perilous, home. Dogs were to be found everywhere in the long battle-line, sleeping under guns and wagons. One battery had twenty. They took cover in the most natural manner, and waited until the "whiz-bang" passed before venturing out again. The small dog who was a good ratter had a princely time. He was carefully looked after by the company to which he belonged. A plague of rats had set in and to exterminate them terriers were god-sends. In fact, terriers eventually were sent to the trenches in carloads, kennels being built for them behind the lines.

Dogs did not monopolize all things in the intrenchments, for cats, chickens, cows, and other animals came with respective claims. Cats figured largely among soldiers' pets. They showed a remarkable disregard of danger, and seemed to prefer trenches to the rest of the lines. A cat would sit and clean herself on the top of a parapet, and only retreat when a bullet or shrapnel sputtered close at hand and upset her toilet arrangements. The whistling and shrieking of shells were commonplaces, but to be sputtered with mud or sand in the middle of washing one's face provoked from cats indignant spits, snarls, and bushy tails. The arrival of a family of kittens became an event of immense importance. Many a small cat that afterward appeared in a soldier's home in Britain had first opened its eyes in the muddy surroundings of a trench "somewhere in France." It had been taken to England tucked inside a tunic or a kit-bag.[8]

All the way from Nieuport to Belfort, but conspicuously in Champagne and Artois, bombardment now set in. This made it difficult for the Germans to decide where the main offensive blow would fall. But in such a combat to keep one's plans entirely hidden was impossible. Aeroplanes could observe a good deal; they could report any large accumulations of men or guns at any point. Nor could spies be entirely eliminated. On one occasion a German air-machine was hit probably

[8] From an article compiled from war correspondence by *The Literary Digest.*

28

threescore times after crossing lines and yet the observer successfully performed his task. Another time a British airman had to drive off four hostile machines before he could complete his reconnaissance. Two officers engaged six German Taubes and disabled at least one. In addition to reconnoitering work and personal encounters, British airmen did service in bombarding German communications. Toward the end of September nearly six tons of explosives had been dropt on various objectives.

The plain around Artois, here a center of the coal industry, was dotted with villages, factories, mine-works and slag-heaps intersected with trenches. For years before the outbreak of the war the coal industry had sunk shafts and bored great tunnels beneath the plain. For nearly twelve months afterward the Germans and their captives had burrowed in hollows and thrown up trenches, so that the ground where not covered by buildings or mining refuse resembled preliminary excavations for a great city. German trenches eight or nine feet deep, mostly cemented or floored and furnished with wooden platforms for musketry and machine-guns, between Lens and Loos, Loos and Hulluch, Hulluch and Haisnes, Haisnes and La Bassée, were supplemented by redoubts and observation posts.

Loos itself, a town which before the war contained 12,000 inhabitants, of whom none but the heroine Emilienne Moreau and a handful of half-starved women and children now remained, was an agglomeration of two-story miners' cottages clustered about an ancient village. The principal street ran west and east, and was now lined by roofless shops and cafés. The parish church, tho reduced to ruins, still served to remind spectators of the antiquity of the place. Conspicuous for forty miles around arose out of Loos the tracery of what was called the "Tower Bridge," 300 feet high, a name given by British soldiers to two square towers of steel girders connected with mining operations, joined two-thirds of the way up by other girders and in a way suggesting the newest of London bridges. This structure was used as a platform for German artillery observers, snipers, and mitrailleuses. For observation purposes possession of "Tower Bridge," which stood midway between La Bassée and Vimy Heights, gave the Germans a considerable advantage.

The attack being correlated with the effort in Champagne under Castelnau, was under the direction of General Foch. Details, however, were left to the two different commands—the French Tenth Army under D'Urbal, and the British First and Second Armies under Haig. On the 25th German positions in the Ypres salient and southwest toward La Bassée were subjected to a tremendous artillery fire. Four attacks were launched, the object being to draw German reserves away from Loos and Vimy. Further to mystify the Germans, Haig assaulted German trenches near Festubert and Givenchy, as if a direct attack on the point of the salient had been contemplated. The fight here was for villages and houses, or for some particular trench before an army could enter the great plain which stretches down to Lille. Every house along the French and German lines had been turned into a fortress. When superstructures were blown to pieces by shell-fire, men burrowed fifty or sixty feet below the cellars and so held on to their positions.

The main British attack was launched on a front of about seven miles south of La Bassée. The village of Loos and the quarries above Hulluch were occupied, the furthest point reached being the slopes of Hill 70. Like the French in Champagne, the British were able to consolidate and hold most of the points gained, the British offensive being supported by a strong French attack between Lens and Arras. Starting from the ruins of Souchez and Neuville, the French penetrated as far as the farm of La Folie, just short of the main road from Lens to Arras. Before the real offensive began the mass of ruins that once was Ypres had been shelled and the adjacent roads sprayed with shrapnel. Everywhere prevailed an atmosphere of tension and expectancy. Just before midnight the great guns began and from thirty miles off sounded like the roll of giant drums. There was no cessation, but sometimes a crescendo, which had the volume of nearby thunder. Every section of the line was engaged. The chief advances were made at Hooge and beyond Vermelles, but the big struggle was just north of Lens. British lines covered Vermelles and Grenay. A hundred

THE SO-CALLED TOWER BRIDGE AT LOOS
Built for mining operations before the war. The Germans long used it as
an observation post. The name Tower Bridge came from the English who
saw in it a suggestion of the London Tower bridge

31

yards beyond lay the Germans. The defense of Lens was in reality a defense of Lille. From a hillock well to the rear of the line could be seen gun-flashes from La Bassée south to Souchez. Sharp hailstorms drifted across the sky, and a wet mist cloaked the horizon. Both French and British were closely engaged, the former against the high ground east of Givenchy, called Vimy Ridge—the old objective of the battle in May, 1915—the latter on a front west of Haisnes to Hill 70, east of Loos.

Immediately in front of the British and French, when the advance began, was Lens, the chief railroad center for the Germans on their front from Lille to Noyon. To capture it would have been to compel the Germans to draw back toward Douai. Its investment would transform La Bassée into an extremely dangerous salient, would be a threat to Lille and would restore to France her lost coal mines. It would also give to France one of the main trunk lines from Paris to the north. Its fall would have made the La Bassée position perilous. The consequence of a British advance might well be a general German retirement upon Lille and Douai, with the Lille-Cambrai-Paris railroad behind them, and the Douai-Lille Canal in front of them most of the distance. Such an advance would have brought the Allies perilously close to the main trunk lines which the Germans used from the Somme to Champagne. Any further Allied advance might have meant a retirement from France, possibly under grave difficulties, especially if a sudden attack should carry the aggressors to the Mons-Cambrai railroad. That was at least an Allied hope—a hope so long deferred, however, as not to be realized until the autumn of 1918.

When, on the morning of September 25, operations began with the advance of the British under Haig, who directed a frontal attack against the German first-line positions north and south of Loos, several positions were captured over a front of five miles, British troops penetrating for 4,000 yards into second-line trenches, up to the outskirts of Hulluch, and expelling the Germans from the mining works between Loos and Hill 70. Beside the gain of ground the day's fighting resulted in the capture of some 3,000 or more prisoners with 21 guns and 40 machine-guns. Simultaneously with this, the main attack, other attacks were made north of La Bassée Canal, and east of Ypres, but beyond holding the enemy and diverting strong bodies of reserve troops toward these points, no advance was made and no results were obtained. Attacks were not pushed home, and were apparently only undertaken as diversions.

While the First British Army was attacking between La Bassée and Lens, the French drove the Germans out of Souchez, and then advanced toward Givenchy-en-Gohelle, gaining a footing on Hill 119, while further south, northeast of Neuville-St. Vaast, the French reached the farm of La Folie. This French army, strongly opposed, was unable to penetrate into German lines south of Loos as far as did the British north of the village, but 1,500 prisoners were taken, and Souchez was left well in the rear. East of Souchez a tiny river of the same name ran among meadows. On the west bank was a coppice called the Bois de Hache, and across the stream a little to the south a larger woodland, called the Bois de Givenchy. Just east of the trees lay the village of Givenchy-en-Gohelle, at the junction of several roads; and south and west were the slopes of Vimy, these slopes not high, the flat top just over 400 feet, but they command Vimy station and the railway between Lens and Arras, and gave a prospect over rolling slopes to the valley of the Scarpe. By September 29 the Canadians had won Vimy Ridge, the French held their position just behind the crest, and all the western slopes and most of the Givenchy Wood. It was a fine achievement, and cost the enemy much in dead, wounded, and prisoners. Canadians at home were justly proud of what their men had done. Conspicuous among them were the Princess Pat's, whose losses here, as they had been at Ypres in April, were appalling.

When finally the intense bombardment at Loos began, the roar produced by an immense assemblage of guns was so terrific that sleepers thirty or forty miles away were awakened. Farther off, when the sounds were dampened by a southwesterly wind, the deafening noise diminished to a low-pitched rumble, broken by louder reports from heavier weapons. British and French science, it was believed, had now given to the Allied armies weapons superior to those

forged in German arsenals. At last the wished-for moment
came when the roar of guns behind ceased and lines of
soldiers, with heads covered with smoke-helmets, and resembling divers in appearance, sprang forward from the
trenches. They moved silently through mist and smoke, and
swept like a wave against German trenches. A British
officer declared later that "hell itself could not be worse."
Nothing "could be an exaggeration of the horrors of that
battlefield; it was, it is, a veritable shambles, a living death
of unspeakable horror even to those who, like myself, were
destined to come through it unscathed—bodily at all events.
Most of the survivors went through a ghastly nightmare
without the relief and joy of awakening." Philip Gibbs
wrote an account of the attack: [9]

"A battalion leaped out of its trenches and ran toward the
enemy's lines with a wild hurrah, the point of attack being the
Village of Loos, some three and a half miles away. The men
reached the enemy's lines of trenches without sustaining many
casualties, and found that the first two lines of barbed wire had
been effectively broken down by the artillery bombardment. The
third line was uncut and was of very strong wire, with great barbs.
The first two trenches were carried with a rush at the point of the
bayonet, a large number of Germans being killed; but the uncut
wire made the first check, and was a formidable obstacle. But our
men, reckless of their lives, and under a deadly fire of machine-
guns forced their way through the entanglement. Rank after rank
streamed up, and at last the great tide of men poured through and
swamped forward to the village, and then three-quarters of a mile
further on, as they ran shouting hoarsely, were faced by the fire
from an enormous number of machine-guns. From every part of
the village there came the steady rattle of these weapons pouring
out streams of lead."

The assault launched from Vermelles was a shock from
which the entrenched regiments around Loos could not recover. An hour and a half after the British attack began,
there was witnessed in some cases the spectacle of German
infantry, in batches of twenty and thirty, surrendering to
one or two men amid the ruins of Loos. Battalions of
Kitchener's new army here gained their first experience of

[9] For the London *Daily Chronicle,* and The New York *Times.*

heavy fighting. They captured a position as strong as many that had been stormed by veterans in the previous year. The price was heavy, but they paid it without faltering. The task was not easy. It meant a charge across level fields, through three lines of barbed wire, past slag heaps; a hand-to-hand struggle for mastery of the German first-line trench; then for the second-line trench; trenches of communication, and dugouts filled with the enemy. These cleared and the trenches won, there remained another dash across fields and a high road studded with visible entanglements until the western edge of Loos was reached; then the silencing of machine-gun batteries, house fighting (with plenty of cellar-to-cellar searches for hidden enemies), and constant pressure through narrow streets eastward to the open fields, beyond where a final rush would carry them to Hill 70, for fresh fighting at close quarters, and the endurance of a galling fire from a kind of "machine-gun fort" until its guns could be silenced. Altogether it was a journey of perhaps three miles. Among the rescued at Loos was Mlle. Emilienne Moreau, a girl

A BRITISH SOLDIER IN A GAS MASK

of eighteen, who had lived through the German occupation and now assisted in bandaging British wounded. She killed with her own hand several Germans who had attacked Highlanders and Territorials. On November 27 she was publicly decorated at Versailles with the Croix de Guerre.

The Crown Prince of Bavaria, in command of the army opposing the British, had brought up reserve troops from Belgium and began a series of vigorous counter-attacks with the intention of regaining the ground the Germans had lost.

He concentrated large reinforcements of men and guns north and south of Haisnes, and succeeded in recapturing Pit 8. During the night, which was lit up by the moon and German star-shells and rockets, the scenes in Loos were ghastly. The attack that day was preceded by a heavy bombardment lasting an hour, but in the face of German machine-gun fire no progress was made. The Germans were firmly established in a redoubt northwest of Hill 70 and finally dislodged the British from Pit 14. They made desperate efforts to dislodge troops from Pit 8 behind the Hohenzollern Redoubt and around this point furious fighting raged through the day. The British, unable to maintain their position as the day wore on, were slowly forced back to the eastern portion of the redoubt. The losses which the British sustained at Loos and the French in taking Souchez, with the enormous expenditure of shells, grenades, and cartridges, induced Sir John French to stop his offensive for the time. September 28 marked the end of the battle

MLLE. EMILIENNE MOREAU
The eighteen-year-old heroine
of Loos

of Loos. No great results had been obtained. The fighting had cost the British heavy casualties. They did not have sufficient reserves immediately available to back up early successes and consolidate positions they had won. This gave the Germans time to rally and counter-attack. The French advance did not take place until six hours after the British, which left the right of the British exposed to a flank attack. The result was a battle which, had it been fought under more favorable conditions, might have changed the aspect of war, but which was to all intents and purposes futile.

Many gruesome details were printed of the Loos battle—

of piles of German corpses at street corners; of bombing parties that fell down steep cellar steps on the bodies of dead men; of living men who were heard calling feebly underneath; and of slow digging into piles of débris to rescue buried men showing signs of life. But the strangest, most uncanny incident was of a British battalion which, in making its way through a captured position, tramped into a deep firing-trench, where they saw a German standing in their

RUINS OF THE HOTEL DE VILLE AT ARRAS

path erect. The first soldier raised his bayonet and then stept quickly on one side. As the man behind him came on, he gave one look, and stept as quickly to the other side. Each succeeding man coming down the trench saw this solitary German, stiffly upright and facing him with a dreadful smile on his face. Not until an observer was within arm's length did he see that a bullet hole was in the German's head. The man had died standing erect, and still smiled as tho the sight of British soldiers was the best joke in the world.

Serious resistance was encountered when the attackers came to a cemetery, which was alive with machine-gun parties, sheltered behind parapets raised among graves. Even tombstones were used as cover. Men who flung themselves on this burial ground rapidly added to the number of corpses as they leapt from one parapet to another, bayoneting as they went, and lost many men. It was three-quarters of an hour before the cemetery was cleared of Germans. The number of corpses then lying among fallen crosses and trampled wreaths far exceeded those in the molding community who lay below. The British beat their way into Loos a step at a time, bearing bombs which they hurled in each refuge. Cellars were packed with gray-coated Germans. Some tried the old trick of pretending to surrender and then shooting point-blank at a British soldier in front. After the taking of Loos the British army sang the praises of guns and planes. No such bombardment had been heard on the British front before. The roar had the power and continuity of Niagara. House windows in the surrounding country kept up a continuous rattle. "It is the sweetest sound in the world," said one of the surviving veterans of the retreat from Mons. "It means that you will get into the German trenches and have a fair fight."

On October 8 the British, after crowding into German trenches, repulsed a German counter-attack. They had known it was beginning when German artillery concentrated a bombardment along the line. This became a terrific ordeal. Philip Gibbs wrote that the trenches "were not only strewn with shrapnel, but German batteries flung out an enormous quantity of high explosives, which made earth fly in all directions." It seemed impossible to live under such an annihilating storm. For a considerable time a German aeroplane remained over the British lines, flying at a great height and directing artillery fire. Shortly after 3.30 the Germans opened with rifle and machine-gun fire until a continual stream of bullets swept across the space between opposing trenches, some fifty yards in breadth. That space was "filled with the smoke of bursting shells and all the reek of battle, including poison-gases and smoke-balls." Suddenly through this dense curtain there loomed up a line of black figures, and then another, and then two more. German infantry were advancing four deep, shoulder to shoulder. The waiting British then knew their chance had come as they fired in rapid volleys machine-guns which sent streams of lead upon shadowy figures. Great numbers of the German infantry fell at once. After a further short advance, others lay down and small groups tried to

THE RUINS OF ARRAS CATHEDRAL

crawl back. Machine-guns and rifles concentrated on these groups and swept the intervening ground so that few escaped. Meanwhile, German artillery had established a curtain of shrapnel and high explosives behind British lines to prevent supports from coming up, while one of their aeroplanes flew no higher than 2,000 feet in directing their guns. British artillery replied and late in the afternoon the Germans slackened their fire. Great numbers of dead were then lying in front of British lines.

After this British drive, Arras, out of 25,000 inhabitants, had some 600, or perhaps 800, still remaining, but there was no house which had not received its shell. Only a few shops remained open. One was kept by a mother and daughter who had never left the town during a bombardment that had lasted practically for more than a year. Contempt for danger was general. H. Warner Allen [10] in October saw in the Grande Place, at Arras, an old woman sitting with her dog in the sun, both fast asleep. The noise of guns meanwhile was incessant. When a big shell appeared, she did not move. On hearing a warning to "take care," she finally moved slowly away, calling the dog to a cellar, a yard or two away, then waited a little, and finally, as if nothing had happened, came back and went to sleep. The owner of one house, on the advance of the Germans, buried under a tree in his garden £60,000 in notes, stocks and shares. Later he returned to dig for his treasure. But altho he dug, and dug, his spade did not strike his treasure-chest. Then he began to dig madly under another tree, and there found the still unopened chest. Arras in October might well have been called a city of the dead if it had not lacked the most impressive mark of desolation—silence. Almost always there were heard the roar of cannon and the wild hurtle of huge projectiles. Great clefts in the cathedral's sides and roof let in a vision of the sky. Part of its masonry threatened to fall at any moment. It hung suspended as if it were lighter than air. Huge arches still remained aloft, balanced fantastically beyond the maddest dreams of architects, each on a single column. Most famous of Frenchmen whose early lives were spent in Arras, was Carlyle's "Sea-green" Robespierre of the Reign of Terror, himself a victim of the guillotine.

When one had seen Ypres he had seen Arras, with the reservation that Arras was built on a bigger scale, and, from its situation as well as from other standpoints, had been an even more beautiful city. G. Valentine Williams, who had visited the place before it was badly wrecked,

[10] Special representative of the British Press with the French army.

described it[11] as formerly "a gem of a city, almost every one of its houses an individual masterpiece of the Flemish builder's art." Reduced now to "piles of rain-soused, mud-stained, squalid, and ugly ruins," time had coated them with "a uniform patina of gray." The massive cathedral "looked as if a giant had kicked it over," its frowning façade sliced away, the interior "piled high with stacks of broken sandstone." Directly you crossed the threshold, you were confronted with splintered brick, charred beams, broken glass, jagged ends of furniture and gaping case-ments, "where a jeweled gleam here and there spoke of a stained glass glory departed." Grass, long, fresh and green, had sprung up between cobbles in the narrow streets, even in the principal thoroughfare with its rows of shuttered or ruined shops. Of civilians who lived in deep and rambling cellars, dug under the Grande Place and other parts of the city, Mr. Williams wrote:

"Long flights of steps lead from the pavement in front of the shops under the arcades of the Grande Place down to these sub-terranean abodes where these wretched people made their homes with such rude comfort as they were able to provide. As you passed the cellar openings you had a glimpse of beds, tables, and cooking pots, an old woman peeling potatoes or knitting, her birds or her cat by her elbow. There were shops, too, where, besides some of the commodities of life brought regularly into the town, you could buy picture post-cards of Arras before and after the bombardment. There were not many shops open, but those which I saw seemed to be general in character and to stock everything from butter to reels of cotton.

"Children in Arras would pop out at you from cellars, from ruins in all kinds of unexpected corners apparently quite reck-less of the danger that was always lowering, heedless of rever-berating explosions echoing from different parts of the city. Like the gamins of Paris during the siege, when a shell fell they rushed to the spot to hunt for the fuse and splinters and to bear them away as souvenirs as soon as they were cool enough to touch. They are a proud and bitter folk, the Arrageois. Fifteen months of war made them so. You saw them standing at their cellar openings, gazing forlornly at the desolation about, thinking maybe, of the ever-lengthening line of crosses in the cemetery in the

[11] In The *Standard,* London.

corner, where the victims of the bombardment were laid to rest. You marked the grave faces of men, the hysteria staring out of the eyes of women.''[12]

[12] Principal Sources : The *Times*, The *Sun*, The *World*, New York ; Associated Press dispatches ; The *Daily Chronicle*, The *Times*, The *Morning Post*, London ; The London *Times'* "History of the War" ; The *Manchester Guardian*; The *Economist*, The *Standard*, London ; The New York *Evening Post*, The *Fortnightly Review*; "Nelson's History of the War," by John Buchan ; The *Literary Digest*, New York.

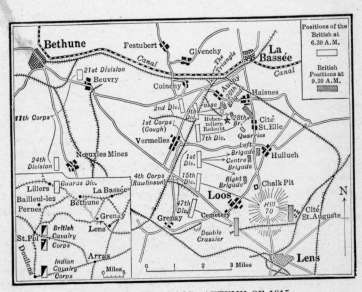

THE BATTLE OF LOOS ; AUTUMN OF 1915

IV

THE HOHENZOLLERN REDOUBT AND GENERAL SIR JOHN FRENCH'S RETIREMENT

October 13, 1915—December 15, 1915

ON the morning of October 13 the wind blew steadily from the west, the air raw and chilly. A thick Scotch mist covered the ground, and the drizzling rain seemed the harbinger of a torrential downpour. As the hours passed the rain ceased, the mist cleared off, and fields were bathed in a warm, autumnal sunlight. To the northwest on the horizon were dimly visible the outlines of the battered town of La Bassée. Along the British front blotches of red marked the presence of what remained of the villages of Vermelles and Le Routoire. Between them and La Bassée rose the lofty chimneys of factories and the black, ugly slag-heaps of Pit 8 and Haisnes. Open spaces, stubble-fields, and cabbage-patches were strewn with unburied corpses and broken weapons. Huge holes recorded the activities of gunners who for a year had been plowing up with their shells this area, once the home and playground of miners and their families. Behind hostile lines groups of miners and peasants were even now phlegmatically toiling at their daily tasks.

Suddenly, at noon, a bombardment comparable with that which had preluded the battle of Loos began. Tongues of fire leaping from the ground flashed as it were a warning to the Germans of a storm of descending shells. In the rear British observation balloons hung motionless. Aeroplanes buzzed forward and back. From hundreds of spots in the German line ascended pillars of black smoke. Fleecy white puffs marked where shrapnel was bursting, a green or pinkish blot—which swiftly vanished—indicating that an asphyxiating shell from answering German guns had exploded. In the distance buildings crumbled away and clouds of chalky smoke told that trenches and dugouts, which a few minutes before had been the refuges of soldiers chatting to each other, had been upturned. An hour passed by and from the British lines near Vermelles a dense cloud of white smoke, fringed below with red and green, drifted toward the Hohenzollern Redoubt. By the time it had left the British trenches it was half a mile broad. Slowly it settled on the redoubt, on a slag-heap behind it, and on the buildings of Pit 8.

Haig had directed the Midland division of British Territorials to storm the Hohenzollern Redoubt, while troops on the right were to attack the Hulluch quarries and trenches between them and the village of that name. The assault met with a certain amount of success. To the east the British captured a trench on the northwestern face of the Hulluch quarries, and, southwest of St. Eloi, trenches behind the Vermelles-Hulluch road and the southwestern edge of the quarries. South and west of Hulluch they gained 1,000 yards of trenches, but were shelled out of them.

In point of strength the Hohenzollern Redoubt was comparable with the "labyrinth" outside Neuville-St. Vaast. Altho simpler in details, it was quite as strong as a position, and all the more strong in not depending on metal cupolas or other mechanical aids. Its nearly impregnable defenses had been found in Mother Earth heaped high and cut deep. Such a defense could be readily repaired under shell-fire, because it did not depend on works constructed of imported materials, but on inexhaustible materials in the dirt ready at hand. The redoubt was a masterpiece of earth construction. It contained a vast number of machine-guns set in dugout positions almost impregnable to shell-fire, arranged so that fire could be concentrated and inter-supported in such fashion that the capture of the fire trenches forming the outer shell of the place was a matter of extreme danger. The Germans welcomed such invasion of their outer shell because they were certain of being able to wreak summary vengeance on interlopers.

The redoubt could have been described as shaped roughly like a big kidney-bean, with its broadest end pointing due northwest, outside the German line. Straight behind was the Béthune colliery, its winding plant practically intact and showing pithead piles of slag. Rows of miners' cottages along the road provided excellent observation-points for German gunners and emplacements for lighter artillery. The "bean" was originally joined on to the German trenches by two communication trenches, which a month or two before the battle had been augmented by "Big Willie" and "Little

CANADIANS IN BRITISH HELMETS ON THE WESTERN FRONT

Willie." "Big Willie" was a strong trench running at an angle from the south end of the "bean" back to the main line. "Little Willie" occupied a similar position from the north end. The whole position was a gentle rise. Across the "bean" from end to end, ran a strong trench, bristling with machine-guns, criss-crossed again with traverse trenches. The very simplicity of the work was its strength. You had here an open gentle rise, without any species of cover. In the dugouts men were sheltered under the heights of three-story houses.

The British front over against the "bean" was roughly 800 yards in length. To the northern end—the "fat" end of the "bean"—ran a long sap (the German trenches being almost 200 yards away), which just failed to get to the junction of "Little Willie" and the main line. The British drove a sap from this about fifty yards back over toward "Little Willie," which also had never been completed, leaving a hiatus of from thirty to forty yards, which incidentally cost a number of lives in traversing open ground. The whole effort, or at all events the main part of it, was concerned with "Little Willie," the British having got "Big Willie" early. Fresh troops were brought up. One regiment which marched by night was immediately thrown into battle. Despite their long march, the men charged what to them was an unknown position and went through to the triangle formed by the saps, and also the corner of the "bean," where they got mixt with another regiment. This first charge resulted in a situation whereby the British were holding "Little Willie" at both ends, but with the Germans still in the center. As the open ground was being swept clean by merciless artillery and machine-gun fire, the British could not get their supplies of grenades, and so the regiment was bombed out of the bits of trench they were holding.

Late in the month débris of the fighting was lying everywhere—broken rifles covered with rust and mud, German knapsacks with their fur lacking, discarded cartridge-pouches, more often than not soaked in blood, bayonets by the score, German and British, and innumerable articles of equipment. The ground was strewn with cartridge-cases, with the safety-pins of bombs, and with splinters of shell. The trench itself showed many signs of the terrific bombardment to which it had been subjected. Great holes had been torn in the parapet, which the British built up again, while here and there some of the many dugouts, with which the bottom of the trench was lined, had been blown in. The open ground that stretched from the redoubt back to the old British line presented a scene of desolation hard to describe.

Out on that strip of shell-scarred field lay many dead bodies, their faces decently covered by overcoats and awaiting burial. Some lay on grass only a few yards from the back parapet.

Owing to the character of the battle-ground and the fine clear day, non-combatants were able to obtain a view of this action from the neighboring countryside. Large numbers of villagers living around slack-heaps and pit-heads did actually go out to watch the bombardment, having been roused to interest in this as a new kind of spectacle, others having become monotonous and familiar to them. This new interest was ascribed to the intensity of the artillery-fire and the smoke-clouds and whitish vapor which were wafted toward the German lines, and stirred the imagination so that peasants climbed to the peaks of black slag-hills and stared off into the mist, where, beyond the brightness of an autumn sun, men were fighting and dying. The Hohenzollern Redoubt loomed vaguely through drifting clouds of thick and sluggish vapor.

Mr. Gibbs [13] climbed one of these slag-hills and wrote that, on the edge of the great battle-ground, "fields were tawny in the golden light of the autumn sun, while the broken towers of village churches, red roofs shattered by shell-fire, trees stript bare of leaves before the wind of autumn had touched them, were painted in clear outlines against the gray-blue of the sky." British guns were invisible. Not one of all the batteries massed over a wide stretch of country could be located by a searching glass. When the bombardment began, it seemed as if shells were coming from every field and village for miles behind the lines. The glitter of bursting shells shot through the smoke caused by their explosion making "little twinkling flashes, like the sparkle of innumerable mirrors and heliographing messages of death." There was one incessant roar "rising and falling in waves of prodigious sound." The whole line of battle was in a grayish mirk, which obscured all landmarks. Even the "Tower Bridge" was only faintly visible.

From these slag-heaps observers had a brief glimpse of the human element in this scene. Across a stretch of flat ground, beyond zig-zag lines of trenches, little objects were seen

[13] Correspondent of The New York *Times,* and The *Daily Chronicle,* London.

47

scurrying forward, not bunched together in close groups, but scattered. Some seemed to hesitate, then to fall, and lie where they fell. Others hurried on, until they disappeared in drifting clouds. No other details than these could be seen of an infantry attack. The Germans were firing shells, some of them curiously colored to a pinkish hue, others orange-shaped and a vivid green, all poison shells, giving out noxious gases. Men fought with fierce valor, and fields swept by shell-fire from heavy guns reached the Germans. They captured the German first line south and west of Hulluch, and swept up to the main trench of the redoubt. The Germans, strong in machine-guns, held on to some of their trenches, while others which the British had captured came under the fire of batteries. There were many acts of fine courage and superb endurance among officers and men.

Compared with the French operation in Champagne, this attack in the north became a lesser operation. The distance covered, however, was about the same, that is, upward of three miles. As compared with Neuve Chapelle, the operation showed improvement. Like the offensive in the Champagne it remained incomplete. The Allies had not broken through, they had not reached their immediate objective, but they had taken positions which, if held, might have led to the retreat of the Germans and the acquisition eventually of points aimed at.

In one of the night bombardments an observer [14] declared that before him there was "nothing but an abyss of shadows," a vast screen, intensely black, like a restless sky-sign where played thousands of luminous streaks, so dense that they formed, in the opaque night, a kind of incandescent bar, extending in an immense line from one end to the other of the field of vision." All these sparkling streaks were in a whirlwind of movement, bursting out in all directions, in incredible profusion, so that the whole horizon "bristled with a shimmering mane of fire that the wind twisted and waved." Before this apparition M. Sem stood "dumb with amazement." Scarcely had one rocket begun to fall when two or three others shot out from the same point to replace it, some straight up to a great height,

[14] M. Sem, the French cartoonist, in *Le Journal*, Paris.

AFTER THE EXPLOSION OF A MINE
Above the mine was a German trench. The hole created by the explosion
was 100 feet deep and 180 feet wide

III.

others sideways, others again in curves or zig-zag, their movements uninterrupted and bewildering. It was a magical spectacle, a giant display of fireworks, over a twenty-five-mile background. The impression of fairy-work was so intense that he was prepared at any moment to see the rockets "spread themselves into multi-colored bouquets, and bow gracefully, as if offering them to the night." Suddenly blinding flashes and tongues of flame would dart furiously out and "split the shadows with a tragic illumination of black clouds that were scurrying in the scared night." Two seconds after, a quadruple detonation would shatter all silences and the tremendous din would "go round the four corners of the horizon, rebound, and come back like a rolling wave, to be tossed on to infinity by all the echoes of the heavens."

Then the noise would move further and grow fainter "like the sound of a train disappearing into the distance." Searchlights would come into play, blazing shafts darting from various points, "as if shot out of mortars loaded with illuminating rays, and pierce the shadow like cannon-balls of light." Brilliant cones would cross each other in the darkness, "cutting out fantastic circles of clearness in which would appear suddenly, lit up as if in a sinister apotheosis, the turrets of the hill of St. Éloi—standing out like two pale phantoms— the mutilated trees of Carency Wood, the skeleton roofs and the ruins of Villers-au-Bois and of Ablain-St.-Nazaire—a

THE RUINED CHURCH OF ABLAIRE SAINT-NAZAIRE IN ARTOIS

complete Dantesque kind of desolation." So the powerful light would sweep up the night, "searching the darkness with the feverish and uneasy haste of a burglar's dark lantern, and then on a sudden palpitate, shiver, and vanish in hiccoughs of light, as if the sky were shaken by Satanic laughter." On all sides rockets would mount in sheaves, to right and left. To the very horizon "guns would dart their flames, and fill the immensity with their deep voices." One could distinctly see shells explode over trenches, and cast showers of sparks and red-hot splinters in the midst of reddish smoke in "a struggle of Titans."

The net result was a gain to the British of nearly seven thousand yards of front and four thousand of depth, tho if one were asked what exact advantage this gain brought, save as a visible sign of military virtue, it would have been hard to find an answer. The most substantial Allied gains were the 3,000 prisoners, including 57 officers, 26 field-guns, and 40 machine-guns. Altogether the losses during three weeks of fighting were not less than 50,000 men and 2,000 officers, a large proportion being of wounded men. For a second time, wet, foggy winter settled down upon the water-logged, clay-bottomed trenches. Little did those who in these trenches spent Christmas in 1914 imagine that Christmas in 1915 would find them in the same position. And yet a move back of a couple of miles at Ypres, and a move forward of the same extent in the south, were all that either side could show for a year's hard work and the loss of many thousand lives.

In the first days of October, Bulgaria joined the Austro-Germans and, as a consequence, a not inconsiderable part of the French and British effectives had to be transported to Saloniki—too late, however, to help the Serbians and still less able to take the field against German, Austrian, and Bulgarian forces. The inability of the Allies to act with vigor in the Near East had made them unable to prevent the enemy from occupying Serbia and Montenegro. This, however, together with the failure to make progress in Gallipoli, and a great mishap to the Anglo-Indian army at Ctesiphon and Kut-el-Amara, reacted on the strategy of the Allied commanders in the west. Such conditions inevitably produced a state of comparative inactivity. There were many small fights and day after day the toll of losses mounted, but no great advantage was gained by either side.

By late October winter along the British front was close at hand. Before midday a white fog would fill up the trenches, steal down the dugouts and drift densely over fields. Perhaps a pale sun would gleam for a few hours, giving a fictitious sense of summer, and then, when darkness came, the mist would creep up again from marshes and woods and chill the air. Another winter campaign, to those who had seen the misery of the first winter in boggy trenches, was a distressing thought—wet mud, ice-cold water reaching above the knees in communication trenches, wind that lasht like sharp whips, ooze and slime in dugouts, water running down through the roofs of broken barns. But it was not to be quite so bad in the second year as during the first—at least not in some sections. Many trenches now had well-bricked floors and drains to carry water away. Forests of timber, too, had been made into logs to build dugouts and to bridge over boggy ways.

The great problem of the winter was the billeting of the new divisions that had come out. In villages behind the firing-lines beyond, or almost beyond the range of German guns, every old barn was requisitioned, and, tho not very watertight and not very clean (rats and vermin resented intrusion), were pretty good shelter against wind and cold. Near fighting lines most barns had been smashed into ruin, like most farmhouses to which they belonged. By the first week in December the British settled down to a winter campaign. For some time it was to be a stick-in-the-mud warfare, for there was incessant work to do in draining trenches, strengthening parapets, riveting walls, tiling or boarding floorways, timbering dugouts. Among the French the walls of trenches were strengthened with hurdles to prevent landslips, the plague of the soldiers' life. Simple but efficient means were taken to provide troops with damp-proof shelters. Ground was carefully beaten down, leveled, and covered with planks or straw. Earthen roofs were strengthened with sheets of zinc, while due attention was paid to ventilation and heating. In the second line, wooden huts were erected with double walls and slate roofs, while in most cases floors were raised above the ground level. Soldiers were particularly pleased with the beds provided, the foundation consisting of wire-netting stretched on a wooden frame, with straw packing and a good supply of blankets. A great feature of these improvised barracks was the charcoal brazier. Coal might be short and stoves thus made ineffective, but in the firing zone there was no scarcity of wood, for shells lopped off great branches in every forest

FRENCH DOG KENNELS BEHIND THE FRONT

and cut down many big trees which, but for the war, the woodman would have spared.

The Germans, too, greatly improved their trenches and dugouts. They were now composed of earth, stakes, and netting, which made them rigid and insured elasticity. Ground around trenches often became green with newly grown grass before winter set in. One could walk through them and yet remain quite clean. Roofs protected men from rain. If an unusually heavy shower happened to penetrate into an interior, the water could be carried away by an arrangement of pipes. Lamps taken from motor-cars provided light, and there were fans, ventilators, and switch-boards. Of smaller trench annoyances few were worse than a plague of rats. Shelters and trenches, no matter where made— whether in woods, open fields, or on mountain sides—immediately became infested. The plague attained considerable dimensions before a really organized attempt was made to deal with it. Many cases occurred of rats actually biting men when chasing them down the trenches. Terriers proved of considerable assistance in destroying them. Trains full of dogs came to the front—whole regiments of them. One train left Paris with 2,700 dogs on board. Poison also became effective. A reward was offered for every dead rat brought in by men in the trenches. In a single fortnight one French army corps disposed of no fewer than 8,000 rats. At a halfpenny a rat this involved an expense of $80 and it was money well spent. The sport of rat-catching on such advantageous terms proved popular.

Romeo Houle was a Massachusetts boy who, when the war broke out, enlisted as private in a French-Canadian regiment. In the spring of 1916 the American Government procured his discharge because he had enlisted when under age and he then came back to this country. He had fought at Ypres, St. Julien, Cuinchy, Givenchy, La Bassée, and in the first-line trenches at Messines. He had also been in the first line at Richebourg and Laventie where he survived as one of sixteen men out of 500. On arriving in this country he gave a striking account [14a] of what war meant to men in the trenches:

"For many months I lived in trenches. I slept daily in dread of bullet, shrapnel, mine, and deadly gas; and nightly in fear of mine and gas—and the man-eating rats. I am one of the few soldiers living who entered the front trenches at the opening of the war and who lived to fight the Germans in the front trenches in February, 1916. Who has seen hell? Who has experienced the horrors of Milton's terrible vision or the slow tortures of Dante's Inferno? God! If Dante's dream-madness were truth, and those seven circles were seven encircling battle lines in northern France or the torn fringe of brave little Belgium, I could stand up and

[14a] In the New York *Times*.

say there is no agony of body or mind which I have not seen, which I have not experienced. I thank God and give Him the glory that I still am sane.

"Gas? What. do you know of it, you people who never heard earth and heaven rock with the frantic turmoil of the ceaseless bombardment? A crawling yellow cloud that pours in upon you, that gets you by the throat and shakes you as a huge mastiff might shake a kitten, and leaves you burning in every nerve and vein of your body with pain unthinkable; your eyes starting from their sockets; your face turned yellow-green.

"Rats? What did you ever read of the rats in the trenches? Next to gas, they still slide on their fat bellies through my dreams. Poe could have got new inspiration from their dirty hordes. Rats, rats, rats—I see them still, slinking from new meals on corpses, from Belgium to the Swiss Alps. Rats, rats, rats, tens of thousands of rats, crunching between battle lines while the rapid-firing guns mow the trench edge—crunching their hellish feasts. Full fed, slipping and sliding down into the wet trenches they swarm at night—and more than one poor wretch has had his face eaten off by them while he slept.

"Stench? Did you ever breathe air foul with the gases arising from a thousand rotting corpses? Dirt? Have you ever fought half madly through the days and nights and weeks unwashed, with feverish rests between long hours of agony, while the guns boom their awful symphony of death, and the bullets zip-zip-zip ceaselessly along the trench edge that is your skyline—and your deathline, too, if you stretch and stand upright?

"Yes, I, Romeo Houle, know the trench. I longed for big adventures, you see, and now, ah, God! I am sick of adventure, for the adventures I have had will plague my sleep until I die."

On December 15 was announced the retirement of Field-Marshal Sir John French from the chief command of the British forces on the Western Front. This left Joffre the only survivor among chief commanders who were serving at the outbreak of the war. Moltke was gone, the Grand Duke Nicholas was gone from the Eastern Front and was serving in the Caucasus (none then dreamed of what he would soon do at Erzerum and Trebizond); and the Austrian generals Auffenberg and Dankl had been among the first to go. Below the rank of commander-in-chief there had been a drastic weeding out of generals in all armies. The hand of Joffre had been particularly heavy. Indeed, he had made wholesale changes before the war actually began and during the first weeks of actual fighting had cut right and left. Of men at the head of the five French armies which took the field—Duball, Castelnau, Ruffey, Langle de Cary, and Lanrezac—two had been removed as soon as the retreat to the Marne began. Ruffey, who failed on the Meuse, gave way to Sarrail, and Lanrezac, who failed on the Sambre, made way for Franchet d'Esperey, later to become the hero of the defeat of the Central Powers on the Macedonian front. Castelnau had failed in the early invasion of Lorraine, but his ability was such that he kept his place and within a few weeks had won a magnificent success before Nancy. Foch, the immortal Foch, who had had a minor command in Lorraine in August, 1914, still remained and had gone much higher up. Of the Germans the first to go had been Hausen, who led the Saxon army on the Marne. Deming, who commanded in Alsace, had also disappeared. Kluck was heard of as convalescing from what gave every sign of being a diplomatic illness. Of British commanders, Ian Hamilton had failed in the Dardanelles, and Smith-Dorrien had been transferred to East Africa. Of the Russians, besides the Grand Duke, Samsonov was dead, Rennenkampf and Sievers had been displaced and Radko Dmitrieff, who took the brunt of the Teuton attack in Galicia, was also out. Neither was there any longer mention now of Brusiloff, who had helped to win the battles of Rawa Russka and Lemberg, but of him something notable was heard a year later. Ruzsky and Ivanoff had survived, and apparently with credit.

A great war usually brings to the front an eminent soldier or statesmen, but seldom does so at the beginning. England's Civil War was well advanced before it saw the advent of Cromwell and Montrose. The French Revolution was four years old before Napoleon's star was seen above the horizon. Great Britain had to survive fourteen years of war to witness the coming of Wellington. In our Civil War we found an exception to the rule in the South, where, almost from the start, two leaders of high genius, Lee and Jackson, sprang into fame; but in the North the rule came back, for Lincoln had to work with a long succession of ineffective generals—

McClellan, McDowell, Burnside, Pope, Banks, and Hooker—before he found in Grant a soldier competent to use effectively the vast resources of the Union, and in Sherman and Sheridan men who could ably support him. It was fair to infer that unless war is originated by a genius like Alexander or Charles XII, there must generally be a long period before a nation can find a leader possest of something which is genius in war. The Punic Wars had long to wait for Scipio Africanus and the Roman revolution long for Julius Cæsar.

When one looked for specific reasons for the going of French it was hard to speak definitely. The outstanding reason plainly was failure to show results commensurate with the size of the British army. The specific reasons were failure at Neuve Chapelle in March and disappointment at Loos in September. The same accusations were made in both instances—lack of preparation by the staff and delay in bringing up reserves. French confest to a state of confusion during part of the operations around Loos. But it was unjust to overlook the peculiar handicap under which the British army under French had labored. It had not had the advantage of veteran staff-officers and intimate acquaintance with Continental ground. It had to create officers as well as men. Furthermore, it was unjust to speak of a British "failure" around Loos as compared with a French success in the Champagne, because, from the German point of view, both attacks had failed. Considering the superior resources Joffre had at his command, the relative gains may not have been disproportionate. Nevertheless, the fact remained that in Joffre the French had found a man of genius, and in Castelnau and Foch men of great talent who might have used the British with greater effect as Foch did so conspicuously in 1918.

French's going emphasized the changed aspect of the war. At the beginning events were decided by leadership and numbers. With the coming of trench-warfare, it became a question of munitions, so that people spoke of the war as something to be won in armament factories. When the problem of munitions had been solved, it seemed once more to be a question of leadership. At Neuve Chapelle British ammunition gave out, and on this issue Lord Northcliffe assailed Lord Kitchener. But there was no shortage of ammunition around Loos. Britain now had to find men, not ammunition. As formerly she had to find guns and shells, so now she had to find a great leader.

The removal of French promised to become as fertile a topic for discussion as the removal of McClellan from command of the Federal forces in our Civil War. There were points of similarity in the two cases. Both were brave and skilful soldiers, animated with patriotic fervor. Both had to deal with comparatively untrained troops. Both fought vigorously and even victoriously on occasions. But both seemed to lack the aggressive spirit and the strategic instinct by which wars are won. The inertia of the British campaign for many months was unquestionable, but there were many who said that in this respect it merely kept itself in harmony with Joffre's Fabian tactics. At the same time, there were men in England who argued that the Neuve Chapelle failure was due to lack of support from Gallic forces; just as it was also said that the French rescued the British from a catastrophe.

Sir Douglas Haig, who succeeded French, had gone out in August, 1914, in command of one of the two army corps which made up French's little force. On September 14, when the first foothold was gained on the north bank of the Aisne, French referred to the "skilful, bold, and decisive character" of the services rendered by Haig, which had enabled the British to maintain their position for more than three weeks of severe fighting on the north bank. Great Britain was then confirmed in the faith that she had in Haig a modern, scientific soldier of front rank. In October when the British forces were moved to the Ypres-La Bassée line and the great three weeks' battle began, the center of the line was in the hand of Haig, who, in the words of French, "held the line with marvelous tenacity and with an energy and valor that gave further proofs of his ability as a leader."

In three great battles—greater than had ever before been fought by a British army—Haig had showed masterly generalship and won unstinted praise. He was then fifty-four years old. He had served through the Nile Expedition of

1898, being present at Atbara and the capture of Khartum. In the South African War he was one of the first to reach Natal, took part in the fighting at Elandslaagte, Rietfontein, and Lombards' Kop, and rode into Kimberley with Lord Methuen. Later he joined Lord Roberts in his march to Bloemfontein, and was present at Poplar Grove, Paardeberg, Dreifontein, Pretoria. After this came many goings to and fro across the Transvaal, the Orange Free State, and Cape Colony when Kitchener was wearing down Boer resistance. He had now assumed command of by far the largest army ever led by a British general. Haig had under him about twenty-five times as many soldiers as Wellington had in the Waterloo campaign.[15]

[15] Principal Sources: Sir Conan Doyle's "The British Campaign in France and Belgium" (George H. Doran Co.), Associated Press dispatches, The New York *Times*, The *Daily Chronicle*, London; The Paris *Journal*, The *Evening Post*, The *Evening Sun*, New York.

COURTESY OF THE MARINE CORPS RECRUITING PUBLICITY BUREAU.

A MACHINE GUN NEST

AIRCRAFT IN THE AUTUMN OFFENSIVE—THE COMING OF THE FOKKER

September 25, 1915—December 15, 1915

IN the Champagne and Artois drives, an Allied aerial army had become no longer a dream of romance, formed as it was in divisions, with battle and cruiser aeroplanes, scouts and torpedo-planes, all armored and carrying three-inch cannon and rapid-fire guns, all made possible through the development of aviation in a field back of the firing-line ten times the size of a large race-track. On entering this field one saw a monster battle-plane thirty feet high, with arms stretching 130 feet across. Further back was ranged a fleet of battle-cruisers and scout-planes, formed into a battalion, twenty planes in a row across the front, and ten deep. Their huge wings made a front half a mile wide. Battle-planes and cruisers were all armed heavily. Each carried both three-inch cannon and rapid-fire guns. Great battle-planes became a center of attention, as the first actual realization of an idea, other aerial dreadnoughts having proved impractical. One of them could fly with a crew of twelve men, with two cannons on the wings throwing three-inch steel projectiles. Trial flights demonstrated that it had the steadiness of an ordinary biplane. The regular crew for fighting consisted of four men and an officer.

As morning approached, after a night of steady bombardment, when officers on the British front were looking at their wrist-watches, and the figure 6 marked the half-hour—half-past six—a wave of men would rise from first-line trenches and every one try to outrun every other. Meanwhile, with the first flush of dawn, birds of war issued from aerodromes. "I think we had eight planes that day to one of the Germans," might say an aviator, and then a plane would be observed to swoop down like a hawk. At all hazards, that aviator was going out to identify shell-bursts. Other planes dropt shells on railroad trains and bridges, to obstruct reinforcements. The first thing was to hold what had been taken. In this effort the turning of wrecked German trenches into British ones, of making new dugouts, traverses, and parapets, and laying out barbed wire defenses, had to be accomplished before the Germans could concentrate and sweep back in a counter-attack. "There has been a good deal of talk," said an officer, "to the effect that the elements of surprize has disappeared from war. It is as vital as it ever was. Only, concealment was never so difficult. Troops and guns have to be moved at night, when the German planes can not note the concentration."

As the attack proceeded, a veritable flock of planes could be seen cutting circles, dipping and turning over the battle-field, as if giving an exhibition of airmanship. Indeed, they almost appeared disconnected from the battle; and yet no participant was more seriously busy or more intent than they. All the panorama of action was beneath them; they alone could really see the battle, if they chose to do so. But each aviator stole only passing glimpses of the conflict, for each was intent on the part he had to perform, which was to see whether the shells of the battery for which he reported had hit their targets. To distinguish whose was the shell-burst that had appeared in a cloud of dust and smoke above German positions, seemed as difficult as it would be to identify the spout of steam coming from some one pipe when a hundred were creating a wall of vapor.

Armored cruiser aeroplanes were small biplanes of high power armed with a cannon and capable of rising almost vertically from the ground at a speed of ninety miles an hour. By October 8 a large number of these were ready. Several had carried on a night bombardment far back of the German line. During the Champagne engagement they hit a German balloon, which exploded in a mass of flames. Battle-planes and cruisers moving in squadrons, both defensive and offensive, attacked German lines of communication, particularly railway junctions, with the object of cutting off supplies and spreading demoralization in the rear.

THE AUTUMN ALLIED OFFENSIVE

Each squadron consisted of nine aeroplanes of all types, including one battle-plane, two battle-cruisers, and six scout-planes. The complement for a squadron was upward of fifty officers and men for the operation of aeroplanes and their transportation on lorries drawn by automobiles, with which each squadron was equipped. About 100 military aviators were under instruction in one school alone. A large number of these schools turned out trained aviators. Observers not absorbed in battle never tired of looking at these monster birds of war. Above the trenches six or seven thousand feet in the air would appear something as big as a man's hand against the blue light of a summer sky, which was an enemy's aeroplane that wanted to see men on the other side building new trenches, moving bodies of troops or transports, and where their batteries were in hiding.

Seven American volunteer aviators took part in aerial reconnaissances in the battle of Champagne—Lieutenant William K. Thaw of Pittsburgh, Sergeant William C. Cowdin of New York, Sergeant Norman Prince of Boston, D. G. Masson of San Francisco, Bert Hall of Bowling Green, Ky., James J. Bach of New York, and H. G. Genet of New York. Five more American airmen at the same time were scouting and raiding on other parts of the French line, and eleven were in training in an aviation school. These twenty-five men formed the Franco-American Flying Corps, which had an office and club-rooms on the Rue de Ponthieu, in Paris. Three of the Americans—Lieutenant Thaw, and Sergeants Prince and Cowdin—were mentioned in the orders of the day, Sergeant Cowdin for having engaged two German aeroplanes. The American corps had two objects—to assist France and to give American airmen experience in war, so as to fit them to serve as pilots for officers in an American aerial service should an occasion arise. The French military administration gave American military volunteers every opportunity to gain this experience.

A battle between a French aeroplane loaded with 90-millimeter bombs and a fast double-engined German aeroplane was an incident of the battle of Champagne while the offensive was at its height. The French machine had just set out to destroy a line of railroad behind the German line when a German craft emerged from a cloud, and the battle began. Almost as soon as it started, the machine-gun on the French aeroplane having jammed, the observer shouted to the pilot, "Dive! Dive!" whereupon the machine plunged in a swift curve. The German, no less prompt, dived too, and continued to fly around the French machine, which was hampered by the weight of bombs it carried. After firing his carbine until his supply of cartridges was exhausted, it having occurred to the French observer that an abrupt landing would be fatal to him and his pilot unless the fuses were removed from the bombs, he coolly set about taking out the fuses, and had just finished the task when a bullet struck him in the back and a moment later another, and then a third shattered one of his wrists. The pilot was hit in the eye by a piece of the propeller knocked off by a bullet, and then wounded in the abdomen and fainted. After this the observer seized the levers and guided the machine into French trenches. Both observer and pilot survived their wounds. The destruction in the Champagne of a German captive balloon, of the type known as "sausage," was another incident of this battle. Determined to get rid of this balloon, by means of which the Germans had obtained valuable information regarding the movements of French troops, an officer had experimented for two months with "fire" balls. The aeroplane which guarded the balloon, moored fifteen miles behind the German lines, was so vigilant that the lieutenant had to try four times before he could rise above it. On the fourth attempt he swooped down in a giddy flight from a height of 10,000 feet, and placed his missiles accurately before the balloon could be hauled down. In dropping his fire-bombs the Frenchman came near enough the earth to be in full range of German aircraft-guns, but he managed to rise safely and so escaped from a perfect hurricane of bursting shrapnel.

After the taking of Loos early in October the British army was singing the praises of guns and aeroplanes. No such bombardment had ever been heard on the British front as that which preceded the attack. There seemed no intervals between the reports of guns. As the attack proceeded, a flock of aeroplanes was seen cutting circles and dipping and turning over the battlefield as if making an exhibition of airmanship. No participant was more busy or intent than they. All the panorama of action was beneath them; they alone could really see the battle if they so chose. But each aviator stole only passing glimpses of the whole; for each was intent on his own part, which was to keep watch and see whether the shells of the battery to which he reported

ADOLPH PÉGOUD'S MONUMENT

Pégoud's air exploits earned him the title "King of the Air." He had been five times mentioned in an Order of the Day. His death occurred in August, 1915

were on the target or not. Every youth in England apparently has wanted to get into the aerial service. So the aviation corps had the pick of men. Promotion was rapid. It took only two months to train a man into aptitude to do the routine work of reconnaissance, but he had to be young. Men did not learn readily after they were thirty, and were very poor pupils after thirty-five.

Occasionally a plane might be observed to sweep down like a hawk which had located a fish in the water. At all hazards the intrepid aviator was to identify the shell-bursts of batteries which he represented. Germans with rifles might have got him, but they were too busy trying to hold back the English infantry. Other aeroplanes dropt shells on railroad trains and bridges, to hinder the Germans from rushing reinforcements. The French aviator Pégoud, whose death was announced in the late summer, had chased twenty-one German machines, most of them declining to fight. Two of them faced him—one on the 28th, and the other, from which he was killed, on the 31st. M. Crémot, whose son by adoption Pégoud was, afterward published Pégoud's diary, describing a journey of December 27 when he lost his way and nearly ran out of petrol:

"Weather cloudy. Morning observation at Verdun. No Boche aeroplane about. 12:20 leave with eight shells for Nantillois. At 4,200 feet over Bras I get into clouds. Fog and rain continue over Nantillois. More than beastly. My machine in all positions. Can see nothing. Am continually wiping my glasses; compass jammed. After one and one-half hours of all sorts of worry dive to get my position. I notice 1,800 feet under the clouds a fine captive balloon and drop my eight bombs. General panic in the company. Several guns are fired at me, and I rise up into the fog. Lost again. Dive down to see, and continue flight at 3,000 feet. Up again among the clouds, and dive down to 2,400 feet. I steady the machine and compass and take the direction S. W. I have an hour's petrol left. Swearing like a pickpocket. It's the limit. I don't know where I am and am fired at. I am 2,400 feet up. Up into the clouds. Down again. Note a rather large station. Am shot at.

"Up into the clouds again. Dive twenty-six minutes later and am again over the station. I'm like a roaring wild beast. Only fifteen liters of petrol left. Don't know where I am; am shot at. I make up my mind, and am going to fly under the clouds at 2,400 feet S.W. till petrol gives out, despite shots. I note a village far off, and as I get nearer recognize Etain. I can use my lungs to breathe now. Saved! Good Heavens, to think how mad I have been with rage. I dive with the motor at full speed. The wind is in my nose. I keep on wiping the glasses and break one case and all. Pass over Etain at 1,450 feet, still diving with motor at full speed. Reach Verdun in fog at 150 feet, and get bail and rain. Can see nothing. One of my eyes is hurting very badly. Land. It's a splendid feeling after all. I can breathe now with my face to the wind and take in lungfuls of air. But to think how I've sworn. Another lesson for me, and I shall keep my eyes open more than ever. Report made at once. Captain astonished, and boasts about it to other officers and makes his report. Food. At my ease, very pleased to be by the fireside at Verdun. Smoke several pipes, which are excellent. Bed.''

After France had developed an aerial force with battle-planes, cruiser-planes, scouts, and lesser aircraft, which officers referred to as torpedo-planes, it became necessary to organize a special aerial service with the exactness of details that armies and fleets are organized with, as to tactics and maneuvers of advance and retreat, attack and defense. All the tactics of the air were in course of time worked out with precision. Official reports referred to these maneuvers as those of an "esquadrille," the French term for a squadron of air-fighters. By the end of October one attack had been made with 65 aeroplanes, two with more than 60, and five with from 20 to 40. A strange device used in these tactics was a battery of twelve small glass bottles, set in a wire rack within easy reach of the operator. The bottles contained a liquid which exploded five seconds after the cork was drawn, emitting a little round puff of smoke, or a short trail of smoke. This was the method used for aerial tele-graphing. The smoke-puffs were dots; the smoke-trails dashes. Thus the pilot talked back to a far-away land battery, in dots and dashes of smoke, telling watchers that their shots were too high, or too low, or too far to the left, or right, and giving them the exact range. Another remarkable development in tactics was the use of wireless, by which aeroplanes were kept in communication with a central station over a radius of 220 miles.

Marked changes in air operations were heralded in December, 1915, with the coming of what was called the "Fokker," a new fast fighting German plane which could maneuver easily and quickly for forward firing. It promised at the time to arrest Great Britain's former superiority in the air. The "Fokker" was the smallest aero-plane that had been used along the battle-front, and was sometimes classed as an aeroplane-chaser. Usually it was only about 24 feet 6 inches long, and had an 80-horse-power motor. It could make about 95 miles an hour, but, when equipped with a 200-horse-power motor, promised to make from 160 miles upward. With the exception of the wings, which were usually made of a new transparent material, making the machine practically invisible, the whole construction was of steel tubing. It carried a pilot and gunner. The armament consisted of a rapid-fire gun capable of more than 600 shots a minute. The "Fokker" was the invention of a young Hollander who lived in Germany. In 1911 or 1912 he had built a weird-looking, uncapsizable monoplane. His "Fokker," however, was quite unlike that early effort in which all attempts at securing inherent stability had been abandoned.

The machine was designed to be under control of a pilot in every position; this made it a dangerous opponent, as it could maneuver with lightning speed. Most Fokkers carried a passenger in front who worked a machine-gun. Others had the gun fixt above the engine. The favorite method of attack for a "Fokker" was to go up about 1,500 feet, and then hang around till one of the Allies' machines appeared in sight below. Then, if of the fixt gun type, the "Fokker" would stand on its head and dive straight for its victim, letting off a stream of bullets as soon as it got within range. By making the descent ever so slightly spiral, the straight stream of bullets became a cone of fire, with its apex at the gun, and with the victim inside, so that, whichever way the lower machine tried to escape, it had to pass through the cone. When the "Fokker" got close to the enemy, if he had not already been hit, it approached directly from behind, firing straight along the body or fuselage, so as to have pilot, passenger, tanks, and engine all in one line of fire. Unless the pursued machine was very quick on its controls and able to dodge like a rabbit, some vital part was bound to be hit sooner or later.

The most reassuring answer to the Fokker menace for the British was the exploit of one of their airmen, on January 17, when he attacked "Fokkers" single-handed and overpowered them. This aviator, who had to his name a long list of successful achievements, was then acting as escort to another aeroplane on reconnaissance duty. Two "Fokkers" had suddenly appeared behind this British machine, when

the escort was 2,000 feet above it. The escort dived immediately and, picking out one of the hostile craft, opened fire
upon it with several rounds, so that it was forced down and
continued to nose-dive for at least 6,000 feet. The second
"Fokker" had climbed in the meantime above his British
adversary, but he was soon chased by him up the sky until
within 100 feet of the German, when he opened fire. After
thirty rounds the German machine made a steep nose-dive,
followed for about 4,500 feet by the British pilot, who saw
him reach the earth at last in a plowed field. The British

A GERMAN FOKKER

This particular machine, captured in France, was brought to New York,
where it was exhibited and used in a demonstration to stimulate subscriptions to a Liberty Loan

pilot climbed again to about 11,000 feet, when he discovered
a German "Albatross" aloft, behind and above one of the
British scouts. It fled after a short encounter. The British
pilot then saw another "Fokker" among a group of British
biplanes on reconnaissance, but forced it out of action. The
third "Fokker" descended at a very steep angle until it
disappeared, still nose-diving, 3,000 feet below.

While this success showed that the "Fokker" was not invincible, it was seen that this type of airplane was a dangerous opponent for reconnoitering machines. But it was
purely a fighting machine, built exclusively for the chase,

and neither stable enough, nor able to carry enough petrol for reconnaissance work. It would lie in wait for scouts coming over its lines, climb very quickly and then make a hawk-like swoop, escaping back to its own lines if it met with serious opposition.[16]

[16] Principal Sources The London *Times'* "History of the War," Associated Press dispatches, The New York *Tribune,* The New York *Times.*

THE RUSTING SKELETON OF A BURNED ZEPPELIN

ON THE WESTERN FRONT

Part VIII

THE GREAT GERMAN ASSAULT ON VERDUN

VERDUN BEFORE THE WAR

I

THE FIRST PHASE: DOUAUMONT AND VAUX AND FORTS WEST OF THE MEUSE — THE COMING OF RUSSIANS TO FRANCE

January 24, 1916—April 30, 1916

TOWARD the end of January the Germans began to "feel" the French and English lines, thrusting one day against the English at Ypres, another against the French in Champagne, and one day making a great din of artillery-fire over the whole front of 450 miles. In a general sense, it had been known that prodigious offensive preparations by the Germans were in the making, but there had been so much feinting, and so many false scares, that public interest had become more or less perfunctory, when of a sudden the tide of action began ominously and dangerously to rise at Verdun. Even then it was two or three days before it was fully believed that the Germans had undertaken, in that sector, an attack of the first importance—one from which they could not recede without serious, not to say disastrous, moral consequences. But it was soon seen that they had elected to put fortune to the touch and pay the price of seeing whether the French line could, or could not, be smashed on the eastern frontier.

It was during the famous "race to the sea," in the early autumn of 1914, that the Germans first established themselves at St. Mihiel, some twenty miles south of Verdun, where the French right had been weakened by the departure for Flanders of the Twentieth Army Corps under Castlenau. The Germans seized the opportunity thus offered to strike a blow, not only to cut the railway between Verdun and Nancy, but to invest the Verdun fortress itself. Their success in getting as far as St. Mihiel filled them at the time with a great sense of triumph. German strategists counted on the Crown Prince's army being able soon to sweep around

Verdun itself, and through the Argonne, and so to join the German army that was operating on the Meuse. Instead of this, the Germans did no more than cut the direct railway line between Verdun and Nancy. For a long time this remained the limit of their success. The Crown Prince, for over a year, tried to break through St. Mihiel and Verdun, but he did not succeed in attaining any objective of strategical or tactical importance. At St. Mihiel he found himself face to face with the natural barrier of the Heights of the Meuse which barred him from making a westward advance.

As a preliminary to the attack on Verdun in February, 1916, there had occurred in January an offensive operation between the Oise and the North Sea. Nothing like sustained German action anywhere on the Western Front had taken place except a year before when a German advance on Ypres was ushered in by the use of poison gas. On January 24, near Nieuport, an attack was now opened with a violent bombardment. As many as 20,000 shells were said to have been fired, but without breaking the defenses. When German infantry tried to debouch from their trenches they were driven back to cover by French artillery. Still another German effort was directed against French positions west of the Arras-Lens road, where there was heavy fighting from January 23d to the 28th, a six-day battle, at the end of which the opposing combatants stood practically in the same positions as before the attack was launched. Among other attacks was one on January 29 south of the Somme. It covered a front of from four to five kilometers between Frise and Dompièrre, when Frise fell into German hands and was retained by them, altho trenches south of the village were afterward recovered.

Beyond air-raids and forays, no further event of importance took place on the British front till February 12, when the Germans renewed their attacks on the Ypres salient by breaking into trenches near Pilkem, but were driven out by bombing parties. This was followed by a heavy bombardment of the British trenches south of Hooge, between the Ypres-Commines Canal and the Ypres-Commines railway, after which, on the night of the 14th-15th, the Germans made

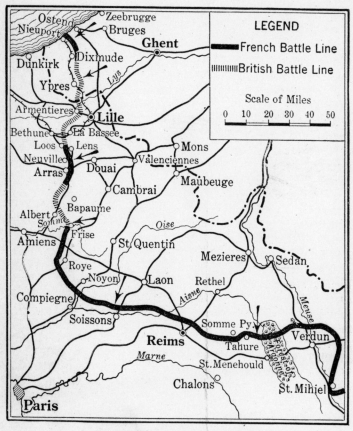

BEFORE VERDUN WAS ATTACKED

Arrows show where the Germans made attacks in the West during January and the first two weeks of February, 1916, the movement being a feint to divert Allied attention from Verdun, the real objective, which was not attacked until February 21

their way into advanced British trenches on a front of 600 yards. The success of this attack was due to an explosion of mines, which rendered trenches untenable. The Germans still had their eye on Ypres, because it barred the way to Calais. Detachments of Germans tried to reach Soissons on February 13, and again on the 14th, but were checked by the fire of French guns. In the Champagne on February 11 the French captured 300 meters of German first-line trenches northeast of Mesnil, and in spite of repeated counter-attacks kept possession of them, but on the 13th they lost a position east of the Tahure-Somme-Py road, and only recovered a portion of it. During the four weeks ending on February 15 the Germans delivered twenty attacks against the French front.

It was still true that, if the Germans could win a great victory in the west—take Calais, Boulogne, and the Channel coast—the moral effect would be incalculable and might lead to the making of that peace which was believed in Germany to have been postponed because of a conviction in Allied capitals that Germany was approaching exhaustion and that the Allies had already won the war. If Germany could have succeeded now, after she had failed in the battle of Flanders, fifteen months before, her success would have been a staggering blow, particularly to France, especially as the Allies at this time were believed to be planning a grand attack for the spring or summer north of Arras and in the Champagne. The German position in France at this time was a deep salient, not wholly unlike the familiar Polish salient which Hindenburg and Mackensen had broken in the summer of 1915. It rested in the west on the fortified city of Lille, and further east on the Argonne ridge now turned into a German fortress. To attack at both ends of the German line, break that line and reach German communications, to envelop and cut off German corps, and so to turn the Germans out of France and Belgium, by a process of envelopment—that was what Joffre had sought to do ever since the battle of the Marne, and that was what Foch finally did in 1918.

The German offensive that was soon to culminate at Verdun became the greatest battle in the west since the Allied drives in the districts of Champagne and Artois in the previous September. On a wide front north of Verdun the Crown Prince had been furnished with an army estimated at from 250,000 to 300,000 men with which to try again. Verdun was the most difficult point at which to smash the French line; strongest of that line of fortified places which faced the German frontier. Why Germany, numerically weaker than her enemies, should have assumed the offensive now, and why she should have assumed it in a theater where

FRENCH SHELLS AT VERDUN
Part of a large open-air storage field where all sizes of shells were kept

the odds were at their highest and the total cost would be tremendous, was a baffling question. To Germany time undoubtedly was more than precious; it had become vital. It was in order to gain time that she had disregarded as "a scrap of paper" an international obligation and had gone through Belgium because the way past Verdun was longer and harder. But the shorter way through Belgium had proved for Germany no thoroughfare to Paris, and now, after eighteen months of precious time and all the wastage of war, she was battering at Verdun once more.

All that winter talk of peace had come from Berlin and had met with a chilly reception, Germany being informed that the real struggle by the Entente had not yet begun. Certain overtures to Belgium—whatever these were, and they were perhaps unofficial—had been answered by a renewal of Belgium's Allied engagements. Germany was not in a position to sit still any longer. She had to consider her own people, who were growing impatient of victories which brought no decision. She had also the prestige of her dynasty to think of, and the whole military and bureaucratic system built around it. Two alternatives confronted her; she might stand as before on the defensive in the West, and look to the East for a decision; or she might attack in the West, and then return against Russia. Perhaps the inspiration for the attack she now made came largely from Falkenhayn, new chief of staff in succession to Moltke, and from Hindenberg and Ludendorff, who had conquered Poland and who believed that a triumph by the same methods could be repeated at Verdun; that Verdun, Toul, and Épinal could be made to go the way of Kovno, Vilna, and Brest-Litovsk.

Germany, to their thinking, had never yet brought into play in the West the full resources of her artillery machine. Attempts, it was true, had failed in the past at the Marne, and in the first battle of Ypres, but Germany had learned the lessons of her failure, and believed that with Falkenhayn to lead her, her new plans, based on an intensified use of artillery, would put the odds in her favor. Verdun was more famous than either Ypres or Arras; besides, it was still intact, and those cities had become mere shells. It was still called a fortress, and had already been desperately battled for. It was less than eight miles from the German lines, and within the area of the Crown Prince's command, so that its fall would have raised the waning prestige of the dynasty, not to mention that of its much discredited and unheroic young figurehead.

In attacking Verdun, Germany really entered a trap, of which she had never dreamed. It mattered not that the trap was of her own making. It was just as truly a trap as if the Allies had made it. To prove her faith in herself Germany attacked the strongest position on the French line, but she got into a position where, to save her reputation, she had to hold on till Verdun fell—or give up a long struggle. To stop would have been to admit to those at home whom her military machine not only wished to impress, but had to impress, that it was no longer capable of the task it had set out to accomplish. Not that German failure to take the fortress would have ended the war in favor of the Allies, but it would have proved, both at home and abroad, that Germany was surrounded by an iron ring, and that, sooner or later, she would have to beat herself to pieces against it in efforts to break through. Germany made the battle of Verdun her greatest effort thus far in the war. Guns that had made short shrift of fortresses in Belgium were brought forward and concentrated there in numbers such as no other section of the battle area on any front had seen. Great guns and small, thousands of machine-guns, masses of infantry, were sent forward in successive waves, only to suffer in time inconceivable losses. The poisonous gases first introduced at Ypres were again thrown forward at Verdun. Liquid fire, shooting out ahead of attacking infantry like so many gigantic dragons' tongues, was employed to sear French infantry as they manned their rifles. Some day Germany's allies and the German public would know how serious and tremendous that German effort was.

Verdun itself was a town of only 20,000 people, but the term was applied to a fortified area of 130 square miles. When the Crown Prince's army began its siege it faced the herculean labor of reducing eighteen outer forts constructed after the most approved plans of modern army engineers. In addition to these there was an equal number of redoubts and batteries, girdling every height in the neighborhood of the town, on both banks of the Meuse. A series of straight lines connecting all forts made a perimeter of nearly forty miles, the longest distance between any two being that from Fort de Marre on the west bank to Fort Douaumont, the most northerly, on the east bank. This line measured six miles, but in the gap were three strong batteries, including Poste and Charny. From Douaumont to Fort Genicourt on the extreme south was a distance of twelve miles. The greatest diameter in the fortified area from east to west was nine miles, which was the distance from Moulainville to Bourrus. The citadel of Verdun dominated the surrounding territory from the left bank on the site of the ancient abbey of St. Vanne. A circle with a radius of ten miles drawn about the citadel before the war would have included more than thirty suburbs and villages nestling in vine-clad surround ings. In the siege practically all these garden-spots of Ver dun were charred by the curtains of fire which swept over the entire region. Some of them, like Fleury and Damloup, under the shadow of Fort Vaux, became immortal on ac count of the frightful toll of life which was exacted in their environs.

The German attack, as initiated on February 21, came as no real surprize to the French. It was a realization of possibilities long foreseen, and for which the French staff had provided means to meet every eventuality. Since Feb ruary 15, the problem of maneuvering and revictualing an army of 250,000 men on the right bank of the Meuse had been under consideration, and had been worked out with complete elimination of assistance from any railways, since the fortunes of the war might not keep railways available. A system of motor-transport had been prepared and or ganized to take the place of railways. The keynote of a battle for Verdun was to be ammunition. On his way west ward from Germany to the front, in March, Cyril Brown [1] passed a continuous procession of ammunition trains, some rolling along through Germany, others crawling over the border into France. He saw them unload their deadly freight at little shot-to-pieces way-stations on strategic branch-lines, well within the range of French guns. Hundreds of field-laborers were straining every nerve and muscle to unload the dangerous merchandise quickly and pile it up into vast mounds, in comparison with which the great quantities of Russian ammunition found by the Germans in Kovno and Novo-Georgevsk in the autumn of 1915 seemed to Mr. Brown "like ant-hills." Other gangs, stimulated by officers, were reloading ammunition into toy-cars, pulled by toy-engines. Among the batteries were a dozen diverging branches of mobile narrow-gage field-railways, "winding away snake-

[1] Correspondent of The New York *Times*.

like." Some of these trains "puffed deep into the fire-zone, where they left loads of ammunition at advanced points." Hitched to miniature ammunition-trains could be seen half a dozen cars, loaded with sections of track, all bolted to tiny cross-ties which only needed to be laid and fastened together.

With an eye to the future, the Germans also had unremittingly pushed narrow-gage tracks close toward Verdun, and so formed a network of ammunition railways. This

FRENCH RESERVES ON THE WAY TO VERDUN

road-building for the transportation of millions of shells was the work of troops. Miles of road with beds of crusht stone had to be built before heavy guns could be brought up. The German front before Verdun resembled the humdrum and well-organized routine of a great engineering enterprise. Mr. Brown's final impression was of heavy artillery boring and blasting away at various points, where infantry wedges would be driven when the time came; of laborious blasting operations till the battle front should crumble and the French fall back behind fortified lines; of monster guns crawling closer and closer on caterpillar tractors; of ground gained in terms of yards and inches only; of an advance that moved so slowly toward Verdun as to seem to stand still; of a concentration of apparently haphazard fits and starts and eccentric jerks that constituted this most unique of military operations, baffling to all except the highest leaders who were in the secrets of the General Staff; of new strategic and tactical methods, uncanny in machine-like inhumanity, and of a wearisome repetition of processes, as merciless as mathematics and as inevitable as the rising tide.

The whole purpose of the German attack was to overwhelm the French with the power of guns, served by ammunition brought on trains on specially constructed railways. No doubt the resources of the French were underestimated by the Germans. They did not know how prodigiously the French supply of munitions had increased. The ratio of this increase was as 1 at the beginning of the war to 31 in February, 1916. The output of large shells rose from 1 at the beginning of the war to 35 in December, 1915, and was more than 44 when the Germans launched their Verdun offensive in February, 1916. Heavy guns were made in April, 1916, at the rate of 33 to 1 at the opening of the war. Of French field-guns the number was more than 23 times what it was when the German rush on Paris was thwarted twenty months before. Thus, as the military importance of Verdun had decreased, the cost of taking it, or of making headway against it, had tended to increase. For the first time since the war started the French were now employing howitzers of the 370-millimeter (14.6-inch) type. Until that time the Teutonic Powers had had a monopoly of big howitzers, and to this fact more than to any other had German successes been due.

The course of the attack suggested within a few days an insufficiency of men for the purpose in hand. Instead of concentrating a great force at one time and place, or striking at the same time in many places, or even repeating blows in one spot over and over again, the Germans struck lightly and successively along the whole front. This was a method least likely to yield a distinct gain at any point, since it was unbinding the twigs that formed the faggot and so unloosed its combined strength. The explanation offered was that, at

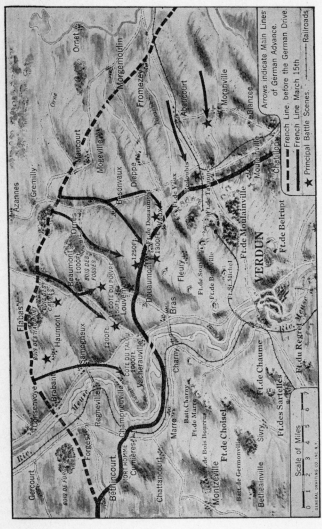

THE FIELD OF BATTLE AT VERDUN

The map illustrates the first phase of the battle—that from February 21 to March 15, 1916—when the French retired from the outer line (Consenvoye to Fromezey) to the inner (Cumières to Moulainville) and then, from strong new positions taken up, inflicted terrible losses on the Germans, chiefly at points where black stars are shown. Forts Douaumont and Vaux were the chief centers of this terrible conflict. Across the Meuse are shown Forges and Le Mort Homme, where the fighting afterward reached great intensity.
The scale of miles shows how far all these points were from Verdun itself

that time, the Germans lacked a sufficient surplus of men to make it possible for them to withdraw some considerable number from any sector elsewhere on the line; and that therefore attacks had to be made in each sector cautiously by troops stationed immediately in each region and having little outside support. The German preparations for the attack in artillery were believed to have been made on a scale surpassing those for any previous offensive on the western front. The guns concentrated in the east a year before probably were not as many as those collected in the upper Meuse valley at the end of February, 1916. But the Russian defeat in Galicia had been due to Russian deficiency in guns and munitions rather than to enormous German supplies. The same conditions did not exist in the west. Verdun, in fact, lent itself to defense in even greater degree than Metz. The German strategy was that of Falkenhayn, and was based on two principles—that no first-class artillery effort had yet been made against the western entrenchments, and that, with adequate concentration, guns might win. As a preliminary the enemy was to be puzzled and distracted.

From the first week of January the Allied front, as already set forth in detail, had been "felt" in all its strength from Nieuport to the Alps. Under cover of these movements Germany had continued to accumulate troops and material in the Verdun hinterland, which was to be the scene of her real offensive, and then at a quarter-past seven on the morning of Monday, February 21, the actual bombardment before Verdun began. The smallest gun was 4-inch, and the commonest 7-inch, but the big Austrian 13-inch also played its part. History had never seen so furious a fire. It blotted out French first lines, shattered communication trenches, tore woods into splinters, and altered the very shape of hills. Following hard upon it German infantry moved forward to what they had been told would be an easy and uncostly triumph. They expected to be in Verdun in four days, as they had expected to be in Paris a few weeks after entering Belgium. On that February morning the air was thick and damp, a raw wind blowing from the east. A short season of premature springtide, which the early weeks of the month had seen, had given place to the cold brume of November. This was perfect weather for the German attack. Their guns, massed far behind in the open and firing by the map, had the exact range of the French lines, while the French guns could not find the Germans, since the limit of visibility was low. It was a sudden, overwhelming blast of fire, precisely directed and fed from accumulations of munitions delivered from no fewer than fourteen new strategic lines, suddenly unloosed upon a front prepared for no more than an average field-bombardment. Its success was planned to be immediate and overwhelming. Soon the French first line disappeared, and German infantry at noon advanced, promenading into possession.

The action started with a general and intense bombardment of the French advanced positions from Malancourt, on the left bank of the Meuse, to Abaucourt, on the right bank; the main volume of fire being directed from the region of Spincourt, where the greatest number of German batteries were massed, against the northern sector of the salient which the concentrated and concealed infantry were in readiness to assault. The bombardment encompassed the Verdun region with a devastating ring of fire on three sides. It destroyed in a twinkling French advanced positions, and removed entirely from the map a number of small localities. It convulsed the countryside like a tornado, vibrated the air and altered atmospheric conditions for miles and miles around, and shattered nerves as well as ground formations.

The advanced positions which the French, under sudden pressure from the Germans, evacuated soon after the ·attack began, had been taken up only for the purpose of protecting Verdun itself from distant bombardment. In the face of an overpowering offensive it had been intended to abandon these outlying posts, remove the civil population from the town, and fall back on the first line of permanent defenses. After the Germans broke through the outer line, the French had second and third lines, both equally strong, to fall back upon. The second line ran from the heights of Montzéville, on the left bank of the Meuse, along a ridge which touches the river at Charny, where it was prolonged on the right bank to the Tavennes bluff which commands the Verdun railway to Metz. On the third line was the Chaume position on the left bank of the river, and the Belleville-St. Mihiel-Belfort position on the right bank, with a continuous chain of fortified works as far as Fort Haudainville. Before the Germans could enter Verdun each position had to be carried at the point of the bayonet after guns had done their work.

Where the ground permitted, the Germans came forward in serried masses, to be met by devastating artillery, mitrailleuse- and rifle-fire. The total forces finally engaged in the attack were estimated as high as from 300,000 to 400,000 men. The French command, while recognizing the strength of the German artillery, refused to believe the Germans were backed by sufficient infantry to hold such trenches as the French might temporarily evacuate under stress of fire. The center of the struggle at first was between Brabant and Ornes. Here dense masses of men, rank after rank, in old phalanx formation, were thrown against French trenches above Haumont, in the Caures wood, at Herbebois and north of Ornes. The Germans were thrown back with losses, except in the woods of Wovrille. Two acute and dangerous French salients, Caures-Herbebois and the village of Brabant, had been left somewhat in the air by the evacuation of a group of twenty or thirty cottages called Haumont. These positions were from three to five miles beyond the outermost of the permanent fortifications of Verdun. The assault proceeded with terrifically increasing intensity and uninterruptedly for seven days, but on the eighth or ninth day the intensity relaxed.

In the meantime, activity increased at other points, notably on the Woëvre Plain, to the southeast of Verdun, and at two points on the line west of Verdun. One of these was at the corner of the western front looking toward Paris. Verdun itself was 140 miles from Paris, but two minor offensive positions, far to the west of Verdun, were 105 and 60 miles from Paris respectively. After two days of rest the frontal attack on Verdun was impetuously resumed, the pressure from the southeast at the same time increased. First opinions apparently were confirmed—that the Germans had made "a fling with fate" and found they could not afford to stop so long as there was any hope of getting through, no matter how great the cost.

THE GERMAN ASSAULT ON VERDUN

By February 23 fighting of great violence was in progress from the right bank of the Meuse to a point southeast of Herbebois. North of Verdun there were infantry actions on a front of ten miles. East of Seppois the French were able by a counter-attack to retake a great portion of the Forest of Cauces. Troops belonging to seven army corps, under the Crown Prince, were engaged along a twenty-five-mile front north. The battle-line reached from Malancourt on the west to Étain on the east, with Verdun in the center but several miles southward. The bombardment of French positions made with thousands of shells was uninterrupted. All available French guns were called into action and responded in kind to heavy shelling by the Germans. In the fighting north of Verdun, which was prest with unabated violence, the Kaiser's troops, despite a heavy fall of snow, made progress toward the fortress, forcing back French lines along the whole front from the east bank of the Meuse to south of Ornes.

"Serious but not disquieting" was the phrase used commonly in Paris to describe the situation. Paris was extraordinarily calm in the presence of the great battle. There were no indications of tension or nervousness, but sober confidence rather in results. The battle on both banks of the Meuse was increasing in intensity, especially in the center on the wooded heights which form a continuation of the Côtes Lorraine. Here the struggle was for the Côte de Talou, a barren ridge commanding the high-road, which the Germans captured in the course of the day, a French counter-attack being repulsed. Simultaneously in the hills east of the Meuse a like movement was in progress. One zone in the neighborhood of the Herbebois Wood, about three-quarters of a square mile in extent, at the end of the bombardment of some hours resembled a field the soil of which had been turned by some new kind of agricultural machine. A veil of smoke and dust floated over the field. An eye-witness described the bombardment: [2]

"Without ceasing shells of every caliber are bursting around us, and the air is torn with incessant explosions. Thousands of

[2] Printed in The London *Times'* "History of the War."

projectiles are flying in every direction, some whistling, others howling, others moaning low, and all this whistling, howling, and moaning unites in one infernal roar. From time to time an aerial torpedo passes making a noise like that of a gigantic rattling motor-car. All these missiles of destruction flying over a fairly wide area burst one upon the other, so dense is the fire. Shell fragments fly on every side from the cloud of smoke and earth, which soon becomes so persistent that it finally covers the earth like a thick fog. With a tremendous thud a giant shell bursts quite close to our observation post, breaking the telephone wires and interrupting all communication with our batteries. A man gets out at once for repairs, crawling along on his belly through all this place of bursting mines and shells. It seems quite impossible that he should escape from the rain of shell which is falling with disquieting rapidity. The enemy's shell expenditure exceeds anything imaginable. There has never been such a bombardment in war before. Our man seems to be enveloped in explosives and shelters himself from time to time in the shell craters which lie thick upon the ground one upon the other. He finally reaches a less stormy spot, mends his wires, and, as it would be madness to try to return to cover, he settles down in a big shell-crater and waits for the storm to pass."

Under this fire the first line and large portions of the supporting lines of French trenches disappeared, and a mass of tumbled earth took their places. Woods in the first line were splintered and shattered "as tho some wild tornado had swept down upon them." Great trees were uprooted and rent and the woods became filled with an undergrowth of splinters and débris.

In Paris the temper of the public as to the final outcome became day by day more confident. For the first time perhaps a consciousness of equipoise in the opposing forces, rather than an intense admiration for a gallant fight against odds, occupied the public mind. After the first days of darkness and disaster along the Belgian frontier, in 1914, the French had begun to realize, faintly, perhaps, the tremendous strength of the German fighting-machine. In the resistance on the Aisne the unyielding wall of German trenches showed them still more clearly how great would have to be their preparations for victory. The Marne, however, had prevented the survival of any legend of actual German invincibility. The fight in Flanders for the road to Calais had shown that, in sticking power, the Allies need fear no comparison with their enemies. In the Champagne were seen for the first time the fruits of war-industries which had covered France with factories. After the first few days of anxious tension during the battle of Verdun, French public opinion began to perceive that here at least the German artillery and German "tackle" had found their equal, if not their master, in the new artillery resources of France.

On the evening of February 25, as the result of Castelnau's

A SURGICAL DRESSING-STATION IN AN OUTER TRENCH
AT DOUAUMONT

visit, and under orders from Joffre, whose chief of staff Castelnau was, and a survey of the situation, Pétain, then commanding in the Champagne, was sent to Verdun to take over direct control of its defense. Pétain, destined to command all the French armies in France during Foch's successful offensive in 1918, at the beginning of the war was one of hundreds of colonels about to retire. He had spent his years quietly in the army seeking neither notoriety nor fame, but performing regimental duties, and sparing neither himself nor his men. Because he had been passed over in promotion lists, and because of his frequent use of a somewhat ironical wit, there had been given to his personality a flavor of bitterness joined to an austerity of life. But he had commanded his regiment so well during the Charleroi defeat, that he had been marked out for promotion. Those were days of wholesale removals of generals by Joffre and promotion was not uncommon. But Pétain got a brigade.

Castelnau having concluded that Vernun could be held, and must be held, summoned to the task his ablest lieutenant in Pétain and Pétain went to Verdun alone in a motor-car, French reserves following. His task was to do what Castelnau had done at Nancy in September, 1914—to hold the eastern gates of his fatherland. He did not arrive an hour too soon. In four days several miles of ground had been lost, and with them gun-positions that made his task still more difficult. Pétain had to reorganize communications which had been terribly threatened, to reconstruct and perfect entrenchments that had been neglected, to bring up supports over difficult ground, to meet the greater man-power of the enemy, and to organize artillery to counteract the hammer-blows of the colossal German concentration. He had to do all this against an enemy who believed a victory had already been won.

An order had been issued by the German command that at all costs Douaumont must be taken and held, since Douaumont was the key to Verdun. Victory was taken for granted when the order was bruited in Berlin. Berlin only wanted the word to fly its flags and make a holiday. When the wearied French lines, after bending back for five days, found themselves reinforced under Pétain, on the morning of the 26th, they launched their counter-attack in which the famous Twentieth Corps of Nancy, the men who, with Castelnau, had held the Grand Couronné, swept from behind a crest of hills and drove back the invaders in the most critical time in the whole Verdun battle. The German aim had been by one torrential assault to sweep the French off the heights before they could reorganize. Had the French yielded, as they might well have done to such a terrific momentum, Verdun would have fallen in less than the four days called for in the German schedule. But the French in first falling back had compelled the Germans to split their en-

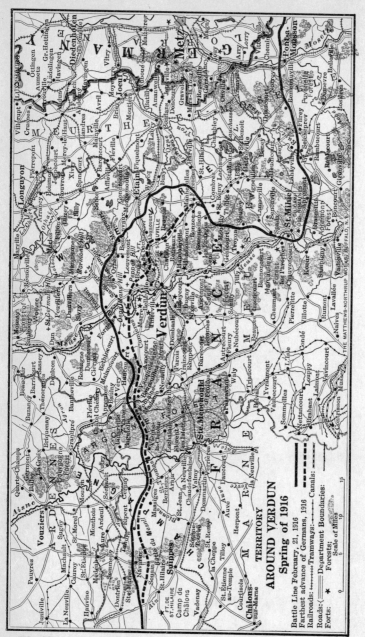

AROUND VERDUN
Spring of 1916

Battle Line February, 21, 1916 ▬▬▬
Farthest advance of Germans, 1916 ▬ ▬ ▬
Railroads: ┼┼┼┼┼ Tramways: ┄┄┄ Canals: ▬▬▬
Roads: ══ Department Boundaries: ══
Forts: ✸ Forests: ▨ Scale of Miles
0   10   15

THE MATTHEWS-NORTHRUP WORKS, BUFFALO, N.Y.

deavors, each part of which now required fresh infantry attacks and new artillery preparations. French guns were fired from positions which the Germans had not registered, and unequaled French gunners handled them. The German momentum did not gain, but declined.

After the Germans had captured the Herbebois Woods, the Chambrette Farm and the Village of Ornes, they found immediately facing them a corner-stone of the permanent stronghold of Verdun—Fort Douaumont—which stood on a protected hill jutting out like a promontory. When, after battering down its armored defenses by heavy artillery, a bold storming attack was made by a Brandenburg regiment, this meant that all the northeastern defenses of Verdun were in jeopardy. Standing on a hill four miles north of Fort Douaumont, Kaiser Wilhelm watched for six hours the bloody struggle for possession of the fort. A raw wind blew sheets of rain and snow across the eminence. Staff officers urged the Emperor not to expose himself on account of a recent illness, but despite entreaties he held to his post, field-glass in hand, protected by a great storm-proof coat, while the Brandenburgs charged the French positions. As Douaumont was being stormed the noise was deafening five miles away. For minutes together there was a continuous crash, huge German shells bursting in and round the town, and French guns answering from every slope. Outside the town from time to time there came a silence of perhaps thirty seconds that was more nerve-racking than the eternal boom of bursting shells. During these silences men waited in tense expectation for the infernal din to break loose again. Never before had so many heavy guns and such superabundance of ammunition been concentrated on a single point. Everywhere on the French line there raged such a storm of huge projectiles as probably had never before been known in the history of war. Practically no small caliber guns were used, the main German artillery being made up of eight- and twelve-inch guns. Officers who had been through the battle in the Champagne declared that the work of French artillery on that occasion was a mere nothing compared with the artillery used by the Germans before Verdun.

Douaumont village is situated about three-tenths of a

mile to the northwest of and below the fort of the same name. It was strongly fortified before the offensive began. Stories were told of protected subterranean chambers, fifty to eighty meters deep, covered by nearby batteries on a ridge running southwestward from the fort. The French could be driven out only after careful artillery preparation and repeated storming assaults. Lying at the base of an elevated peninsula, forming a salient from the fort northwestward of the main line of the outer girdle of permanent fortifications, it became a mere scrap-heap, mingled with the shell-torn trunks of trees.

German artillery, after a pause of sixty hours, returned to the attack against the Douaumont positions on March 1. Douaumont, which was 1,200 feet high, was the highest hill above Verdun, and commanded the whole surroundings. On March 2, from 10 A.M. until 3 P.M., the village was covered with so great a number of shells that the Germans believed they had annihilated the defenders. Having covered their heads with helmets, infantry went forward, but machine-guns and rifles stopt and decimated the assaulting waves. On March 3, the French bombarded Douaumont and soon converted the village into a heap of stones. French artillery charged at night, battalions of selected troops throwing themselves against German barricades all of which gave way. The village was again in French hands. On the 4th, the Germans resumed the offensive. A furious battle lasted from daybreak until the night when the village was once more taken by the Germans, and the French line was reconstructed 200 meters in the rear.

Baron von Reden, writing from the front on February 29 [3] declared that "a new page of history had been turned here before my eyes—a tenfold magnification of the picture of the battle of Sedan." While only a part of the battle around Verdun could be seen by him, "yet this section was titanic in extent." He said of the attack on "the strongly fortified and far-dominating Hill 344," that as the infantry advanced, "a frightful fire from some far-distant French flanking batteries laid a checkerboard pattern of bursting shells on the foreground, through which the brave troops

[3] In the Berlin *Tageblatt*.

stormed with indescribable defiance of death till at last they reached the top of the hill.'' But the French having laid a fierce concentric fire upon this important hill, possession of which was decisive for the terrain on both sides, the German troops ''were completely cut off for two days as on an island and forced to hold out,'' which they did despite everything, and held out until a whole strip of the front was in their possession. Karl H. von Wiegand [4] quoted Paul R. Krause, son-in-law of Field-Marshal von der Goltz, as

FRENCH DUGOUTS BEFORE VERDUN

describing on March 2d, the scenes he had witnessed around Verdun:

''Hour after hour, day and night, the thunder of the big guns in what was perhaps the greatest artillery duel in the history of the world, rolled in from around Verdun like the ponderous roaring of gigantic waves continuously breaking on some rock-bound shore. The roar of battle was at times heard 200 kilometers or about 124 miles. Fascinated by the wonderful spectacle almost the entire population of the towns and villages of the western slope of the Vosges, in the Meurthe Valley and in Lorraine, sus-

[4] In The *World* (New York).

pended work to watch and listen to the deep-throated cannon, which made the earth tremble for a radius of many miles.

"People seemed hypnotized by the spectacle. Not only German civilians but a large portion of the French population; wounded who came from the hospitals far back of the reserves; officers and men of the lines of communication back of the army, and officers and men of the columns of supply and ammunition trains, were assembled on the Lorraine heights overlooking the Woëvre plain, and almost silently looked into the veritable hell of thunder-roars, fire and smoke beyond.

"Several stories high smoke, earth, and débris shot into the air where the biggest shells exploded. Each time it seemed as if an unusually gigantic wave had broken there on the cliff. It was impossible to conceive how human beings could live through that fire. Tons upon tons of steel and iron projectiles were raining upon that short sector with marvelous accuracy, wreathing the ridge in jagged flame and smoke. Numerous columns of French prisoners and wounded passed us. The French were in a state of apathy as if stupefied, utterly dazed. They said no human being could long exist in that hell; that the shock when the big shells struck the reinforced concrete or steel armored plates, the air pressure and concussion from the terrific explosion, and the constant trembling and shaking of the ground were so terrible that it stupefied the mind and paralyzed the nerves."

French artillery officers estimated that, during the first four days of the struggle, the Germans discharged 2,000,000 shells, most of them of heavy caliber. The number of projectiles fired by the French was probably as great. The whole theory of operations was to pulverize defenses at long range, drive out or kill defenders, and then occupy the ground by massed rushes of infantry. The principle of the defense was to search out the heavy pieces of the adversary with equally heavy shells, to withdraw from demolished first line works, and then, when those deserted trench-webs were approached by attacking forces on the run, to catch them with multiplied enfilading artillery and machine-gun fire. At times the fire was suddenly suspended, and the attackers engaged in hand-to-hand infantry clashes.

The Germans used several kinds of liquid-fire projectors. One was in the form of a small tank carried on the back and filled with a composition-liquid which seemed to be mostly kerosene. Attached to the nozzle was an igniting apparatus, the liquid being projected by means of a hand-pump. The radius of action of the oil depended on the skill and physical effort of the man who projected it, but it was ordinarily from sixty to ninety feet. Some French soldiers were burned to a crisp by this flaming liquid. Other chemical weapons used by the Germans were asphyxiating shells which spread vapors that irritated the eyes, and incendiary shells.

Near the end of February had been undertaken an attacking movement in the Woëvre plain. The northern part of that rich, fruitful country, had been in French hands since September, 1914. The German advance now swept over its fields and through its extensive woods, first in snowstorms and then in a spring thaw. Field-batteries galloped past in the open and heavy guns advanced, producing unaccustomed pictures everywhere. Among the fresh troops with which the French in violent counter-attacks sought vainly to withstand the advance from Douaumont to Hardaumont, were seen Moroccan regiments. From the Lorraine Heights a German war correspondent [5] wrote:

"We could overlook the Woëvre plain and see far behind in the background that hell of smoke and fire in which an unprecedented artillery fight for the forts and fortified positions of Verdun was raging. Clearly visible on the horizon rose a bare ridge of heights on the right bank of the river towering above the Meuse heights, and in the valley behind lay Verdun. At the northern point of this ridge, which was also the highest point, a faraway garland of white shrapnel-clouds looked like the silhouette of the fortress which we had conquered. In the immediate neighborhood of this fortress of Douaumont the battle was raging with particular fierceness. Even from our distant point of observation we could recognize this from the white powdery clouds which were wafted hither and thither.

"But how can we describe the hell on the height of the ridge to the left of Douaumont, upon which for miles the French artillery positions extended? Upon them the fire of our heavy and heaviest guns was directed. As high as a house columns of dust, earth and smoke rose from our bursting shells, and it was almost incomprehensible to us t' at men could live there and fight."

[5] Of the *Local Anzeiger* (Berlin).

On March 5, further west across the Meuse, the Germans emerged from positions around Forges and began a long-expected flank offensive. It was about eight o'clock in the morning when their gray clad columns started from the Forges wood and the village of Drillancourt (west of the wood) toward Forges. Whenever Prussian regiments debouched from the lower angle of the hill and the shelter of the wood, they were met with fierce machine-gun and rifle-fire. They were also subjected to the enfilading salvos of French field-guns from Béthincourt and Dead Man's Hill. After a furious bombardment, the Germans entered Forges, and despite repeated French counter-attacks, pushed forward up the grassy slope of Hill 265. Five regiments were sent to the assault. They were repulsed twice with great losses, but the third attack was successful. At the close of the day the French still held the upper heights of Goose Ridge (*Côte de l'Oie*) and the approaches to the road from Forges to Cumières. French officers estimated the attacking forces at not less than 20,000. More than fifteen different battalions were identified by the French. All day the Germans fought to gain a footing in the important village of Béthincourt, which lies in a hollow, overlooked by both combatants. When night fell their last columns were being thrown back by the French, who fought with indomitable tenacity. The heavy losses among German officers were explained by the fact that, for the first time in many months, officers up to the rank of general had on the Kaiser's order led the men into action instead of following them.

On March 10 the battle at Verdun was going on with undiminished intensity, but without causing any radical change in the respective positions of the opposing armies. Fighting was proceeding for definite possession of the village of Douaumont. Reinforcements, brought up by the Germans after this phase of the battle began, had raised the total forces utilized by the assailants probably to half a million—such at least was an Allied estimate. Particularly violent were attacks made to the north of Verdun, around Douaumont, at the village of Vaux and at Fort Vaux. Here the Germans were thrown in solid formation against French trenches at the foot of slopes dominating Fort Vaux, but the French brought their curtain of fire into play and drove back the attacking forces. Northeast of the fort the Germans essayed an assault against the village of Vaux, from which they had previously been driven by the French, but here they were repulsed. An attack on the outskirts of the village of Douaumont was similarly beaten by French artillery and infantry-fire.

Three weeks of terrific conflicts ended in disputed possession. One week the question was as to Fort Douaumont—whether the Germans had taken it or whether the French still held it? In efforts put forth by one side to capture and by the other to save it, a presumption was created that Douaumont was a "key position," but when the French yielded and the Germans finally took it, the effect on the combat as a whole was almost imperceptible. Next week there was a like suspense over Fort Vaux, which the Germans one day were reported to have taken at a dear price, against which came the French assertion that the Germans not only had not captured Fort Vaux or the village of Vaux, but had never stormed the one and were repulsed from the other. Fort Vaux was only two miles from Fort Douaumont to the southeast, but it was hardly any nearer Verdun.

Major Moraht, the German military expert, estimated the French losses at this stage of the attack at 70,000 to 80,000 and the German losses as low; but if the offense had not cost a greater sacrifice of men than was required of the defense, the result was a reversal of experience in war. If the German casualties had not been at least twice as heavy as those of the French it would have been remarkable. An explanation might lie in the fact that the battle of Verdun was an event characterized by new experience. Powers of offense and defense, developed to the utmost, here met as for a supreme trial. It was the most terrific impact of the war, and it came after a long preparation as to means and conditions with problems which could be solved only by the outcome. An inelastic, muscle-bound, direct and headlong mass was impigned with terrific momentum upon a body which was fully prepared to receive it, and which, for tactical and temperamental reasons, had elected to offer a resistance that in quality was flexible instead of rigid. In other words, a German iron-mass was launched and a yielding French body received it with commanders who from the moment the fighting began were opportunists. If one applied the mathematical law of impact, he would have expected that the elastic body would suffer the greatest alteration of shape at the first shock but that it would rebound further, and would ultimately make the greater effort to recover its original form.

Never before in this war, or in any other war, had artillery and heavy guns been employed as they were at Verdun. On this point at least all the evidence agreed, no matter from which side it came. In the first four days of the attack, when the Germans fired 2,000,000 shells, whole woods were reduced to kindling, a river disappeared in one place; the top of a hill was literally blown away in another. The third week left the outcome as uncertain as it was at the end of the first, save that the arrested rate of German progress had to be treated as significant. One of the peculiarities of the attack, from the first, was that it was launched frontally against the Verdun salient, whereas good tactics always before had insisted on taking a salient on two sides at once instead of on the head; to squeeze it together rather than crush it from the apex. It was French military critics who seemed to think this was a blunder, and that the Crown Prince was responsible for it. It was a question to be left for future decision, on evidence not at that time available.

The offensive thus far had resulted in important net gains. While at some points the Allies had been able to regain parts of the ground, the Germans clung tenaciously to many positions despite all efforts to dislodge them. The attack was then resumed with an advance by the German center, as far as Fort Douaumont, followed by a swing of the German left which brought the line to Fort Vaux. By a third movement an advance was made by the right German wing on the west bank of the Meuse. Through this combined movement the Germans expected to have Verdun closely encompassed on three sides and every part of it under fire. The eventual reduction of the fortress seemed inevitable, provided the French did not launch a serious counter-offensive and the Germans did not run short of men and ammunition.

The result of the blow on the west bank was to win a triangle, less than a mile deep, between the brook of Forges and the Béthincourt-Cumières road. It sharpened the Béthincourt salient, but it did not secure the keypoint of the Mort Homme. On the east bank most of the Wood of Hardaumont had gone, and the Germans were up to Vaux village, but they were no nearer retaking the village of Douaumont. Up to now the attack had lost perhaps twice as many men as the defense. The original German plan had gone astray. The battle of Verdun, as conceived by Falkenhayn by the end of the first week had been lost. That swift surprize which was to have given the Germans the city—and thereby a resounding advertisement for German arms—and which in certain circumstances might have broken the French front, had died away into a war of trenches. By the middle of March, it was clear that Verdun, even if it fell next day, would have been bought at far too high a price. The essence of war is to win something from an enemy at a fair price. In every battle both sides have losses; if the loss to one side, whether in position or in men, is greater than the loss to the other, the latter has won.

The German schedule, according to numerous German prisoners, called for an entrance into Verdun on March 2, or two days before the opening of the new German loan subscription on March 4. Verdun had not been entered on that date but Douaumont, with its old fort had yielded and sufficed to give an aspect of hopefulness to the Verdun offensive. Occasional attacks kept up the hope of victory until the closing date for subscriptions on March 22, after which the attacks on Verdun plainly slackened, altho they were continued for many weeks. Thus a loan was made at Verdun, but the commission was paid in the blood of perhaps 100,000 killed and wounded. To deny the success of the loan, as some among the Allies did, was to doubt the obvious. Perhaps less was raised than in the phenomenal subscription of August, 1915, but still it was enough to carry on the war for several months longer. The loan proved that there was still plenty of borrowing capacity in German Government credit.

Berlin's confidence in gaining Verdun was reflected as late as March 27 by Karl H. von Wiegand,[6] who wrote from the German lines north of Verdun on March 27 that "with almost glacier-like force, irresistibility, and steadiness the vast army of the Crown Prince is slowly enveloping Verdun." He said that probably not far from 1,000,000 men had been battling on both sides around Verdun, and "never in the history of the world have such enormous masses of artillery been engaged in battle at one point." On the forty mile semi-circle firing-line around Verdun, from the Meuse above St. Mihiel to Avocourt, the Germans probably had two thousand, perhaps 2,500, guns in active service or in reserve. Were each gun fired but once an hour, there would have been a shot every second. As probably half the guns were of middle and heavy caliber, the average weight per shell was certain to be more than twenty-five pounds. It followed that, even in desultory firing, 160,000 pounds, or from four to five car-loads of iron, were raining on the French positions every hour. The tremendous amount of artillery used by the French was estimated to be almost as great as that used by the Germans. The conclusion was that more than 6,000 cannon, varying from 3-inch field-guns to 42-centimeter siege-mortars, "were engaged in hurling thousands of high-explosive shells hourly in the never ceasing, thunderous artillery duels of the battle of Verdun."

In the sixth week of the assault two miles of line between Vaux and Douaumont saw a resumption of the German attack, being the fourth major assault on the Verdun front, but it was thrown back after it had scored partial gains, French troops delivering one of the few extensive counter-attacks they had thus far undertaken. They regained positions in the Caillette wood and in Vaux village, loss of which had seriously threatened their line of defense. As a result the situation north of Verdun and east of the Meuse, for the time being, was brought back approximately to where it was on March 11 so that the tactical situation remained the same, but the failure of a fourth assault had

[6] Correspondent of The *World* (New York).

for France a larger meaning. It gave further proof that
the French stronghold could not be won by the Germans
without a sacrifice of men exceeding its value, and perhaps
surpassing the power of Germany to bestow. Infantry
masses had been used by Germany four times, with all the
losses that such a course in the face of an entrenched
enemy, entailed, but without breaking the line of defense,
a line moreover which was neither the last nor the best
still standing between the attack and its objective. When

EFFECTS OF SHELL-FIRE IN VERDUN

some intimate history of the Verdun struggle came to be
written the battle for Caillette wood promised to rank as one
of its most bloody and thrilling episodes. After a hurricane
of French artillery fire, there was left a shell-torn ground,
covered with débris, over which neither horse nor cart
could go.

Unless some barrier rose swiftly, a French counter-attack
already massing might sweep the assailants back. Under
heavy fire, the Germans, disdaining cover stood at full
height making a chain that stretched openly across hollows

and over hillocks, a fair target for French gunners, who missed no chance. Again and again great rents were torn in that line by bursting melinite, but as coolly as at maneuvers the iron-disciplined soldiers of Germany sprang forward from rear shelters to take the places of fallen comrades and the work went on. Gradually another line came in and doubled the chain as upheaved corpses formed a continous embankment, each additional dead man giving greater protection to his comrades. The work of resistance ended after fearful cost. As the vanguard sullenly withdrew there burst along the whole length a havoc of flame directed at the advancing Frenchmen who dashed forward, but the barrier still held. As evening fell German working-parties burrowed like moles in a maze of trenches.

Here had been seen a radical change in the tactics employed by the Germans. One saw the massed formation that was to mark many later German offensives, companies of men hurled one after another at a single point, with just sufficient interval to give a succeeding attack the full force of a definite blow. Had it not been for the rapid-fire French guns, probably nothing could have withstood the shattering impact of that resolute body of humanity. The rapid-fire gun found nothing to compete with it. A dozen of such guns, operated by fewer than fifty men could melt the ranks of a charging company as if they were wraiths of battle-smoke. About a thousand Frenchmen stood off 15,000 Germans coming on in four columns. No less enthralling was the story of men on the crest of the "waves" that beat against fortifications. A German officer named Ross[7] found so overpowering the impressions burned upon men's memories by these attacks that they "cared mainly to keep silent about them and to forget them." But he was induced to say:

"What are we fighting f r; why are we lying under shell-fire for days on end, freezing, thirsting, in mud and water, between the dead and the dying; why do we hourly greet death if not for you at home? I do not speak of myself; I am still alive and unwounded. I speak for the thousands who are shielding Germany's

[7] In the *Vossiche Zeitung* (Berlin).

hearth with their bodies, who are silent without expecting either thanks or recognition, simply doing their duty, and a hundred times more than their duty. I do not call them 'heroes.' That word is worn out. They are more than heroes. There is many a weakling among them who in peace-time ran from a biting dog, yet who lies now, under a murderous shell-fire in trenches which are shot to pieces, without murmuring, and leaps toward death on signal without hesitation, without fear, almost without consciousness. These men are dying for you daily, hourly."

As to how long the Germans could keep up an offensive on such a gigantic scale there was wide difference of opinion. The Allies said the Germans were every day suffering enormous losses, and that they had by March 15 used up two-thirds of 300,000 men. But unofficial reports from Berlin claimed that the German losses amounted to "only a few thousand" and that the Allied reports were "fantastic." According to the British, the Brandenburgers who stormed Fort Douaumont lost 40,000, but the official German casualty list gave only 202, of whom fifty were killed. There was also great discrepancy in the accounts of early operations at Vaux. The fighting on the western side of the Meuse seemed at this time more important than that on the eastern. A sufficient advance there could have cut off Verdun from Paris, which so far had been kept in communication one with another by railroad and a double stream of automobiles.

The Meuse pursues a winding course north of Verdun. In one of its loops lay the village of Champenville, which the Germans had taken. Just north of this the river makes a curve to the east around Forgès and Regnéville, two villages which also had been taken by the Germans. Beyond these points the way to Verdun was barred by two strongly fortified heights, the Côte de l'Oie and Le Mort Homme (Goose Ridge, and Dead Man's Hill) both over eight hundred feet high and dominating the plain and ravines across which the Germans had to advance. They were about two miles apart, with adjacent lower hills known as the Bois des Corbeaux, or the Crows' Wood covered with timber. Barbed wire stretched from tree to tree had made of it a veritable entanglement, concealed batteries covering all the approaches. In spite of these obstacles, the Germans penetrated the

Crows' Wood and had begun to ascend the slope of Goose Ridge, when the French drove them out by raking the wood with their 75's and charging with infantry. Later the Germans gained the wood and threatened the French line south of Béthincourt. During the next week the Germans made no perceptible progress, altho they attacked on both the eastern and western sides.

On March 29, 30, and 31 they had delivered a series of assaults to the west of the Meuse, several miles away, which were designed to divert French reserves. Pétain had permitted the Germans to seize Malancourt knowing his chief risk was not there. When soon afterward the main attack fell in the east on Vaux and Caillette he still had his reserves in hand. Having captured Malancourt, the Germans shifted their offensive to the sector around Le Mort Homme. With heavy forces they attacked the French line between Hill 295 and Le Mort Homme and succeeded in entering French first-line trenches. A vigorous counter-attack by the French almost immediately expelled the invaders. Another attack by the Germans, delivered a little later, was declared by Paris to have been completely defeated. The Germans made no attempt to debouch from Malancourt after they had occupied the village.

The heavy bombardments of preceding days northwest of Verdun greatly slackened. There was only moderate activity by big guns to the north and east. About four and one-half miles northeast of the fortress the Germans penetrated the Caillette wood, just outside Fort Douaumont, but as already stated, after a violent bombardment from part of this wood the French, in an immediate counter-attack had driven them back. Another attack was delivered against that portion of the Avocourt wood held by the French, but here the French barrier-fire and machine-guns held the Germans. The French by April 2 had entirely evacuated the village of Vaux and drawn their lines south of the town, to points in its immediate outskirts.

The Germans had not been brought to a full stop, as the British were at Neuve Chapelle or the French in the previous autumn in the Champagne. Nor was the fate of Russia being repeated in France. Six weeks had passed since the Germans launched their attack. In May, 1915, they had marched in that length of time nearly one hundred miles from the Dunajec, had recaptured Przemysl and were on the eve of reoccupying Lemberg, while further south they had advanced sixty miles from the Carpathians, and were winning the passages of the Dneister. In contrast with Mackensen's drive the record of six weeks around Verdun showed an advance forward of perhaps three miles on a front of not much more than twenty-five. The only appreciable German gains were made west of the Meuse, where the attack at first had bided its time for nearly two weeks,

A RUINED STREET IN VERDUN

while the first assault was being delivered east of the river.

A zone like the one conquered east of the river had been gained west of it, by a series of short movements, so that the line on both sides had been made continuous. Attacks had alternated on both banks, with the rate of advance inconsiderable when measured by standards in the Russian campaign, but important when compared with former sapping and deadlock in the west. The capture of one village at a time, like Malancourt, or Vaux, showed that the energy of the German attack had not yet spent itself, altho the rate of advance was not such as to threaten Verdun in the immediate future. Hardly a day passed west of the Meuse without some German step forward. Two days after the capture of Haucourt Silesian and Bavarian troops stormed two strongly fortified supporting points, lavishly protected by fields of wire-entanglements and trenches, south of Haucourt and on the right bank of Forges Creek. Storming troops also took the so-called Termiten Hill, extending a kilometer south of Haucourt along the road from Montfaucon to Esnes. The attack, launched after a strong artillery preparation, was an excellent example of cooperation between artillery and infantry, trained to efficiency.[8]

Disappointed in a sharp advance, the Germans, instead of going back into siege warfare, were still using the method of continued battering. The principle of wastage, which had obtained along the whole front for nearly a year and a half, was concentrated on a small portion of the line. It was a prolonged test of nerves carried on in the open. It had become a question of outstaying one another in sustained collisions. Formerly it had been a question which side could pour in the most terrific deluge of shells in the course of a single day or of a couple of days. Now the problem was one of continuous artillery fire lasting for months. The capture of Verdun would have materially improved their position in France, but only from a defensive point of view. Such an achievement could not have contributed materially to the chief aim of a German offensive in France, which was to break the Allied line and sever connection between the mass of the French forces defending central France and the French and British forces operating in northeastern France and across the Belgian border. The Germans at Soissons for eighteen months had been much nearer Paris than they would have been had they captured Verdun. The easiest and shortest road to Paris started from the Aisne, not from the more distant Meuse.

After a little over six weeks, with brief lulls in the fighting, the feature of the battle which stood out most conspicuously was its relentless continuity. There had been nothing like it on the Western Front. The British drive at Neuve Chapelle and the great Allied drive at Lens were

[8] Karl Rosner in the *Lokal-Anzeiger* (Berlin).

quickly brought to a stop, exhaustion of artillery supplies having ended the forward movements, but at Verdun the Germans lavished fire as it had been lavished nowhere else since the war began, and followed up the bombardments persistently with infantry attacks. Men and material were used with a prodigality unprecedented. Under a similar attack Russian lines in Poland had yielded; the fortresses of the Polish and Baltic Provinces had been evacuated and Russian forces driven back to the line of the Dwina and the Pripet marshes. Serbia, in about the same length of time, had been cleared, the Serbians hardly having a chance to rest in their flight from the banks of the Danube over the mountains to the shores of the Adriatic.

For the first time in history aeroplanes at Verdun took part in the actual fighting; they were used not only against other planes but against troops. When the Germans were bringing up a battery to shell Pepper Ridge (Côte du Poivre) an air squadron dropt bombs from an altitude of less than a thousand feet, killing thirty men and nine horses. With other horses wounded or frightened, the guns could not be moved and soldiers had to abandon them and run to cover. In one day the French reported twenty aerial engagements northeast of Verdun. Sometimes these were duels in which a score of *avions* participated, the new German "dreadnaught of the air," the "Fokker" biplane, turning out to be not as invincible as at first feared.

The most famous of the French airmen was Sub-Lieutenant George Guynemer, barely twenty-one years old, who at the outbreak of the war was a high-school student. He had offered himself for the army but being rejected by the examination board, set himself to learn flying. In August 1915, he obtained his pilot's license, and in December brought down his first German machine, a "Fokker." He then devoted himself to single combats with German aeroplanes, acting both as pilot and gunner. In one duel he chased a German to a height of two miles, where the air was so cold that his machine-gun would not work because of the freezing of the oil. Guynemer then dashed against the German machine and both fell. The German was crusht to the ground, but Guynemer recovered control at a height of

1,500 feet and alighted safely. For his exploits he was awarded the Legion of Honor, the Military Medal, and the War Cross. On the ribbon of the cross were embroidered eight palms, one for each German aeroplane he had brought down.

One reason that the German onslaught on Verdun now slackened was because these air-raids interfered with German lines of communications with supply dépots in the rear. The army attacking Fort Vaux received ammunition and reinforcements over a railroad that ran *via* Conflans and Metz. One night seventeen French aeroplanes from Verdun flew over this line, dropping forty large caliber shells on the station at Conflans and fourteen on Metz. All the aviators returned to their base unharmed. On another night forty-two shells were dropt on the station at Brieulles which fed the northern sector of the investing force.

The only gain recorded by the Germans in a week was Malancourt. While this success made good reading for the civilian population in Germany, it was without meaning in a military sense. Malancourt, of itself, had no value. It merely brought the Germans a few yards nearer a French position that was causing them trouble, and was only a small plateau, amounting to little more than a hill-top, about 500 yards to the southwest. This hill-top was not a part of the main French position like Le Mort Homme, but it had tactical value and was a point the Germans wished to clear away as they had cleared other advanced French posts. Foot soldiers once again, as through history, had become the decisive factor in war. Torn to pieces by shells, their front ranks melting under cannonades, waves of German soldiers flowed incessantly over their comrades' bodies, until at last Joffre unleashed his waiting legions and man fought man as of old. Two facts stood out clearly, the first that German artillery could not silence French, and second that, if sacrifices were ignored and reserves were sufficient, infantry could advance despite artillery and, be checked only by infantry.

Had Germany succeeded at Verdun, she probably could not have escaped ultimate defeat, for sooner or later the Allied workshops would have delivered the needed

quantity of guns and munitions and the Allied army would
have attained a sufficient numerical superiority. Then would
have come a series of blasting attacks, terribly expensive,
but culminating in a German reverse. In the last resort
only infantry could have saved Germany, but her infantry,
from the banks of the Marne to the Riga swamps, had been
wasted like sand. The ground was of no especial value. Indeed, Verdun itself could have been laid in ashes without
affecting the essential military situation on the Meuse front.
So long as French lines held every gain in territory merely
called for another effort and another sacrifice on the part
of the attacking armies.

Tactically, Pétain was master of the situation. He had
followed the traditional French practise of holding his first
line lightly, or surrendering it under attack, and of winning
it back, if necessary, with a counter-stroke. Thus, when a
desperate push was made, he was prepared to fall back a
little, provided he could take sufficient toll of the enemy.
In such fighting the losses of the defense were only a half
or a third of those of the attack. In certain cases, such as
the Douaumont crest or the Mort Homme, where the position
was vital for his plan, Pétain was prepared to push the
counter-attack with resolution, and lose men on the same scale
as the enemy; but his general purpose was to incur no
needless losses, and to make the enemy pay heavily for
every yard of ground surrendered. No village, or crest,
not even Verdun itself, was immune from his grim attitude
of bargaining. The Germans could have any ground they
wanted—so ran his argument—provided they paid a high
enough price. He knew it was the destruction of the German forces, not the sacrosanctity of strips of land, that
could gain for France the victory. April 9-10 marked the
culmination of the German effort. By the middle of the
month the French themselves had taken the offensive—at
Vaux, Haucourt, and the Mort Homme. It was no general
counter-attack—that was not the French strategy—but the
winning of a position here and a position there.

So ebbed the first phase at Verdun, already the longest
continuous battle in history. It had stretched from late
February into mid-April. When the first shots were fired,

"the copses of the Meuse Heights were brown and leafless," when it closed "young green was breaking in waves over the scarred soil, almond trees were blooming, and waterside meadows were gay with marigolds." On that arc of thirty miles a million men had stood to arms. To the observer from any point—from the ridge of Charny, the southern forts, or the shattered Verdun streets—they seemed to have been swallowed up. Only the dull unceasing rattle of guns, fleecy puffs of shrapnel on ridges, and mushrooms of dark smoke, told of a struggle going on with an endless stream of transports choking every road as the might of France moved up to lines of defense.

The result was already a French victory. If Verdun represented a less critical moment than the Marne, it was far more deadly as a struggle, and it bit deeper into German strength. Of all that she set out to win Germany had gained nothing. She had not broken the French front; she had not set foot in Verdun city, she had not lured the British into a premature offensive; she had not taken considerable toll of the French. She had, however, compelled the expenditure of large stores of shells, and thereby had delayed the Allied offensive, and she had won a few square miles of barren highlands. But that was the sum of her achievement. Of losses those of the French up to the end of April was probably under 100,000 men and the German over 200,000. The British at Loos had lost in a week between 40,000 and 50,000 men fighting with nine divisions on a front of four miles.

Germany's tactical plan was sound, but the soundest plan may miscarry. When an immediate success was denied her, she continued to spend herself for victory which every day became of diminishing value. Verdun to her was worth a price, but it was not worth any price; and it was beyond doubt not worth the price she paid after February 26th. Tactically, she probably overrated the power of artillery in action. Her successes against Russia in the East, against an ill-equipped foe, her success against Serbia, a small people, had distorted her vision. She was inclined to regard infantry as a mere escort for guns. But infantry wins decisions; its rôle is the principal one. An artillery "preparation" can

never be more than a means to the occupation by infantry of
an enemy's trenches. It was clear time and again that Germany's men had not the stamina, or the *élan*, to complete
the work which the guns began. The German infantryman
was tried too far; his nerve was weakened by impossible
demands. Germany treated her human material as if it
were a lifeless mechanism, and human nature reacted and
foiled her plan.

In manuals Verdun was spoken of as a first-class fortress,
facing German Lorraine, on the road from Metz to Paris.

AROUND VERDUN NEAR DOUAUMONT

Outside the fortress proper, spreading like the rays of a fan
toward the Germans, lay sixteen or more detached forts,
where, after amazing feats of strategy, valor and invention
and enormous losses, only two detached forts, Douaumont
and Vaux, had been reached. All the rest of the fighting
so far had been outside the girdle of detached forts. For
nearly half the time the city of Verdun had been on fire
from shells dropt into it by big mortars, but it had been
abandoned by civilians and its great fortress was practically
undefended, having been "unclassed" and disregarded after
Liége and Antwerp. The battle took place almost entirely
outside of forts. The fighting was on hill-tops, and in

ravines, forests, village streets, and open spaces. Seven weeks after the beginning of the battle, Verdun was still surrounded by a chain of forts that averaged five miles from the center of the town. Whereas to the east of the Meuse the Germans in four days had covered a distance of three or four miles from their original line to the edge of the fortress line; to the west of the Meuse they had taken four and a half weeks in traversing a smaller zone, and were still a good three miles from the fortress line. The Crown Prince's supreme effort for the capture of Verdun had spent itself.

One of the most dramatic occurrences since the beginning of the war took place in the midst of these operations at Verdun. On April 20, to the neutral world's surprise, it was learned that a Russian force had actually landed in Marseilles and was on its way to the Western Front, a fairly open road running north through Lyons straight to Verdun. At Berlin, this event was taken as a sign that French resources were running low. Quite the contrary was the case. The number of men whom the Czar, owing to the long sea-voyage, could send to France was bound to be small, if not incommensurate with any military results hoped for. France, had she really been in straits, had forces of her own at Saloniki that she could have drawn home. The expedition was generally taken rather as a formal pledge of Russia's fidelity to the Allies. If expectations of a separate peace with Petrograd were still entertained at Berlin, this move was meant effectually to dispose of them. Had Joffre been in any actual need of Russians, they could have been brought to France without the world being any the wiser, but care was taken to give much publicity to their arrival. A censorship which had concealed the departure of the Russians from home could have concealed their arrival in Marseilles.

In the view that the expedition was a sentimental one, was found an answer to the question why it was necessary to bring men across 3,000 miles, or 10,000 miles, of sea when large British forces were available for the French on the Western Front. The British had not only taken over a section of the French line as far south as the Somme, but their line had turned the corner of the Oise and extended as far south and east as Soissons. From having only one-tenth of the Allied line in the west they now had one-fourth; and this change, involving elaborate and complicated maneuvers, had been accomplished without the world's knowledge, until Joffre chose to make it public in formal thanks to the British for their hearty comradeship.

It was plain that, if the British army could more than double its line, it could easily have spared to the French line as many men as debarked from the Russian transports at Marseilles. The Russian expedition had a moral rather

© INTERNATIONAL FILM SERVICE, N. Y.

RUSSIAN SOLDIERS ARRIVING AT MARSEILLES

than a strategic purpose. The French knew that the war must be decided on the Western Front and felt that Russians had come so that all elements aiding the Allies might be represented when the decision was reached. The Russians were looked upon as heralds of happenings of great moment. One of the greetings they received was the appearance in a daily Russian newspaper which had been started for their benefit and in which was given news that Trebizond had been captured. Other preparations included a Russian church.

The Czar's troops had come from European Russia by way of the Trans-Siberian Railway and Dalny. On April 25 another contingent arrived at Marseilles and was received with all military honors. Its coming was greeted by the flying of flags and blowing of whistles from the craft of many nations in the harbor and by a large crowd massed on the quay. The Russians marched through the streets on their way to Camp Mirabeau amid a tumultuous welcome from crowds on pavements, balconies, and housetops. These men belonged to the same class of sturdy young soldiers as the previous contingent, and occupied the same quarters at Camp Mirabeau, the others having already gone forward to Camp Mailly, near Troyes, on the Seine, ninety miles southeast of Paris.

The manner in which troops for this war had been transported from the four corners of the earth to battle on the fields of France, Serbia, Mesopotamia, and Gallipoli, quickened the imagination and commanded the admiration of observers as had no similar military enterprises in history. While lacking the spectacular elements of Xerxes's crossing of the Hellespont, of Caesar's voyage to Britain, of Hannibal's crossing of the Alps, of the march of 10,000 Greeks as recorded by Xenophon, or of Napoleon's expedition to Egypt or of his march into Russia and its calamitous retreat, yet the staggering problems involved in bringing thousands of fighting men across great oceans were almost staggering. Because her colonies were so widely scattered and her command of the seas carried with it greater responsibilities, Great Britain had become the chief long-distance carrier. She brought South-African troops from Cape Town to Calais and her troop-ships semi-circled the globe, a distance of nearly 11,000 miles, in order to bring Australians from Melbourne to Marseilles, by way of Suez. She brought Ghurkas from Bombay to Bruges; Indian garrisons from Calcutta to the gates of Constantinople; Canadians from Montreal to the Marne, and volunteers from New Zealand to Saloniki. From her own shores, in the meantime, there went forth a stream of English, Scotch, Irish, Welsh and other British troops to France, Serbia, Gallipoli, Suez, and Aden. The distances between these many points aggregate more than 50,000 miles, or twice the circumference of the earth. France also sent soldiers thousands of miles by sea, Marseilles being the chief port of embarkation for troops bound for Saloniki, Gallipoli, Albania, and Serbia, while Turcos whom she brought from Algeria served to swell the ranks under General Joffre in northern France.

The coming of the Russians to France recalled vividly certain reports widely credited during the first month of the war that Russian troops were then crossing Scotland and England bound for France, having reached Scotland from Archangel. These reports were remarkable for their persistence during several weeks. London clubs and London newspaper-offices became split into two camps—those who scoffed at the rumor and those who implicitly believed it. The report began in an unassuming fashion. It was said that a certain number of Russian Staff-officers had come to England to get in touch with the military plans of their British and French Allies. Then a certain small number of troops were spoken of and, before long, these had swelled to two, three, or even more army corps. Many denials were forthcoming, but the story continued to gain ground. Men were prepared to bet anything that the Russians were in England or had been there and were now in France. In at least two London newspapers, it was firmly asserted that Russians were going to make their appearance in the western field at a crucial moment. In one office, after every possible means of investigation had been tried, the news-editor was prepared to bet 25 to 1 that there was not, and had not been, any Russian force in England.

When the story was at its height, the favorite theory of the amateur strategist was that Cossacks had been landed at Ostend and Dunkirk and were going to make their attack in the rear of the German line of battle at the psychological moment when the Germans were busily engaged on their front with the French and British. Hundreds of people said Ostend was swarming with Cossacks. Many persons were prepared to say they had actually seen hordes of Russians, scattered over the south of England on night duty. One man asserted that the Russians were mounted and carried bayonets; that they were infantry and carried swords. Others had been awakened from sleep by the tread of thousands; one person in Peterborough said he had seen 20 army trains pass in one direction in an hour; Yarmouth was kept awake all one night by the march past of 250,000 men in astrakan tunics; a whole train had gone through Redhill laden with field-cannon of a pattern unknown to the British Army.

After repeated denials that any Russian troops had entered Great Britain efforts were made to ascertain the cause of the persistent reports. According to a high official they probably owed their source to the fact that several Russian officers, detailed for staff and observation duty with the French and English armies, had actually passed through Britain accompanied by their orderlies and servants, all in uniform. Villagers in Scotland who caught sight of these Russians started reports of a Cossack movement across Great Britain. Among explanations of the great myth was a statement, put forth long afterward, that Kitchener had started the story and craftily promoted its spread, in order to shake German nerves.[9]

[9] Principal Sources: An article by Garet Garrett in The New York *Times* and one by the "military expert" of The New York *Times,* The *Evening Sun* (New York), The *Daily Chronicle* (London), Associated Press dispatches, The *Evening Post* (New York), The Cologne *Gazette,* Baron Karl von Reden in the Berlin *Tageblatt,* "Nelson's History of the War" by John Buchan, The London *Times'* "History of the War," Karl Rosner in the *Lokal-Anzeiger* (Berlin), Max Osborne in the *Vossische Zeitung* (Berlin), Karl H. von Wiegand in The *World* (New York), *The Literary Digest, The Independent,* The *Tribune,* The *Journal of Commerce,* New York; "Germany in Defeat" by Count Charles de Souza, *The Fortnightly Review* (London), "Bulletins" of the National Geographic Society.

THE SECOND PHASE—HILL 304, DOUAUMONT AGAIN AND THE FALL OF FORT VAUX

May 3, 1916—August 30, 1916

WEST of the Meuse the safety of Le Mort Homme seemed assured by the first of May because for the moment, it looked as if the German offensive on both banks had worn itself out. The French General Staff announced, in a semi-official review, that the check of the enemy might be regarded as final, but this judgment turned out optimistic. In the first week in May the Germans made ready to launch another attack, aimed at the capture of Hill 304, the tactical key to the whole of the Verdun defense-system west of the Meuse. If the Germans could have succeeded in driving the French off this hill, and in establishing their batteries at the top, the Mort Homme position would have been enfiladed and no longer tenable. The whole length of the Côte de l'Oie would then have fallen into the enemy's hands, so that this commanding ridgeway could have been used as an offensive *point d'appui* for attacking the Côte du Poivre, on the east bank.

The second phase of the battle divided itself into three main episodes. First, the attempt of the German right wing to carry Hill 304 and Le Mort Homme, to press the French back on their last position—an attempt which succeeded in its immediate, but failed in its ultimate, purpose. Second, simultaneous with the first, a vigorous counter-attack by the French on the Douaumont ridge. Third, a concentrated German assault from Douaumont against the last line covering Verdun, which gave them Fort Vaux, Thiaumont, and for a moment the village of Fleury, and which brought them within four miles of the walls of Verdun.

After inaction there began on May 3 a steady, violent bombardment of the northern slope of Hill 304. Not only were French front lines bombarded, but the crest of the slope behind them became a mass of spouting volcanoes. All that night the fire continued; trenches were obliterated, and the defense sheltered itself as best it could in shell-holes. There was a lull on the morning of the fourth, and then artillery began again, and continued with increasing fury till afternoon. At four o'clock reconnoitering parties of German infantry advanced, but were driven back by French rifle-fire. Altho the Germans occupied a considerable stretch of the first lines north of Hill 304, the French at Le Mort Homme on the same day pushed their left horn forward.

On May 7 came a more formidable assault, delivered on all three sides of Hill 304, from the wood of Avocourt, the direction of Haumont, and the ravine of the Esnes stream between Hill 304 and Le Mort Homme. An intense bombardment began at dawn, and a barrage cut off all communication with the rear. That fight for Le Mort Homme was one of the most costly incidents of the whole battle. The Germans between Avocourt and Cumières used at least five divisions, partly drawn from the First Bavarian Corps, which had lately been on the British front. Their losses were heavy, the ravine of the Esnes being cumbered with dead. There were slopes on Hill 304 and on Le Mort Homme where the ground was raised in meters by mounds of German corpses. The French casualties altho high, were small in proportion to the German. This success brought the Germans half a mile nearer Verdun; but every yard of that advance had been dearly paid for. When the battle was over there was a visible slackening of the German offensive.

By May 10 another great assault, the ninth against Verdun and the third west of the Meuse, was begun with its object the capture of Hill 304. Two or three divisions, including fresh Pomeranian troops *d'élite* were employed. The immediate occasion was the development of a strong French offensive in another quarter, leaving Hill 304, as the Germans thought, neglected. Seven attempts in all were made here. The culminating one of the series, carrying the Pomeranians up a ravine and brook, led to the top of the

BATTERED CASEMATES NEAR FORT VAUX

divide between Hill 304 and Le Mort Homme, whence they were expelled by the French. The German gain amounted to an insecure tenure of trenches still swept by French fire on the north and northeast slopes of Hill 304. The total German loss was placed in excess of 15,000 men for a week's effort. No position had been captured; only the fringes of positions.

Two months had passed since early successes had ended with the capture of Vaux village. Each resumption of the fighting became a cause for increasing wonder in the world outside of Germany. The only explanation was that this new effort was intended, in some spirit of desperation, to be a supreme blow. Germany was a duellist who, feeling exhaustion and loss of blood, redoubled her effort in a forced last spurt. Redoubled activity occurred among the French. Auto-trucks loaded with troops and munitions arrived. Pétain had converted the whole Verdun sector east of the Meuse into a gigantic heap of subways and deep cuttings along which troops could advance unperceived and without harm. George la Hir [10] visited and described them:

"Under ground in quarries the darkness was absolute save when bursting grenades showed brief visions of carnage and terror. It was an extraordinary journey. Altho the bombardment from both sides was tremendous, shaking the earth, we were completely sheltered, now moving along in deep-cut galleries, and now in actual tunnels, above which at intervals we could hear a strange thud, followed by a roar as a shell fell harmless in the open air. Twice we rested in wide, deep caverns, where the men were allowed to talk and smoke without fear of enemy aircraft. They joked and chatted freely as if engaged in a practise march instead of being on the verge of a terrible battle. Only here and there a nervous laugh or yawn marked emotion that was impossible to control. When the signal came for the men to emerge—the combat seemed the most savage of the war. Men fought amid stone-heaps, hand to hand, or at ten yards' distance with grenades like children playing ball. The balls were bombs, deadlier than those with which anarchists used to set a whole city in uproar.

"By May 24, the Verdun deadlock had changed to probably the most terrific pitched battle in history. Fully half a million

[10] Correspondent of The New York *Times*.

men were engaged altogetLer. Whole regiments melted in a few minutes, but others took their places, only to perish in the same way. 'It is a battle of madmen in the midst of a volcanic eruption,' was the description given by a Staff Captain. The valley separating Le Mort Homme from Hill 287 became choked with bodies. A full brigade was mowed down in a quarter of an hour by machine-guns. While the scene there was appalling it was dwarfed by comparison with the fighting around Douaumont. West of the Meuse men died in the open air, but at Douaumont in the horror of darkness, they fought in tunnels, 'screaming with the lust of butchery, deafened by shells and grenades, stifled by smoke.' ''

The great interest of the Douaumont battles lay in the fact that no other portion of the operations gave so clear an idea of the real cause of German failure to break through. The great fact was that the Germans had underestimated the fighting spirit of the French soldier. When the hour of an attack drew near, all Frenchmen knew the price of it. They remembered the fighting at Neuville-St. Vaast, the offensive in the Champagne, the hand-to-hand struggles in the Bois des Caillettes; and they knew the efficiency of German artillery. The French center had allotted to it the big job, which was to carry the ruins of the fort; the right and the left were to take enemy trenches east and west, and endeavor to surround the position. When they all dashed forward there was no singing, and they did not form a battle picture. They bounded from shell-hole to shell-hole, from obstacle to obstacle, lying down, disappearing, rushing forward, some falling never to get up again. At noon a staff aeroplane reported that a fire was burning on Douaumont fort. One regiment had taken only eleven minutes to carry three lines of enemy-trenches and reach its objective. On the left all German trenches west of the fort as far as the road from Douaumont to Fleury had fallen into French hands. The northeastern angle was still in German hands.

The renewed fighting at Douaumont showed that the spirit and dash of French infantrymen were as great as ever. Infantry streamed out of trenches in open order and advanced faultlessly upon the plateau. Once they got inside the fort, the garrison made a most determined stand and hung on to positions in the north and north-east with grim intensity, waiting for a counter-attack to come. They had not long to wait. The rest of the day and night were filled with the roar of battle as fresh counter-attacks followed one after the other. Time after time strong bodies of infantry were launched against the fort from west, east, and north. Two fresh Bavarian divisions were finally triumphant, and on May 24 the ruins of Douaumont were again in German hands. The whole Verdun front was now ablaze. From Avocourt to Vaux the Germans hurled regiment after regiment of new troops upon French lines in a supreme endeavor to break through.

On May 23 the situation on the left bank had again become extremely critical; in fact, the whole battle of Verdun was an unending series of critical days. Time after time the Germans stormed the most forbidding positions, over corpses of hundreds who had failed before them. Time after time regiments which had reeled and melted beneath the deadly sputtering of mitrailleuses reformed and returned to obvious destruction. The French were not long left in possession of a recaptured line. Before night it fell again under counter-attacks. This effort was most pronounced to the west of Le Mort Homme. A surgeon saw in a redoubt 200 French dead, fully half of whom had more than two wounds. Those he was able to treat seemed utterly insane, kept shouting war-cries, their eyes blazing and indifferent to pain. German dead lay heaped in long rows. One observer thought there were a few thousand in the space of 700 yards.

May 30, the one-hundredth day of the Verdun battle, was marked by the beginning of another great battering against the whole western section. Infantry moved out of the Corbeaux Wood against French trenches between Le Mort Homme and Cumières. French guns drove the Germans back in disorder. Five hours later a midnight assault was made, but it met with no better fate. The Germans had resumed a violent bombardment from Avocourt to the Meuse. In the last big attack on this section over sixty heavy German batteries had been engaged, but the number in the attack on May 31 was higher. The fighting began in the neighborhood of Hill 304. Large forces, estimated at the strength of two army corps, were flung into an attempt to complete its capture and drive the French out of trenches on the southern slopes. Two separate attacks failed. Troops gathering for a third effort were caught and dispersed by French guns west of the hill. The best troops of the Germans were understood to have been employed in an attack on Cumières, a little hamlet numbering some twenty houses, and only 250 yards long. All the Germans gained was a portion of a trench 200 yards long.

After this failure the High Command instructed the Crown

UNDERWOOD & UNDERWOOD, N. Y.

A FRENCH CEMETERY NEAR THE VERDUN BATTLEFIELD

Prince to transfer his efforts to the right bank, and use Fort Douaumont and works constructed round it as a starting point for a further advance, with the object of driving the French off the Douaumont plateau and forcing them back to the Côte de Belleville, where their last and most formidable line of defense was situated. Before this could be done it was necessary first to capture Fort Vaux, situated on heights overlooking a deep ravine which extended from Damloup in a northwesterly direction to the western spurs of the plateau.

Its guns not only dominated the ravine but were in a position to bring an enfilade fire to bear on troops advancing from Fort Douaumont to Fleury. It was necessary to capture this tactical point before attempting any ulterior operations, and the Germans decided to undertake the task.

On June 1 the attack began with a bombardment which was described as one of extreme intensity, in the course of which German infantry debouching from west and east of Fort Douaumont, seized positions on the north side of the ravine and descended into it. Fighting went on all through the night, the Germans capturing the village of Damloup, under the cliff on which Fort Vaux was situated. The same day they got a footing in the northern part of the Bois de la Caillette, north of the Vaux ravine. In the afternoon infantry swarmed up the south spurs of the cliff and attempted to rush the fort by a *coup-de-main*, but at first failed. Undaunted by defeat, the Germans returned to the attack and succeeded late at night in penetrating into the ditch of the fort, which had been battered to pieces by German guns. Here they remained four days, unable to enter the interior of the fort, which was held by a battalion of French infantry. The defense had clung to their posts throughout a storm of shells rained into the fort at the rate of 8,000 a day. To escape the shells the garrison retreated into bombproof refuges. Here they held off till the fort was surrounded and the water supply cut off, when further resistance was beyond the limits of human endurance. The surrender took place in the early morning of June 7.

Thirst was one of the most terrible trials to which soldiers on both sides were subjected. Letters captured on German prisoners continually referred to it. Troops were entirely isolated by curtains of shell-fire on a narrow front, making all movement impossible. Darkness was the only protection; but in June the nights are short, and shells were continually blazing. Isolated men succeeded in giving relief at terrible risks. Tiny supplies of water only could be carried. The task of providing with water 400 men who had taken refuge in the fort was wholly beyond their power. Yet the fort was held for four days when a limit to human endurance came. The last message sent by Major

Raynal, commander of the fort, ran as follows: "We are near the end. Officers and soldiers have done their whole duty. Vive la France!"

June 6 was the final day. In the morning a few wounded, who were determined not to be taken alive, escaped through a grating and crawled toward French guns, but several were killed. The defense of this fort was one of the finest examples of French doggedness. Departing from a rule which up till then had always been observed not to mention

MADAME RAYNAL BEING DECORATED AT THE INVALIDES

an officer in a *communiqué*, the French Government held up to admiration Major Raynal. Indeed, before the fort fell, he was promoted to the rank of commander in the Legion of Honor. Major Raynal's defense moved the Germans to admiration. On his removal to Mainz they permitted him to retain his sword. From them he learned of the honor bestowed upon him by the French Republic. In further recognition of his gallantry the insignia of his new rank in the Legion of Honor was conferred also upon his wife. The value of Vaux in the general reduction of Verdun proved small, but its fall was the necessary preface to the beginning of a direct operation against Souville. It was realized everywhere that the French at Verdun were fighting for time. As Sir Edward Grey pointed out, they were fighting, not for France alone, but for the whole alliance. If the French had failed there, the arch of Allied cooperation might have tumbled to the ground, the machinery of victory would have been flung out of gear, and many a month probably have been added to the duration of the war.

Long before June the struggle had ceased to be a battle for Verdun and had developed into a process of murderous attrition. It showed the wearing-out tactics which, for a year and a half, had obtained on a four-hundred-mile front, now concentrated within a twenty-mile area. One might almost say that by common consent the opposing leaders had decided to try attrition with 40,000 men to the mile instead of only 5,000 men to the mile. This plan gave commanders a much narrower field to worry about, it simplified their problems, but it did not change the purpose of the war, which was to see which side could continue to lose the most men without moral breakdown. As the contest for more than a year had been a matching of casualty lists, it hardly mattered whether these lists were filled from a narrow sector around Verdun, or from a line extending from the North Sea to Switzerland. Dead Man's Hill and Hill 304 are several miles north of the line on which the French would have made their last stand to hold Verdun. Possession of them was valuable to the French because it permitted them to deliver a flanking fire on the Germans when attacking across the river, but the view in Paris had been from the outset that these hills would willingly be "sold to the Germans" for a heavy cost in casualties.

On June 8 the French War Office, in an official statement, admitted the occupation of Fort Vaux by the Germans. Its capture, according to the German official statement, took place under a storming action in which guns and 700 prisoners were taken. Thus a problem to the Germans still was to push across five or six miles of ground, every foot of which would be defended. Vaux was, nevertheless, testimony to the extraordinary resourcefulness and persistence of the German attack. If the battle of Verdun had been the only operation necessary in the war, its occupation by the Germans—that is, occupation of the ruins that once were Verdun—could have been predicted, after three months, perhaps, or after half a year more. The essential of German success was that their efforts against Verdun should not be interrupted.

After a brief respite for tired troops there set in on the east bank a series of new assaults no less savage in character than those which gained Fort Vaux. The objective point was a heavily fortified position, not unlike the Hohenzollern redoubt on the British front, which went by the name of Thiaumont Farm. It lay about a mile southeast of Fort Douaumont. Against this farm no fewer than fourteen bayonet charges were directed. Fully 50,000 Germans, including a division never before brought into action at Verdun, were deployed on a front scarcely two miles in length. Despite a frightful cost in casualties, two battalions managed to dig themselves in a few hundred feet in front of their original lines and cling there until reinforcements, flung forward in dense waves, came to their aid, but no dent was made in the French defense.

After dark, when the fire of the 75's would necessarily be less accurate, the Germans sent another full division into the slaughter-house, but after two more bloodily contested rushes, the fighting died down from sheer exhaustion of the combatants. Counting the new divisions which the Crown Prince had thrown into the fray the Germans had now had thirty-nine divisions (approximately 780,000 men) "completely or partially demolished" in the nearly five-months-old battle for the fortress city. In this time the Germans had won many local tactical successes, and had made notable advances toward the town on both sides of the Meuse; but the price they had paid was still incommensurate with its value. It was estimated from documentary evidence and reports of prisoners that up to May 15 the German losses of all kinds had amounted to 370,000. Had these casualties continued on the same scale up to June 15 the losses would have been not less than 450,000. French losses had also been heavy, and particularly in prisoners, owing to the tenacity with which French troops held on to exposed positions long after the continuance of the defense had become tactically hopeless; but the roll of killed and wounded was smaller than that of the Germans, who had been continually attacking.

Berlin had looked for victory in a fortnight; then in a month; in two months, or in three; at the outside, in four. The four months ended on June 21, and not even the nearer defenses had been breached. Observers often said, and France still scarcely denied, that Verdun eventually would fall if the price could be paid. Yet success seemed less likely on the twenty-second day than on the fifth. In two weeks a new Russian onslaught in the East, following the recovery of the Russian army from its disaster in the autumn of 1915, had taken four times as many prisoners as the Germans claimed at Verdun and was calling German reserves to that imperilled front. Some writers for nearly two years had been calling the battle of the Marne Germany's Gettysburg, her warning of certain defeat. Her check at Verdun again invited that American comparison.

On June 30 the French recaptured the Thiaumont works. After a terrific struggle the Germans were dislodged from a place they held for seven days. There was heavy fighting also near Hill 304 when, in a terrific attack, the Germans captured a fortified work in the first line of French trenches. But this success was not won until after the garrison had been buried under a storm of shells. Then the position was recaptured by a brilliant counter-attack. The Germans on the same day delivered a powerful attack on French positions in Avocourt Wood, but the effort was checked.

By the middle of July, Verdun, after a period of comparative quiescence, once more for a time divided attention with the great Franco-British battle begun on the Somme which had been in progress for a fortnight. Both French and German reports indicated that the fighting on the Meuse was scarcely less desperate and stubborn than on the Somme, the Germans having once more attacked on both sides of the Meuse, after an artillery bombardment said to have been equal to that preceding the fall of Fort Vaux.

THE GERMAN ASSAULT ON VERDUN

Denser German masses stormed the approaches to Fort Souville which was the seventh great assault since the battle began. They kept up a violent bombardment throughout the night, but made no infantry attacks. The violence of the attacks gave evidence that Germany was determined to continue fighting regardless of her critical position on the Somme. Eighteen days had been spent in the preparations. She had brought up guns and trench-mortars, shifted more troops from the west bank, and hurried fresh supplies of ammunition to the Souville-Damloup sector. The French turned loose a sheeted fire into the advancing German ranks and took terrible toll with "75's." Only at one point, near the intersection of the Fleury and Vaux roads, did the German attack gain ground.

By the end of July the great struggle for Verdun, the longest continuous battle as yet fought, had fallen for the time being into a struggle of second-rate importance. In a five months' combat some 3,000 heavy cannon had been brought into action; two millions of men had attacked and defended the stronghold; perhaps 200,000 had lost their lives, and the end was not in sight. The second anniversary of the beginning of the war found Germany on the defensive. Verdun proper still lay in ruins, but still untaken. Within the ramparts built by Vauban, where barbed-wire trenches covered the favored promenade and play-ground of old families, in gaping walls and cracked cellars, one had glimpses of twisted bedsteads. Red roofs, where any roofs remained, were littered with tiles torn up and shattered by explosions. In streets were scattered earth and stones.

Verdun had not suffered as Ypres suffered, but the work of making the town uninhabitable had been thoroughly accomplished. Hardly any building remained untouched. In the center where the bombardment was heaviest, little remained, but much had come to light of the ancient city which Rome had made one of the sentinels of her empire. German guns had laid bare a Roman wall, the existence of which had been quite unsuspected. It lay uncovered along the whole mile and a quarter of its circumference. From this old wall stretched out the circles of defense of successive civilizations. First came grass mounds and masonry fortifications built by Vauban; then an inner line of forts which were modern when this war broke out; then trench after trench, field after field, of barbed wire seaming the plain and mounting in terraces upon hills toward their crests and ridges. Stubbed fields which once were green woods were marked by trailing veils of smoke and fume which rose also on trenches that no longer existed. Men huddled under what cover they could find, in craters and mines. The country for miles around was blasted and scorched; in every village there were ruins.

GENERAL CHARLES MANGIN

Mangin under Nivelle, had a command at Verdun during the later operations in 1916. At the historic meeting with the British under Kitchener at Fashoda in 1898, he was present with Marchand. Marchand also was still living and in active service in the West

The condition of Verdun itself was almost indescribable. The town had been built on slopes descending to the Meuse. On its west bank was the famous citadel, on a natural hill, flat on the top and constructed into a fortress. Great powder chambers had been dug into its depths. Long galleries with openings on hillsides connected these chambers. There was now not one inhabitant left in the town. It had become a deserted city. The only sign of life was a soldier now and then going through a street on an errand or with a message.

Parts of the town were heaps of ruins. In other parts houses reared their fronts, but gaping shell-holes showed that probably little was left of their interiors. Verdun was like Pompeii—a dead city.

Since the end of June it had been evident that the defenders of Verdun were to get relief. Along the whole line trench raids were carried out, the Germans kept constantly on the alert and made to feel that something was coming, but where no one knew. Then suddenly, on July 1, the storm burst. Events in the Verdun region became affected and controlled by Franco-British operations on the Somme. Sir Douglas Haig, in a dispatch dated in the following December, pointed out that one of the main objects of the Somme battle had been achieved, when Verdun was relieved. Not only were the Germans forced to abandon Verdun, but the Somme operations so altered the situation on the Meuse that the French were able to recapture much ground lost and to seal quite definitely the defeat of the German Crown Prince.

On July 15, General Mangin, famous already as a hard-hitter, began a series of minor attacks on Fleury which gradually spread along the whole front on the right bank. By August 1 it became evident that a French offensive of some importance was in progress of development. Thiaumont was in the hands of the French on the fourth, won at the point of the bayonet and held against a gray line driven against it in unending surges. Twice the French took that shell-plowed, lead-sown field-work, and when forced out, they won it back. Thiaumont in peace was not even a village, but merely a small farm along the road between two villages, Bras and Fleury. When Liége and Namur had taught the world that forts of concrete were not to be relied upon, this farm was made into a marvelous labyrinth of trenches, of hidden gun-emplacements, tangles of barbed wire and catacombs of underground shelters. As such it was a prize for an army which held it and a constant menace to an enemy. By August 4 it had changed hands six times. To take it the Germans had sacrificed three divisions— 36,000 men. Thiaumont seemed likely to go down into history as sharing, with the open slopes leading up to Fort Douaumont, the gruesome distinction of being the bloodiest spot in the world. On August 8 it was again in German hands.

All France believed the battle of Verdun had now entered upon its final phase. The attacks had lost their dash, but artillery still roared uninterruptedly day and night from behind German lines. The French thrust was netting gains such as neither side had registered since the first phase of the attack. After five and a half months the combat had become one involving the retention by the Germans of the outer rim. The French strengthened their positions on the Poivre heights and for a short time held the Thiaumont redoubt, whose capture more than a month before had been hailed in Berlin as ushering in the last act of the drama. Unbroken in spirit, the French army showed itself sufficient in numbers for its task. It was, however, easy to exaggerate the value of French progress. So far they had taken nothing which materially changed the situation. But it was not possible to overestimate the value of the fact that it was the French and not the Germans who were on the offensive.

Nothing better illustrated the gravity of the strain under which the Germans were staggering than the change before Verdun. To abandon the attack upon the heights of the Meuse was not only to admit to the German people the failure of their most costly operation in the war, but to lose a valuable pivot on which the withdrawal of the German western front might some day be brought about. The attack had not been abandoned, but the Crown Prince had been compelled to send a number of his regiments to the Somme and he was no longer able to continue his offensive, or even hold the ground he had won. After a pause, a series of demonstrations were made, principally on the east bank, leading up to a strong effort to make headway southward toward Souville. As a whole this movement was a failure. The French, after breaking repeated assaults, were able to make a more satisfactory advance, both immediately north of Souville, where they reached the borders of Fleury village, and to the northwest, between Froide Terre and the Côte du Poivre. In a three days' offensive the French had regained all the ground the Germans took several weeks to conquer. They took positions for a depth of about a mile from the slopes of Souville fort to the approaches of Hill 320, as well as in the woods east of Vacherauville, and in the Vignes ravine. They also installed themselves in positions southwest, south, and southeast of the Thiaumont fieldwork and captured the redoubt itself.

The conditions of fighting before Verdun developed a new type of soldier called "the couriers of Verdun." They were men who maintained communication between troops in the midst of *mêlées* and officers commanding from the rear. The battlefield into which they darted with orders or after information was a desolated zone where nothing but thick smoke, sometimes black, sometimes white, gave any appearance of life. Except during the brief period of an infantry-attack it was to all appearances deserted; the sharpest eye discovered no movement of humanity. The earth was everywhere furrowed by freshly stirred earth, but no one saw the hand that stirred it. Occasionally a form was seen going over this desert land something after the manner of

FRENCH OFFICIAL PHOTO.

MASS IN A VAULT AT FORT DOUAUMONT

a rabbit, bounding into sight out of herbs and above uneven ground only to disappear again; leaping from obstacle to obstacle, from ditch to ditch, from shell-hole to shell-hole as it approached the front line, at times vaulting, at others crawling, and sometimes kept motionless for considerable periods by showers of projectiles sent over from the other side of the line. This was the messenger of the modern battle; he was never more needed nor more useful than at Verdun and the type may bear the name for years to come of "the courier of Verdun."

No telephone line could resist the incessant bombardment

that dug up the soil and leveled all field-work along the whole line in front of the fortress. Consequently to assure communications between the front and the rear became a difficult problem. Communications by carrier-pigeons became uncertain, and optical signals were insufficient for various reasons. Nothing was certain except a man messenger and to transmit information and orders across the beaten field required something extraordinary in the way of a man. He had to be an athlete, with good lungs, and, above all, he had to have a stout heart. The courier of Verdun was unable to use communicating trenches, where he would be out of sight of the enemy, because that line was always crowded with soldiers going to or from the front line, with wounded carried back, with men of the commissary department carrying provisions to men on guard. That was too slow a route for the courier of Verdun; he had to take his chances of being sighted and hit above ground.

The first formidable obstacle to pass was the zone that was beaten by "drum-fire," where eight-inch, six-inch, and four-inch shells were bursting with formidable explosions, sending showers of shrapnel over the whole zone. In going through this the courier saw everywhere the spectacle of death, stumbled over corpses, sometimes ran into a cloud of poison-vapor before he crossed it; once through, he was within range of the smaller German guns and the quick-firers. For the whole distance of a mile or two miles, according to position, his nerves were at highest tension, his mind on the end of his mission and at the same time on the obstacles that were multiplied each instant in his path. Some of these couriers got through untouched; some crawled back to the starting-point, bruised or maimed; some never returned to tell the story of their heroic effort. The couriers of Verdun were all volunteers, selected from a considerable number of men who offered themselves for the dangerous mission.

The Verdun battle cost the French very dear. There was hardly a village throughout France which did not contribute to the defense. In spite of a censorship, the country as a whole knew only too well what was the price of the

Meuse struggle. There were moments when all seemed lost. It became commonplace, both in France and in Great Britain, to say that the peoples of the two countries had shown themselves infinitely superior to their governments. Directly responsible for the later plans was General Nivelle, who was appointed to supreme command in France six months later, but was not to retain it long. From the beginning of May, Nivelle was in direct command in succession to Pétain, who had superseded General Langle de Cary in

A FRENCH OFFICER'S QUARTERS ON THE MOSELLE

command of the central group of French armies which included the Verdun area. Pétain's successor at Verdun had a long record of pre-war service in the colonies. He was an old "Polytechnique" man, and had specialized in the use of artillery. Less than a year later the honor of appointment as Chief of Staff came to Pétain.

On August 30 news was received that the Kaiser had removed Falkenhayn as head of the German General Staff, and had appointed Hindenburg in his place. Among neutrals and the Allies Falkenhayn's dismissal was accepted as Germany's admission of defeat around Verdun.

It came more than six months after the beginning of that gigantic adventure, when rumor had it that Falkenhayn believed Verdun could be taken at a cost of half a million men. He had spent the half million, and they were the *élite* of the Kaiser's armies, but Verdun had only turned out a military defeat whose consequence could be observed in the Picardy drive in western France, in the Russian advance, and in Italian successes in the Trentino and on the Isonzo.

While the recapture of Thiaumont on the last day of June, the 130th day of the struggle, was taken as the logical end of the battle of Verdun, fighting followed for weeks, but this was only the backwash of a great action, the last efforts of a baffled enemy who had lost strategic purpose, and the first forward movement of the defense. The battle had destroyed the bulk of Germany's free strategic reserves and had tided over months of waiting during which the Allies were completing preparations. The scene now shifted from the sheltered Verdun uplands to the green hills of Picardy, from the Meuse to the Somme. Over Verdun, as over Ypres, there will brood in history a strange *aura*, the influence of a supreme sacrifice, of splendid resolution, of unyielding fortitude, of tens of thousands who died before her gates.

All over northern France the "lift" brought to the French by the final results at Verdun was unmistakable. Confidence was everywhere newly evident. Frenchmen did not say that Verdun was the beginning of the end; they did not forecast the prompt collapse of Germany, or an immediate end of fighting about Verdun; they did not regard the victory as a Waterloo, or a Sedan, or any other foolish thing; but they did calmly see in Verdun the chief German failure since the Marne, and failure in a fight in which the Germans had laid down all the conditions in advance and had advertised as a victory what they did not achieve.

The long duration of the campaign of the German arms at Verdun was due to "tactical and strategic" considerations, at least so the German papers maintained. One, published in New York,[11] said in May that the German plans did not contemplate the taking of Verdun before August, and that the be-

[11] Called "The Fatherland."

sieging army was then three weeks ahead of its schedule. The methods followed in attack, said another, had been "voluntarily decided upon in advance." Already they had inflicted gigantic losses on the French in killed, wounded, prisoners, and booty. Long after obvious defeat some of the most influential German papers published long articles to prove that all was well at Verdun. A staff officer on furlough wrote in the *Berliner Tageblatt:* "Reviewing the whole series of operations before Verdun, we see that, since the beginning of the offensive on February 23, we have gone forward by steady, victorious stages." The military expert of the *Frankfurter Zeitung* emphasized the fact that "patience had to be exercised," final success in the circumstances could only "mature very slowly." Germany's enemies had made the greatest possible effort to attain a solid coordination of their strategical action, but "had been forestalled," and this had been "too easily forgotten by those who seemed unable to tear their expectant and hopeful gaze away from Verdun." Everything was proceeding according to schedule, said the *Kölnische Zeitung.* There was no need for impatience. Battles occurred either here or there "because our Supreme Command chose its own place and time and compelled the enemy to give battle where we wanted it." One phase of the operations was "linked on to another according to our scheme," and the pauses had not been dictated by the Allies, but had "proceeded from our own intention and the direction of our will." The writer said he did not mean to say that "the enemy's will did not come into the question at all, for such a view would not be in accordance with the nature of war which is a two-sided and not a one-sided activity"; he wished to make the supreme point that "we stick to our purpose in order ultimately to achieve it." German strategists protested that a decision had not been counted on and that the gains were worth what they had cost. Views such as these make strange reading now.

Berlin's claim that more than a million men, two-thirds of them French, fought for Verdun, was exaggerated. The French had not 800,000 or half of 800,000 on their line at Verdun, or in reserve behind it. A conservative estimate of the French forces engaged and in reserve was 300,000. Neither the French nor the Germans could munition and maintain any larger forces in that sector; nor could either have made use of them because of the character of the country. When the Germans asserted that they were outnumbered on the Western Front, and had been for a long time, they were telling a truth which had not been disputed. Germany's indirect bid for peace at this time, viewed alongside her estimate of French losses, gave new strength to the argument of those who believed Germany was approaching the point where her military reserves would be exhausted. There was sound reason for believing that Germany might not be able to hold her lines for six months longer if the wastage continued to be anything like the average for previous months of the war. The whole Verdun campaign had been planned by the Crown Prince's mentor, General von Haeseler, oldest of all German generals still in service, and who, when Verdun had become a failure, went into retirement. Haeseler's achievement in the war had been the conquest of Antwerp in October, 1914.

Verdun, a mighty episode in itself, was commonly thought to be only the prelude to a final act in the war drama. Above the grim orchestration of guns on the Meuse there came from behind the curtain such vague sounds and scurryings as immediately precede the darkening of a playhouse and the upflare of footlights. England hurried through conscription. Russians came across fifteen thousand miles of land and sea to take their place on the front. Fresh Canadian forces crossed the Atlantic. Australians were ferried over to France from Egypt.

At Verdun, as elsewhere on the Allied front in the west, the French 75's played an important part in saving France. Some French officers estimated that these little guns won the battle of the Marne. It was also their opinion that at Verdun it was the "swarms of little bees" that came from the 75's that stung the German columns to death on the bloody slopes of that famous field. If there ever was a weapon which had a personality it was this gun. Other field-guns, as Stanley Washburn remarked,[12] "seem cynical

[12] In The *Times* (London).

VERDUN AT THE END OF THE WAR

© UNDERWOOD & UNDERWOOD, N. Y.

and sinister, but this gun, like the French themselves, has nothing malevolent or morose about it." Its whole atmosphere was "one of cheerful readiness to serve." Killing was a part of its impersonal duty. With a speed of fire of thirty shells to the minute, and with a well-trained crew serving it with clockwork regularity, the 75 resembled a machine-gun rather than a field-piece in action. So exquisite was the adjustment of the recoil that it was said a coin, or even a glass of water, could be placed on the wheel while the gun was in action without being jarred off. In one of the battles on the Russian front a battery fired 525 rounds to the gun in a single day, which seemed at the time an extraordinary rate of fire. When this fact was mentioned to a French captain in the west, he laughingly replied to Mr. Washburn, "I have fired from the four-gun battery 3,100 rounds of shells in forty-five minutes." "How long do your guns last at that rate?" he was asked, for the theory before the war was that a field-piece did not have a life exceeding 8,000 to 10,000 rounds of fire. The officer placed his hand affectionately on the gun and said: "This is a brand-new gun which I have just received. The one whose place it has taken had fired more than 30,000 shells and still was not entirely worn out. You may be surprized at this speed of fire, but there have been 75's in this ~~~ that have fired 1,600 rounds in a single day."

No commercial or manufacturing people in the world, no matter how well organized or how efficient, could manufacture shells at the rate they were consumed in one of these modern battles. It was estimated that two batteries of French 75-millimeter guns could use up in one day the output of 5,000 men for a week. The depletion of shells, therefore, was a serious matter to an army contemplating an offensive. The French had a great reserve of shells when the Verdun battle started, and were manufacturing at an estimated rate of about 250,000 a day of all calibers. But in two days' fighting in Loos and in the Champagne they had used up nearly 2,000,000. How many they used at Verdun after February 21 no one knew or could even approximate. It was probable that the German reserve supply, in spite of all the offensive work they did, had been greater than that of the French. But their expenditure, particularly of heavy shells, had been much more lavish. The French apparently did not use as great a proportion of heavy shells as the Germans, principally for the reason that there was no such necessity. The Germans had to pound intrenchments to pieces and ruin them; the French had to disable men. The German problem was by blasting to make every shelter held by the French a shelter no longer; the French problem was to put out of action as many men as possible as they came forward. The former required heavy artillery; the latter quick-firing light artillery and machine-guns.

Verdun was not attacked, we may feel fairly certain, with the main idea of raising the Crown Prince's lost military reputation by a showy victory. It was not assaulted as a means of opening Paris. It was not beleaguered solely with the intention of breaking up French and British plans for an allied offensive at some other point. Nor was the blow a desperate, random effort, dictated solely by an approaching collapse of German power. Equally certain it is that Verdun was not especially coveted for remote economic reasons, such as the control of the adjacent iron ore basins of Briey. Each consideration might add a little to the desirability of attacking Verdun, but not all of them together would have wholly sufficed. The Kaiser's leaders believed they could reach Verdun not so much by waste of men as by use of artillery. They deliberately planned the operation so that much artillery might take the place of men. This they did logically and systematically, as they did all things. They calculated that they were now outmatched in men on the Western Front and could not therefore fight deadly campaigns without further cutting down their already inferior forces. In output of artillery-munitions they remained superior to the French and British combined; therefore they devised an offensive which relied chiefly on artillery and made a minimum demand on infantry.

Verdun became the grave of Germany's claim to military invincibility. The original conception of the attack was a stultification of the Kaiser's reasons in August, 1914, for incurring the odium of violating Belgian neutrality. His plea at that time of military necessity in using Belgium as a stepping-stone to Paris, broke down when his armies tried to do in 1916 what he had said was impracticable in 1914. The French owed their victory at Verdun to their unaided efforts. They fought during the great long-drawn-out battle as they never fought before, with a courage due to a good cause, and with a confidence inspired by conscious strength. They never showed any sign either of flinching or of yielding. In Pétain they found a commander who was as skilful as he was resolute. They had said early in the assault, *"Ils ne passeront pas"*—"they shall not pass"—and the Germans did not pass.[13]

[13] Principal Sources: "Nelson's History of the War" by John Buchan, *The Fortnightly Review*, The *Evening Sun*, The *Times*, New York; The London *Times'* "History of the War," the "Military Expert" of The New York *Times*, The *Daily Mail*, The *Daily Chronicle*, London; Associated Press dispatches, The *Tribune*, The *Evening Post*, The *Literary Digest*, New York.

BARBED WIRE IN A LORRAINE WOOD

THE LATER PHASE: DOUAUMONT AND VAUX
RECOVERED—JOFFRE A MARSHAL—AS
TO NIVELLE AND PÉTAIN

October 29, 1916—December 18, 1916

FOUR months after the Somme offensive got under way—
that is, on October 24—the French under Nivelle
struck a sudden and smashing blow north of Verdun. Breaking through the German lines on a front of more than four
miles, they advanced at one point almost two. Fort
Douaumont and Douaumont village, the scene of savage
earlier battles, and the Haudromont Quarries, as transformed into a fortress, were captured and the great redoubt
on Thiaumont Farm was taken. Violent German counter-
attacks were delivered but failed, the French maintaining
their positions. Among 3,500 prisoners taken by the French
was the German commander of Fort Douaumont. Nivelle's
stroke accomplished a twofold purpose. It definitely removed the German menace and it halted the massing of a
German army on the Bapaume-Péronne line for a counter-
attack against Haig on the Somme. The German lines were
thrown back two miles at the point where, in the summer,
they had made their nearest approach to Verdun. The
battered Fort Vaux, southeast of Douaumont, was the only
important work on the northeast front that now remained in
German hands. With this resumption of the French
offensive the last vestige of the German's dream of reaching
Paris by way of Verdun was shattered.

The operation falls naturally under two headings—the
battle of Douaumont and the battle of Vaux. Around
Douaumont it was very much more easy than around Vaux,
and much more decisive, since it was largely the success of
the Douaumont fighting which rendered inevitable the fall
of Vaux in the last stages of the engagement. The honor
of carrying the Douaumont fort was given to three battalions

of the Moroccan Colonial force that had earned this privilege by its conduct at Dixmude and Fleury. The Moroccans met with unexpected resistance at the outset, having to recapture portions of their own line before they were able to start for the fort. The incident was curious as an illustration of the surprize which even a modern battle may contain. The French had found it necessary, in order to increase the efficiency of their heavy gun bombardment, to evacuate certain portions of their line at points which ran too close to their artillery targets. The Germans, taking advantage of a fog, pushed through, and when the first of the three Douaumont battalions advanced, it found that it had to clear out its own trenches with grenades before it could get going. This did not take long. The Modat battalion reached its first objective without much delay, and dug itself in, while the Croll battalion swept past and pushed beyond the fort, leaving it to be carried by Major Nicolay's battalion.

During four weeks all French thoughts and actions had been concentrated on this attack. In a replica of the fort, erected on training-ground in the rear, they had fought the action time after time in anticipation of finally taking the fort. Each man knew the exact spot for which he was to fight; each knew the nature of the obstacles he would have to overcome. The battalion, moreover, had been specially equipped for its task. It moved out in thickening fog, and had, like most of the troops throughout the day, to rely upon a compass for its direction. Disaster nearly overtook the men owing to an error in the compass, caused probably by the attraction of a revolver or some other piece of metal. Thus misled they were moving far from the direct line of advance when suddenly the fog lifted and two German prisoners who came in pointed out the rising height of Douaumont in the distance.

The fort consisted of two stories, covered with a tremendous cuirass of sand and armored cement. This shield had completely defied the efforts of the German bombardment in February, but beneath the repeated blows of the great French sixteen-inch howitzer shells it gave way in three places. Two casemates and one of the first-story corridors were pierced, and the upper works, such as observation stations, turrets, counterscarp walls, etc., were completely destroyed. The moat was filled up, and the outer tunnels were blocked by the tremendous fire concentrated upon the fort. In three days 400 tons of steel and high explosives fell upon it. No less than seventy-one of these huge missiles were flung upon the fort. Twenty-two of them fell in the immediate neighborhood of the fort, twenty-three inside the outer wall, and twenty-six upon the fort-building itself. This tornado of shell stirred up the ground as if it were a whisk going through cream, and left it twisted

FRENCH ANTI-BARBED WIRE GUN
Note the revolving knife used to cut the wire

and mangled in fantastic shapes so that it resembled a stormy sea suddenly frozen into immobility. The battle of Verdun, begun on February 21, 1916, had at the end of the year brought the French back almost to the line from which they were first forced.

The French success, while possessing importance as an achievement in itself, when measured by the number of prisoners taken, and for its possible effect on the situation on the Somme, was perhaps most significant as a demonstration of the reserve striking power of the Allies in the west. It had been the custom in German quarters to speak of

France as now "bled white." That the blow around Verdun should have been delivered at the same time that the heaviest fighting in the Somme campaign was under way, argued effectively that French resources were not yet exhausted. German resistance had, however, been weakened along the line of greatest German effort. Battling in rain, mists, and clouds of smoke the French had recaptured Fort Douaumont in less than three hours. The entire operation was witnessed by General Joffre.

The French had launched this supplementary offensive at Verdun eight months to the day after the beginning of the Crown Prince's effort in February. Within six hours they had recaptured important positions east of the Meuse, all except Vaux. French aviators had established the fact that many German batteries on the Verdun front consisted of a single gun and others of only two or three. Since the beginning of the Allied Somme offensive the only German reinforcements that had been sent to that battlefield were drawn from Verdun. Reports of casualties showed that those of the French were less than the number of prisoners taken. A large proportion of the men were only slightly wounded. Three lieutenant-generals who, under command of Mangin, led the attacking divisions, were all lieutenant-colonels at the outbreak of the war, and had been singled out by Joffre for promotion on account of technical ability, energy and initiative.

This exploit demonstrated once more how this war was all one battle, the Battle of Europe. As the Roumanian division had been repulsed, the Verdun division had come to its rescue, cooperating with the Somme division. Railroads had narrowed a continent to the size of what used to be a battlefield. Germans could send divisions from the Somme to the Dobrudja, just as Napoleon, at Waterloo, sent them from Hougomont to La Haye Sainte. Knowing they could not advance on the Somme, and that their only chance to extort a victory was to destroy Roumania, the Germans had launched their heaviest forces there. When Roumania cried for help, the French assailed and dashed on Germany's weakened Verdun lines. The victory of Nivelle was the victory of one wing in the great European battle; the losses

GENERAL NIVELLE

Having retaken Forts Douaumont and Vaux at Verdun when acting under
Pétain in the late autumn of 1916, Nivelle, in the following year, was
made Commander-in-Chief of French armies in the offensive in Champagne,
but was afterward superseded

in Roumania were the loss of another. Verdun served notice on Germany that she had another front to be protected.

The French victory was a triumph of character. The defense of Verdun by France throughout those many weeks surprized all save those who knew at first hand the spirit in which France was fighting. Every one had expected brilliant French charges, but a dogged, sullen, tenacious hanging on—this was what took the Allied world by surprize no less than Germany and cost the Kaiser at least half a million casualties and a great defeat. What Nivelle did was to reconquer practically all the positions which actually menaced the French and so terminated the great chapter of which Verdun had become a subject in the war. That chapter in French history became what Saragossa was in Spain's battle against Napoleon. In those few days the French took almost all the ground of prime military importance which the Germans had taken in months. Verdun had practically been restored to the condition of a bulwark against German invasion. Like the Marne, Verdun was a French triumph. Neither in the earlier nor in the subsequent success did France receive any aid of real importance from an ally. Half a million German casualties, a quarter of a million French casualties—this was the measure of the cost of Verdun. At a terrible price France had saved herself and after a colossal sacrifice the Germans had won nothing. The decision of the Marne was confirmed at Verdun; the day of deliverance for France might still be long in coming, but the peril of conquest had been adjourned without date.

By November Fort Vaux was evacuated by the Germans. The only German occupant when the French entered it was a nondescript dog, who was treated with all the honors of war. Germans left behind, according to an estimate, a million cartridges, 3,000 meat rations, 3,000 bottles of mineral water, large quantities of anti-tetanus serum and other drugs unobtainable outside of Germany. With their artillery in place a Fort Vaux garrison could now dominate the entire Woëvre plain, whence new lines of German entrenchments became vaguely visible several kilometers off, in low, marshy ground.

One of the most interesting statements made by any one in authority in Germany was made by Hindenburg in the early summer of this year to an Austrian press representative, a circumstance which gave to the interview a political tinge, since the world knew the condition of Austria, with her lines shattered and the Russians pouring through and capturing men by thousands. Hindenburg's statement as to the condition of affairs in France was one which Germany had been making, in one form or another, since the beginning of the battle of Verdun. It was a condition which Germany devoutly wished were true, but nothing that had yet happened gave any indication that it was true. Hindenburg said: "France was bled white on the hills of Verdun." Yet before the glow of the Verdun fire died out, the world saw the French take the lead in the terrible fighting on the Somme, and while the Somme fighting was at its height, saw enough reserve-force left to strike another blow at Verdun which snatched from the Germans in a short fight of a few hours all that they had gained after months of fighting.

French troops on December 18 again made an effective thrust. Striking at German positions between the Meuse and the Woëvre, north of Douaumont, along a front of six miles, they forced back the Crown Prince for almost two miles. More than 7,500 prisoners and numerous guns were taken on the first day. The French next day continued their offensive and made further gains. The prisoners taken finally numbered 11,387, including 284 officers; 115 guns were captured or destroyed; 44 trench-mortars, 107 machine-guns were taken with much other material. Four villages were occupied, and the better part of six enemy-divisions were destroyed. The French losses for the first day were in the neighborhood of 1,500. In the later days the total mounted higher, thereby proving Nivelle's point; for he had argued that it was only when the line grew stationary that losses came, and that an attack, kept up continuously, had to be economical—a truth of significance for the future. This success was no sudden gift of fortune, but a result foreseen and planned for—a triumph of generalship and calculation as well as of fighting prowess. The

episode took its place in the history of the war "like some
noble lyric interpolated in a great drama."

"Nivelle has answered Von Bethmann-Hollweg," were
words that went through all France, the reference being to
the Chancellor's peace proposal of December. The cry was
mingled with singing of the "Marseillaise" in many parts
of the western field. Nivelle, who had planned the operation some time before he became aware of his promotion to
the post of Commander-in-Chief, had decided to carry it
through in person, despite his assumption of the duties of

A PROTECTED AMMUNITION MAGAZINE BEHIND FRENCH LINES

high command. The effectives engaged were under the immediate control of Mangin, who gained new honors in Foch's
victories of 1918, and was now assisted by Maud'huy. Each
of four divisions covered a little over two of the ten kilometers of front. The initial bombardment was of terrific intensity, several batteries participating. So well did the shell-
fire keep step with the infantry that in most cases the latter
found it unnecessary to seek momentary shelter by throwing
themselves at intervals flat on the ground, the usual pro-
cedure in bayonet charges. Fortified machine-gun redoubts

in Vacherauville and fortlets at Hardaumont and Bezon-vaux were the chief obstacles to progress, but so overcome were the Germans by the high explosives and shrapnel that continually broke over them, that their resistance was seldom more than nominal.

Nivelle's action was not part of the general Allied offensive; it was an individual thrust made at a time when there was the greatest chance of success. It was also an eloquent reply to official statements from Berlin as to the impregnability of the German line in the west. From the peninsula of the Meuse to the heights of the Woëvre the Germans now did not hold a single position of any importance or of any value from which they could advance. The blow was proof of the basic unsoundness of the theories of Falkenhayn, Haeseler and the Crown Prince as to the possibilities, from a German standpoint, of the western field, and equally showed the unsoundness of the theories of Hindenburg that he was free to do what he would in the east, since the western situation was under control. This success, however, did not mean a breaking of the German line. Twelve square miles did not look very large when compared with the amount of territory in France which the Germans occupied.

Joffre, whose place in one sense Nivelle had now taken, was idolized by the poilus. There was no misunderstanding of Joffre's remaining position. His title remained the same as before—Commander-in-Chief of all the French armies—while Nivelle was Field-Commander of the French armies in France. Joffre in a real sense was more important than before. Inasmuch as the war was to be conducted on bigger lines, the whole nation coming in close touch with the active army, he was to become the technical adviser of the War Council. Meanwhile, it would be Nivelle's task to execute offensives, wage battles, and generally occupy the center of the scene. The choice of Nivelle was the result of long deliberation filled with a realization that, no matter what the future brought, it was "Papa" Joffre who had won at the Marne; it was he who had made the army bigger and stronger than at the beginning of the war, despite its sacrifices, and his name would remain forever one of the most glorious in French history.

Nivelle was one of the youngest generals in France, but no French generals were very young. He was sixty-one, but could pass for forty-five. He was big, tall, and powerful, without an ounce of fat. Except for the trimness of his waist-line, and his face which was unlined and almost youthful in its freshness, he was regarded as a type not unlike Joffre—a much younger Joffre, untired by the responsibilities of high command. Since May, Nivelle had

A FRENCH OFFICER'S SHELTER ON THE EASTERN FRONTIER

been in command of the Verdun defenses, completing the work of Pétain, who had been advanced to command the armies in the Champagne, and was one of numerous discoveries made by Joffre. At the beginning of the war he was a colonel in command of a regiment of artillery and about to be retired. He resembled the authentic portrait of Cardinal Richelieu, in action alert, and while given to gesticulating, gave an impression of reserves of energy, both physical and mental. He had also the reputation of being a strict disciplinarian and possibly the greatest gunner in the French army. He spoke English, having had an English mother, and was fond of reciting English war-verse, like "Hohenlinden," "The Battle of the Baltic," and "The Burial of Sir John Moore," the last of which he had translated into French.

The struggle at Verdun had been the making of Nivelle. When the battle entered its fourth month and the French took German trenches at Haucourt and Haudromont quarry, and recaptured a part of Fort Douaumont, the recapture was effected by Nivelle, who took advantage of the German concentration of effort on Dead Man's Hill on the other side of the river until artillery resistance practically prevented further German advances. When Fort Vaux was lost the French held stubbornly to trenches in the neighborhood, and after Fleury fell the Germans were again driven out of the fort. Altho the Germans reached the inner girdle of forts late in June, they had kept a precarious hold against small counter-successes won from time to time by the French. Finally, in October, the French retook Douaumont, and early in November Vaux also fell before Nivelle's stroke. His last success, the retaking of points that the Germans had gained in their first onset, the capture of over 10,000 men, and the taking or destruction of over eighty guns, gave to him and his new high command a prestige that promised much to the French cause.

Just after Christmas the whole Entente world was delighted to hear that Joffre had been made Marshal of France. Napoleon had said that a soldier of France always carried a possible marshal's baton in his knapsack. Just as Ney, Soult, Massena and Murat owed nothing to birth, so was it true of Joffre, a marshal worthy to be named with, if not above, all these. Louis Napoleon had cheapened the marshalship. Bazaine had added nothing to the rank and Mac-Mahon had been glad to forget his military career when President of France. Marshal Forey had long since been forgotten, even in Mexico. Joffre was the first marshal to be named under the Third Republic. General Chanzy, shortly after the war of 1870, had been offered a marshal's baton, but refused, saying the "distinction of a Marshal of France must be kept for a victorious general, who will have the honor of commanding in a war of reparation." The Government, in appointing Joffre, had not forgotten Chanzy's words. The last living French marshal was Canrobert, of Crimean fame, and the last marshal appointed by the Second Empire was Lebœuf, the luckless Minister of War in 1870. Mac-Mahon pre-deceased by a few years Canrobert, who died in 1895. Since Canrobert died there has been no living Marshal of France.

Joffre was the three hundred and twenty-fifth marshal France had created. The dignity dates back to the twelfth century, when it was held second to that of High Constable of France. For centuries, or until Francis I, only two living marshals were permitted, but their number was increased later to sixteen and so remained until the Revolution abolished the title. Napoleon, in restoring it, enacted that it could be received only by a commander who had vanquished a foe in a pitched battle, or had captured two fortified places. A Marshal of France holds his dignity for life. He wears a general's uniform, with three rows of oak and laurel leaves embroidered on a cocked hat and sleeves, and carries a baton, which, according to Francis I's regulation, has to be twenty inches long, and bear at one end the marshal's name, and at the other the inscription, *"Terror belli decus pacis."* [14] His baton, under the Monarchy, was covered with blue velvet and bore gold fleur-de-lys, and under the Empire, bore gold beads. Marshal Joffre's baton is embroidered with gold stars. The French Government determined after the battle of the Marne to confer this supreme honor on Joffre. On September 21, 1914, a regulation was published specifying that the pay of a Marshal of France, if any were named, would be fixt at 30,315f 79c per annum. [15]

The battle of Verdun, which thus had dragged from February 21, 1916, to the 16th of December, ranked next to the battle of the Marne as the greatest event of the war. Like the Marne, it represented the checkmate of a supreme effort on the part of the Germans to end the war swiftly by a thunder-stroke. It surpassed the battle of the Marne by its length, by the fury with which it was carried on, and by the huge scale of the operations. It came after a year that

[14] A terror in War; a glory in Peace."
[15] About $6,000.

had been rich in successes for the Germans. In the West they had held firm against Allied onslaughts in Artois and in Champagne and in the East their offensive had been fruitful. Galicia had been almost completely recovered, the kingdom of Poland occupied, Courland, Lithuania, and Volhynia invaded. To the south they had extinguished Serbia's opposition, had saved Turkey, and won over Bulgaria. These triumphs, however, had not brought them peace, for the heart and soul of the Allied Powers lay in the West—England and France. It still remained for Germany, seeking victories, to attack and annihilate the French army, and then came Verdun, the object of which to Germany was to win a decisive victory in the West, starting a tremendous onslaught which would bring the war to a triumphant close.[16]

Verdun, which by holding out saved France—and by saving France saved the Allied cause—became two years after the German assault for the Allied nations a shrine at which they paid homage to France. They had deposed at Verdun votive offerings in the form of the highest declarations and medals for military valor which they had had the power to confer. France herself paid the first tribute by conferring on the city the cross of the Legion of Honor, to which was added the Croix de Guerre. Other allied nations followed. In the Citadel were pinned, on a velvet cushion, in addition to the Legion of Honor and the Croix de Guerre, the Russian cross of the Order of Saint George; the British Military Cross, the Italian gold medal for military valor, the Belgian cross of the Order of Leopold, the Serbian gold medal for military bravery, the Montenegrin historic Obilitch gold medal and the plaque, collar and grand cordon of the Portuguese Order of the Tower and the Sword. Above the jeweled and decorated cushion was hung a glistening gold sword from the Mikado of Japan. King Albert of Belgium made a journey to Verdun that he might pay his tribute in person. On a hill just outside the city he pinned various Belgian decorations for military valor on the breasts of individual defenders. King Victor Emmanuel left Italian soil for the first time since ascending the throne of Italy in order that he might also pay his homage in person. Prince Arthur

[6] Raoul Blanchard in *The Atlantic Monthly*.

MARSHAL JOFFRE IN FULL UNIFORM

III.

of Connaught made the pilgrimage on behalf of King George of England, and President Bernardino Machado of Portugal went there in person, taking with him the high insignia of the Order of the Tower and the Sword.[17]

[17] Principal Sources: The London *Times'* "History of the War," The New York *Tribune,* The "Military Expert" of The New York *Times,* "Nelson's History of the War" by John Buchan, Lincoln Eyre in The *World* (New York), The *Evening Post* (New York), The *Daily Telegraph* (London).

FRENCH TRENCHES ON THE MEUSE

IN VERDUN—FIGHTING FIRES CAUSED BY GERMAN SHELLS

ON THE WESTERN FRONT

Part IX

ALLIED OPERATIONS IN THE NORTH BEFORE THE SOMME BATTLE BEGAN

HAIG, JOFFRE AND LLOYD GEORGE AT THE FRONT
At the left is Albert Thomas of the French Cabinet

156

I

MONTHS OF WAITING, WITH MINOR ENGAGEMENTS—THE INSURRECTION IN IRELAND

December 19, 1915—August 10, 1916

AFTER Sir Douglas Haig took over Sir John French's command in December, 1915, activity continued on the British front, but only as minor operations. Within five months, and mainly while the Germans were throwing themselves in vain against Verdun, some hundreds of local actions took place, of which two or three occurred every week. The effect of this was to retain opposite the British lines an active body of German troops proportionately more numerous than the German troops engaged on any other front except Verdun. Among the more important actions were February to March fighting in and about the Ypres salient and on the Bluff, March to April fighting at St. Eloi, and German gas attacks in April. In the first of these actions German attempts to advance ultimately failed, and the British advanced their line. At St. Eloi the offensive was British, and in the long run it was frustrated. Of the various German gas-attacks none led to a consolidated success. The Germans, however, were only feinting on this front. Their real purposes were revealed on February 21 at Verdun.

Some of these engagements, which, from Berlin, were designated as "fierce drives" on the part of the Germans, were set down by Haig as "sharp local actions." They revealed certain points in the German line which needed readjustment. The strategy of the line still remained what it was when the British created their salients at Ypres in October, 1914; at Neuve Chapelle in March, 1915, and at Loos in September, 1915. For a distance as great as that on which the Germans could feed their line with men and munitions, a British offensive at Ypres had to dominate the front in Artois. Lille, Lens, Douai, and St. Quentin were the natural objectives. Airmen of the Allies found that the Germans had rebuilt the French fortifications at Lille, Rochambeau, Maubeuge, Landrecles, Hirson, La Fère, and Laon, while in the south they had prepared three lines of defense for use in case an offensive should be delivered in the Champagne. In May the British had 450,000 men on the line and the Germans 500,000. The Germans kept the bulk of their forces on the firing-line, but the French and English, unless attacked, did not keep more than a third of theirs exposed in the normal condition of a dormant front. They depended on the vigilance of officers on the first line to notice any signs of an attack. Reserves could then be brought up. Thousands of lives were thus saved during daily artillery duels.

Meanwhile, the French for four months were resisting the tremendous German assault on Verdun. The comparative inactivity of the British at this time led many to feel that the British should improve a great opportunity to break through while the Germans were being weakened elsewhere. French people, when they saw their sons falling by thousands on the hills of the Meuse, sometimes asked earnestly, "What are the English doing? Why don't they counter-attack? They might easily draw off some of the troops which the Crown Prince is hurling on us." But it was mainly from the uninstructed classes that complaints of this sort came. The more intelligent French had confidence in the loyalty of their British ally and in the closeness of the understanding that existed between the two general staffs. Since at Verdun the Germans were said to be losing three men to the French one, intelligent Frenchmen did not require much reflection to see that, for the British in the north, by an offensive in March, to repeat the error made by the Germans at Verdun, would have been a disastrous way of neutralizing the fruits of French resistance. Moreover, for administrative and military reasons, it would have been impossible for the British to have dispatched any appreciable body of men to Verdun to fight with the French.

British assistance took the more practicable form, the more fruitful, if less glorious, form, of an extension of their line in France, and the consequent release of French troops for service at Verdun. Joffre, in replying to a telegram of congratulation from Haig, said the French Army thanked the British "for the expression of hearty good-will which it had been good enough to address to us while the great battle of Verdun is proceeding," and added that, from the fierce struggle going on there, the French Army was convinced that it would achieve "results from which all the Allies will reap an advantage." He remembered that a recent call on the comradeship of the British Army had "met with an im-

BRITISH SHELLS ACCUMULATED IN A STOREHOUSE
The entire storage shelter, of which the area shown was a part, covered ten acres

mediate and complete response." That "complete response" was the relief afforded to the Tenth French Army by the British troops that took their place north of the Aisne.

Critics of the British did not know how well in accord the British were with the French all this time. Bonar Law declared, in a French newspaper, that the British Army was completely in accord with Joffre, and was prepared to move "whenever the French headquarters staff saw fit to have it do so." This statement was cited as a sufficient answer to the charge of British indifference to French losses before Verdun. From the outset, military authorities in Paris insisted that it would be playing Germany's game for the British to move before the psychological moment arrived, and scouted anti-British criticism as idle or malicious gossip. Observers about this time were contending that for weeks there had been unmistakable signs of a British offensive impending, but that it would not become active until the German forces facing them had been seriously reduced from losses at Verdun, or until propitious offensives had been begun by the Allies in other quarters of the long fighting line. While the struggle above ground and under its surface went on thus uninterruptedly, but with varying violence, air and sky were also embraced in the area of conflict. Observation balloons ascended, and airships and aeroplanes crossed and recrossed the immense front of battle.

Early in March occurred the extension of the British front. A British corps thus relieved a French corps in occupation of that part of the Allied front which lies between Loos and Arras. The British line now extended in unbroken continuity from Pilkin, opposite Boesinghe, on the Yser Canal, to the Somme, a few miles south of Albert. No formal announcement of this extension was made in either the British or French *communiqués*, but in a dispatch of March 23d, Haig incidentally mentioned the activity of the British artillery in the region of Souchez. It was afterward ascertained that British had replaced French troops as thus indicated, thus setting free a French corps to reinforce the army fighting around Verdun. The British now occupied a front of about ninety miles, or a quarter of the entire western front. Even before the German campaign against Verdun began on February 21, a British offensive had been generally expected by visitors to the British concentration camps, parade-grounds, and storehouses. Subsequently the gigantic proportions of the German offensive at Verdun had diminished the chances of success for an immediate British offensive, since the defense of Verdun would of itself make great inroads on Allied accumulations of munitions and men. In the defense of Verdun, the French, save for veterans transferred from the western sector, had not gone beyond the use of local reserves. A reserve force of 1916 men and conscripts of the 1,000,000 men of 1917, besides a veteran Territorial army of another million. had not yet been touched.

By the middle of June public opinion in Great Britain reached the conclusion that great events were impending on the western front, if not in every zone of the war. Joffre's visit to London, conferences between British and French Ministers, Premier Asquith's and Colonial Secretary Bonar Law's announcements that British help had been proffered to the French some time before, the fact that Kitchener when he lost his life was bound for Russia—all these events had helped to create a universal feeling of expectancy. The Entente Allies were known to be in complete touch by wireless. Their military operations and grand strategy were in more instant and thorough coordination than they had ever been before. High hopes were raised in all Allied circles and in many neutral ones. That the Germans were soon to be driven out of France was, however, expected by few trained observers.

Early in July was published a statement that seven hundred and fifty-three communes or townships had by that time been partly or totally destroyed through military operations in France since the beginning of the war. These figures were made public by the French Ministry of the Interior with a view to ascertaining the total damage caused by hostilities. These communes were distributed over eleven departments of France, including those in the Ardennes, still occupied wholly by the Germans, who were in possession of 2,554 towns out of a total of 36,247 in all France, or 7 per cent. Houses to the number of 16,669 had been totally destroyed and 29,594 partly destroyed. In 148 communes the proportions of houses destroyed exceeded 50 per cent. The public buildings destroyed in 428 communes included 331 churches, 379 schools, 221 town halls, 300 other buildings, and six bridges. Of these buildings fifty-six were classed as historic monuments, including the town hall of Arras, and the cathedral and town hall of Reims. Three hundred and thirty factories which supported 57,000 persons had been destroyed.

While the British held the line from the Yser to the Somme and thence south of the Somme, and extending to the Oise, the French under Foch were holding perhaps thirty miles. Between the Yser and the sea French and Belgians held rather more than fifteen miles. Allowing for curves, the whole line might cover 150 miles between Nieuport and Noyon.. Portions of the line held by the British covered the sectors from which an offensive could be expected to move. The region occupied by Belgians supported by French troops was a swamp, following two years of inundation. The German sector in front of Foch was too strong to hold out much hope for a successful drive by the French. Resting, as the German flanks did here, on the fortress of Péronne, the Somme marshes at the north, the Noyon Hills on the south, it was an exceedingly difficult front to break.

The Belgian sector and the Foch sector, those about the Yser and west of Roye, had been in the main inactive since the battles of the Marne and Flanders in 1914. The Germans after the Marne had made a great effort to move west from the Oise on Amiens and turn the French flank; and had failed at Roye and Albert in one of the most desperate of the western operations. More familiar was the German thrust at Calais which was checked at the Yser, when the sluices were opened and the country flooded. The British afterward made their first effort to break the German lines at Neuve Chapelle in the spring of 1915. Here they almost reached the Aubers ridge, the key to Lille, and a few months later they attacked to the south of La Bassée, reached Loos and almost succeeded in turning the Germans out of both La Bassée and Lens. The French in June made a terrific assault on the German front south of Lens and northeast of Arras, took the Lorette heights, some villages west of the Vimy ridge, including Souchez, and gained a foothold on the Vimy ridge, but could not make further progress.

The progress of the Russian drive in Galicia and Volhynia in the early summer of 1916 had been watched in France with painful eagerness, not only because of its own importance, but because it was felt that that campaign was only a part of a vast movement contemplated for all fronts. In London the utmost which many observers hoped for in 1916 was the defeat of Austria, a virtual elimination of the Balkans and the driving back of the Germans a considerable distance on the Western Front, the final defeat of Germany being delayed until another year. Great Britain was believed to have 4,000,000 men in northern France. Of these, two million five hundred thousand had seen no fighting. They had been held in reserve awaiting the great offensive. Meanwhile, 1,500,000 were in the trenches holding a line eleven

FRENCH OFFICIAL PHOTO. © COMMITTEE ON PUBLIC INFORMATION.

A FRENCH TRENCH WITH A METAL ROOF

miles long from Arras to Neuve Chapelle. Both the British and the French were erecting hundreds of new base-hospitals. Near Ypres within a few weeks forty-five hospitals had been established.

The Germans, expecting this offensive, were reinforcing their lines. From Knocke in Belgium, in the second week of June, troop-laden tram-cars were going toward the front "in a never-ending procession, and were covered with green boughs to prevent the Allied airmen from detecting them readily." A French statement, much quoted at the time, was that "the Germans in front of Verdun were maintain-

ing an attitude of expectation in view of the menace of
events which they felt were becoming more and more imminent.'' This was commonly interpreted to mean that the
big Allied drive would start at the strategic moment, when
the momentum of the Russian drive should have left the
German commanders with no choice but to have their line
smashed either in France or in Russia.

Great Britain's activities all through the spring and early
summer of 1916 were those of complete preparations for an
important offensive. When the war began Kitchener had
said two years would be needed for England to become
really prepared. By June, 1916, in addition to her "superior
fleet,'' it was pointed out by Lord Rosebery [1] that five millions of British were in arms; that a million and a half of
men and a quarter of a million of women were turning out
munitions; that the daily expenditure was approaching five
millions; that a debt was piling up so formidably that by
March, 1917, at the rate in March, 1916, it would reach the
almost incalculable figure of £3,440,000,000. In the presence of
these facts it was a grave error to say England was "taking
the war lying down.''

In the first half of that eventful year, 1916, the war was
entering upon a new phase. In unexpected quarters both on
land and sea, after a long period of stagnancy, events had
followed one another with startling rapidity. Around Verdun for over three months the Germans had been battering
French defenses, but, except in the latter part of February,
had made only costly local gains; it had become a question of
advancing by yards, not by miles, and then only after
enormous sacrifices. In May the Austrians had turned their
strength against the Italians and, after inflicting severe losses,
seemed on the point of breaking through their northern lines.

On May 31 the British and German fleets had met off the
coast of Jutland and here, for the first time, an opportunity
had come to measure their strength in a general engagement.
The result was inconclusive. Both sides suffered severe losses,
the British heavier than the Germans, and the Germans
heavier than they were willing to admit. If British naval
prestige suffered, Germany found herself still blockaded by

[1] In an introduction to Mrs. Humphry Ward's book, "England's Effort."

an impenetrable wall of British dreadnoughts and cruisers and the German ships never ventured out again. In the meanwhile the Russian giant had awakened, and in June Brusiloff's armies had captured over 50,000 Austrians—more prisoners than the Germans had taken around Verdun since February 21—had driven the Austrians from the fortress of Lutsk, which they had held since the previous August, and were driving home their advantage over a two hundred-mile front. The immediate effect of the Russian drive had been to paralyze the Austrians in their campaign against Italy. Thus, by June, had come a sudden change everywhere except along the British line in France, where sharp fighting around Lens was chronicled in a few lines only in daily official bulletins. But there had been much local fighting along this line for half a year.

These events and the battle of Verdun to some extent had made onlookers forget that to the west, northwest, and south of Verdun, from Switzerland to the sea, heavy field-artillery was seldom, if ever, silent for any long interval in the six months between January 1 and the beginning of the western allied offensive on July 1. Bombing and mining operations and flights and duels of airmen were also the rule and not the exception. The daily casualty lists, if not very numerous, showed that there were continuous encounters with the Germans, altho none was of any magnitude. It was known to the Allies that their resources in men and material would eventually be far greater than those of the Central Powers, and there was no military reason why they should be drawn into a premature offensive, which, if unsuccessful, might lower their prestige among neutrals and cause disappointment to the British, French and Italian nations. They believed that for the moment it was their best plan to play a waiting game.

Meanwhile tragic events that concerned the Western Front had occurred in Ireland, and were believed in Allied quarters to have been timed to synchronize with the Verdun attack. Sir Roger Casement, who for years had been prominent in the British consular service, was arrested near an Irish port, on or before April 21, while seeking to land from a ship laden with munitions of war intended for insurrectionists in Dublin. Sailing under a German commission, this ship was disguised as a merchantman. Sir Roger had been associated with a small band of Irishmen who hated England because of traditional grievances, rather than present injuries, and who held that every means of revolt, however violent, was justified. They had combined themselves into an association called the "Sinn Fein," founded about 1905, and were the political heirs of the Fenian movement of fifty years before. They dreamed of an independent republic for Ireland. Two days after Sir Roger's arrest riots were re-

LIBERTY HALL IN DUBLIN—A HEADQUARTERS
OF INSURRECTIONISTS

ported in Dublin and telegraphic communications were cut. It was understood that the rebels were in possession of a large part of the city: By April 27 the uprising had so spread that all Ireland was placed under military law, and large contingents of troops were sent over from Wales. Next day the post-office, Stephen's Green, and other parts of Dublin were in the hands of the Sinn Fein. Sniping was prevalent and fires broke out. On April 30 the "Irish Republic" which the rebels had proclaimed and which had had an existence of 120 hours, was overthrown, and its leaders surrendered unconditionally. Save for occasional sniping, Dublin thereafter enjoyed peace. Next day scattered remnants of the Sinn Fein surrendered. In all over 1,000 prisoners were taken and were rapidly brought to trial. On May 3 occurred the first executions. By May 10 thirteen men had been executed. The casualties of all kinds —soldiers, civilians, and rebels—were about 1,000. Of these 400 were killed. Of the troops and constabulary 124 were killed, 388 wounded, and 9 missing, or 521 in all.

Sir Roger, altho a north of Ireland Protestant, had been an active figure in other conspiracies organized by ex-

RUINED BUILDINGS IN SACKVILLE STREET, DUBLIN,
DUE TO THE INSURRECTION

treme Irish revolutionists. In his early career he had done excellent service for the British, especially in connection with the exposure of cruelties in the Kongo and in the Putumayo rubber industry in Peru, and as a reward had been knighted and pensioned. Thomas F. Woodlock,[2] of New York, voiced the views of many Irishmen in this country in saying that this revolt was "the cruelest blow that had been struck at Ireland's hopes in over a century." He believed, however, that those who struck it, tho erring deeply in their judgment—foolish, indeed, beyond words—struck,

[2] In The New York *Times.* Mr. Woodlock was formerly editor of The *Wall Street Journal.*

as they thought, for Ireland. He believed that those who were "sickened at heart by the tragedy" should not allow themselves to be led into a wrong judgment as to the ultimate causes from which it had sprung and the shoulders upon whom should fall the blame. The blood shed in Dublin he said was "upon the heads of that section of the English people who supported Sir Edward Carson and the Ulster Orangemen in their utterly lawless attempts to cheat the Irish people of the home rule that had been fairly won from the English democracy." English "unionists" in the early part of 1914 "had openly backed an armed rebellion against the law of the land."

On May 3 Premier Asquith announced in the House of Commons the execution on that day of the leaders, Pearce, "provisional president of Ireland"; James Connolly, styled "Commandant General of the Republican Army"; Thomas J. Clark, and Thomas MacDonagh. Casement was to be tried. Three other men were sentenced to three years' penal servitude. Taken to London, Casement and Daniel Bailey, his soldier confederate, were indicted for high treason on May 26 by a grand jury after due consideration of the evidence. Harold Begbie [3] described Sir Roger as entering court "quickly and jerkily, his eyes glancing in every direction, his hands fidgeting at his coat, his lips working, his eyebrows twitching." He was a tall, handsome, aristocratic looking man, extraordinarily dark, thin to the very bones, and looked "desperately ill." He cast his eyes at the magistrate, bowed with real politeness, recognized a friend in court, bowed to him with a momentary smile, which flickered away almost immediately, and then seated himself, "half turning at the same time to the other prisoner, as if inviting him to be seated, too; as if, indeed, he would put this other prisoner at his ease." Then he "folded his arms, worked his neck about in its turned-down collar, bit his lips, and looked at the prosecution." The thick black hair of Casement, with two or three flecks of white over the ears, was brushed straight back from the forehead, which projected over large dark eyes so surrounded by shadows that the pupils were indistinguishable at a few paces. The nose was

[3] In The *Daily News* (London).

aquiline and small. A short moustache covered the upper lip, and a little grizzly beard, with an upward tilt at its fine point, covered the chin. It was a face "not only aristocratic and fine, but spiritual." The man was more than bronzed; he had been "baked by scorching suns to a darkness which was almost Indian." And yet no one could have mistaken him for an Eurasian. Casement's trial came off late in June. He was found guilty of high treason by the jury who deliberated less than an hour.

POST-OFFICE BUILDING IN DUBLIN AFTER BEING DESTROYED BY FIRE BY THE INSURRECTIONISTS

Many efforts were made to save Casement's life, but late in July the sentence of death by hanging was confirmed by the Court of Criminal Appeal. Adherents of John Redmond had forwarded to Premier Asquith a petition for clemency signed by six bishops, twenty-six members of Parliament, and fifty-one other persons, including a number of educators, and Pope Benedict interceded in Casement's behalf. Irish Nationalists urged that he was not a traitor but a sincere man inspired by Irish patriotism. Strenuous efforts were made in the United States and Ireland, and even in England, to secure a reprieve. Some of them sought to obtain action by President Wilson.

The hopes of the condemned man's friends were finally extinguished when Lord Robert Cecil, Minister of War and Trade, announced that the Government had determined not to grant a reprieve. Lord Robert declared that Casement was much more malignant and hostile to Great Britain than were the leaders in the Sinn Fein revolt, and that there was no ground which could be brought forward in mitigation of his offense. Casement was hanged in Pentonville prison on August 3. Two hours before the execution a crowd of men, women, and children gathered before the prison gates. Twenty minutes before Casement mounted the scaffold when the great prison bell began to toll, the sound was greeted with cheers from the crowd, mingled with groans. At nine o'clock the crowd had swollen to such proportions that it extended for two blocks from the prison front. At one minute after nine, when a single stroke of the big bell announced that the trap had been sprung, it became the signal for a mocking, jeering yell from the crowd, but this soon died away.

© BROWN & DAWSON.

SIR ROGER CASEMENT

Men recalled, as a similar incident in a great war, the attempt of General Hoche during the French Revolution to land a force of men in Ireland, at Bantry Bay. Hoche was one of the ablest of the French Revolutionary generals, and was in command of a splendid veteran force. Ireland from north to south, and from east to west, was at that time disaffected. Had Hoche, the man who had already pacified La Vendée, actually landed in Ireland at the head of his efficient troops, there might have been an exceedingly serious struggle, altho even then the British fleet had sufficient control of the sea to determine an eventual victory in favor of the United Kingdom. But, under a general of the capacity of Hoche, and with the whole of the United Irishmen ready to join him, such a struggle would have been serious. It was in this attempt that the Irishman, Wolf Tone, became involved. Tone, like Casement, was arrested by the British, but after being condemned to death, he managed to commit suicide before his execution. Like Robert Emmet, Tone made a speech after his trial, which usually finds its way into collections of Irish oratory, along with Emmet's, altho it ranks far below that classic among impassioned speeches.[4]

[4] Principal Sources: The *World,* The *Times,* The *Tribune,* New York; The London *Times'* "History of the War," Associated Press dispatches.

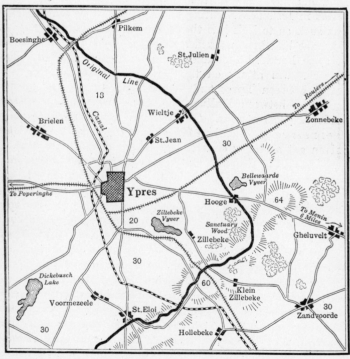

THE THIRD BATTLE OF YPRES—JUNE 2 TO JUNE 18, 1916
For an account of this battle, which occurred mainly around Hooge and Sanctuary Wood, and in which Canadian troops bore a conspicuous part, see the following chapter from pages 176 to 185

II

A THIRD BATTLE OF YPRES—CANADIAN VALOR AND KITCHENER'S DEATH

April 27, 1916—June 29, 1916

BY early May the Germans were showing marked activity in the Ypres region following earlier and rather serious attacks on April 21 and 27—each more than mere trench raiding. Then came a great Zeppelin raid over Great Britain, a naval raid on the English east coast, and the armed revolt in Ireland. Fighting along the British front, in fact, was such as to look like the beginning of a big drive. The Germans had kept massed against the British an aggregate of some hundred thousands of men, with heavy guns and cavalry. An attack on the 29th was launched at several points between Ypres and Souchez, the most serious effort occurring between Hulluch and Loos, where the Germans made two gas attacks. They gained a footing on support lines near Loos which had been heavily bombarded, but were driven out again by counter-attacks from Irish troops. This activity of the Germans was no doubt intended to convince the French that the Verdun battle had come to an end, but when the storm again burst around Verdun the French were fully prepared for it, the disposition of their troops having undergone no numerical changes.

Of the Irish troops in this fighting Philip Gibbs [5] noted as "a splendid coincidence" that, on the night when the Sinn Fein were trying to besmirch the honor of Ireland in the streets of Dublin, Irish battalions at the front in France were on the fighting line, and by great gallantry "gave proof to the world that the heart of Ireland was loyal." On April 27, when one of the Irish brigades was holding the chalk-pit salient south of Hulluch, the Hohenzollern redoubt was attacked and the Germans were bombed out of one of

---

[5] Correspondent of The London *Daily Chronicle* and The New York *Times*.

the craters. Through the darkness, faintly lighted by thousands of stars, throbbed a great glare when one of the German mines exploded to the west of Hulluch, and another lurid flame zig-zagged across the fields to the northeast of Vermelles. Mr. Gibbs wrote:

"There was no sleep that night. Irish officers going their rounds warned the sentries to keep a sharp lookout by a quiet word or two. Irish soldiers in the dugouts behind the front line of trenches exprest the thought that perhaps before dawn the enemy might make an attack upon 'the boys up there.' These Irishmen kept cool. In the trenches they were as stolid as their English comrades, with a grim joke or two. It was no joke just before dawn when the enemy's guns concentrated upon the Irish sector. Irish officers kept up the spirits of the men. The guns ceased about 5 o'clock that morning, a queer silence ensued in which many birds were singing high in the blue sky of a brilliant morning, when slowly, on the light northeasterly wind, came from the German trenches a thick sluggish volume of smoke. The Irish boys grabbed the helmets they carried in little satchels slung across the shoulders. A headdress like that made them look like queer beasts.

"Far from being demoralized by the poison-gas, the Irish spirit was fiercely aroused and they poured a heavy rifle-fire into the German soldiers as they came rushing forward. Many fell and the others were checked by the barbed wire. So the Dublins shot them down before they could break through. An officer and forty dead Germans lay there entangled among broken strands. The Irish organized a counter-attack. Within half an hour the enemy was driven out, leaving many dead. An officer with four men of an Irish brigade in this sector advanced up the trench into which a German patrol had gained a footing and without any other aid put the enemy out of action. A third gas attack was attempted but failed to reach the Irish and floated back in a swirl of wind to the enemy's lines."

From the end of April until the beginning of the Somme offensive—that is, for eight weeks—fighting on the Western Front was continuous, but it yielded no important results. Fighting also went on continuously in the Argonne and Champagne region, and at many little points the French straightened their line. Since the second battle of Ypres the Germans had made use of poison-gas, lachrymatory shells and flame-jets, but after the first use of gas at Ypres, where it came as a surprize and so enabled the Germans to gain some success, it became only a small factor in warfare, since the Allies had fully armed themselves against it. Every man carried a helmet which, filtering out the noxious gas, enabled him to breathe air, which passing through chemicals, was rendered fit for respiration. One of the latest German developments was the introduction of ''stink'' gas, so called from its odor, but not in itself dangerous. It was sometimes mixed with poison-gas. Lachrymatory shells, as their name implied, produced a copious flow of tears. To guard against it goggles were introduced which, in the latest pattern of helmets, formed part of the helmet.

On the night of May 15, on the Vimy Ridge, the British advanced and seized the German forward line over a length of 250 yards, and inflicted considerable losses. Vimy was important to the Allies, as it dominated ground to the east over which the British would have to pass in any future advance. On May 21 the Germans tried to recapture positions at the north end of the Vimy Ridge. After a heavy bombardment, which lasted well on into the afternoon, their infantry penetrated the front line of British trenches on a front of 1,500 yards, and to a depth of 100 to 300 yards. Several lines of the British position over a length of a mile and a quarter were captured, and during the night counterattacks were repulsed and eight officers and 220 men, with four machine-guns and three trench-mortars taken. On the next day the British guns, in their turn, subjected the enemy to a bombardment, but nothing more was done. During May 27 the British bombarded German trenches to the southeast of Neuve Chapelle, and destroyed some stores at Guillemont. The Germans for their part directed a bombardment lasting twenty minutes west of Fricourt, and one about Serre. The British sprang five mines, three about Hulluch and two southeast of Cuinchy, and the Germans exploded one near the Hohenzollern Redoubt and another on the Vimy Ridge. On May 30 the Germans continued their general bombardment, the one about Neuve Chapelle being particularly heavy and lasting eighty minutes. This was followed by an infantry attack which penetrated British trenches and took some prisoners, but a counter movement drove the Germans back. North of Béthune the Germans sprang a mine and British troops occupied the near lip of the crater. There was some activity near Loos also.

This sort of conflict was followed early in June by another at Ypres which has been called the third battle of Ypres. Round Ypres there had already been two severe battles, the first from October 20 until November 11, 1914, the second from April 22 to May 13, 1915. On June 2, 1916, the ground over which the battle was fought was roughly confined between the Ypres-Menin road and the neighborhood of Klein Zillebeke.[5a] Possession of Ypres was

CANADIAN OFFICIAL PHOTO.

REMOVING WOUNDED FROM VIMY RIDGE

still considered of sufficient importance to the British to justify them in hanging on to it, because if it should fall into German hands it would be necessary to draw back the front line of British trenches, north and south of it, for a considerable distance.

Few cities in the path of German devastation had suffered more than Ypres. At the beginning of the war there were few more picturesque towns in Belgium than this thriving community of 17,000 inhabitants, a majority of whom gained a livelihood from the production of Valenciennes lace. They were among the earliest sufferers. The great Cloth Hall of Ypres, now in ruins, which had been

[5a] See map of the Ypres neighborhood on page 171.

the most considerable building of its kind in that country, was begun in 1200 by Count Baldwin IX of Flanders and was under construction for more than a century. Within a stone's throw of the hall stood the famous thirteenth century cathedral of St. Martin, which, during two years, was reduced to a shell of crumbling stone above the grave of its famous bishop, Jansen, father of the great religious revival known as Jansenism, that spread through this part of Europe during the first half of the seventeenth century. Both the Cloth Hall and the cathedral had been completely restored only a year or two before the outbreak of the great conflict.

After breakfast on the morning of June 2 the British were observed to be in high spirits, going about their tasks of digging, repairing, rifle-cleaning, and general tidying-up. Then, at twenty minutes to nine o'clock and without any warning, "hell broke loose," the detonation becoming overwhelming. It did not come from one part, but from the whole length of the opposing line opposite the Canadian division. It not only deafened the ear and paralyzed the nerves, but instantly the firmament became blackened. For the next few minutes men groped about in darkness, unable to hear any word of command, clutching rifles and waiting for what would happen. Two generals attempting to reach a communication-trench found their retreat cut off. Behind the front line a high wall of descending shells, screaming, crashing, exploding, emitting clouds of noxious smoke, seemed to shut off all chance of escape. Moments passed that seemed hours, and then iron and steel missiles rained and exploded in the front line, scattering death and destruction. Nothing could live for long in such a storm. Sides of trenches crumbled and fell in. Men held on, however, darting from one devastated section to another in order to gain a refuge, while a mine would explode leaving a grim crater.

From an opposite trench swarms of gray-coated Germans began to spring. Fully accoutered, and with overcoats and full packs, they advanced on the run, yelling wildly, as if convinced that amid those battered mounds and ditches not one human soul had escaped. Then a wonderful thing happened. Out of the earth there sprang up a handful of soldiers, two officers among them, and, running forward with rifles and pistols, they bade defiance to the Germans. On they ran, and, having discharged their weapons, flung them in the very faces of the Germans. Death was inevitable for these men, the only remaining occupants of the British front line, but it was better to die thus than to be shot in a ditch or finished off with a German bayonet.

The battle began at 9 A.M. when the Germans opened a bombardment against that part of the British front which lies between Hooge and Hill 60. The bombardment lasted four hours. At noon the infantry attack was launched by Württemberg regiments, who penetrated into first-line trenches against the resistance of the Princess Patricia's Canadian Light Infantry. Three commanding officers were killed in a hand-to-hand fight in the trenches and another was wounded and taken prisoner. The Germans continued their attack during the night and pushed through the British defenses to a depth of 700 yards in the direction of Zillebeke, the Canadians having retired on their supports to organize a counter-attack, which, after a bombardment equal in intensity to that of the Germans on the previous day, was delivered at 7 A.M. on the 3d. The Canadians fought their way back to their trenches, which they found battered to pieces, with hundreds of German dead lying about unburied, some of the trenches being untenable. Altho they failed to recover all the ground lost on the previous day, they pushed the Germans back for a quarter of a mile and consolidated their new line.

Except for a continuous artillery duel, there was then a lull in the battle till the afternoon of the 6th, when the

WHAT REMAINED OF FRICOURT VILLAGE

enemy began another heavy bombardment on the British position and north of the village of Hooge, while southeast of Zillebeke, between the Ypres-Commines railway and canal, the bombardment was maintained with the same intensity as before. Between 3 and 4.30 P.M. a series of mine explosions took place at various points at a 2,000-yard front, north of Hooge, these being the signal for a general infantry attack, which was unsuccessful except at Hooge, where the Germans captured the British front line trenches running through ruins of the village. There was a lull in the infantry fighting till 1.30 A.M. on the 13th, when the Canadians made another counter-attack with the intention of regaining their former positions between Sanctuary Wood and Hill 60. The Germans fell back under the impetuosity of this attack. Trench after trench was retaken, three officers and 158 men being made prisoners. Sanctuary Wood and Hooge were still in German hands, but elsewhere the British line was intact.

The initial success achieved by the Germans on June 2d was further proof, if such were wanted, of the enormous power which artillery exerted on the modern field of battle. The bombardment came as a surprize to the Divisional Commander, who clearly had no suspicion of its imminence. It was possible to effect an artillery concentration without discovery because a movement of men was less easy to hide from the observation of airmen than a movement of guns. The latter could be brought up at night and placed in concealed positions till the moment for action arrived. When, on the other hand, a large movement of troops took place, they betrayed their presence by a corresponding movement of supply wagons and other transport accessories. It thus had happened that the German bombardment began without an equality of artillery strength on the British side.

Contemporary narratives agreed as to the suddenness with which the bombardment began over the whole area attacked, and the terrible, and, so far as this front was concerned, the unprecedented severity with which it continued, without interruption, for over four hours before an infantry attack was made. A weapon the Germans were now using was sometimes known as the "5-9," but every other sort of gun was employed, including heavy howitzers, naval guns, and trench-mortars, with high explosive, shrapnel, and lachrymatory shells. In a position such as this, at the angle of a salient, the place attacked could be subjected to a concentrated fire from all sides, but, quite apart from this local

VETERANS AMONG CANADIAN TROOPS
These troops who had already fought at Neuve Chapelle, and in the second battle of Ypres, were still to fight at Festubert, Givenchy, Messines, Sanctuary Wood, Paschendaele, Amiens and Cambrai. The picture shows them marching through Montreal after the war closed

condition, the immense weight of artillery used, in proportion to size, in all attacks on this front, gave to the fighting a new character. Artillery-fire was not now used merely to demoralize the enemy or break up formations. It was used to annihilate, to obliterate every form of defensive work, and to make life itself impossible on every yard of the ground attacked. The troops engaged included units of the Princess Patricia's Light Infantry, the Canadian Mounted Rifles, the Royal Canadian Regiment, and the Canadian Infantry. The northern end of the line attacked, just south of Hooge, was held by the "Patricias," and there, in Sanctuary Wood, was fighting of the most desperate kind. The "wood" afterward was a mere ghost of what the name implied. There was little greenery or shelter; nothing but a certain remnant of ragged stumps and bits of splintered poles. To the south, occupying the middle of the ground covered by the German fire, were battalions of the Canadian Mounted Rifles. Here the trenches were out on flat ground in a region where the soil a few feet below the surface became water, so that defensive works of any depth, capable of resisting modern shell-fire, were impracticable.

The lines in front were held by a battalion of the Canadian Mounted Rifles. Other battalions came up later to assist them through the barrage. Few things finer have been seen in war than the way in which they came. If one could imagine Zeppelin bombs dropping at a rate of scores to the minute over every acre of a given area, and continuing unceasingly for hours, until before the end there was no spot where holes in the ground did not coalesce, and none where every sort of structure on the earth's surface was not a shapeless lump of ruin, one would have some idea of what this type of artillery bombardment meant. When the German infantry advanced they came, not charging, but in regular formation, as if to occupy untenanted ground. In Sanctuary Wood next day, when the British pushed through in a counter-attack, they found the ground covered with German dead.

Even more splendidly dramatic were some of the scenes along the trenches. After the long bombardment the Germans heralded their infantry attack by blowing up mines, which besides the wreckage they wrought at that particular point caused considerable loss of life. The actual advance of the German infantry from the trenches was preceded and partially concealed by a smoke barrage. To the dazed and broken remnants of the men in British trenches the Germans were not visible until close at hand. Of one battalion few men who remained had any rifles left that were fit for use even if the men had been fit to use them. But when they saw the Germans close at hand they climbed from the trenches to meet them and, some blind and deaf and staggering, charged pitifully to their death with no weapons but the broken rifle-butts, bits of entrenching tools, and in some cases bare fists. Among innumerable gallant deeds one deserves to be recorded. It was that of a private from Saskatchewan. Under the awful artillery-fire to which there was no replying with rifles, he had busied himself in caring for the wounded. He had bandaged one officer, two non-com-

BRITISH OFFICIAL PHOTO.

BRITISH TROOPS MOVING IN A SUNKEN ROAD

missioned officers, and two privates, and was looking after them as well as he could behind a bit of battered sand-bag breastwork out in the open, when the fragment left of his company was told to fall back but he refused to go. He had set up his private hospital there, and one of his wounded privates was a pal from his own small town in Saskatchewan. So he stayed with his pal. Philip Gibbs wrote of scenes he witnessed among the Canadians at Ypres:

"Yesterday I spent some hours with the Canadian officers and men who faced the fire. These men had been holding their ground for forty-eight hours under shell-fire more severe than any bombardment that has been seen upon our front except at Vimy, and as I listened to their stories of the battle, I stood in the presence of men who had escaped from the very pits of that hell which has been invented by human beings out of the earth's chemistry, and yet had kept their reason, and their courage, and their pride of spirit. That was wonderful.

"Earth below them opened up into great craters as high explosive shells burst continually, flinging up masses of soil, flattening out breastworks, and scattering sand-bags into dust. The bombardment continued without a pause for five hours, by which time most of our front trenches had been annihilated. At about a quarter-past one the enemy's guns lifted a little, and through the dense smoke-clouds which made a solid bar across No Man's Land appeared a mass of German infantry. They wore their packs and full field-kit, as if they had come to stay. They died to a man, fighting. It seemed to me one of the most pitiful and heroic things of this war, that little crowd of men, many of them wounded, some of them dazed and deaf, stumbling forward to their certain death to oppose the enemy's advance.

"No one can say," said one of their officers "that the Canadians do not know how to die. It is a tragedy that so many of them have fallen in this battle under that devilish shell-fire, but the splendor of their courage will live forever."

This fighting at Ypres fell into two distinct actions. The results of the first have already been told; with a counter-attack this phase ended. The next three days formed an interlude, and then came a new and well-defined attack, that had been in preparation for weeks. The section of the line south of Hooge, which had stood firm in the earlier attack, together with an extension of the line through Hooge, was intensely bombarded that day from noon onward. The barrage of fire, put up at the same time, was particularly directed at Ypres itself, of which the ruins were then still further subjected to demolition. At 3 P.M. five mines were exploded under and about the British front, giving proof of long preparation, and German infantry advanced under cover of the explosion. The attack was not wholly successful, tho some trenches in the ruins of Hooge were seized and occupied. The northern part of the British line stood firm. Nor did the Germans reach their objective on the south.

After this action no further infantry fighting was recorded, altho no day was free from heavy artillery-fire from both ends. By the end of a week heavy British guns had silenced hostile batteries. The casualties on both sides were severe. On the night of June 4-5 five raids were carried out by English, Scottish and Welsh troops in the neighborhood of Cuinchy and Givenchy. All had been planned with care. A dash to the trenches was made. After that the work was brief, but exciting, depending on the cool courage of individual men working on a general plan.

Just south of where the Canadians made their stand a maple copse was visible. The earth was all torn and seared, but a surprizing amount of fine timber was still standing. During those two fierce days' fighting wounded men were crawling about or lying motionless for hours on the ground, either helpless or in order to avoid observation, having lost their way. One man spent two nights on his back in No Man's Land without food, drink, or succor. Another was thrice buried by the effects of a minenwerfer shell, which plowed up the surrounding earth, and was thrice dug out by a passing officer. Machine-guns were repeatedly buried, and then rapidly and diligently excavated and brought again into action, much to the enemy's discomfiture. Little by little in after time the threads of the story of the third battle for Ypres were to be gathered up and individual acts of daring and heroic self-sacrifice brought into the light of day. The German had apparently done his worst. He had given a violent tug at the loop, and if he had shortened it by a few inches, he had also made it stronger. Precisely what new schemes of frightfulness he was meditating the British did not know, but his latest exploit cost him thousands of lives and yielded him a dismantled church and a few battered cottages at Hooge. Elsewhere on the British front numerous raids, adroitly planned, became the order of the day.

Fighting in this region now became of more normal and quiet character. It was chiefly artillery-fire with occasional small raids of no great importance; but on the 10th the German bombardment against the Ypres positions became violent, British trenches north of the Ypres-Comines railway, between the hours of 1 and 3 P.M. being severely punished, as was the ground south of Hooge; but there were no infantry engagements. The next day, during the morning, there was a further bombardment of Ypres and ground to the south of it, also of British trenches north of the Menin road, while in the afternoon the main attention of the German guns was directed against the Canadian positions from Hill 60 to the north for a distance of 1,500 yards. But again there were no infantry attacks of importance. June 12 was an uneventful day with only a heavy bombardment between Hill 60 and Hooge by both sides; but the 13th saw a vigorous counter-attack delivered by the Canadians to regain ground lost on June 2-3. At half-past one the Allied fire lifted and the infantry dashed forward. The enemy poured out a severe barrier-fire to prevent the approach of the British, but so great was their impetuosity that they pushed through it and quickly gained their objective before the sun rose. The British set about consolidating heavy artillery-fire, and during the next twenty-four hours clung bravely to the position they had gained. Once the Germans massed infantry for an attack, but they were met by such a hail of fire that no attempt to advance was made.

On the morning of June 22 the Germans sprang a large mine in the neighborhood of Givenchy, just north of La Bassée Canal. This was followed by a heavy barrage-fire behind the British line, under cover of which the Germans penetrated the British front on a narrow space. Suddenly there was a terrible roar, the earth opened, and a huge mass of timber, soil and sand-bags was upheaved and fell back with a crash into a vast crater, 120 feet across, and the trenches in its neighborhood, destroying the parapets and replacing the well-ordered construction by a cleared space and a deep pit. Then came artillery-fire, pounding the position and seeking by a veil of shells to cut off all access to it, followed by three distinct assaulting parties, who rushed forward to occupy the mine-pit. Welshmen—some of whom had been blown up and others dazed by the shock—closed on the flanks of the raiding party and drove them back, fighting hard, into the crater, out of it, and back to their own trenches.

ALLIED OPERATIONS IN THE NORTH

A preparatory bombardment of German lines, intended to pave the way for the great advance of July was begun at the end of June. From Ypres to the Somme the German position was subjected to a hail of projectiles, generally distributed, but also concentrated at various points, so as to leave them in doubt as to where the attack, which they quite appreciated was coming, would really be delivered. The German reply, except for short intervals, and against a few places, was ineffectual. The British fire was one of devastation intended to destroy Germans, their batteries and trench defenses, blow up their ammunition dépôts, and bombard far back their resting-places and lines of communication. Raids were made on German trenches, inflicting losses. Some of these attacks were covered by gas, and at one place where they had been employed the trenches when entered by the British were full of German dead. No less than a dozen successful raids were made by the British between June 28 and 29. The prolog of the play then came to an end, and in a couple of days the grand drama would begin. All this time battle raged round Verdun and in the Champagne, while further away, in Alsace, there was more or less continuous fighting. The Allies were about to begin a more real offensive on the Somme.

While the death of any one man could not have affected vitally the issues of the war, while neither Kaiser, Czar, nor King, neither Hindenburg nor Joffre, carried on his shoulders any strictly single responsibility, and while such a war as this was not to be settled by any one man's genius, nevertheless the death of Lord Kitchener on the night of June 5, by drowning, off the Orkney Islands, after the warship on board which he was bound for Russia had been torpedoed, or hit by a mine, moved the British public profoundly. Earnestly the nation mourned his death and acclaimed his fame. Kitchener was on his way to Russia to consult with Russian war-leaders about munitions and plans. His vessel, the *Hampshire,* an old-type British cruiser of little war value, was blown to pieces. Whether the ship was sunk by the Germans, or even whether the mine was a German mine, was uncertain. The *Hampshire* went down, almost instantly, at eight o'clock in the evening. Officers and crew were said to number between three and four hundred—a small complement for a ship of the *Hampshire's* class. With Lord Kitchener were lost his staff. How Kitchener died was described by the last man who saw him alive, a seaman named Rogerson. After the explosion occurred, Kitchener had gone calmly out of the captain's cabin and mounted a ladder to the quarter-deck. There Rogerson saw him "walking about collectedly and talking to two officers." All three were wearing khaki and had on no overcoats. Kitchener was watching the preparations for abandoning the ship, which were going on in an orderly way. Rogerson continued:

"The crew went to their stations, obeyed orders and did their best to get out the boats, but that was impossible. Owing to the rough weather no boats could be lowered. Those that were got out were smashed. No boats left the side of the ship. What the people on shore thought to be boats leaving were rafts. The men did get into the boats as they lay in their cradles, thinking as the ship went under the boats would float, but the ship sank by the head and when she went under she turned a somersault forward, carrying down with her all the boats and the men in them. When I sprang to a raft Kitchener was still on the starboard side of the quarter-deck, talking with the officers. From the little time that elapsed between my leaving the ship and her sinking, I feel certain that Kitchener was on deck at the time she sank."

When news of the tragedy reached Edinburgh, it was learned that not more than a dozen people in the city had been aware of the fact that the Secretary of War and his staff two days before had passed through that city on their way to the port from which they sailed on their last journey. On his train, a night express from King's Cross station in London due in Edinburgh at 4 o'clock in the morning, Kitchener had a sleeping saloon. At that early hour there were few people in the station at Edinburgh, and fewer still knew the names of the travelers on this train. One or two railway officials only were aware that Kitchener was on board. After a few minutes' stop the train went on by the Forth Bridge route to Perth and the north of Scotland.

Perhaps the thing that one might say first of Lord Kitchener was that he, more than any other man, served in

Britain as a symbol of the will to bear and do in the terrible first months of the war. When there had been a whisper that Lord Haldane might go back to his old post, Britain and Britain's Allies alike felt a sense of apprehension, but all this was dispelled when the fact was established that "K. of K." was to go to the War Office. In the months that followed, when England had to create out of nothing new armies with officers, a system and a machine, it was Kitchener who in the public mind stood for the success of that tremendous undertaking. The very posters that bade men enlist bore the face and name of the man who had conquered the Sudan and brought civilization back in the land where Gordon perished.

FIELD-MARSHAL (VISCOUNT)
KITCHENER

Never in history, probably, not even in our own Civil War, had there been a more voluntary rising of a nation than that which answered the call in Great Britain in the early months of the war. Those who volunteered were numbered by millions. The task that was Kitchener's was in magnitude beyond that which any other general had confronted. In character it was like that which was faced by the elder Carnot, the "organizer of victory," in France, and by McClellan in our Civil War. It was the task of finding guns, officers, and munitions, not for an army, but for a nation long given over to habits of peace. Mistakes were made. Kitchener himself was responsible for some, but the main mistake was not his. While the miracle itself was performed men criticized incidental mistakes. Before he died almost 5,000,000 men had joined the colors. The work was completed by conscription as we in the Civil War had recourse to the draft. This was the great, enduring, British fact in the war, and it was the fact that men would hereafter associate with Kitchener.

Following so closely on the naval battle off Jutland on May 31, which the Germans continued to hail as a great sea victory over the British fleet, altho the German fleet retired to port whence they never again ventured out to challenge the British, the sinking of the *Hampshire,* with Lord Kitchener and his staff, made a tremendous impression in Germany. Morning papers in Berlin devoted columns to a review of Kitchener's career and what Kitchener meant to England. The substance was that Kitchener embodied the traditionally tenacious bull-dog qualities of the. British, iron determination and great energy. He was pictured as Great Britain's most capable military leader and Germany's most inveterate foe. The blow to the British from his loss was compared to what Germany would feel if Falkenhayn and his staff or Hindenburg were killed. He was declared to have been England's one real hope. The German Navy Department did not claim credit for the destruction of the *Hampshire.* No reports from submarines in the area where the cruiser sank had been received, therefore nothing definite could be said. The impression, however, in navy circles, was that it was not the work of a submarine, but of a mine. The fact that the disaster occurred in a very rough sea argued against the U-boat theory.[6]

[6] Principal Sources: The *Morning Post* (London), *The Fortnightly Review,* The *Times* (London), The London *Times'* "History of the War," Associated Press dispatches, "Bulletins" of the National Geographic Society, *The Outlook* (New York), The New York *Tribune.*

ON THE WESTERN FRONT

Part X

THE ALLIED DRIVE ON THE SOMME

A BRITISH GUN IN THE SOMME BATTLE

I

THE PREPARATIONS AND THE FIRST FORTNIGHT'S FIGHTING

July 1, 1916—July 14, 1916

EARLY in June surprized comment was continually heard on the prolonged delay in launching a real British offensive. Turko-German forces in Asia Minor had by this time been put completely on the defensive; Russia had attacked fiercely and with conspicuous success on the Eastern Front; Austria had been diverted from her offensive against Italy, and at Verdun the Germans had obviously failed, altho for political and strategical reasons they still went on making sacrifices. In these conditions, so favorable to a British attack, war on all that part of the Western Front where the British held a line of 90 or 100 miles from Ypres in Flanders to the Somme in France had continued, it was true, but only on a plan of slow attrition. It seemed altogether probable that for weeks and even for a month a British offensive could have been made effective in that territory in a high military sense, whether tactically it should succeed or fail. Opposed to the British had been forty German divisions, perhaps 800,000 men, altho English writers thought the number had been gradually reduced by demands for Verdun to not more than 500,000 men. In any case, the British force was larger, and probably much larger, than the German. That the British alone were equal if not superior to the Germans in artillery equipment, was also generally assumed. Therefore it could not be for lack of strength that Haig delayed an offensive. There was apparently as much mystery and conjecture in England about the delay as there was anywhere else.

By the end of June, however, evidence was strong that a general British offensive was at hand. An official statement from the German Headquarters Staff on June 26, spoke of the fighting for two days on the British and northern French fronts as "important," while bulletins of the British War Office, altho scanty in details, gave the impression of a concerted attack at many points, together with constant and heavy artillery-fire. All this was understood to be in preparation for a greater attack soon to follow and for which all were impatient. Traveling along roads one now saw heavy guns and field-guns arriving. New British troops flowed in from French ports, passed and disappeared for a while, to be found afterward in fields and billets, looking more hardy than before, and burdened with stories of trench life and raids. Every one felt that Germany was no longer on the offensive, except for defensive purposes. It was not so much a grip at the throat that she was feeling as a steady and squeezing pressure on her every physical part. Central Europe was being prest on one side by Russia, on another by British and French armies, on a third by Italy. Germany also had a fourth side, one where a pressure, at once the hardest and most severely felt of all, had been exerted for nearly two years by the British fleet.

When Brusiloff's Russian attack began, in the early summer of this year, there was much speculation as to whether it was intended to relieve Austrian pressure on Italy or German pressure on Verdun. It later appeared that it was not for either purpose, but was the beginning of a general Allied movement on all fronts. Whether it was intended to originate the long expected drive or not, no one knew. The point was that, by an almost simultaneous movement on three fronts, Germany was about to be assailed in a general attack. Our Southern Confederacy had been slowly strangled for two years by a blockade before the squeezing process was put in execution by Grant in the East and Sherman in the West. The resemblance of those months in our war to the situation in the World War was striking. If Brusiloff should prove to be the Russian Sherman and Haig the British Grant, we should have had not a resemblance but a parallel.

The most striking feature of the drive was the extraordinary preparations that had been made for it. Seemingly nothing that could have been done was left undone. The collection of ammunition, the assembling of artillery, and the concentration of troops were only one phase of the preparations. Bases for various supplies were prepared where they would be most easily accessible when the advance began. Emergency hospitals were constructed and enclosures built for the reception of prisoners. Extra motor-lorries in great numbers were provided for transport work over roads which were continually being improved by thousands of workmen. Red Cross motor-ambulances were made ready for handling large numbers of wounded. Engineers worked out an elaborate scheme whereby water could follow men into the German trenches all along the line. Gun emplacements back of the German front lines were prepared and routes of least resistance for reaching

Ⓒ COMMITTEE ON PUBLIC INFORMATION.

INFANTRY RESTING EN ROUTE TO THE FRONT

these points decided upon. Plans for the consolidation of captured territory were elaborately considered, and provisions made for the immediate clearing away of great quantities of débris of every description such as always strews a battle-ground.

When the attack got under way, intense but methodical activity prevailed for miles behind the front. Motor-lorries bringing supplies passed in steady streams back and forth along the roads. Wounded were moved swiftly but with great care to base hospitals miles away. Scores of thousands of soldiers were kept busy handling supplies, making provisions for calls from the extreme front, and clearing and consolidating ground taken. At points back of the line where

British and French forces joined, operations were carried on side by side. In various towns one saw great numbers of French and British motor-lorries using the same streets. Bodies of khaki-clad and blue-uniformed troops passed each other continually as they went about their duties. Each was under control of its respective army commander, and there was no confusion in the work. Foch and Haig cooperated much as Prince Eugene and Marlborough had worked together in the campaign of Blenheim, and as Wellington and Blücher in that of Waterloo. Foch's position was that of commander of the French troops on the northern front. He had been ordered to keep in close touch with the British, and do all that was necessary to coordinate the operations of the two armies. With Haig he had got into most friendly relations until the whole scheme of actions on the Somme became the result of consultations.

Some further idea of the magnitude of the preparations could be gathered from the fact that over 1,800 wells had been sunk in that particular region before the first attack began. But the greatest of all proof was seen in the Parc des Buttes, which was only one of eight similar munition depots situated directly behind the line just out of shell-range and connected with batteries by new railroads and a continuous train of auto-camions. The shell supply at this dépôt covered several acres. The number of shells of all sizes was staggering. On an average day several hundred loaded freight-cars and auto-camions were sent forward. An enemy aeroplane sailing above could never have recognized the place for what it was, the greater number of the shells being placed below ground, while those above were under a canvas roof of the same color as the ground and arranged upon sloping sides so as to cast no shadows. One saw going into bomb-proof shelters thousands of beds and window-shades for huts. There were cast-iron observation turrets, with slits for rifles and mitrailleuses, and curved cast-iron tops for underground tunnels. Rolls of barbed wire posts and barbed wire sheets covered acres of ground. Vast quantities of tar roofing-paper were seen. Acres were covered by flooring for trenches, trench-beams, planks, and stakes made into forms to fit the needs of underground life. Attached to each dépôt was a fleet of armed aeroplanes which patroled the sky day and night. One could see hundreds of new hangars along the countryside. New big guns often reared their huge snouts aloft, and were the most striking features of the landscape.

A sinister object was one of these great guns which her crew regarded tenderly and named "Birdie." It was a 400-millimeter (15.7) mortar that could throw projectiles so heavy that only twelve of them could be carried in an ordinary freight car. It had a weird disguise of paint. An instrument could move its nose a considerable number of degrees to the right or left and it could be fired every two minutes. Its twin companion, named "Desire," was similar in appearance and caliber. This unlovely pair while in transportation formed the main burden of a railway train which also hauled dozens of ammunition-cars loaded with shells. Each gun had a crew of twenty-two men. The train's equipment included a complete wireless outfit and two aeroplanes for scouting and defense. On a track adjoining this train was seen another outfit, the star favorite of which was "Julie," a coast gun of 300 millimeters (11.8) caliber, and the longest gun ever mounted on a train. "Julie" had a revolving platform, so that she could turn completely around if necessary, and the exceptional range of 25 kilometers (15.6) miles. On account of its long range this gun was used chiefly against German munition depots, bridges, convoys, and other places that had been picked out by aeroplanes, rather than in throwing projectiles against trenches.

The most considerable offensive the British had before undertaken was the drive at Loos, in September, 1915, in conjunction with a similar French effort in the Champagne district. The British then captured Loos and claimed to have

CANADIAN OFFICIAL PHOTO.

BRITISH NAVAL GUNS IN LAND OPERATIONS

taken 20,000 prisoners and many guns, but were unable to press home their advantage because reserves failed to arrive. The British official losses in the battle of Loos were 60,000 men. That the British public was prepared in 1916 to face a roll of dead and wounded on a vaster scale was indicated by the comments of British newspapers in anticipating the offensive on the Somme. Political and military leaders warned the nation that the smashing of the German lines could not possibly be accomplished without an appalling loss of life. It was indeed asserted that the British authorities were prepared to face a loss of hundreds of thousands, if in doing so they could achieve their object, which was to drive the Germans out of France and Belgium.

The line in Picardy selected by the British ran northward from Albert to a point about eight miles south of Arras, being part of that section of the Western Front which ran roughly north and south from the North Sea through Belgium and northern France, before it swung sharply south and east to the Swiss border. Albert lies seventy miles northeast of Paris. In former actions there had been much heavy fighting over this ground, but not to the same extent as further north, where lay the battlefields of Arras, Loos, Neuve Chapelle, Ypres and Dixmude. The region chosen lay almost entirely within the level plain of the Department of the Somme, on a dry, chalky soil, with few natural obstacles to an advance. Before the war most of the villages taken had been inhabited by weavers, the open country devoted to sugar-beet cultivation.

Picardy, an ancient province of France no longer on maps, was now divided into four departments—the Somme, the Oise, the Pas-de-Calais, and the Aisne. It contained two battlefields whose very names quickened the pulse of all Englishmen. It was at Crécy that the Black Prince won his spurs, and at Agincourt that Henry V, commanding his yeomen with their cloth-yard bows, overthrew the flower of French chivalry. Picardy is a treasured name in romantic literature and in French history; it has a literature of its own of the twelfth century, and its soldiers have been among the most valiant of France. The province was a natural battle-ground for French and English in the Hundred Years' War—the war in which

Crécy and Agincourt occurred. Its shores extend along the North Sea and English Channel, from above Calais to a point below Dieppe. In the fifth century it was the heart of Merovingian France. Clovis made Soissons his capital; Charlemagne made Noyon 'his principal city and lesser Carolingians similarly honored Laon.

If an observer had stood on a small knoll, about three miles north of the town of Bray-sur-Somme, and looked north he would have seen, almost at his feet, a shallow and tortuous

SIGHTING A BRITISH GUN FOR ACTION

valley, running in the main east and west, with a single line of railway winding along its course. Beyond this hollow ran a range of hills, so small that in the general geography of Europe they did not count as hills at all, but only as details in the surface drainage system of the great east and west European plain which one can cross by train from the Pyrenees to Warsaw without passing through a tunnel. That little range of hills is only ten miles long, and its highest point less than 550 feet above the sea. While it has sometimes been called a plateau, it has, in miniature, all the salient features of a mountain range. It is composed of a stiff yellowish clay, and is dotted with a dozen villages, isolated farms, and six or seven thick woods of irregular shape, with well-defined edges, looking rather like patches of fenced cover in a bare park. Across this range of hills the British fought the Germans, northward and northeastward, during July.

To appreciate some of the difficulties and inevitable delays of the enterprise, one had only to step down from a post of observation, after a successful drive had been made, and examine what remained of the German line. The first trenches had been so shattered that in most places it was difficult to judge of their quality, or even to say for certain which holes in the ground were scraps of unfilled trenches and which were pits made by shells in the open. The recognizable portions, altho good, were not extraordinary specimens of trench-digging. They had been made in a favorable soil which could be cut like cheese, needed little support, did not crumble in the wet, and baked almost to brick in hot weather. What were really remarkable, for their military value, were some of the communication trenches and the dugouts. One, at least, of the surviving communication trenches was a tunnel more than a hundred yards long, completely lined with timber, and carried so deep underground as to be secure against everything except mining. Another tunnel acquired fame in 1918 when American troops—Twenty-seventh and Thirtieth Divisions—fought brilliantly for and captured it in their break through the Hindenburg line on the St. Quentin Canal.

The larger dugouts were entered through a steel door; from it one descended a thirty-foot staircase, in which the face and tread of each step were made of wood. At the foot of the stairs were spacious rooms in which floors, walls, and roofs were closely boarded. The connecting passages were equally well finished. A second thirty-foot staircase led down to a second group of rooms treated in the same way. In one dugout where an extension was being made when the line was captured, was to be seen an ingenious mechanism for sending up excavated earth, ready packed in sand-bags, for use in trenches above. Another was arranged as a hospital with two tiers of bunks, as in an English hospital-ship, to hold some thirty patients. Each of these larger dugouts would easily house a whole platoon and give it complete security under severe artillery-fire unless a high-explosive shell or mortar found its way in at the door.

Another striking detail of the German defenses was the skill taken in providing effective posts for snipers. A typical post, near Fricourt, was the mouth of a small, deep manhole, such as is used in American streets to give access to sewers. It reached the surface near the highest point of a piece of high ground, where the opening was screened by the casual-looking débris of a broken cart. At the bottom of the manhole a tunnel connected it with trenches. Each manhole

EAST INDIANS IN PRAYER ON THE WESTERN FRONT

of this kind was well squared, full timbered, and fitted with convenient iron rungs. Like dugouts, it suggested that German troops in the trenches had done an amount of manual labor which, to any one else who had had to organize trench fatigue-work, seemed remarkable. Apart from trenches, each successive German line included a chain of fortified villages and woods. Among the ruins of Mametz could be seen the remains of a typical improvised fort, in the oval basement of a large cottage, from which machine-gun fire could be directed through loop-holed walls toward almost any point at every stage of their progress. House-to-house fighting, in any case notoriously trying, was practised by the Germans with unquestionable method and energy in Picardy villages, as was also the defense of woods complicated with barbed wire, which, from the nature of the ground, could not easily be destroyed by artillery-fire. In these chalk-bed shelters, occasionally forty feet under ground, German batteries were so well hidden that the Allies were sometimes surprized at the emergence of German soldiers from ground which they had apparently swept clean with fire long before. In most cases the Germans were well protected by reinforced concrete casements, from which they could be reached only by bombs or bayonets. But in others they met the charge of the Allied infantry by coming out on parapets and using machine-guns in the open to rake advancing lines.

As early as June 27 intensified artillery activity had been accepted in Berlin as heralding the long-expected British offensive, but German military circles were described as "calmly confident that Great Britain's greatest effort would meet the fate of previous offensives." There was, however, keen interest in seeing Kitchener's new armies in action. The general opinion was that a supreme test of strength between the British and Germans would occur during the summer and that it would mark the climax of the war. News then came of a slackening in the intensity of the bombardment around Verdun, and of gains by the Russians in Volhynia, while in the Trentino region the Italians continued to force back the Austrians at various points between the Adige and Brenta, in the Garina and Arsa valleys, between the Posina and Astico, and along upper regions. Northeast of Verdun, the French recaptured ground north of Hill 321 and around the Thiaumont works, and northwest of Verdun carried out a heavy bombardment against the Avocourt sector, but were prevented from launching an infantry attack from the east of Hill 304. In the Champagne, the Germans occupied French positions near Tahure but later were driven out.

Almost at the hour when the new Italian rush began in the Trentino, British artillery on July 1 broke loose against the German trenches from La Bassée Canal southward to the

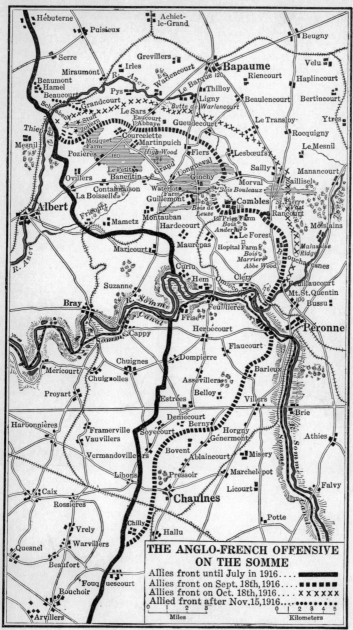

THE ANGLO-FRENCH OFFENSIVE
ON THE SOMME

Allies front until July in 1916....
Allies front on Sept. 18th, 1916....
Allies front on Oct. 18th, 1916....
Allied front after Nov. 15, 1916....

Miles

Kilometers

THE ANGLO-FRENCH OFFENSIVE
ON THE SOMME

224

Somme. Both British and German official statements commented on the violence of this attack, which in certain sections approached the intensity of the drum-fire that precedes an infantry blow. The steady shelling of the German line from Ypres to the Somme was continued for five days. Apart from raids in which British troops penetrated trenches and brought back prisoners, the object of this fire was simply to kill Germans in large numbers, and to save British man-power as much as possible; to destroy German batteries; break up defensive works; blow up ammunition stores behind lines; bring down observation balloons; reach the Germans in and beyond their communication trenches in billets and rest camps, and generally to cause destruction to the German offensive powers over a wide area. It was known from various sources that British gunners were successful in many of their objects. At various points from Neuville-St. Vaast southward to the Somme, the bombardment had its effect. The zone of shell-fire was wide and far-reaching. All along the lines shells burst. La Boisselle was slashed with fire. Above Fricourt was a continual flash of bursting shells through the smoke which shrouded it. Only a few German shells answered British batteries.

From one of the hills a correspondent [1] watched the beginning of the offensive after he had witnessed the preparations for weeks. With deliberate and methodical precision the gathering of human and mechanical material had proceeded everywhere along the whole line included in a preliminary bombardment. Overwhelming as was the power of guns, a grim and significant spectacle was the sight of detachments of infantry in field-fighting equipment, moving forward until finally dugouts became hives of khaki about to swarm forth for battle. Each officer had maps and directions in detail of the part his unit was to play in the complicated scheme. Men had sewn to their uniforms insignia to designate units amid the dust and smoke of action.

As a battalion marched they sang the same tunes they had sung on drill-grounds at home after responding to Kitchener's call. There were quiet and undemonstrative English, speaking with Yorkish or Cornish accents, or

[1] Of the Associated Press.

maybe breaking out in gibes in the slang of the London cockney. There were brawny Scots, with kilts and steel, mushroom-shaped helmets, suggesting medieval men of arms. An Irish battalion could have been heard whistling not only Irish songs but "The Marseillaise." Men realized that fearful work was ahead of them. Ridges and hills, rich farming lands and numerous villages rolled away to the eastward. To the north one could see almost to Dommecourt and to the south as far as Bray, near the banks of the Somme. Every village within range of vision was to be fought over, as had been those in front of Verdun. Something more than a mist rose from dew-laden fields and hid landscapes.

From 6 o'clock to 7.30 all guns along a twenty-mile front were for the first time firing their fastest in a chorus of final blasts, cutting wires, and demolishing trenches. The trenches were hidden by a curtain of smoke, punctured with vicious flashes. Toward that curtain, which shrouded every form of destruction within the power of man, reserves were moving forward. Far above were observation balloons, motionless in still air, and a squadron of aeroplanes flying to their work and spotting targets for artillery. At 7.20 o'clock rapid-fire trench-mortars added their shells to the deluge pouring upon first-line German trenches. At 7.30 the guns lifted their fire to the second line of German trenches, as if answering to the pressure of a single button, and men of the new British army leaped over their parapets and rushed toward the wreckage which guns and mortars had wrought. They were visible only a moment before they were hidden by the smoke of a German shell-curtain over what remained of trenches. Germans, said a British Staff Officer, had now to yield to "two years of our preparedness against forty for the Germans."

Soon nothing was to be seen from the hill except smoke flashes, through which was visible a figure of the Virgin atop the tower at Albert, which, tho struck by a shell early in the war, was still in place, tipping at an angle, but showing dimly. It was not long before ambulances were coming down roads, and batches of half-starved prisoners were being brought in, too dazed to appreciate their escape after having been marooned for five days in dugouts without food. Haig delivered the concerted British attack along a sixteen-mile front extending from Gommecourt to Maricourt. As days passed the bombardment became intenser. It fell everywhere on the front; German trenches were obliterated at Ypres and Arras as well as Beaumont Hamel and Fricourt. From Gommecourt a mile or two south of the Somme the fire was especially methodical and persistent. It seemed as if a complete devastation had been achieved. Villages had become heaps of rubble.

COMMITTEE ON PUBLIC INFORMATION.

STARTING A FRENCH BALLOON AT THE FRONT

There was a curious exhilaration everywhere. Men felt that the great offensive had come, that this was no flash in the pan, but a movement conceived on the grand scale as to guns and men which would not cease until a decision was reached. A detailed description came from the pen of one of the editors of the *Berliner Zeitung am Mittag*, who had been an eye-witness of an advance. He gave a picture of the destruction wrought by incessant big-gun fire:

"The bombardment brought another surprise in the shape of

aerial mines of unheard-of calibers, which were thrown in incredible numbers. The explosion of the aerial torpedo shattered by its tremendous detonation the windows of the bomb-proofs, and threw up a massive pillar of black earth—perhaps a hundred yards. This showered the whole neighborhood with roofs, bricks, and earth. This was a regular Vesuvius eruption. The destructive effects of this uninterrupted throwing of the heaviest mines were almost immediately visible. The work of day and night for nine months was destroyed in a few minutes. Report after report arrived of bomb-proofs demolished by aerial torpedoes burying the inmates. The trenches became rapidly leveled; communication between the sections was difficult. The third lines were so heavily shelled that it was impossible to traverse them.''

South of the Ancre heavy assaults were delivered against Thiepval, Ovillers, and La Boiselle, but British troops found themselves up against formidable positions, and the most they could do was to secure a firm footing in the approaches. On the left, between Gommecourt and Beaumont Hamel, where their artillery had been less successful than south of the Ancre, no substantial gains were obtained. On the second, Fricourt was captured, and on the following day, after a fight that lasted sixty consecutive hours, La Boiselle fell. North of the Ancre the attack was abandoned in order to concentrate an effort against the German front south of that river, and widen out the northern face of the Peronne salient. On the fourth, many local points of vantage were secured. In the evening General Haig reported that more than 5,000 prisoners had been brought in since the beginning of the movement. Owing to the slow progress made, in comparison with the French south of the Somme, rumor gained ground in London that the British advance had been checked, but this proved baseless, as on July 7 British troops successfully stormed a formidable work known as the Leipzig Redoubt, which was the key to the Thiepval position, while further south the village of Contalmaison was carried by storm. On the eighth an advance was made through the Bois de Bornafay to the Bois des Trônes, an important tactical point, and for the possession of which severe fighting took place during the next three days.

A part of the assault comprised nocturnal expeditions of

patroling parties into German first-line trenches, an essential feature now in any attack on fortified lines. The first thing in order, however, was the destruction by heavy artillery of German concrete shelters as perfected with consummate skill, the second being to reconnoiter and make sure that the destruction was complete, for a single machine-gun left intact under a shelter could alone stop an infantry assault. Next came the destruction of barbed-wire defenses, since it was only after this had been done that infantry could be

FRENCH OFFICIAL PHOTO.

THE FRENCH "SOIXANTE-QUINZE," OR "75"

Tommy Atkins knew this gun better as "pa-pa-pa-pa." The "Soixante-quinze" could be fired as often as twenty-eight times a minute

prudently ordered to attack. In these operations British troops showed the Germans, as well as the French, something new in the tactics of siege operations. It had formerly been calculated that 80,000 shots from field-guns were necessary in order to make sufficient breaches in barbed-wire defenses to permit a single army corps to go through. But the fire of the heavier British guns in leveling trenches and destroying concrete shelters and machine-guns became far more effective than that. In amount of ammunition expended and in territory involved, the Somme offensive exceeded anything of the kind previously known in the war. More than 1,000,000 shells were fired daily in preliminary bombardments, extending over a front of ninety miles. Employing an enormous number of guns, the British maintained a continuous fire, leveling German trenches and destroying concrete fortifications sheltering machine-gun squads, while hurricanes of shells were directed against barbed-wire entanglements.

Following daylight artillery storms raiding parties at night dashed out to complete the work of destruction. Many prisoners were taken, many machine-guns destroyed or captured, and the defense demoralized. Frederick Palmer remarked that, "There were times when a fortune was being fired away every hour; when a sum which would send a youth for a year to college, or bring up a child, went into a single large shell that might not kill one human being as an excuse for firing it; when an endowment for a maternity hospital was represented in a day's belch of destruction from a single acre of trodden wheat land."[2] The German artillery-fire was heavy at some points, but in most cases it seemed half-hearted. The British appeared to fire two shells to the Germans one. A new type of British mortar was capable of such rapid fire as both to cut wire and smash trenches. The sky at night for a space of from twenty to thirty miles was made brilliant from dusk to dawn. One could witness scenes of grandeur under a cloudless and moonless night with broad sheets of flame and ugly flashes and darts of fire over an entire area of more than eighty miles, from the Yser to the Somme, where British guns were shelling German lines. Lincoln Eyre[3] wrote:

"All the horizon beyond the ground where I stood to-day was darkened by the fumes of shells. Not a minute passed without

[2] In his book "My Second Year of the War" (Dodd, Mead & Co.), Palmer at that time was the accredited representative of the American Press with the British Army and Fleet. When General Pershing sailed in June, 1917, Palmer went with him as a member of his staff with the rank of Major. His title of Lieutenant-Colonel was acquired in the last year of the war, when still serving on Pershing's staff.

[3] In The World (New York).

the crash of high explosives. Raids that followed this shell-fire killed many of the enemy and brought forth sufficient prisoners for the identification of regiments and divisions confronting the British. Some prisoners said they had had no food for three days, owing to the barrage-fire, which prevented supplies from reaching them by communication trenches. Immediately in front of where I stood I counted twelve British kite-balloons posed above the lines so that observers could see far across the German trenches to their battery positions. Time was when I used to see 'German sausages,' as we called those balloons, starting down upon the Allied fields. But to-day there was not a single hostile balloon opposite those twelve British ones. Rapid-fire destruction of six of them had. I fancy, caused the hauling down of others. The purpose of these bombardments, is to kill Germans. Behind the dead is a great living army, strongly intrenched and able to strike back heavy blows.''

Within twenty-four hours after British battalions north of the Somme and French units immediately north and a considerable distance south of the river, debouched from their trenches, ten Picardy villages had again become Allied territory, and each of which, with a normal population of from 100 to 500 persons, had been transformed by the Germans into an armored and cemented stronghold like the Hohenzollern Redoubt and the Thiaumont Farm. The speed with which men flung themselves across 500 yards between their own trenches and the German earthworks was such that German machine-guns, already depleted by a week-long bombardment, scarcely had time to get into action before their operators were bombed or bayoneted into submission. Silencing machine-guns was not the only task. In Dompierre the Germans had constructed, besides ordinary trench-lines, dozens of little dugouts and underground block-houses, in each of which men were able to resist death or capture for hours. Special platoons of French, armed only with grenades and knives, were obliged to force their way into these dens, and there, in the darkness, to wrestle and stab the defenders into submission. Owing to the stubborn courage with which the Germans fought, few prisoners were brought to the surface after these struggles under the earth. The percentage of dead everywhere along the front was large. In Dompierre 1,500 German bodies were counted as against 700 prisoners. Special correspondents vied with one another in vivid descriptions of the fighting, but it was a private soldier in a North Country regiment who told of the launch of the Allied offensive in terms that perhaps went furthest home, for he spoke, or wrote, in the language of his own people:

"Aye, it were half-past seven when we started, sir. 'Twas in a kind of a bit wood, ye know, sir. The third line like, we was; B and C company bein' afore us, ye see; we could see them movin' in the open like, past the wood; till the fire caught 'em, an' they went down like grass. I was beside the Colonel in the front trench. I carried bombs, ye see. The Colonel, he was to go wi'the last line, after us.

"But when he sees the second line cut down that way, an' our time come—Oh, damn! says he—just like that—and he ups an' over the parapet. 'Come on, me lads,' he said—like that an' just that moment he was hit, and kind of staggered, an' afore I could get till him like, he fell backward into the trench again. I doubt it killed him. But we had to go. I had me bombs. We was singing 'John Peel' like mad, all but two or three near, who saw the Colonel, an' cheerin' to raise the dead.

"I got a bullet in me arm here directly, I was on the parapet, an' somehow it made me stumble like, an' I fell. But I went on as quick as I could, me havin' the bombs, ye see. But ye'd have wondered to hear how loud our lads were singin' an' cheerin', like at a football-match. Aye, twas a pity I lost me rifle an' bayonet an' me cap an' all when I fell then. But I'd the bombs, ye see. I knew well we'd need the bombs.

"Wonderful thick them bullets flew, to be sure. There's nae trees left there now I'm thinking. It was just past their first line I got this one in me hand. A bit sore like, that was, more'n the arm; but not so very bad but what I got on all right; till this third one got me here, and I fell in a shell-hole near by the second line. The pity was, I could ha' used me bombs, like: aye, I could from there, but I was afeard of killin' our own lads. But Lance Corporal——, he took 'em on from me, an' I lay a long while.

"Near along evening time I could see our stretcher-bearers comin' out behind, an' hoppin' back wi' a wounded man when they could. But them Boches is dirty devils. They saw the stretchers, an' every time the bearers showed up they turned a gun on em, an' they swep' the ground very low to kill off the wounded. They got all our stretcher-bearers that way after a bit, just one after the other, as they tried to work. They've no decency like, they Ger-

BRITISH SOLDIERS HOISTING A SHELL INTO A 15-IN. HOWITZER

III.

mans. So I just kind o' humped myself along, as ye might say. But they fired when they saw a move, and then I got into a trench, an' they couldn't see me crawl.

"I came to where the dead lay blockin' the way, an' I didn't like to crawl on top o' they. But I saw they was Huns, an' outside, ye see, the bullets come pretty thick, so I crawled on 'em till I found I was on one of our own lads. I couldn't crawl on them, an' I got out again, an' then I don't seem to mind much after. 'Twas after dark I got in, an' the M. O. at the dressin' station, he said, 'You're all right, lad,' he said, like that; and he give me a cigaret. Aye, an' a stretcher-bearer helped me out through the wood. I reckon 'twas their machine-guns checked us like. But them behind us got through with some of ours what was left. Our boys is all right, ye see. They're not afeard o' the Boche—not at all."

Many villages in this part of France had a complete system of catacomb-like cellars. The Germans had made the fullest use of cellars, extending them into elaborate subterranean barracks and fortified positions. The value of underground habitations in such a bombardment was obvious. Complete destruction of a village overhead only increased the thickness of the protective covering. At Thiepval, after the British had taken it and passed on, the Germans issued from secret hiding-places underground and with machine-guns took the British in the rear. The capture of Herbecourt and the outskirts of Estrées carried the French advance about six miles beyond the point of departure. The French lines were now only three miles from Péronne, the defense of which had been greatly weakened by the capture of Moreaucourt Woods. This was the strongest fortified position of the German second line on the entire front. By the evening of the fifth German second line positions on a six and one-half-mile front south of the Somme were in French possession. On the sixth and seventh the Germans, reinforced, delivered a series of counter-attacks which were all repulsed, while the French consolidated their new positions. On the eighth, fighting in conjunction with the British, the French captured the village of Hardecourt, north of the Somme, and next day assaulted the German position at Biaches, south of the Somme. This brought them within half a mile of Péronne. On the eleventh they stormed Hill 97, and occupied the Maisonnette farm on the Summit, which brought the first phase of the French offensive to an end. The total captures amounted to 235 officers, 11,740 men, with 85 guns, 89 machine-guns, and 26 trench-mortars.

The fact that Germany had lost the offensive did not mean that she had ceased to be a formidable foe. None could tell what her temper might be under the shadow of defeat—whether she would fight to the last ditch, or seek to save the utmost she could from the wreckage. The great current of the war had obviously changed. Humanly speaking, there was no power visible that could turn it back into old channels. The end might, however, still be far off. Thus it was that, in the first week of the last month of the second year, Germany was put on the defensive on all fronts—a circumstance new in the conflict. The Central Powers were attacked on the east by the Russians, on the south by the Italians, and on the west by the British, French, and Belgians.

In this drive the snake-like line that had dangled from Belgium through France for twenty-one months was at last shifted some miles eastward. The actual distance advanced during the first week was not much greater than the space gained by the British at Neuve Chapelle in March and the French in the Champagne in September, 1915, but the prospect of a permanent success was better, for the largest army Britain ever had in all her history was in this field and both French and British for the first time were supplied with artillery and ammunition on a scale at least equal to the Germans. Altho the French lost heavily at Verdun, the Germans were weakened more, not only by greater losses, but by the men whom they were compelled to sacrifice during the year on other fronts, in Russia, Galicia, Serbia, and Turkey.

At Le Creusot, the center of the French war munitions works, the output of the iron torrent which was deluging the Central Empires was now surpassing all expectations. At the outbreak of the war these works employed more than 15,000 hands, and their great shops, covering hundreds of acres, were connected by a network of nearly forty miles of railroad-tracks. After the war began this plant was enormously increased. Le Creusot lies in the center of one of the richest coal- and iron-mining districts of France. Its coal-beds were first discovered in the thirteenth century, but it was not until three hundred years later, in 1774, that the first iron-works were established. Just before the war began the city had 35,000 inhabitants, nearly half of whom were employed in armor-plate factories, gun-shops, locomotive-

FRENCH DISPATCH-BEARER'S CAR
Note the splashes of mud and the wheels without rubber tires

works, and ordnance-plants. Le Creusot was admirably situated with respect to the French frontier, for while it was not so far from the firing-line as to occasion undue delay in the transportation of munitions, it was sufficiently removed to be well beyond the danger zone. It was 135 miles, in an air-line, southwest of Belfort, and 175 miles south of Verdun. This was not the first war in which the works of Le Creusot had played an important part in furnishing France with arms. During the conflict of the Crimea and the

Franco-Prussian War its factories produced enormous quantities of munitions.

Nothing more clearly showed the successful defense by the French of Verdun than the undisturbed manner in which for weeks the French General Staff had been busy accumulating guns, ammunition, and men behind the Somme for an Anglo-French offensive. Foch's armies had been virtually recreated. He had received, in addition to the army under General Fayolle, some of the finest troops of France, including Moroccans and Colonials. Opposed to the French at the beginning were twenty-seven German battalions, belonging to several divisions, but reinforced until the number of battalions had been brought up to thirty-nine.

Lincoln Eyre [4] obtained details of the advance by French storming divisions over four miles in a straight line from trenches west of Frise, thence through that village, the Méréaucourt Wood and the Chapître Wood, to Feuillères. It took fifty hours to traverse those four miles along which were stations transformed by German labor into powerful strongholds, augmented by the obstacle presented by a "buckle" in the Somme. The Somme's regular course is east and west, but just north of Frise it makes an abrupt hairpin loop northward, the sides of the loop about two miles in length and the width about three-quarters of a mile. Before the offensive, French trenches ran from north to south immediately east of the western side of the "buckle." Much of the French artillery was further west, across the river. Therefore, when the infantry left the trenches and started for Frise, six hundred yards due east of them, they risked being deprived of adequate artillery support because of the difficulty of moving heavy guns forward across the shell-sprinkled river. The number of French batteries south of the river was such that the handicap imposed by the "buckle" was no real hindrance to efficient and sufficient gunnery activity. An officer in a French line-regiment who took part in the first day's attack and was wounded in the knee, wrote from a field-hospital: "I have been in the war from the very first day; I have

[4] Correspondent of The *World* (New York).

taken part in every great offensive and defensive action—
Artois last year, the Champagne and Verdun—but this is
different and more terrible than any of those. The artillery
organization is more wonderful than ever. For several days
before the first attack the earth trembled as in an earthquake. We are stronger and better organized than the
Germans, wonders tho they have been and with a big kick

SHELTERS ON THE SOMME

still left in them, but we will never stop now until they are
finished.''

The French in five days of the offensive made more
progress than the British, owing partly to the more difficult
ground that faced the British, and partly to the fact that
stronger forces were opposing them in a belief among the
Germans that the main attack in these operations would be
on the British front. Despite their slower progress the
British successfully beat back heavy German counter-attacks
delivered both day and night in the region of La Boiselle

and Thiepval, and, generally, between the Ancre and the Somme, where the British were making steady progress. It was estimated that the German losses in the battle of the Somme by ˙July 5 had been 60,000. The capture of guns was comparatively small, however, because the Germans, in anticipation of the offensive, had withdrawn their big artillery to longer ranges before the battle began.

The battle of the Somme was eventually to assume the proportions of the biggest battle ever yet fought on the Western Front; but its maximum strength had not yet been reached. The Germans were throwing men into the resistance as fast as their means of transport would permit, and while many of the troops were reserves in the strict meaning of the term, the bulk of them had been hurried on from other theaters of war. Berlin believed that a severe check had been administered to the French and that, since the opening days, Haig had been unable to make any important gains. Forced to abandon shell-wrecked first-line positions, the Germans had retired to their second line north of the Somme, where they threw back time and again British infantry assaults. It had been well understood in Berlin that the British were about to resume the offensive, perhaps with greater violence than marked the first days; but the manner in which the German wall had withstood the first shock inspired the greatest confidence in Berlin.

Never before, however, had the Allies been able to drive at Germany from all sides at once, and the situation was frankly recognized in the Fatherland as serious. Signs of anxiety were seen in a Berlin dispatch passed by the German censor from Karl H. von Wiegand,[5] which impelled the New York *Times* to say, "If von Wiegand talks in this way, the end must be nearer than had been thought." Von Wiegand had long proved himself "a faithful reflector of military sentiment and opinion in Germany." He was "impregnated with it," and repeated what he heard "with entire fidelity and not the slightest consideration for how it would strike outsiders." That the German authorities were preparing the people for the "inevitable" was suggested in his statement. He wrote that "now ˙for the first time in the

[5] Berlin correspondent of The *World* (New York).

war, the military initiative has passed to the other side,'' and added:

"Germany is fighting on the defensive almost everywhere; even westward of Lutsk, Linsingen's counter-offensive has slowed down. Only at Verdun the German Crown Prince is keeping up a slow but strong offensive pressure, gaining ground literally foot by foot, and even the combined offensives of the Allies east and west have not yet been able to divert the Germans from that goal. Germany is fighting day and night against superior numbers in the west, with a heroism and bravery to which the other side is giving a lavish tribute of praise. In the east the thin, anemic line of Hindenburg, Leopold, Linsingen, and Bothmer is struggling against almost overwhelming odds—often four or five to one. Fresh armies, drummed up out of Russia's hundred and fifty millions and equipped with ammunition from the arsenals of Japan and America, are beating against those thin lines with the ceaselessness of the sea, that cannot be otherwise than discouraging to the stoutest hearts."

Nevertheless there were close observers who warned any one who expected to see the British break through successive German lines, jam a million men through the breach and march to the Rhine, that they would "soon be disillusioned." This offensive would apparently be Verdun over again, with the Allies in the rôle of attackers and the Germans launching counter-attacks and succeeding here and there in regaining a trench or a wrecked village and holding it for a day or for two days, or for three days, at a hideous cost in lives. That the decision would be slow and uncertain, and that no immediate *coup* could be looked for was an opinion held by many thoughtful minds, remembering the great recuperative power of Germany, even with the burden of her Austrian ally. A titanic struggle was promised in Picardy before there could be even a glimpse of a decision. But it was now clear that the war-councils of the Allies in Paris and London, in Petrograd and Rome, had been "no mere conventional affairs." The enemies of Germany felt that the day they had long looked forward to had come and that they could begin to exert the full force of their united superiority in men and resources.

German writers took serious note of the changed situation. The *Frankfurter Zeitung* referred to the French advance on Péronne as "remarkable," and added:

"We know we are only at the beginning of the battle. The first pushes usually are dangerous, but it stands to reason that the introduction of very important reserves by the attacking armies, which is to be expected to a certainty, will impose a very heavy task on the defenders. There is no question that the British will attempt to profit in their new offensive by the experience they gained through failure at the battle of Loos."

The Cologne *Folkszeitung* said it was the feeling of the German people that, if only the Allied offensive could be held up, Germany would accomplish a great deal. Other German journals exprest themselves similarly and indicated confidence that the Entente Allies could not really menace the German lines anywhere. At the end of the first week, Dr. Max Osborne [6] said the Germans could see with satisfaction that, after initial local successes, the enemy had come no nearer to their goal. Osborne added:

"What an army has to endure in such a defense exceeds all conceptions. We have become so accustomed to these unheard-of performances of our troops that we think nothing more of it and must leave it to a later time to estimate what it means for half the German army in the west to stand at bay against the united forces of France and England, fresh armies of 1,000,000 men, the last of the Belgians, and expeditionary corps from the four quarters of the globe, and the ammunition factories of half the world. All manner of signs indicate we may have to figure on an extension of the attacking front.

An outstanding principle of strategy established by the war was the value of artillery of all kinds on a scale heretofore never dreamed of. In its use Germany early proved her foresight and skill. So great was her preparation and the power of her thrust that her drive through Belgium and northern France in 1914 barely missed its ultimate object— the capture of Paris, and the elimination of France as a fighting force before others of the Entente Allies could put their forces in motion. It was only by the most heroic

[6] Correspondent of the Berlin *Vossische Zeitung*.

efforts that France and Great Britain had turned back the tide of German invasion at the Marne and later at the Yser. It was by these successes that they gained a breathing-space in which to make the preparations necessary for the successful prosecution of the war. Germany had demonstrated the power of artillery in a way that was a revelation to the rest of the world. The walls of Liége and Antwerp had crumbled under her fire and the same results had followed the concentration of artillery in the East Prussian, Polish,

A DEVASTATED TOWN IN THE SOMME REGION

and Carpathian campaigns. The Allies had been slow to understand the meaning of this. The British had failed at Neuve Chapelle and at Loos, and the French in the Champagne offensive, not because they did not have enough guns, for they had partially learned the lesson as to guns by that time, but because they did not have shells and other high explosives in sufficient quantities. Accordingly they had to sit down for a year or two in order that preparations for their next offensive might be carried to a point beyond chance of failure.

Official reports on the production of arms and ammunition in France showed how this gigantic artillery offensive was made possible. If the figure 100 be taken as representing the power of daily production of various arms and explosives at the outbreak of the war, then by the end of March, 1916, the comparative production was as follows: Machine-guns, 9,850; rifles, 23,700; seventy-five millimeter guns, 2,530; powder, 445; other explosives, 2,560, and superior-caliber shells, 5,460. This growth of several thousand per cent. was proof of wonderful cooperation between State and private enterprises. Furthermore, reports stated that the number of guns for other Allied armies had increased in like measure. Using the same scale as a basis for comparison the number had reached 2,740 per cent. for heavy cannon. The Allies had no trench-guns at first, but they had them now in the proportion of 196 when compared with heavy cannon. Such figures gave ample explanation of the long delay in the Allied offensive and were a triumph of French initiative and industry. Shipments from America had played a small part, and that part was constantly decreasing.[7]

Karl Rosner [7a] reported that violent English attacks on the road from Albert to Bapaume continued uninterruptedly for forty-eight hours, had increased to unheard of violence. Approximately fourteen kilometers long, the attacking front "presented a picture of one immense battle, swaying now one way, now the other." The British had "a colossal numerical superiority," and "were hurling attacking wave after wave, division after division, against our defenses, staking everything on a renewed, embittered effort to wipe out the failure of the first offensive by widening the strip of ground so far gained by them, in order to give the wedge driven into our lines a broader front." What German troops performed in stemming this attacking flood "belonged among the most glorious deeds of this war." Repeatedly in the course of these charges of unheard-of embitteredness, the British succeeded in temporarily getting a footing on the edge of positions they strove to take, but so

[7] The *Journal of Commerce* (New York).
[7a] Correspondent of the *Lokalanzeiger* (Berlin).

far "we have invariably succeeded in tearing their achieved success away from them by our counter-attacks." The French were mainly pressing forward in the region of Estrées and Belloy, and against Barleux. There, too, the attacks followed one another like waves. A stubborn battle raged incessantly, "in which the enemy's embittered passion for gaining ground and the loyal and glorious firmness of

ONE OF THE LARGEST OF FRENCH GUNS

our defenders measured strength," while their attempts to storm positions continued to be "checked by our barrier-fire." Mass storms in the sector from Belloy to Barleux "collapsed with frightful losses." The offensive, Rosner thought, had not yet reached its last horrible climax of intensity.

A stiff action on July 14 produced the largest single

gain the British had yet made. After artillery preparation an infantry attack was launched and the German line southward at Montauban was completely eliminated, until the new line extended so that it was almost straight. At its deepest point the day's advance was over a mile. After the British had made an advance sufficient to protect themselves, they switched the section under fire to a point to the east so as more thoroughly to keep in touch with the French. This move greatly improved the French lines. It formed against the Germans a little pocket just north of Curlu. The British were now slowly and steadily working north toward the Albert-Bapaume railroad, one of the main national highways. Should it be reached, the German line west of that point would be seriously affected.

When the Anglo-French attack began, the German line in Picardy was a great half-circle or salient, bulging out between Arras and Estrées, and reaching its extreme westerly point a little north of Albert. Both Albert and Arras were now in British hands. This advance cut off nearly half the German salient and carried the Allied line a little east of the longitude of Bapaume. Instead of holding a wide salient, the Germans occupied only a narrow salient, with the French and British well in their rear. In effect the operation had driven a deep wedge into the German lines on a front of perhaps fifteen miles and to a depth of about four. This was the first phase of the great Allied offensive of 1916. After it was accomplished there were several days of quiet when the French and British consolidated their new positions and brought up heavy artillery.[8]

[8] Principal Sources: "Nelson's History of the War" by John Buchan, The *Times* (New York), The *Morning Post* (London), *The Fortnightly Review,* The *World* (New York), The *Daily Chronicle* (London), The *Journal of Commerce* and "Bulletins" of the National Geographic Society, New York.

II

FIVE MEMORABLE WEEKS, WITH PÉRONNE AND BAPAUME AS OBJECTIVES—HINDENBURG SUCCEEDS FALKENHAYN

July 14, 1916—August 22, 1916

THE British attack on the Somme after the second week of July took a direction wholly different from what it formally had been. Originally both the French and British advanced from west to east, but now the British made their attack from south to north. As the two forces advanced, they steadily narrowed the salient and, as they narrowed the salient, the position of the Germans inside of it became more perilous, since they were increasingly exposed to the danger of being isolated and their line of retreat cut off. Primarily the important thing was to retain in true perspective the nature and objects of this western offensive. It was not intended to be at once, or soon, a knockout blow. Should the German line crumble sensationally, that would have been a success not contemplated in the original design which was to wear down the Germans, partly by mere slaughter and the capture of effectives, partly by forcing them to keep their reserves continually in motion and to meet incessant attacks delivered in widely distant areas.

The most interesting feature now was the part played by the British who seemed to have settled down to the work that the world had long expected of them. They pushed ahead at a pace that equaled the advance of the French south of the Somme. Practically all the gains the British made for weeks were made after the direction of their attack had been changed. The gains on July 15 totaled a depth of about four miles over a front of six and a half miles. Since the first of July the British had acquired twenty-five square miles of territory, or about one-fifth as much as the Germans had taken since the battle of Verdun began in February. Considering that this offensive had for its ultimate object the clearing of Germans out of France and Belgium, and that it was not a merely local movement, it as yet had not carried far. But, locally, the gains were of importance —the local object was control of the Albert-Bapaume road, and later of Bapaume itself. The measure of British success, therefore, was its influence on these two objectives. On the day when the British broke through the second German line, Philip Gibbs [9] wrote:

"The men poured through and surged in waves into and across the trenches. Every man among them was a grenadier, provided with bombs, and with supplies coming up behind, it was with the bomb, the most deadly weapon of this murderous war for close combat, that the men fought their way through. While men were cleaning up the dugouts in the first-line trenches, other men prest on and stormed their way into Longueval village. The great fires there had died down and there was only the glow and smolder of them in the ruins, but the machine-guns were still chattering in their emplacements.

"In one broken building there were six of them firing through holes in the walls. Scottish soldiers rushed the place and flung bombs into it until there was no more swish of bullets, but only smoke clouds and black dust. Longueval was a heap of charred bricks above ground, but there was still trouble below ground before it was finally taken. There were many cellars, in which the Germans fought like wolves at bay, and down in the darkness of these places men fought savagely, seeing only the glint of each other's eyes and feeling for each other's throats, unless there were still bombs handy to make a quick ending.

"And while wounded men crawled backward, bleeding, from shell-hole to shell-hole, unwounded men crawled forward in the same way, some in groups, others alone, keeping their bombs dry and ready for use. There were machine-guns sweeping the southern end of the woods with crossfire, and with bursting shell overhead it was a place of black horror in the night, but these English boys kept crawling on to gain a yard or two before the next crash came, and then another yard or two, and at last they came up to the German line and flung themselves suddenly upon the German machine-gunners and German riflemen sheltered behind earthworks and trunks of trees.

[9] In The *Daily Chronicle* (London) and The *Times* (New York).

THE ALLIED DRIVE ON THE SOMME

When, as sometimes happened on the Somme, a squadron of cavalry, British or Indian, intruded upon the mass of motor-trucks and tractors drawing guns, Colonel Frederick Palmer [10] noticed how "they brought picturesqueness and warm-blooded life to the scenes." He thought "such a merciless war of steel contrivances really needed some such ornament." Sometimes cavalry at such times would facetiously refer to themselves as the "Dodo" band, or say they were like the bisons "preserved in the Yellowstone Park in order that the species might not die out." Except-

© COMMITTEE ON PUBLIC INFORMATION.

TRACTOR HAULING AN AMERICAN GUN IN FRANCE

ing a dash made in the Champagne, and on the Marne, not since trench warfare began in 1914 had cavalry had any chance. Aeroplanes had taken their place as scouts; machine-guns and rifles their place as a rear-guard, and aeroplane patrols as a screen. On the Somme, cavalry had a taste of action owing to the British success of July 14, which took the Germans by surprize between High and Delville Woods and left them "staggering with their second-line trenches lost." Gunners then rubbed their eyes as they saw horsemen pass and infantry stood amazed as they saw them crossing trenches, on their way up the slope to a ridge. The wonder was that any came back alive. In the casualties

[10] "My Second Year of the War" (Dodd, Mead & Co.).

were about the same number of horses as men. Riders who lost their horses, mounted horses that had been made riderless. A percentage of one horse in six or seven had been hit. Some were killed and others only wounded, but "there were enough deaths to cast a spell of gloom over the adventure; and yet just enough to show what a gambling hazard is war and to give the fillip of danger."

According to advices reaching Paris, the capture of Orvillers was signalized by heavy German losses and desperate fighting. The importance of the place lay in that it covered the main road from Albert to Bapaume and in its situation on the British left flank which rendered its reduction necessary to safeguard advances further south. After six hours of concentrated bombardment by hundreds of heavy guns, the attack began at dawn from three sides, a section of men from Orvillers Wood being the first to penetrate the village. The British plunged into the ruins, chasing Germans along the passages. In one underground retreat they captured twenty-five Germans, survivors of a full battalion, "who had not tasted food for sixty hours." In another stronghold survivors were found nearly dead from thirst. Corpses were seen everywhere. At one end of the village where two little forts defended its entrance were more than 800 bodies, "horribly mangled by the incessant shell-fire."

Near the central market-place a half-ruined house proved the final center of resistance. Here for fully half an hour a terrible mitrailleuse-fire beat off all attacks. Then bombers, crawling foot by foot, managed to throw their missiles into the loophole. For a moment the defense's fire wavered, and the British charged, led by a wounded subaltern whose left arm was almost severed at the shoulder. There was a short hand-to-hand struggle, after which the few survivors, when unbayoneted, threw down their arms, while a subaltern whistling "Tipperary" stood in the doorway, waiting for an ambulance to remove him to a dressing-station. Only 126 living prisoners out of nearly 6,000 men remained. One non-commissioned officer said many had "gone mad from shock and strain and had run amuck until killed by their comrades in self-protection." As the tattered, exhausted prisoners marched to the rear an order rang out, and swiftly formed khaki lines "presented arms in homage to the defenders' courage."

The German General Staff in the third week of July issued an appeal to the people of Germany for confidence in its conduct of the war. "Never has the world experienced anything so stupendous as the present battles," said this appeal; "never has an army braved what ours has braved." Neutrals were startled by this appeal, coming as it did from the German official world. The Government and the Great and General Staffs were all asking the German people to trust them. On all fronts their enemies were making progress and Germany was definitely on the defensive, with France, Russia, Great Britain, and Italy each advancing. Germany could not break out in any new place. She had come to a point where she must hold what positions she had and do this with all her strength against superior numbers and equal preparations. Only two years before she had expected to reach Paris in six weeks. French, Belgian, and British armies were soon to be destroyed. On the soil of France and before the gates of Paris, Sedan and Waterloo were to be repeated. In this tone German official reports had been framed.

There had been nothing more significant since the war began than this appeal to the German people to trust the Government. Many German illusions had gone by the

FLOODED COUNTRY ON THE SOMME NEAR PERONNE

board. There was no longer a decadent France, a helpless Britain, or an inert Russia. Instead there were British, Russian, and French armies breaking in waves of fire and steel against German lines, and the German people were begged to trust the army as the instrument that was defending the walls of the Fatherland, which was a far cry from the attitude of August, 1914. A military force that had expected to make the German people masters of the world had gone down on its knees to ask them for a measure of confidence. Perhaps a million Germans had already died; thousands more were dying daily, east and west; other millions were hungry and Paris, Calais, Moscow, Suez, and Verdun, as German dreams and goals had become the fictions of yesterday.

When the Allied offensive was in its fourth week it had plainly settled down to a war of attrition. Each side could rush the other's trenches after an artillery preparation but only at terrible cost. Undeniably, the Allies had the better of the struggle, but so for weeks had the Germans at Verdun, where their attacks were finally stopt by need of troops elsewhere to hold back French and British in Picardy. Much had been gained in proving the value of Kitchener's levies; but there was no sign as yet that the Allies were within sight of that long desired hour when they could break through the German lines and resume warfare as practised in other days. It was in its indirect results that, next to the wearing-down of the German forces, the Allied offensive was telling most. It was preventing the sending of troops to the east to hold off the Russians; it was straining the nerves and resources of the German General Staff, and it was hourly crushing the morale of the German people, who must now have realized that their hopes of an early and separate peace with France—which they had been told was to be the result of the capture of Verdun—were without foundation.

As days passed there was no abatement in the struggle north of the Somme. In counter-attacks the British succeeded in regaining most of such territory as at times they lost, and in addition dispersed with artillery-fire bodies of Germans massed for other attacks. North of the Somme

THE ALLIED DRIVE ON THE SOMME

French infantry established new lines along the Combles-Chery narrow-gage railway. South of it troops stormed and captured an entire first-line trench between Barleux and Soyecourt. The advance north further straightened the French line to confirm to the British advance, while the attack south was another gain in a campaign to clear the Germans from the bend of the river. Every foot of German positions behind lines captured by the British north of the Somme was carefully and slowly drenched with a destructive fire of high explosives. Giant British shells were dropt on German works from guns stationed miles to the rear. British artillery of large and small caliber, acting in unison, systematically pounded German lines. The roar of guns became continuous. From a height a short distance in the rear, Wilbur S. Forrest [11] obtained an excellent view of Fricourt, Contalmaison, Mametz, the Mametz Wood, Bazentine-le-Grand and other positions taken by the British. Later with others he traversed the valley of the Somme and entered the ruins of Fricourt, once a German stronghold, but stormed and captured by the British early in their offensive. He said:

"Imagine a giant steam-roller passing over any American town of 2,000 inhabitants and you get an idea of Fricourt to-day. The little French town has been literally wiped off the map. German dugouts and shell-holes represent the spike-holes of a huge steam-roller. The rest of the town is flattened in débris. Here and there from the hole of a battered-in German dugout comes a sickening stench that tells of piles of corpses. The scene at Fricourt is typical of that in any of the other villages blotted out by high explosives.

"High British officers say that the purpose of the British offensive is not speed, but to recover by slow, steady pushes every yard of invaded French and Belgian territory at a minimum expenditure of human blood and by a heavy expenditure of powerful explosives, of which there is an ample supply. Fighting must go on below as well as above ground. The Germans have catacombed all villages to escape shell-fire. At Bazentin-le-Grand, for instance, the underground caverns sheltered 1,500 men.

"The entire Anglo-French front on the Somme offensive, as far as the eye can see, literally swarms with men and material."

[11] Correspondent of the United Press.

After a brief pause a main thrust by the French was made to the south. The French now struck against one side of another salient, the famous Noyon salient, where the Germans were nearest Paris, a distance of about sixty miles with Le Fère as a center. From Craonne, its eastern end, to Noyon, its northwestern end, was fifty miles. From La Fère to the front west of Noyon was about twenty-five miles. The prime object of the French here was, by pushing south and east, but mainly south, to get behind the German troops in the salient and compel them to retire from Chaulnes, Roye, Lassigny, and Noyon in order to avoid being enveloped and compelled to surrender. The Germans in Chaulnes were already in difficulties. The British were then holding the north side of the Bapaume salient with troops about Arras. Thus each ally was attempting to squeeze the Germans out of a salient and the Germans were fighting desperately to prevent them. The Noyon salient was much larger than that of Bapaume; the distance across the neck of the latter from Arras to Péronne being not much more than twenty miles, as against fifty from Péronne to Craonne. Thus the task of the French was greater, since they would have to advance much further before they could accomplish the same result, but, if they succeeded, they would recover a much greater bit of territory. The important thing to recognize was that both the British and French had thus far only made a beginning. They had not been stopt; indeed, a further advance might take Bapaume and turn the Germans out of Chaulnes and Roye; but neither of these results would necessarily be followed by sweeping changes.

By July 22 the Germans had begun to lose certain advantages furnished by nature. With the impending capture of Foureaux and Delville Woods their forces would be swept out of what remained to them of natural covers. That explained the tenacity with which they clung to these places, which were being reduced by British artillery-fire to acres of blackened stumps and holes in the ground. The British at the same time were encountering the full strength of the third-line positions of the Germans with their bomb-proofs and shelters, to build which they had had plenty of time uninterrupted by artillery-fire. Trench-stormers found the

Germans in many cases burrowed underground in labyrinths with roofs reinforced by steel plates and concrete. Only the heaviest artillery-fire could have any effect on such defensive structures. In the Péronne sector the French now had the advantage of fighting from heights with the Germans below them. They had advanced beyond much marshy ground.

Another attack was begun by the British along a seven-mile front from Thiepval through Pozières and Longueval,

WHAT WAS LEFT OF CHAULNES

as far as Guillemont, just north of Trones woods. Haig's infantry had captured the outer works of Pozières and Longueval, but the Germans, in a heavy counter-attack, regained the northern end of the village. During the next day the outskirts of Guillemont changed hands twice. The Germans fought with their utmost strength to prevent the British from advancing to their third-line positions, but the Australians, firmly established in Pozières, got astride the road in the direction of Bapaume. A German counter-attack against the French front proved unsuccessful. Berlin declared that along the entire line the attacks of the British were thus far fruitless and that they had suffered heavy casualties. Around Pozières and Foureaux Wood the combatants came to grips in hand-to-hand fighting, the attacks being unusually stubborn and at many points on a front of twenty-five miles. At Foureaux the British threw cavalry against the Germans. With the village of Poziéres in their hands, and having strengthened their positions temporarily by the capture of two strong trenches west of the village, the British rested before attempting again to throw their forces against the Germans, who were blocking their advance toward Bapaume.

The British put on Delville Wood the heaviest concentration of shell-fire in a given area yet directed against field-fortifications. Gunners were amazed when they computed its volume per minute. There must have been three shells a minute falling on every yard, the purpose being to leave nothing standing, nothing living. Not a single German sniper in a tree, not a German machine-gun, was to survive the tornado of blasts. German officers taken prisoners bore witness to the work of gunners. "Your artillery," said one of them, "is better than anything I have seen, even at Verdun." German officers were surprized that "an army of amateurs," as they still called the British, had produced scientific artillery-work in so short a time and paid tribute to the daring of field-gunners. "They came up," said one of them, speaking of the Memetz Wood attack, "like charioteers in a Roman circus, at full gallop." Many horses were killed, but the men were reckless of danger, placing their batteries in the open as if at maneuvers. There seemed little doubt that the German army was now standing up under frightful losses. A correspondent of the Berlin *Vossiche Zeitung* emphasized the importance of the operations of which the battle thus far was regarded as only the opening stage:

"After two years of war the angel of destruction is passing through the ranks of the German army with a fury and mercilessness as if the death-lance of battles had just begun. We feel, as two years ago, the raging storm of the enemies' united power. It is now a question of life or death for our nation. The root of this war is the deep meanness of human nature, which can not bear another power growing up alongside itself without trying to destroy it.''

Among many points of similarity between the Allied offensive on the west and the attack on Verdun, was one essentially different. Verdun could be definitely marked down in phases, each phase representing a period of exhaustion in shells, making necessary a shift in the attack from one side of the river to the other. These periods came with regularity, and altho the attacks were practically continuous, they were not so on any given section of the line. The French attacks south of the Somme had the same characteristics, but the British attacks were different. After the first few days there did come a period of quiet, which lasted for several days; but the attacks became continuous. Night and day shells were rained into German lines. The British supply-system was something that had not been seen before in this war. It was probably the most perfect thing in the way of a transport service yet developed. To have a shell was one thing, but to have it where and when it was wanted was another. The fact that the British were able to keep their shell-supply at the front was now the most promising thing in connection with their part in the great offensive. They had never been able to do this before. At critical moments in every former battle either men or guns failed them when success was almost within their grasp.

The destruction at this time of a certain German fortified work on the Somme was marked by a tragic episode. An order had been given to destroy the fort at whatever cost. In less than six hours more than 2,500 shells were fired and the defenses finally all gave way in clouds of dust and smoke. Infantry then went forward and Germans positions were taken. French artillery officers, in examining the ruins, discovered amid a mass of débris a Bavarian officer lying with his chest crusht and at the point of death. He seemed to collect himself and began to speak softly, and a Frenchman knelt at his side to hear what he wished to say. Thirty-two men, he explained, had originally occupied the place. After the bombardment began half the men became victims of an awful death. Two were decapitated. Of three others near whom a shell exploded not a vestige remained. The survivors crouched at the bottom of the subterranean shelters and there awaited their fate. When another terrific explosion came these men were thrown together in a confused heap and almost immediately flames shot up from the underground cavern. A moment of indescribable terror ensued in which the man in command went mad. Shouting wildly at imaginary enemies, in the sinister glare of flames, he set furiously upon his own men, killing one after another, and then was himself burned to death. Of all these the Bavarian officer alone survived. Determined not to die by the hand of his chief, he had scaled the ruins, clung to a sloping side of the works, but only to be buried under a block of stone. He died soon after the French officers found him, in the hospital to which they had carried him.[12]

Real Allied success was regarded as relatively unimportant now, save as it might be the foundation for success later. The Artois-Champagne operations in 1915 had extended over only a week, but in the third week of the Picardy fighting every one recognized that the offensive was to go on indefinitely. It resembled the Verdun, more than the Champagne, struggle. It was an effort to wear through, not to crash through—a wearing, not a driving, attack. Should the British finally get Bapaume and the French turn the Germans out of Chaulnes, Roye, and Noyon, something real would follow. Some twenty miles east of Bapaume and southeast of Arras, at the intersection of roads, lay the considerable city of Cambrai, one of the great railroad centers of that region. After Bapaume, Cambrai was the real objective of the British. If they could get it the whole German position west of the Oise would be in peril. The fall of Cambrai, from all appearances, would have meant the retirement of the Germans from France, from the Argonne to Picardy, or from south of a line drawn from Vouziers to Lille, which, in fact, was what it meant in September, 1918.

Less than twenty miles east of the French line was St. Quentin, one of the big industrial cities of northern France

[12] *La Liberte* (Paris).

and an ultimate French objective. If the British could get Cambrai, the Germans would probably have to quit St. Quentin; if the French could capture St. Quentin, while it might not imperil Cambrai, it would mean that the Germans must leave France, south and east, as far as the Argonne, evacuating La Fère, Laon, and the Champagne south of Rethel. Should the British get Cambrai, they would be able to cut all the main lines of German communication west of the Argonne and the Germans would have no choice but to retire behind the Belgian frontier from Lille to the Meuse. France would then be liberated, save for some parts in Lorraine. The British had got half-way to Bapaume and once Bapaume was taken they might advance on Cambrai. Unless they were able to do that, the Germans would have successfully checked the offensive. Should the British get Cambrai before snow fell they would accomplish all they had dared hope for, but it would mean something like half a million casualties. The British, however, had the men to pay the price; the French had not, and the Germans had not. This whole Allied operation was like a flood beating on a dike and wearing in to make a breach. If the flood ever got clear through, it would spread rapidly.

The Kaiser on July 22 was seen at the Western Front by Karl H. von Wiegand,[13] who declared him to be in excellent health. Reports current that he was in ill-health and broken down were fables. During the entire war he had "never looked better." Mr. von Wiegand, who was one of the few civilians who attended church where the Kaiser at that time attended, sat near him one day and thus had an excellent chance to study and observe him. He described him as follows:

"Kaiser Wilhelm has aged considerably; his hair has turned very gray. His face, while reflecting earnestness, is at times remarkably fresh and vigorous. His expression has become more serious, his manner more grave. Except for his hair he does not look older than his years. One receives the impression that no one is more conscious of his responsibilities than is he. Attired in a field-gray uniform, he sat in a plain, large wooden armchair directly in front

[13] Correspondent of The New York *World*.

of the pulpit. Behind him were two rows of officers from the head-quarters staff on a small raised platform; to his left other officers were standing, and to the right were fifteen sisters. Of these and the several hundred soldiers who stood during the service none was a more attentive listener than the Kaiser. Only when the organist started at the wrong moment, which caused him to glance in that direction, did he take his eyes from the little white cross on the black draped pulpit. After the service the Kaiser stood under the trees by the roadside while the soldiers who had attended the service stepped by in review. He then talked with military representatives of the Kings of Saxony and Württemberg. I stood about fifty feet away. The Kaiser was describing to them what he saw on the Somme front. At times his face became almost fiercely earnest; gesticulating energetically with his right hand, he occasionally emphasized words by bringing his fist down on his leg. His entire attitude was one of great forcefulness."

On July 23 the main fury of the attack was on the left, where Pozières and its windmill crowned the slope up which ran the Albert-Bapaume road. The village had long ere this been pounded flat, the windmill was a stump, and the trees in the gardens matchwood; but every yard of those devastated acres was fortified in the German fashion with covered trenches, deep dugouts, and machine-gun emplacements. The assault was delivered from two sides—a British Midland Territorial Division, moving from the southwest in the ground between Pozières and Orvillers, and an Anzac division from the southeast, advancing from the direction of Contalmaison Villa. The movement began about midnight, and the Midlanders speedily cleared out the defenses which the Germans had flung out south of the village to the left of the highroad, and held a line along the outskirts of the place in the direction of Thiepval. By the evening of the next day most of Pozières was in British hands. By July 26 the whole village was British, and the Midlanders on the left had taken two lines of trenches. The two divisions joined hands at the north corner, where they occupied the cemetery, and held a portion of the switch line where they lived under perpetual bombardment. The Germans still held the windmill, which was the higher ground and gave them a good observation point.

THE ALLIED DRIVE ON THE SOMME

On July 28 the Germans, thrown back in two counter-attacks on the Delville Wood and at Vermandovillers, while the British gained at Delville, High Woods, and Pozières, found themselves unable to take up an offensive. Sharp hand-to-hand fighting continued at many places. The military pounding was tremendous, but Haig reported that "nothing of importance" had occurred. All news went to show that the British were maintaining their superiority in hand-to-hand fighting, which was gradually driving the Ger-

HINDO-CHINESE LABOR IN FRANCE
Brought from French colonies to cultivate the soil while Frenchmen were at the front

mans from the last of the high ground between Albert and Bapaume. In both Pozières and Longueval it became literally a case of every house being a fortress. Under terrific artillery-fire the British steadily wore through the enemy's third line. Their wedge, first driven in at Pozières, was widening. Their growing superiority in men, guns and supplies facilitated their ability to attack where and when they pleased, while the German counter-attacks were growing less. The fact that each counter-attack was followed by a gain for the British showed how great was their superiority. Without spectacular charges, without any general attack along the front, the British, with grenade, knife, and bayonet, were slowly cutting down the defenders of the crest of the ridge, and forcing their way across it.

The French and British were now attacking in sweltering, midsummer heat, the first real hot wave of the season having struck northern France. Every day the Germans were increasing the number of their guns and men in the Guillemont sector, which was among the last portions of high ground they held. Ten German battalions, or 10,000 men, occupied a front of 2,000 yards. Part of the British attack struck from Trones Wood and another on the flank. The Germans tried to man machine-guns after a British bombardment and resisted bitterly, fighting under a broiling sun as if every inch of ground was precious. The British got possession of the railroad-station, which they had reached in a previous attack, and some of the attackers got into Guillemont, reaching a church where the Germans, swarming in dugouts, outnumbered the advance party which was fighting against them on all sides. It was a hide-and-seek conflict amid village ruins with indescribable ferocity.

The British finally had to retire from the edge of Guillemont, but made good a considerable advance southward on the flank of the town where, through a hot night, fighting continued. Perspiration that day "made white watercourses in the dust on men's faces." Eyes looked out through masks so thick that faces "seemed to be covered with some kind of armor." Motor-trucks passing on the road were like "fantoms in thick clouds." Gunners, stript to the skin, served guns at top speed. In that mixture of dust and shell-smoke, breathing was difficult. Men in the first line, with no dugouts and no shade except that made by clouds of shell-smoke, and often exposed to the full blaze of the sun, found their steel helmets about as hot as skillets off a fire. The haze of dancing heat-waves in a lifeless air hid many positions from balloon observers. Artillery observation became almost as difficult as in a fog. It was hard at any distance to tell dust-covered French blue from dust-covered English khaki.

THE ALLIED DRIVE ON THE SOMME

Details were given out in France on August 2 of the deportation on Easter Sunday of this year, at an hour and a half's notice, of 25,000 citizens from Lille, Roubaix, and Tourcoing. The victims were chosen by an officer in charge of the deporting party. Each person singled out for deportation was permitted to have sixty pounds of baggage, which it was recommended should consist of utensils for eating and drinking, a blanket, good shoes, and personal linen. If any one exceeded this weight his or her baggage was to be thrown aside. Each bundle was to be made up separately for one person and supplied with a tag showing the address, name and number card. When at their destination the deported persons were permitted to write to their relatives once a month. Premier Briand, Viviani's successor, sent copies of a "Yellow Book" with a covering note to all neutral Powers, in which he said:

"About 25,000 French subjects, young girls of between sixteen and twenty years of age, young women, and men up to the age of fifty-five, without distinction of social condition, have been torn from their homes at Roubaix, Tourcoing, and Lille, separated without pity from their families and forced to work in the fields in the departments of the Aisne and the Ardennes. Girls whose hands showed signs of work were taken in preference to the others; servant-girls were taken nearly everywhere, and in many cases their mistresses, declining to be separated from them, went with them to share the unknown future. The proportion of women taken was between 20 and 30 per cent. Two hundred schoolgirls of fifteen were taken away, but on the whole it was the laboring classes who suffered, and in some instances young girls of good family who had been removed have been sent back.

"The raids were accompanied by terrible scenes of grief and sorrow, and not a few elderly people lost their reason when they saw their daughters being carried off. Some of the men, especially of the Landsturm, seemed to be conscious that they were engaged in shameful work; some of the officers, too, admitted that nothing could ever cleanse the German flag from this fresh stain put upon it. Indeed, it is said in Lille that a number of officers and men are in the Citadel awaiting their trial for refusing to dishonor themselves.

"Detailed evidences as to where they were all sent was not forthcoming, but the majority appeared to have been scattered between Seclin and Templeuve down to the Ardennes. There they were employed in various labors—some on the soil, others road-mending, some in the manufacture of munitions, or in the digging of trenches. But the fact which was most appalling was that the women were employed in cooking for German troops, and as servants to German officers. Inhabitants were forced by threats and deportations to make trenches, bridges, roads, and railways; to work in factories and mines; to make sand-bags for use in trenches. They were forced to work during long hours for no pay, in conditions of the utmost misery, without food, liable to flogging and to other punishment. They were deported to work in mines and factories of the Rhineland and Westphalia.''

This matter was considered calmly by the official *Norddeutsche Allgemeine Zeitung,* which stated that the French population affected by the emergency measures "declared itself to be quite satisfied to the fullest degree." The Allies were blamed for making such measures necessary. That paper, an official organ, added: "The German administration caused many thousands of French inhabitants of both sexes to be removed from the great cities in French Flanders. It is intended to go on doing this in future. The necessity for this action the French and their Allies owe to themselves alone."

The two years of war now completed were marked by a notable contrast between conditions as of August 1, 1916, and those of a year before. Germany, in August, 1915, had gone forward with the greatest campaign of the war. The magnitude and extent of her conquests, as Hindenburg had said they would do, had "astonished the world." That triumphal eastern march had continued almost to the gates of Riga, which had been evacuated by the civil population. Other facts were that Lovcen and Belgrade had been bombarded, some hundreds of thousands of Armenians massacred by Turks and Kurds, Brest-Litovsk occupied and Bulgaria mobilized against Serbia. Against these achievements the British could point only to small gains north of Loos and east of Kut. Bad as the record in August was, it soon became worse. Bulgaria declared war against Serbia; the offer by the Entente Allies to Greece of Cyprus, on condition that she would discharge her treaty obligations to

Serbia, her ally, was refused; the French army was forced to retreat from Serbia; Doiran, forty miles northwest of Saloniki, was occupied by the Bulgars, while as a visible sign of Teutonic progress the first Berlin-Constantinople railway express train started from the German capital with a flourish of trumpets, confirming the highest Teutonic hopes, and overawing the neutrals of southwestern Europe. These events, however, had blown into a consuming flame the smothered fire of British wrath. Great as had been the results of voluntary enlistment in Great Britain, they were found inadequate for the task the British had before them. Not until the twelfth hour, when the fortunes of war were at their lowest, had the British Government, urged by the nation and by Britain's Allies, assented to obligatory military service. Probably all Britain felt that the most difficult and decisive achievement of the war had been the voluntary abandonment by the British race of the luxuries of pacifism and acceptance of the hated burden of Continental military discipline.[14]

In August, 1916, Germany was on the defensive. In far-off Armenia, in Volhynia, in Galicia, in the Baltic provinces, in northern France, in the Trentino, the troops of Russia, France, Great Britain, and Italy were attacking her. Meanwhile, there was every promise of a new offensive from Saloniki aimed at Bulgaria and designed to liberate Serbia, and further promise of an early entrance into the war on the Allied side by Roumania and Greece. It was no longer possible, as it had been in 1914 and 1915, for Germany to move troops from east to west, or from north to south, as one field after another became interesting or unimportant. On all fronts with equal pressure the flood was beating upon her battle-lines. Three times she had sought to destroy one of her foes at a time—at the Marne, in Russia, and at Verdun. Each time, by a single colossal blow, she had aimed to put one of her great opponents out of the reckoning, as Napoleon disposed of Austria at Austerlitz, of Prussia at Jena, of Russia at Friedland. But France was still standing erect, unbroken. Russia was returning to the charge with numbers and efficiency that evoked wonder in

[14] Dr. E. J. Dillon in The *Daily Telegraph* (London).

Berlin, while Great Britain had millions where she had tens of thousands in August, 1914, and hundreds of thousands in August, 1915. As the year advanced, it became more and more clear that, even when Germany had outnumbered her foes on the Western Front, she had been beaten, first at the Marne, and then in Flanders. After that she gave her western foes more than a year in which to recover and then she tried again, only to be beaten more decisively at Verdun, for in that offensive she did not gain ten miles in five months. To balance the miles of French territory that Germany still occupied—in all less than 8,000 square miles—France and Britain had taken a million miles of German colonies, swept the seas clear of German ships and isolated Germany as no nation had ever been isolated before in modern history.

Current compilations of the cost of the war in two years showed how utterly beyond previous conceptions the figures were. An estimate of $50,000,000,000, as the total cost to August 1, 1916, was a figure that could be handled by the tongue, but not by the mind. It hardly helped the imagination to know that the amount spent by Great Britain in two years was ten times as great as the cost of our four-year Civil War. A Wall Street compilation placed the total loans of the Central Powers at $12,124,500,000, and the grand total of war loans at $39,191,254,110. Meanwhile the casualties for two years of war were estimated at 13,557,627.

There were, however, no complete figures for losses, only estimates based in part on official returns, in part on various news dispatches, and in part on computations made by Major-General Hugh L. Scott of the United States Army. For the first year of the war the casualties had been placed at 8,673,805. The French Minister of the Interior, M. Malvy, made public the extent of the damage thus far done to property in those portions of France occupied by German troops, the figures being the result of an official investigation conducted by his department. Data were collected from 754 towns and villages, in which it was found that 16,669 buildings had been entirely wrecked and 25,594 partially wrecked. The worst sufferer was the Department of the Marne, where 15,106 buildings were damaged and

3,499 totally ruined. In Pas-de-Calais, which came next, 13,542 buildings were damaged and 6,660 completely razed. In 148 communes more than 50 per cent. of all the buildings within the commune limits were destroyed, and in 74 communes the wrecked buildings were more than 80 per cent. of the total existing. Public buildings were wrecked in 428 communes, the damaged edifices including 221 city halls (Mairies), 379 schools, 331 churches, and 306 other structures of a public or semi-public character; the public monuments damaged totaled 60. Fifty-six of the edifices destroyed were classed as "historical," among them being the city hall and departmental archives of Arras and the cathedral, Archbishop's palace, church of St. Remy, and city hall of Reims.

On August 1, 1916, a month had passed since the Great Allied western offensive began. Since that Friday morning, July 1, when men looked at their wrist-watches and said, "It is half-past seven," there had been no day's pause in fighting until July 31; when, for the first time, there had been no infantry attack. After the first break through the German line between Fricourt and Montauban, and the partial break north on the left, the fighting had been a harder struggle as each day passed. It was never an easy triumphal progress from one place to another, even when Germany was in retreat to new positions. It was intensive

DEVASTATION IN NORTHERN FRANCE

fighting, in which every bit of ground, every bit of broken dinglet, every earthwork, almost every shell-crater, had to be attacked, sometimes twice or thrice, by determined troops. The Germans fought stubbornly, not yielding any ground until forced to do so by a superior determination.

The second phase of this fighting had become known as the "Battle of the Woods," when British troops were called upon to capture Trones Wood, Bernafay Wood, Caterpillar Wood, Mametz Wood, and Bailiff Wood, which had to be done before any great effort could be made to break the second German line. By this time the Germans had brought up great reserves of heavy guns and were hurling enormous quantities of shells in steady barrages along the British line. British battalions had to advance through this fire when they captured Mametz Wood and Trones Wood, and had to hold them under terrific bombardment by day and night. The tide of battle ebbed and flowed in and about those woods, and it was a tide of blood. After five weeks the Anglo-French offensive came to one of those halts which were a familiar detail of operations in this war, when an attack had failed to pierce enemy lines in the opening thrust. Berlin was justified in its assertion that the effort to pierce the Somme front had so far failed; and it might have been warranted in a belief that the effort had permanently failed; but of that there was no proof as yet.

There was now probably no more dreadful region in all France than that which lay about and beyond Orvillers-La Boisselle. No adjectives could describe its hideousness. La Boisselle was no more than "a flat layer of pounded gray stones and mortar on the bare face of the earth." Of anything like a village, or even of buildings, there remained no semblance whatever. The whole earth's surface before and around had been torn into shell-holes and seamed with lines of trenches, now all white because the soil here was chalk. Such land as remained unscarred was almost bare of vegetation, with only here and there a thin coat of sickly grass, or a dusty tuft of cornflower, mallow, or white camomile. Crowning a gentle slope were a few ragged stumps or fragments of tree-trunks ten feet high, with bits of splintered lower branches sticking from them, standing gaunt against the sky to mark where Orvillers used to be. Beyond was uproar, the sky above constantly full of the rattle of machine-guns and the noise of exploding shrapnel. Orvillers was more utterly destroyed than any other village in this battle area. No village could have been destroyed more completely, because there was nothing left of it but cellars, mere holes in the ground. Of superstructure there was none. It was estimated that the dugouts at this place could hold, and did hold, 2,000 Germans. In one, eighty dead Germans were found.

The failure of the German counter-attacks on British positions around Pozières was in line with what had occurred around Verdun, altho on a more extensive scale. The Kaiser's soldiers did not "come back" at Pozières as sharply as they had been in the habit of doing at Verdun. Nowhere was there that sharp rejoinder by which the Germans hitherto had testified that, wherever they had got their teeth in, they would not let go. At the same time, it was declared that in Germany more than one million new troops were in training in barracks. The youngsters of the 1917 class, which, according to advance mustering, now expected to yield close to 500,000 high-standard troops, had not yet been called to colors, and there was no possibility of their being mustered before 1917. Of the 1916 class only 60 per cent. so far had been called to the colors. They were receiving the same thorough training as in peace times, and formed an *élite* army equal in quality to the first line that took the field at the outbreak of the war. In addition more than 1,000,000 able-bodied men between the ages of nineteen and forty-five could be thrown into the field. Mustered and found physically fit, they had not yet been called to the colors. The age limit for active service had been raised from forty-five to fifty, but for this at present there was neither necessity nor probability of need for them. Over 4,000,000 men between the age of eighteen and forty-five would altogether be available. These figures were held in German military circles to justify the German War Minister's statement that Germany's requirements in men were fully covered for a war of indeterminate length. Such had been the confidence of Germany in the early summer of 1916.

It was not until after the battle of the Somme that this confidence appeared in any way to have been shattered.

East of the Somme, with French guns roaring a morning salute and German cannon thundering replies, the German Emperor, on August 12, unexpectedly appeared in a little village behind the front, reviewed a hastily improvised parade and decorated a number of officers and soldiers. He addrest the men briefly, and was then whisked on to the most advanced position. His visit was known beforehand only to a few high officers and came as a complete surprize to the troops. Upon a broad level plain, flanked by a French château, all the troops in the immediate neighborhood were soon collected. With the Emperor was Prince Eitel Frederick, besides an admiral, and several generals. The troops were drawn up in, a hollow square. His majesty was described as "looking trim and fit, tho perhaps somewhat wearied." He quickly passed in review, shook hands here and there with officers whom he knew, and saluted soldiers who stood at present arms as correctly as they would have done at a parade in Berlin.

In August Cyril Brown [15] had an opportunity of viewing the whole twenty-five-mile Somme front from a high vantage point where a far-flung parabolic battle-line was unrolled before him "like a painted scroll." The center was marked by giant smoke-pillars of burning Péronne, where German soldiers, at the risk of their lives, under heavy French shell-fire, were dynamiting blocks of houses to stem the conflagration. Far to the north "the smoke-pall of battle festooned the British front, and just north of the Somme there was a sea of smoke where the French and German artillery were grappling with drum-fire." Just south of Péronne was the village of Blaches, in German hands, and close to it "one of the burning points of the Somme battle, now smiling in sunlight and comparative calm, the small hill of La Maisonnette, whose toll in blood approximated the human sacrifice laid on the altar of Notre Dame de la Lorette." From his vantage ground, Mr. Brown could see the German and French first lines, "a tangle of trenches chiseled sharply in the checkerboard pattern of the Somme landscape" and even

[15] Correspondent of The New York *Times.*

French second and third lines. It seemed to him as if the battle of the Somme were already "entering the last phase of transition to trench warfare." A straight silver thread —the Somme Canal and the winding green-edged river— was at the observer's feet.

French and British troops, in a combined forward movement on August 16, took German trenches totaling three miles in length and in one place a third of a mile in depth. In impetuous bayonet-charges, Allied infantry captured

SCENE IN A FRENCH VILLAGE AFTER IT HAD BEEN
RETAKEN BY THE FRENCH

hundreds of German prisoners. The gains by the Allies were the most important that had been made on the French front in weeks. They practically assured the occupation of Maurepas, where the French already had a foothold, seriously threatened the village of Combles and put the French nearer the village of Berny, to the south. The French made the greater gains in this combined assault. North of Maurepas they and the British worked together. They took an entire German line of trenches on a front of almost exactly a mile. At some points this trench line

reached as far as the road from Maurepas north to Guillemont. South of Maurepas the attack was made entirely by
the French. There the aim was to occupy all the German
positions between the former French front and the road
from Maurepas south to Cléry. It succeeded completely,
driving out the Germans along a front of a mile and a
quarter and a third of a mile back. These gains put the
British and French a little less than two miles from Combles,
a railroad town and the junction of five roads, toward which
they had been driving.

Perhaps the most important advantage the Allies had in
the Somme offensive was the superiority of their air-service.
Squadrillas of airplanes went forward to bring down or
drive back German aviators and destroy their "sausage"
observation-balloons. These raids were carried out before
infantry advances began. The importance of the airplane
mastery the French had obtained became evident. It
meant that, in this offensive, the costs in life and limb, inevitable to an attack upon modern field-works, were reduced
to a minimum, and that the whole depth of the French
front became comparatively immune from effective bombardment.

The curve in the British lines between Thiepval and
Pozières had been a menace to the British since Pozières
was taken, but the menace was eliminated on August 22 by
the taking of trenches in the German salient on a front of
about half a mile. The gains were south of Thiepval and
on both sides of the Pozières-Miramont road. The British
lines were now extended to within 1,000 yards of Thiepval,
thus decreasing the "Leipzig" salient. On August 23 the
British captured more ground on the Thiepval ridge, driving back the Germans for 200 yards. This height, strongly
fortified and guarded by a network of trenches, was slowly
yielding to the pressure of Haig's guns and infantry. On
August 24 was captured an important portion of territory
within the area of the "Leipzig" salient immediately to the
south of Thiepval. The particular trench seized, on a length
of about 700 yards, after the German position had been penetrated to a depth of 300 yards, was known as the "Hindenburg trench," a name applied to it out of compliment

to the general whose wooden effigy for so long a period had had nails hammered into it where it stood in Berlin. The British had not only had to traverse open country in their direct assault, but to work up on the left through a maze of trenches. They had also to secure a transverse sector of the stronghold known as the Königstrasse, which formed a point of juncture with the Hindenburg trench.

Prussian Guards, the Emperor's pet troops, fought with skill and bravery. They proved themselves expert bombers, but in the end were beaten. Some of them lurking in dug-outs came forth and absolutely declined to surrender. In this way many were killed. In an early stage of the fight the trench was heaped up with German dead. From one dugout there emerged a Prussian company commander with a number of non-commissioned officers and men who declined to surrender and a terrific combat at once ensued at close quarters. Then a counter-attack was ushered in by a prolonged and intense bombardment. The Germans knew the British were then in the Hindenburg trench, and were able to "register" on it with precision with their "heavies" and their shrapnel. British artillery apprized of the situation turned on a tornado of shell-fire. Machine-guns from the newly conquered trenches joined in, until the counter-attack was smashed and pulverized.

A correspondent [16] who saw the fighting below Thiepval under advantageous conditions, described it as the most wonderful spectacle he had seen in this war. Bombardments had occurred over a much larger front and attacks had been made on a grander scale, but nothing had been more intense. Well hidden from German view, he lay with others in holes near a narrow spur of ragged trees which were once a wood. On the further edge of these remnants of trees ran the British first-line trench, from which the attack was delivered, and from 300 to 400 yards beyond, running directly across the line of vision on the opposing slope, were German lines along the lower side of the salient. It was all "as plain as if you looked out on your own grounds," in that sunlight of a perfect summer evening. Straight ahead, beyond the top of the slope, was another fringe of blasted tree-trunks, hav-

[16] Of The *Times* (London).

ing a few shattered branches; that was where Thiepval lay out of sight. No word could describe the battle that ensued. "One could hardly set oneself to describe the end of the world." In the course of his life he had seen "many gigantic things, like typhoons, prairie-fires and forest-fires and most of the great volcanoes of the world, and some battles, and the fall of Antwerp"; but as a spectacle, for the splendor and the power of it, he doubted if anything ever resembled what now went on before him for twenty minutes. He wished to shriek, to bite his fingers, to do he knew not what, but "all one could do was to drum one's heels on the ground and gasp." How many guns were at work he did not and could not tell. But they began all at once breaking suddenly on the sunlit silence. In ten minutes hundreds of shells had plunged upon one spot of earth. In twenty seconds it seemed as if there had been thousands:

"Hurricanes, whirlwinds, thunderstorms, and gigantic conflagrations, bring them all together and concentrate them on all in a ring of a few acres, and you will have only a suggestion of what went on immediately before our eyes. One almost sobbed from sheer exaltation, for the over-mastering sensation was astonishment at the power of it—at the power of British artillery and the splendor of its accuracy. We could concentrate here on less than 1,000 yards the guns which ordinarily have charge of miles of enemy front. So terrific was it that, above all the roar of the explosions, the sound of the shells passing overhead filled the ears with a shrieking louder than any wind. As for the ground where the shells fell, it simply was not. Rent and torn in every direction, it heaved itself into the air, not in spurts or bursts, but universally in one great dust-storm. There was no ground, no trench, no brown earth or green; nothing but chaos, swirling and incredible, until the smoke grew and blotted even chaos out."

After the early weeks of Verdun, France had said: "They shall not pass," a phrase which became a creed; and the Germans did not pass. Now after seven weeks Germany was saying of the Somme: "They shall not pass." On the Somme a system of sometimes three and sometimes five lines of trenches covered bases which fed the German lines south and southeast, while outposts protected lines of retreat into Bapaume. With Bapaume and Péronne in the Allies' hands, the Germans knew they would have to retreat from a front encircling Noyon, while, with the loss of Douai, Cambrai, and St. Quentin, they would have to give up the Champagne. There were no such key-positions at Verdun, where the operations were local in effect. Those on the Somme were general and far-reaching. At Verdun, in over five months, the Germans had occupied 120 square miles of territory, pierced a twelve-mile front to a depth of five miles, and captured two of the nineteen permanent French positions. To do this they had perhaps lost 300,000 men, and attained none of their objectives. In seven weeks on the Somme the Allies had occupied seventy square miles of territory, pierced a twenty-six-mile front to a depth of eight miles, and threatened the most vital German bases on the Western Front. They had done this with a smaller loss of men, for there was no comparison between the preparatory artillery assaults on Verdun and those on the Somme—no comparison between the killing capacity of the respective defenses. The offensive at Verdun had long since reached its maximum; silent guns at Pont-à-Mousson were all that covered the forts of the great Lorraine stronghold. But the offensive on the Somme still went on.

On August 24 the French captured the village of Maurepas and advanced more than 200 yards to the east on a front of one and a quarter miles. On the same day the British, who were blasting their way toward Thiepval, pushed their lines 300 yards nearer the town and captured a German trench 400 yards long, together with many prisoners. The new French line east of Maurepas now extended from the railway north of the village of Hill 121, to a point southeast, and the fall of Thiepval was near at hand. By a series of small, sharp attacks in short rushes after enormous shell-fire, the British had forged their way across a tangled web of trenches and redoubts until they were just below a row of apple-trees which still showed a broken stump or two. Below the southern end of the village they had bitten off the nose of the "Leipzig" salient and taken the "Hindenburg" trench, barring the way to the southern entrance of the village fortress. The Thiepval garrison was in a death-trap.

Thus ended inconclusively those first weeks of memorable fighting in Western Europe. In July the war had entered upon a new phase—its fourth great phase, counting the Marne, the Russian campaign, and Verdun as the three others. Germany in two years had not only failed to conquer her foes, but her foes had found themselves sufficiently strong in men and munitions to undertake to conquer Germany. German preparations and efficiency in those two years had overbalanced the numbers, wealth, and sea-power of the Allies, but she no longer had any such advantage. As yet the Allies had failed to conquer her; indeed, they had failed to show just how they were to conquer her in the end; but they had almost reached the Gettysburg stage. It took nearly two years of war after Gettysburg for the North to bring about Lee's surrender at Appomattox, but it was to take two years and more to force the Germans out of France.

© AMERICAN PRESS ASSOCIATION.

GEN. ERIC VON FALKENHAYN

The Allied and neutral nations were startled on August 30 when from Berlin came news that the Kaiser had dismissed Falkenhayn and appointed Hindenburg in his place as Chief of the General Staff. He had thus substituted a popular hero for an imperial favorite, had replaced a latter-day tactician with a veteran of three wars. The change was referred to as a victory of tried age over impetuous youth—for at fifty years or so Falkenhayn was a mere stripling compared with Hindenburg, the revered "Old Man of the Lakes," who was in retirement and almost an outcast in his profession when the war broke out, a soldier distinctly of the old school. In his teens Hindenburg had fought in the Austro-Prussian war of 1866 and as a young man had served in France in the Franco-Prussian War. Nearly ten years before the World War began, he had been retired from the army for physical disabilities. But his interest in the war-game had remained as keen as ever. War was his life and the science of war had been his life study.

When the Germans, under commanders of the new school, overran Belgium, pushed back the French, harried the British and marched onward to the tune of "Paris in six weeks!" this "Old Man of the Lakes," in his study at home in Hanover, was poring over maps, not those leading to Paris, but maps leading to Moscow, and he offered his services to his Emperor, but was told courteously that when they were needed he would be duly informed. Hindenburg's time came after the Russians overran and began to lay waste East Prussia in the early autumn of 1914. He was called to take command in East Prussia where he administered to the Russians among the morasses of the Mazurian Lakes an utter defeat near Tannenberg. Hindenburg's name was thereafter on every German tongue. Cities were named for him, busts, portraits, and a huge wooden statue were raised in his honor, and Tannenberg Day became a festival.

FIELD-MARSHAL VON HINDENBURG

Of different sinews from Hindenburg was Falkenhayn. A descendant of one of the oldest and noblest houses in the empire, he traced his ancestry to the eighth century. Nervous, brilliant, excitable, and good-looking, he was past-master of the new school of Prussian soldiery. At fifty he had become Chief of Staff to succeed Moltke, a veteran of the old line, who was retired after the battles of the Marne and the Aisne on account of "ill-health." With actual war-experience limited to the expedition against the Boxers in China, Falkenhayn had betrayed no lack of confidence when thrust into supreme command. His dismissal now was regarded in Allied and neutral countries as Germany's acceptance of a verdict of defeat at Verdun. It came more than six months after the beginning of that gigantic adventure and when the German failure was fully proved. If Falkenhayn paid the price of failure at Verdun, it was still true that to his credit—at least officially—stood the greatest achievements of the German armies in the war, achievements large enough, perhaps, to excuse even so big a failure as Verdun—the conquest of Poland, of a goodly portion of western Russia, and of Serbia, all of which were carried out under his auspices. The Mackensen "phalanx" which smashed the Russian line in Galicia was usually described as a Falkenhayn idea and it was Mackensen in Galicia who had made Hindenburg's advance possible in northern Poland. Most German faith in ultimate victory was now based on the huge enemy territories which the Kaiser's armies held, and of these five-sixths had been acquired under Falkenhayn.

It was not so much Hindenburg the man as Hindenburg the national hero and ideal whom the Kaiser placed at the head of the General Staff. It did not follow, because Hindenburg knew the Masurian swamps as well as the palm of his hand, and had bagged Russians by hundreds of thousands, that he could bring the same minute knowledge to bear on a couple of thousand miles of German war-front with similar decisive effect. While about him was seen the popular halo of victory, the victories he had to his credit were by no means the greatest that the German armies had won. Rather it was his personality which imprest his countrymen. His great bulk, his massive, unemotional face, his curt economy of words—these appeared to the German people when in adversity, as an embodiment of fundamental national traits of rugged strength and patience. Brilliant strategists and technicians all had failed Germany. For the problem of *durchhalten*, which confronted her, she now had recourse to the man whose very physical dimensions suggested that *feste Burg* to which a nation encompassed with enemies could turn for refuge in her hour of need.

252

THE ALLIED DRIVE ON THE SOMME

In Berlin the appointment was regarded as "a measure of such far-reaching military and political consequences that, even at this close range, it is impossible fully to discern its significance." The investment of Hindenburg "with practically dictatorial power" was the most popular thing the Kaiser had done. There was more enthusiasm over the field-marshal's elevation "than over any victory since the earliest months of the war." While the change was precipitated by Roumania's entry into the war, as much as by the Verdun failure, it was impossible to say whether the decisive factor was military necessity or the certainty of a tonic effect on the morale of the German nation. Both considerations were undoubtedly important factors, but the magic of Hindenburg's name was the most compelling factor.

Falkenhayn's fall was regarded in some quarters as one of the most dramatic incidents of the war. It not only marked the triumph of Hindenburg over his younger rival, but, what was much more important, it indicated that a perception of the real gravity of the German situation was dawning on the Emperor and his advisers. No one mistook the meaning of the sacrifice of the courtier soldier in favor of the gruff old field-marshal, who had not always been in the Emperor's good graces.

No artifices could longer conceal the results of divided counsels and the dissipation of forces. Falkenhayn's removal was tantamount to an open confession of failure, as well as a humiliation for the Crown Prince whose instructions in military matters had come from him. Indeed, Falkenhayn was said to have owed his earlier appointment as War Minister largely to the Crown Prince's influence. No one had been more frequently than Falkenhayn in the company of the Emperor and the Crown Prince. He had been entrusted with all kinds of important confidential commissions, had traveled with the Kaiser in special trains and within a few weeks of his fall had accompanied him to Cologne Cathedral, during his journey from west to east.[17]

[17] Principal Sources: The *Daily Chronicle* (London), The *Evening Post,* The *Times,* The *Tribune,* New York; the "Military Expert" of The New York *Times,* The *Daily Telegraph* (London), *The Sun* (New York), The *Times* (London), Associated Press dispatches and "Bulletins" of the National Geographic Society, New York.

GUILLEMONT, COMBLES, AND THIEPVAL—THE "TANK'S" ARRIVAL

September 2, 1916—September 27, 1916

IN August the French and British armies had been almost within sight of Péronne and Bapaume and yet those towns did not fall. English papers explained that the advance was not intended as a "knock-out blow," but to wear down slowly the Teutonic lines and eventually to force a general retirement. Most London papers commented optimistically on the situation, and stated emphatically that the advance, altho slow, would finally result in a general withdrawal of the German line, but all warned readers not to attach undue importance to local successes.

German military circles had been a little puzzled at the choice of this particular point for a Franco-British drive. Whatever had been the original purpose, it now possest, they said, only academic interest. That German commanders had brought the advance to a standstill by September was an opinion held by most German papers. Owing to the extraordinary length of the Western Front, from the North Sea to the Swiss frontier, it had not always been possible for the Germans to have reserves so well distributed that they could meet a strong push with the necessary force at every place. The Allies on the Somme had reckoned on this when they began their offensive with great superiority in numbers. But the Germans as soon as they could bring up the necessary reserves and the artillery, believed the Allies would be "compelled to halt." The Allies, they maintained, had sacrificed thousands of men in achieving nothing considerable after making an initial offensive stroke.[18]

Berlin asserted that the Allies on both fronts had lost

[18] *Deutsche Tagezeitung* (Berlin).

more than a million men in killed, wounded, and missing, since the grand offensive opened with the Russian attack in June. Against these losses they had to show only the conquest by the Russians of the Bukovina and some Galician territory, the capture of Gorizia by the Italians, a shallow thrust into the German position on the Somme and the occupation of mountainous Transylvanian territory by the Roumanians. The Allied losses were listed in Berlin as follows: Russian, 600,000; British, 230,000; French, 150,-000; Italian, Serbian and Roumanian combined, 50,000. Some Austrian experts, and a number of Germans, estimated the Russian losses at more than 800,000, and the combined British and French losses at more than 400,000—all probably exaggerated figures. Anglo-French forces might score further local successes on the Western Front and the Russians might advance at some other points in the east, but any additional gains "must be made at such a frightful additional cost in human lives, and with such an extravagant waste of munitions, that the people of the Allied countries would cry for peace."

The British view was that the offensive by the Allies had achieved formidable results on every side. Probably the main burden henceforth would fall on Great Britain, but she was quite prepared for it. The conditions of victory were comprised in men, warships, munitions, and money, and in three of these elements of power Great Britain's contribution would continue incomparably the greater. As for men, she expected to put at least six millions through her fighting services before the end of the war, and more if needed, which as an achievement was something gigantic and far beyond anything else recorded in her history. The Allies believed they could wear down any possible German counter-attack and again take the offensive. They meant to "crush inward on converging lines, and they were determined to effect a thorough settlement on German soil." [19]

Quite inadequate conceptions of the magnitude of the British achievements in the war had at this time prevailed in America. The appeal of France had been so simple and direct that America's sympathy and admiration for France

[19] J. L. Garvin in The New York *Tribune*.

had not gone astray, but so much had been heard of British mistakes and shortcomings that Americans lost sight of the magnitude of what Britain had been doing. By common consent among the Allies the creation of England's volunteer army, with the mobilization of the industries of the nation for the support of that army, was the most marvelous achievement of the war—always excepting the victory of the French and British on the Marne, which still remained the miracle of the war.[20] Before conscription was adopted almost 90 per cent. of the available men in England, Scotland, Wales, and Ulster had volunteered. Great Britain had assembled, trained, equipped, and officered a volunteer army of about 4,000,000 men. No one who had not seen this for himself could form any conception of the gigantic proportions of that task. England by the voluntary action of her people had done in two years what it had taken Germany and France two generations to accomplish with the most drastic measures of conscription and organization. England had been turned into a veritable armed camp. Soldiers were seen everywhere. To equip and munition this army over 4,000 factories had been operated by the Government, or were under its control, many of them built since the beginning of the war. At least 2,000,000 people were engaged in the manufacture of munitions, and in other activities directly connected with the war. Since the outbreak of the war, the production of munitions in England had been multiplied at least fiftyfold. In two years England had spent over $9,000,000,000 on her preparations, and loaned about $4,000,000,000 more to her Allies and Colonies. After allowing for all the blunders and delays, this mobilization of the energies of the nation had been accomplished with a promptness and a universality of sacrifice and service for which history probably afforded no parallel.

On September 2 the Allies made gains on the Somme that exceeded any they had scored since an intensive defense of the German lines had been organized. The advance was made on a six-mile front to a maximum depth of nearly a mile, over territory defended as elaborately as Verdun itself

---

[20] Statement by Paul D. Cravath in an interview with a New York *Times* reporter on returning from Europe in August, 1916.

and thus constituted an important day's work. The capture of Cléry village, an outpost of Péronne, the chief single point in the French success of September 2, was accompanied by the capture of Leforest hamlet and an approach in a single bound to the edge of Combles. On the British side the complete capture of Guillemont and an entry into the neighboring village of Ginchy carried forward the northern extremity of the advancing armies. Of the village

A GERMAN TRENCH ON THE SOMME AFTER IT HAD
BEEN BOMBARDED

of Guillemont only one wrecked and battered building, apparently a barn, remained in a waste of masonry pounded into the earth. How even a fragment of the walls of that one building still stood was a mystery. Some queer chance had kept it tottering on its feet when everything else had not only fallen but had been pounded to nothing. The ruins were full of Germans lurking in holes. All around the edge of the village were strong positions held with machine-guns.

On the southwestern and southern sides were deep dugouts. Before the attack the Germans had thrown into or about the British front lines gas-shells to the number of probably 10,000, but the shells did not seriously impair the vigor of the attack.

The most intense struggle was in the region of Falfemont Farm and Wedge Wood. Due east from Guillemont was a strong, narrow wood, on high ground, known as Leuze Wood, a conspicuous object in the landscape. From the lower end of this wood, nearest to Guillemont, the high ground ran southwestward in a narrow spur some 500 yards, with a narrow valley or ravine on either side. In the left-hand valley—that is, the one near Guillemont—lay Wedge Wood, a small, wedge-shaped patch of trees. On the slope of the right-hand valley was Falfemont Farm. On this little patch of ground throughout the afternoon, along the sides of the little valleys and upon the spur itself, there raged as stubborn fighting as had perhaps been seen. Almost immediately before the British reached Falfemont Farm, the ruined site of which was once a considerable farmstead, came a counter-attack. The Germans came on almost in a solid line, from Leuze Wood, over high ground toward Wedge Wood and the farm, until they topped the edge of the ravine where the guns took them. The dark, solid line first wavered at one end, then gaps appeared in it, and it broke into bits, withered away and disappeared. Those who were not killed or wounded flung themselves down to take cover in shell-holes or among the herbage on the edge of the ravine. The capture of Guillemont and an advance to Ginchy by September 5 were treated as a completed operation.

The points which emphasized the gain made were, first, its greater extent as compared with previous progress on the Somme; next, its situation in the most difficult part of the Somme front and toward the most important direction; and, finally, its accomplishment in the face of German expectation and intention to prevent it. In extent, the advance fell only slightly short of equaling the entire previous gains made on the six-mile front from Cléry to Ginchy. A mile's progress in ten days, the rate set, if continued, would carry the offensive in eight months a distance of twenty-five miles, or to Busigny, an obscure railroad-station, where the direct line from Cologne to St. Quentin, the chief supply line of the German Aisne front, intersected a line from the Champagne to Lille, the short, direct route taken by German reserves in passing from the Champagne front to the Artois front. The arrival of the Allied forces at this point would cut down the supply of munitions for some sixty miles of the German line, from Chaulnes to Craonne.

Foch, shifting his attack on September 6 from north to south of the Somme, reached the outskirts of Chaulnes, the main support of the German line in the sector from Péronne to Roye. The French also threw forces against the railway from Chaulnes to Roye, thus cutting one of the two roads which supplied the Roye salient. The gains were made after heavy counter-attacks had been beaten back. Assailing the Teuton line on a front of more than twelve miles, Foch's troops carried the greater part of the village of Berny-en-Santerre, northeast of Chaulnes, and the northern part of Vermandovillers, to the southwest. The British meanwhile endangered the German grip on Combles. Haig's troops captured the Leuze Wood, less than a mile northwest of Combles. This gain, in addition, imperiled Ginchy, which lay well west of the new French line, and left the Germans the alternative of withdrawing or surrendering.

This victory held the promise of speedy developments around the two towns toward which the Allied offensive was immediately directed, Combles and Péronne. Foch attacked on a front of nearly four miles, but the main advance was along the middle section of that front for a distance of more than a mile and a half. Along that section the French drove forward about two miles. Hitherto the Allied line, pressing against Combles and Péronne, had run in a southwesterly direction on a fairly even course with no forward salients. The new French success thrust forward a wedge nearly two miles wide and more than that deep, so that Combles found itself "pocketed." The Germans had now to face west, south, and southeast. The southern face of the wedge in the same way threatened Péronne from the north. The highway to Bapaume had been cut. Every mile which the French could push forward would mean the severance of another of the three remaining highways running north from Péronne and including the road to Cambrai.

To what extent the steady yielding of the German lines on the Somme was involuntary, to what extent it was a part of the plan which the advent of Hindenburg as chief had brought into the field, namely, the abandonment of the German lines in the west for a concentration and a decision against Russia or Roumania, were vital questions now. Outside observers could only conjecture, but the feat performed by Foch, if it could be repeated, would make it plain that the German defensive on the west was no longer rigid. At Soyecourt had occurred a great battle of the old-fashioned kind, a battle of armies in the open, a battle of bayonets between great forces. Armies had gone forward to meet each other just as they did in feudal times, but on a vaster scale. The feudal baron ran no great risk when he advanced to meet his foe, gallantly scorning advantages of position, and that was just what the French and Germans now did, with much more courage. The French came out of the trenches cheering and singing, and the Germans rushed to meet them. At Soyecourt the French charged with the bayonet, took machine-guns, and turned them on their former owners. The British, at their end of the line, fought in the same way. Aviators who looked down upon the scene saw it as a mad football scrimmage of struggling figures. There had been such fighting before in this war but never on such a scale in the west. Brigades had fought hand-to-hand, but here armies were fighting. It was a great battle, a clean-cut victory. The Germans were not able to retrieve their losses as they had so often done before. They made small gains here and there, but no such fight to regain their place as they had been accustomed to make. Their resistance was brave and vain, but their recuperation languid.

There had now been a gradual development of a strategic plan until the Allied operations on the Somme and at Verdun had become part of one great battle. The headquarters of Joffre became like some vast clearing-house, which linked the offensive conducted by Foch with that carried on by Nivelle. It was no mere coincidence that, within fifteen minutes after the units of the Tenth Army fought their way into the mound of masonry which had been Berny-en-Santerre, the regiments of the army of Verdun were storming German trenches in the Vaux-Chapître and Chenoise Woods north of Fort Souville on the Meuse. The two attacks, separated by hundreds of miles of firing-line, were interlocked even to the extent that the generals in charge of each knew to the minute when the first was to reach a conclusion and another was to begin. Heavy

GERMAN HUTS NEAR THE MEUSE
Here, not far from Thiaucourt, Germans lived for four years

artillery miles behind lines and innumerable field-guns tucked away in close proximity to trenches crusht German earthworks and armored bastions into fine powder during a forty-eight-hours' cannonade. At 1.45 fuses were lengthened, and infantry sprang from trenches. Without even the usual halts for getting their second wind in dodging shrapnel, French battalions sprinted full tilt across shell-scarred fields intervening between them and a village half a mile away. In German trenches little sign of life was usually found but much rapid-fire activity was necessary to stamp out the resistance of machine-guns and grenade-throwers lurking in underground shelters.

On September 6 the village of Berny became part of France again for the first time in nearly two years. The fighting continued among a few battered houses to which the Germans still clung south of the road from Berny to Estrées, but by 5 P.M. French possession of the village was assured and infantrymen settled down to dig themselves in. The capture of Berny made for the strategic domination of Barleux, the last stronghold of the Germans on the plateau overlooking Péronne. More important still, perhaps, was the taking of the railroad from Roye to Péronne, for this was the principal means of communication behind all the front south of the Somme. No sooner had the conflict waned in the Chaulnes region than the tide began to rise in the Verdun zone, where a twenty-four-hours' artillery preparation sufficed to pave the way for the regiments which Nivelle hurled against the German positions on a line almost a mile long in the wooded districts south of Fort Vaux. Every objective was reached in this engagement, and 250 prisoners and dozens of machine-guns were seized.[21]

Advancing along a front of six miles north of the Somme, on September 8, the French and British forces struck the greatest blow they had delivered in weeks. In a joint attack the Allied forces extended their lines nearly half a mile at every point and brought them to the outskirts of Combles. During this attack the Allies were again on the offensive on all fronts, and the respite which the Germans had had while the Roumanian question was being settled was ended. At a time when Austro-German armies were being driven from vital positions on the Iron Gates of the Danube, and when Germany had sent 50,000 men to avert disaster, Russia, Italy, and now Britain and France were applying pressure. This Allied success on the Somme carried the British front 500 yards east of Guillemont from Ginchy to Falfemont Farm, and extended the French lines almost on top of Combles and as much as half a mile east of their former positions in the district between Combles and Cléry. Guns now threatened Combles from the west, south and east. By

21 Lincoln Eyre in The *World* (New York).

capturing Cléry the Franco-British troops accomplished what the French alone had found too difficult a task. Foch's soldiers had entered Cléry before, but counter-assaults pushed with vigor had succeeded in turning them out.

For ten weeks it had been a ceaseless body-to-body struggle on the Somme. There was nothing of chance in this fighting. On the field, as a whole, the question was only one of power and its right application—sheer grit, fighting quality, and staying power. The actual extent of territory won by the British was somewhere in the neighborhood of thirty-three square miles, but if all the lines of trench-defended shell-craters, and lines of fortified positions, as on sunken roads, the edges of woods and villages, could be strung out end to end and measured, they would have been found to reach for hundreds of miles—300 or 400 miles was one estimate. Rough calculations showed that the total expenditures in those eighty days, on the part of Germans and British, had been between 20,000,000 and 25,000,000 rounds of artillery ammunition. These figures included shells of all sizes, from those of ordinary field-guns to those fired by large guns, and huge howitzers, gas-shells, tear-shells, incendiary-shells, shrapnel, and high explosive of every description. To these had to be added many hundreds of thousands of trench-mortar projectiles, millions of bombs and hand- and rifle-grenades, and untold millions of rifle and machine-gun ammunition. The grand total of missiles fired ran into some tens of millions; and this took no account of gas-clouds, flammenwerfer bombs dropt by aeroplanes, and other miscellaneous instruments for the destruction of human life.

Continuing the drive toward Combles and Péronne, the French on September 12 captured Bouchavesnes, midway between Combles and Péronne. Early next morning they pushed further eastward, capturing in a bayonet-charge the Bois l'Abbé Farms, near the Péronne-Bapaume highway. The positions carried by the French were the last of a strongly fortified German third line between Combles and Péronne. All the positions behind this line had been built under the unceasing fire of French artillery, and consequently were not nearly as strong as the old lines. Foch was believed to be nearer a striking victory over the Germans than at any time since the Somme offensive began. Combles was under fire from two sides and half-way surrounded. Péronne itself had been cut off from direct communication with Combles, and the French, driving eastward on a front of nearly four miles, established themselves almost directly north of the city. The capture of both Combles and Péronne within a fortnight was confidently expected, provided Foch continued his hammer blows north of the Somme.

In the capture of Hill 145, two miles southeast of Combles, the French went over its summit with bayonets and grenades and drove the Germans down the slope. From the new position thus acquired French artillery could completely dominate Combles, while the British were shelling the town from the northeast. According to military critics the key to the Bapaume-Péronne road passed into the hands of the Allies when the British took Ginchy, which was the pivotal point whence the line turned south. As Ginchy was strongly fortified its capture was necessary to the taking of Combles, just as the capture of the latter was essential to the bagging of Péronne. This explained the extraordinary efforts the Germans made to recover this ground.

Now took place on the Western Front a battle in the open field, where tactics and maneuvers of troops, rather than assaults on trenches, won an advance. This, more than anything else, served to show the extent of the French gains in the Somme offensive and the advances they had made. Between Combles and the Somme there was a gap of more than four and a half miles running clear through German lines of fortifications that had been two years in building. The French, debouching through this gap, defeated the Germans in a series of maneuvers in the open country and drove them back a distance varying from almost two miles on the north to a little more than 600 yards on the south. This encounter was in three parts, and was fought by troops battling veritably for their homes—for the French soldiers engaged were mainly from the invaded districts. Two nights of unremitting cannonading demolished the German trenches.

3

A FRENCH ATTACK ON GERMAN TRENCHES ON THE SOMME

III.

THE ALLIED DRIVE ON THE SOMME

From Combles the Germans tried to hit the French in the flank, but artillery, moving forward with infantry, held them in check, while infantry seized prescribed positions and entrenched. This was the second stage of the battle and the first part of the fight in the open field, the second part being an advance of the center and right wing. The extreme right debouched from Cléry and took Hill 70, in front of Feuillancourt, while the center, linked up with the left wing, seized the Péronne-Bapaume road south of Bouchavesnes.

A FIRE-PROOF CHURCH IN NORTHERN FRANCE

The line was completed by the advance of the right wing connecting the positions with Hill 76. The French now encircled Combles on the west and south, while the British menaced it on the north. Foch's troops were on the borders of Mont St. Quentin, the last point from which the Germans dominated Péronne, and had cut the main road.[22]

By next day the French offensive had achieved what the Germans believed was impossible. It had driven a wedge

[22] Dispatch from Fred. B. Pitney to The *Tribune* (New York).

through the original German front and definitely broken the line of fortifications across France from beyond the northwestern frontier to the limits of Switzerland. This achievement filled the battle-weary troops with an enthusiasm unknown to them since the battle of the Marne. Great as was the moral value, the strategic effects were even more important. High-road No. 37, one of the great arteries feeding the German front, had been cut between Bapaume and Péronne. By their advance beyond Hill 76 the French now menaced, and already swept with their artillery, the main road from Paris to Lille *via* Cambrai, the loss of which was expected to force the German High Command to consider seriously the necessity of that shortening of the front which was expected to mark the beginning of the end. Péronne was now under French fire from the north, west, and south, which cut it off from all communications except along trenches or by dangerous night transport. The latest, and in a sense the most complete, of recent French successes at the Somme, was an example of the fashion in which the French had learned to coordinate their movement of troops with their artillery preparations. For the second time in a relatively brief period they had made an advance on a considerable front, and this advance had enabled them to take possession of one of the most important highways.

Directly east the French extended their positions to the southeast and carried the farm of Le Priez, which the Germans had organized into a stronghold guarding Combles on the flank. Combles was now completely isolated, altho it was not surrounded. The British were striving to close the loop by pushing forward from Ginchy, but their task was arduous. They made some progress on September 14, but they still had to conquer a mile of strongly fortified ground. Communications with Péronne had been cut and roads leading to Combles and Péronne were raked by Allied guns. It was not quite correct, however, to say that all communication between Combles and Péronne had been cut off, because communication could be made by a circuitous route, but this would take a long time in travel. For practical purposes the statement was not far amiss. In so far as it referred to the ability to transport ammunition-trains, under French pressure, communication between the villages was at an end.

On September 15 the British struck their heaviest blow in the Somme offensive. Before it was completed, Haig's line had been pushed forward along a six-mile front, penetrating in some places to two miles. The villages of Flers, Martinpuich, and Courcelette were carried by storm, on the front from Pozières to Ginchy, and the greater part of Bouleaux and High Woods lying between. Combles was pocketed. The British stroke carried all the high ground between that stronghold and the Albert-Bapaume road, thus bringing Haig's line up to Foch's. Meanwhile, the French continued an incessant battering and won 500 meters of trench north of Le Priez farm, thus cutting off Combles from the east. The British advance was accompanied by an inferno of artillery-fire. Shells were poured out north of the Somme until they made another record in expenditure of munition. Numerous air-battles were fought. British fliers brought down thirteen German planes. The first effort was made against the ridge from Thiepval to Ginchy. The thoroughness with which the artillery-fire had been carried out made the task easier, but fierce resistance had to be overcome. With the dash and precision that had characterized the French operations south of the river, the British troops rushed at these heights and succeeded in winning the ridge.

British army officers all spoke of September 15 as the best day for British arms that had been known since the offensive on the Somme began. With the exception of the attack on July 1, the attack on September 15 was the most

PARISIANS WATCHING A GERMAN "TAUBE"

extensive of all that had been made in ten weeks of fighting. The slow, plodding work of earlier weeks, which included the taking of Ginchy and Guillemont, had had for its object control of all the high ground from the region of Thiepval to a junction with the French on the British right. The Germans fought hard for every foot of it. Delville Wood, High Wood, and the rib of earth which a windmill crowned beyond Poziéres, had been steeped with blood under the heaviest kind of shell-fire. Germans wrestled with Britons, not for a piece of farmland, but for military and human mastery. The British push was largely downhill. Hence they put behind them high ground whose slopes gave shelter for their guns and whose crests gave observation points for artillery-fire. All sorts of men from the ends of the earth took part in the conflict. In the same dressing-station could have been seen Canadians, Australians, New Zealanders, Englishmen, Scotsmen, Irishmen, Newfoundlanders, and Americans. With them went into action armored motor-cars called "tanks," "which looked like so many prehistoric monsters in a skin of modern armor with engines inside." Among the men were Canadians from Montreal, Toronto, Winnipeg, and Vancouver. There were men with the accents of Missouri and New England, and others who, on the soil of France, hailed one another in the French of Quebec, a battalion of men of the kind one sees in times of peace working farms in Quebec, or bending over the benches of a factory in New England. "We had luck with us and we forced it," said one of the Canadians. "It was up to us to do so, that's all." The Americans in the Somme battle were men who had gone to Canada and enlisted for service in Canadian regiments.

For the first time in the war the French used an aeroplane squadron to lead a successful attack. At the village of Boucharesnes, north of the Somme, twenty fast armored aeroplanes, each mounting three machine-guns, charged the German lines before the infantry left their trenches. Flying high above this charging air-column were French aviation officers, who directed the attack several hundred feet below in much the same manner as an officer directs an infantry charge from a sheltered dugout. French fliers swooped low over the German lines as the artillery-fire lifted and raked the German trenches with a murderous hail. As French infantry came on with a rush the aerial chargers drove forward to the second phase of their work, flew along roads, turning machine-guns on German reserves that were being brought into action along highways leading to Bouchavesnes. This new use of aeroplanes proved so successful that it was expected to play an important part in future operations. British fliers apparently had used the same method successfully in the British advance against the Germans the day before.

Heavy rains temporarily cut short operations on September 21, the only activity of Foch's troops being an energetic shelling of German works. Heavy assaults on the British were beaten off and little ground was gained. Hindenburg was said to be personally in charge. The fighting was extraordinarily fierce around Bouchavesnes, Bois l'Abbé, and at Combles. Next day the French began an attack on Combles, which was a stronghold forming the apex of a sharp salient north of the Somme. In two sudden attacks they won a point on the outskirts of the village and carried trenches to the east. The British moved their line still closer toward Bapaume, breaking through two lines of trenches on a mile front and so straightening their line between Flers and Martinpuich. It was now announced officially in Paris that the number of prisoners taken by the Anglo-French forces on the Somme from July 1 to September aggregated more than 55,800. Of these, 34,050 fell into the hands of the French.

The advance of the Anglo-French had revealed more clearly than before the German system of trench architecture, which was undoubtedly the most remarkable and elaborate method of housing troops ever evolved in the long history of warfare. Twenty, thirty, and even forty feet below the surface of the ground Allied soldiers found abandoned villages, lighted with electricity, with spacious and well-equipped quarters for officers and men. In one underground apartment there was a hospital with thirty-two beds and an operating-room; in another there was convincing evidence that its occupant, an officer, had lived there with his wife and child. The whole German idea of trench-life was different from everything before known. The German front was like one huge straggling village, built of wood, and strung out along a road 300 miles long. Their houses, underground, of one or two floors, had been built after official designs, drawn out in formal plans. The main entrance from the trench-level was sometimes through a steel door of a pattern apparently standardized, so that hundreds had come from a factory as one order, missing parts being easily replaced. A heavily timbered doorway had been made to proper measure. Outside the front door you found a perforated sheet of metal, serving as a doormat or scraper. Inside, a flight of from twelve to thirty-six·steps led down at an easy angle, the treads of stairs and the descending roof of the staircase formed of stout timber, with double sills. The walls were of thick planks notched at the top and bottom to fit the frames, and strengthened with iron tie-rods, running from top to bottom of the stairs and with thick wooden struts at right angles to them. At the foot of the stairs a tunneled corridor ran straight forward, perhaps fifty yards, and out of this opened rooms and minor passages. In many dugouts a second staircase, or two staircases, led to a lower floor, which might be thirty or forty feet below the trench-level.

All these staircases, passages, and rooms were completely lined with wood and as fully strengthened as the entrance staircase. In one typical dugout each section had its allotted places for messing and sleeping, its place for parade in a passage, and its own emergency exit. Another, near Mametz, was designed to house a company of 300 men, with the needful kitchens, provisions, and munition store-rooms, a well, a forge riveted with sheets of cast-iron, an engine-room and a motor-room. In officers' quarters were found full-length mirrors, comfortable bedsteads, cushioned armchairs, and pictures. One room was lined with glazed "sanitary" wall-paper.[23]

On September 25 Allied troops stormed forward along a fifteen-mile front north of the Somme. In a blow as heavy

[23] Lieut.-Col. F. G. Newcomb of the Royal Engineers in The New York *Time*

as any they had struck in Picardy, they captured three towns, broke through several lines of trenches and took a large number of prisoners. British and French moved forward in a combined attack. Haig's troops assailed the German line from Martinpuich to Combles, a distance of six miles, while Foch's men advanced from Combles to the river, a distance of nine miles. Strong obstacles faced the British, but before the battle was over they had moved forward a mile along the whole six-mile front. Morval and Lesbœufs, lying directly south of Bapaume, fell, and with them several lines of new trenches that had been built since the Allies broke through the original defenses. Morval was the hub of a furious battle. This village had been converted into a veritable fortress, a maze of underground passages, trench lines and wire-entanglements. Situated on a hill, its capture became a formidable task. But the suddenness of the dash and the thoroughness of the artillery preparation found a way into it.

By these gains Haig's line was brought to within three miles of Bapaume and more positions along the important road from Albert were carried. The seizure of Morval cut the last road from Combles. This, in conjunction with the French advance, made the encirclement of that village complete. Further south was Mont St. Quentin, the key to Péronne, the objective of the French, who advanced along the whole line from Bouchavesnes to the river, which brought them within half a mile of Mont St. Quentin and extended their hold on the national highway. In this fighting the British took half of Morval, all of Lesbœufs, and advanced their line on a front of 8,000 yards for an average depth of 1,000 yards, while the French stormed Rancourt and pushed their lines to the outskirts of Frégicourt, a mile east and a little north of Combles. The German stronghold of Combles was now virtually isolated.

Frederick Palmer [24] went over the ridge in the Devil's Wood and Ginchy region, to gain which the British had fought for two months, walking two miles through an area which reverberated to the blasts of great guns, picking his

---

[24] At that time Colonel Palmer was the accredited representative of the American Press at the Headquarters of the British Army and Navy.

way between bursts of flame from crashing batteries and moving around rows of cannon. On the other side of the ridge he saw guns where he had never seen them before—on lower levels which the British had won by persistent siege-work, where the guns were close up to British infantry listening to their thunderous chorus as they prepared for the charge in the next day's attack. In his return Palmer decided he would not pass through that wilderness of British guns while he had hearing left. Every one of them was firing at top speed. He chose to descend into a gallery which took him past batteries that for two miles were pouring out a raging tempest of gun-fire. From the ruins of trenches, whence the battle panorama stretched before him, Palmer had a near view of French gunners who were feeding shells into gun-breeches as grain is fed into a threshing machine with the mechanical precision of automatons. Shortly after noon infantry rushed forward under cover of a final intensive chorus from artillery. The ridges in front and on either hand were flecked with racing sparks of flame. Within an hour Palmer thought at least fifty thousand shells must have been fired within his sight.

At the appointed time waves of infantry surged forward to the attack. Then the tremendous fire of German guns "swelled to its utmost volume until the whole field was lost in vast clouds of smoke." The attacking infantry vanished in that grim pall, "while high overhead scores of 'sausage balloons' and hundreds of aeroplanes, their wings gleaming like silver in the brilliant sunlight, strove vainly to see what was passing beneath them." Then across dead fields arose a signal from Morval which said that the British infantry had reached another goal and that another village had been taken. A man at a telephone in a nearby signal-station would call out the capture of strong points "with the enthusiasm of one who scores a hotly contested game."

Combles, the pivotal point in the German line guarding the approach to Bapaume on the north, and Péronne on the south, fell on September 26 when French and British troops swept in from three sides after the capture of Morval and Frégicourt had broken through the German defenses, overrun the town and carried all before them. Combles, with its marvelous subterranean passages and powerful fortifications, had been caught in the grip of the Allies who, coming from north and south, had already advanced far beyond the place and cut off communication with the rear, except in a narrow strip covered by Allied guns. The town was found filled with the bodies of Germans who had fallen fighting.

The capture of Combles became a certainty when French cavalry patrols, advancing northeastward, and English cavalry patrols, thrusting southeastward, met east of Combles and so completely encircled the village. The Germans had so fortified every house, especially cellars, where machine-guns were installed, that the Allies were forced to employ siege-methods. They completely encircled the town with heavy artillery, which gradually closed in with every advance of the infantry-lines. Judged by the enormous quantity of artillery massed against it and by the number of shells rained into it, Combles could boast of having undergone one of the most terrific sieges in history.

It was only on reaching the most advanced artillery lines that one could grasp mathematically the method which had rendered successful the Allies' tactics of advancing by heavy artillery. While troops were tugging guns forward, a veritable army of soldiers sank a tortuous winding roadway several feet below the surface of the ground, paving it with bricks from nearby houses wrecked by artillery-fire. Over this sunken road munition caissons, screened from German

LOOS, IN THE QUARTER WHERE A CHURCH ONCE STOOD

observation by the depth of the road, drawn by four, six, and even eight horses, dashed along with an incredible number of shells necessary to feed advanced lines of artillery, which could be reached in no other way. Back from these advanced lines were thousands of soldiers methodically transforming what had been on preceding days caisson-roads into highways capable of sustaining huge automobile convoys, which were bringing up heavier munitions for heavier artillery. Behind these automobile-fed artillery-lines was still a third army of workmen steadily constructing railways on which to bring up artillery so gigantic that not only it but its shells could be transported only on especially constructed railways. If Combles fell before a methodical, heavy-artillery advance and encirclement, it fell also before this methodical construction of roadways transformed from dirt or brick-bedded wagon-roads to full-gaged, rock-ballasted steel railways. Combles being several miles in advance of the French line of observation "sausage balloons," the final observations resulting in the capture of the village had to be entrusted to aeroplanes. In great numbers they circled above the village like a flock of huge vultures waiting only the certainty that life was extinct before swooping down and seizing the prey.[25]

The final dash against Combles developed into some of the most savage fighting of the war. Germans caught in the southwestern angle of the village stuck to their machine-guns bravely and died at their posts. The French, advancing through the cemetery on the southeast, were repeatedly counter-attacked by Teuton detachments, who stormed their lines in the face of certain death. The few Germans who escaped retreated hastily toward Sailly, falling back a distance of more than two miles. The capture of Combles was one of the most picturesque incidents in the whole course of the Somme offensive. All night long fierce fighting had been in progress at various points on the front, and with dawn the battle broadened out to include the whole British left. Combles fell in the morning as the sun rose on a perfect summer day.

About mid-day on September 27 the British left had its

[25] Henry Wood, United Press Correspondent.

turn in the region of Thiepval, which lay at the other extreme of the battle-front from Combles. Here the Germans, in their dugouts and galleries, fought with the skill and stubbornness which characterized them in all this kind of warfare. "They stick like glue to their dugouts," said one British soldier, "because they know that once they are pushed back we do not give them time to dig any more." A blackish heap of dirt on the crest of a ridge was all that remained of Thiepval. Its capture was an unexpected

A FRENCH 80 MM. GUN WHICH COULD THROW AN AIR MINE
WEIGHING 236 POUNDS

stroke. While the Combles attack was in full swing, there suddenly had come a heavy assault on Thiepval which caught the Germans off guard. Before they had time to form to meet it, the British had taken this obstacle to their advance. At Thiepval above ground there was nothing to see but black and broken tree-trunks, with lopped branches. Men could not have remained alive above ground when British guns hurled upon it a stream of heavy shells which burst all over the village with violent upheavals of earth and vast clouds of curly black smoke filled with death. The

German garrison kept below in a long series of vaults and tunnels which they had strengthened and linked up and dug deeper in a way that would have surprized old French farmers who had kept their wine and other stores down there for centuries.

The infantry attack began after a great bombardment, which was continuous for twenty-four hours, rising to infernal heights of shell-fire. The attacking troops leaped out of trenches and advanced in waves, the right wing swinging around from Mouquet. It was on the left that the men had the hardest time. One battalion leading the assault had to advance directly upon the château, while from cellars beneath came waves of savage gun-fire. They were also raked by the enfilade fire of machine-guns from the left top corner of ground where the village once stood. Many deep dugouts were blown in at the entrances, so that the Germans were forced to come up on the other side, the British smoking them out or digging holes to tease them. It was like rat-hunting, but they were dangerous rats those Germans, of life-size, and often desperate. When the British got around them and down into their tunnels, the Germans surrendered in hundreds. Nine hundred and ninety unwounded men and forty wounded were brought down as prisoners; others were killed on the way by their own barrage. Some dugouts were filled with dead and many lay above in shell-craters. All through the night until early morning the last remnant of the garrison held out in the northwest corner of Thiepval, until they were swept into a net by separate and gallant assaults.

One of the most remarkable of the "tank" adventures occurred in the direction of Gueudecourt, where the attacking troops were held up in the usual way by the raking fire of machine-guns. They made two attacks, but could not go beyond the screen of bullets. Then a "tank" crawled along, rolled over the trench with fire flashing from its flanks, and delivered the trench into the hands of the infantry with nearly 400 prisoners, who waved white flags above the parapet. The "tank," as if exhilarated by this success, went lolloping along quite alone in search of more adversaries, and only stopt for minor repairs when surrounded by a horde of German soldiers who closed upon it with great pluck, for it was firing in a most deadly way, and tried to kill it. They flung bombs at it, clambered on its back, tried to smash it in with batters of rifles, jabbed it with bayonets, fired revolvers and rifles at it and made wild pandemonium about it until British infantry arrived, attracted by the tumult, and drove the Germans back. But the tank had done deadly work. Between 200 and 300 killed and wounded Germans lay about its ungainly carcass. For a while it seemed as if the tank was out of action, but after a little attention and a good deal of grinding and grunting it heaved itself up and waddled away. These "tanks" proved to be terrible engines of war, doing grim work. The men inside took high risks with astonishing courage. They were of the same breed as the flying-men who circled in flocks over and beyond Thiepval, "ridiculously low down," as one officer observed, swooping like hawks over German batteries, so close sometimes they did not dare to fire.

In the capture of Combles and Thiepval the Allies realized the most important strategic gain made since the beginning of the Somme offensive. The British were now only two and a half miles from Bapaume. They had removed the most serious obstacle to an advance over a road which, while not the main line, was extremely important as a subsidiary and constituted the next objective in operations north of the Somme. The worst thing that had happened to the Germans was the effect produced on the morale of their troops, who had been ordered to hold out in death-traps. Altho they fought well and were brave men, as soon as the British swept across their trenches and sunken roads and entered villages, the German garrisons came out of their underground places and surrendered. They could have fought longer and harder, perhaps, but only with their backs to walls asking for death. One by one their strongholds had fallen, Courcelette, Martinpuich, and Flers, and now those other places, Gueudecourt, Lesbœufs, Morval, Combles, and Thiepval, had fallen.

Extraordinary aerial activity had prevailed, with both armies directing the fire of batteries, inflicting damage on enemy works, breaking up troop-movements. French aviators on September 25 engaged in forty-seven separate combats above that shell-scarred plain of Picardy. Nine German machines fell victims. The French flying squadrons conducted nearly a score of successful raids on German posts, throwing down no less than five hundred shells. Never were such numbers of planes employed, and never had they played such an important part as in the battle of the Somme. The wastage of British planes was supplied by new ones that flew across the Channel from England. The record time in crossing the Channel at the narrowest point, where the distance is twenty-two miles, was eight minutes.

The significance of the capture of Combles and Thiepval lay in the fact that the Germans were caught in a trap. Ever since the beginning of Allied attacks in the west, dating from Neuve Chapelle, in March, 1915, the Germans had taken a chance at being caught in traps with an eye to the very large profits that would accrue if the trap did not quite close upon them. It was this kind of trap that had inflicted enormous losses on the British at Neuve Chapelle and later at Loos. What the Allies had since learned was to coordinate their movements so as to leave no ambushes in their rear. That was the principal meaning of Combles and Thiepval.

The Allied gains on the Somme were important also for the light they threw on the probable nature of the trench problem the Allies had to face as they pushed forward. It had been a commonplace to speak of France and Belgium behind the German lines as gridironed with trenches all the way back to the German frontier. The Allied task was described as an unceasing steeplechase with ditch hazards at every mile of the course. But the comparative ease with which on the Somme they had now pushed forward a mile or a couple of miles at a time, showed that, if there were new trench-lines to cross, they were by no means as formidable an obstacle as the original front along which a deadlock had been established for nearly two years. When one read of the elaborate nature of the German underground system of fortifications, of which part was now in Allied hands, it was plain that no such vast labor could have been expended again and again on every mile of ground occupied by the German armies. If one could trust certain accounts of French unpreparedness around Verdun, the contrast between the situation there and that on the Somme was great. Around Verdun the first German rush had been over the easiest portion of the French defenses, while on the Somme the Allies broke through what was probably the strongest German line.

More significant than the final details of the taking of Combles were the two weeks devoted to encircling it. But more significant than the encirclement was the fortnight of artillery-battering which preceded the infantry assault and conquered the ground before they set foot on it. The Allied artillery-service on the Western Front was the chief means of the offense. It alone made effectual infantry action possible. The conspicuous fact about this artillery service was the failure of the Germans to bring up any artillery capable of withstanding it. In this complete supremacy of the Entente artillery, as exemplified at Combles, were found the chief assurances that the offensive would continue.

"We employed for the first time a new type of heavy armored car, which proved of considerable utility," said Haig in his report of the battle before Combles on September 15. The topography of the country over which the action was waged had permitted these cars to dash down a gentle slope, plow through hedges, and even to hurdle narrow ditches and mounds, the cars being extremely mobile. Altho the Duke of Westminster had used armored cars with success in Egypt, this action before Combles was the first occasion when they had been employed on the Western Front. Whether they would eventually supplant cavalry was a question which the military now considered. Haig's

A ZEPPELIN THAT FELL INTO A FRENCH FOREST

reports showed they had made an extremely favorable impression, after having been much whispered about in army circles. Some of the British referred to them as "tanks"; soldiers handling them called them "willies."

The object sought in them was to operate a heavily armored motor-car in a shell-torn and roadless wilderness of trenches where a vehicle on ordinary wheels could not be used. British writers tried to imagine the feelings of German infantry in their shell-shattered trenches "when, in the uncertain light of dawn, they first saw advancing upon them an array of unearthly monsters cased in steel, spitting fire and crawling laboriously but ceaselessly over trenches, barbed wire and shell-craters." There had been nothing more wonderful even in this war, than the spectacle of that advance toward the German lines at Combles.

Some Germans were fighting stubbornly, from behind the ruins of a sugar factory, when one of the new monsters, dubbed "Crême de Menthe," went lumbering out toward the Teutonic positions, spitting fire. It advanced upon a broken wall, drove up against it heavily until it fell with a crash of bricks, and then the monster rose above the bricks and advanced straight through the ruins. From its sides came flashes of fire and a host of bullets, and then it trampled around over machine-gune emplacements. It crusht machine-guns under its heavy ribs and killed machine-gun teams with deadly fire. Frederick Palmer wrote that, when the Germans found this strange creature with its hide of steel had been stalled, "curiosity and a desire for revenge became a fillip to their courage," and they went after it "with the avidity of prehistoric man stalking a wounded mammoth whose bulk was fast in one of the alleys of the cave-dwellers." No such scene had ever before been seen on this Western Front, marked as it had been by bizarre fighting. Colonel Palmer added:

"While the tank's machine-guns blazed right and left some of the Germans managed to creep along the trenches under the forelegs and hindlegs of the crouching beast. Then they swarmed over it looking for an opening through which to strike at its vitals. They fired their rifles into joints and bombed it all over, but to no more avail than burglars trying to reach the inside of a battle-ship-turret with a jimmy. All the while the tank's machine-guns kept busy at the human targets in reach while its crew, chosen daredevils, concluded to stick until they starved or the Germans found the proper can opener to get them out. Finally the British infantry in the rear, seeing the tank in distress, refused to wait on any general's orders that they should remain at the objective which they had gained. They were out to save that impounded tank and with a cheer they rushed the Germans and overwhelmed them. When the crew heard the laughing and shouting in English they opened the door and called out: 'We are all right if you will only get us some more juice so that the old girl can have a guzzle of her proper drink and we can take the road again.' So the infantry formed a line in front of the tank determined to defend her to the last man, while a runner was hurried back for a can of gasoline. The gasoline arrived safely and the beast, having taken a swallow, ambled back into reserve amidst wild cheering.''

These cars were in effect small, movable fortresses on wheels, with armor sufficient to protect them from infantry-fire, and carrying sufficient machine-guns for offensive as well as defensive work. They were huge, grotesque bulks, and some of the men who watched them maneuver about could do nothing but sit down and laugh at each new antic they performed. Germans emptied rifles at them, but on they kept rolling till they reached the first German trenches, then sat themselves complacently astride and swept them with fire in both directions. Secure as they were in the toughness of their hide, they could thrust themselves into close quarters where unprotected infantry could never get. In woods they crashed their way through undergrowth and climbed over, or broke down, barricades, contemptuous of machine-guns and of rifle-fire.

The surprizing thing to Colonel Palmer was that so few casualties occurred among the crews of tanks, who had gone out prepared to die but "found themselves safe in their armored shells after the day's fight was over." This was true whether the tanks went across a line of German trenches, developed engine-trouble, or temporarily foundered in shell-holes. Bullets "merely made steel-bright flecks on the tank's paint and shrapnel equally failed to penetrate the armor." There was no indication of any guiding human intelligence, let alone a human hand directing a tank. The sight of these engines of war soon "became part of the routine existence, and interest in watching an advance centered on the infantry which they supported in a charge." Had the tanks accomplished nothing more than they did in the two great September attacks, "they would have been well worth while," said Palmer, who believed they had saved twenty-five thousand casualties, since that loss must have been the additional cost of gaining the same ground by unassisted infantry action.

That our own famous "cheesebox on a raft"—that is, the *Monitor* of the Civil War—which revolutionized naval warfare, might find its land counterpart in these land-monitors, was an opinion soon exprest. They made their first appearance by advances across trenches and shell-craters, through wire-entanglements and stone-walls, and led infantry in an attack which pierced the German third line of defense and administered what Haig characterized as "probably the most effective blow that has yet been dealt the enemy by the British troops." Altho casually mentioned in official bulletins of that day's fighting, in unofficial reports they came in for a wealth of allusion almost as vague as it was picturesque. The new juggernauts, as one editor called them, had "all the ear-marks of having burst full into the fray out of the pages of Mr. H. G. Wells, or M. Jules Verne." They were again described as "land-dreadnoughts," "mobile fortresses," "steel tortoises," "prehistoric monsters," and "toads of vast size." They "stamped down dugouts like wasps' nests, and climbed barricades like elephants." Their gait was generally described as a waddle, but in some accounts they were said to have "crawled, walked, and lopped." According to German reports, the "cruelty" of these monsters "was equaled by their efficiency." Haig reported that they caused "indescribable demoralization in the enemy's ranks." In one short hour, said a correspondent of the London *Times*, "the tanks did more military service, killed more of the enemy, and had a greater influence on the war than all the Zeppelins." He predicted that before the war was over both sides would be building "other monsters, each huger and each more horrible

THE TANK AND ITS PROGENITOR

The central picture shows the farm tractor, with caterpillar wheels, from which the propelling apparatus of the tank was derived. In the lower picture, this origin is clearly apparent. The upper picture shows a tank making its way over difficult ground than the last, until there would be battles of whole fleets of land-dreadnoughts and terrestrial monsters.'' Despite their terrible effectiveness, they ''tickled the risibilities of all ranks,'' and even German prisoners ''began laughing when they recalled their first glimpse of them.''

Credit for the adoption of this weapon was given by Lloyd George to Winston Churchill, the former First Lord of the Admiralty. He, it seems, ''took up with enthusiasm the idea of using them, but met with many difficulties before he succeeded in convincing the military authorities.'' Berlin did not take the cars at first with much seriousness. Imprisoned crews were said to have declared that they were a ''complete failure,'' since they were able to advance ''only at the rate of a mile an hour, and therefore became excellent targets for artillery.'' Berlin instanced a case of seven machines that started in an advance but only two of which reached their objective and these ''were completely put out of action by shell-fire.'' Their occupants declared them atrocious contrivances to travel in, because of the noise, smoke, and heat and the treacherous ground over which they had to move when in field service.[27]

Much speculation as to the tank's origin, near and remote, was indulged in. Peoria, Illinois, claimed the honor of having actually built such cars years before, fitted with caterpillar tractors, to meet some of the difficult problems of modern farming. Except for their armor, their machine-guns and their crew, thousands like them had been in use in the United States in plowing, digging ditches, and in other labors. Since the war began about 1,000 Peoria caterpillar-tractors had been sold to the British Government, but Peoria had had nothing to do with coating them with armor or with installing machine-guns in them. All that was done in Europe. Germany had some of these Peoria farm tractors before the war began, and some had been sent to France and others to Russia. Until their appearance on the front as armored cars, they had been used in the war but only to tow big guns. Germany used about forty of them before Liége. Those sent to England weighed about 18,000 pounds each, and had 120-horse-power.

[27] The Overseas News Agency.

Speaking broadly, this tractor crawled on two belts with corrugated surfaces, one on each side of the body, the corrugated surface being on the ground. On the inside of the belts, on each side of the body, were two lines of steel rails, making four lines in all. These rails were in short sections, jointed and operated over a cogged mechanism that actually laid them down with their belt attachment as the tractor moved ahead and picked them up again, so that the car ran continuously on its own self-made track. The short joints in the rails made it easy to turn to right or

INTERNATIONAL FILM SERVICE, N. Y.

TANKS GOING INTO ACTION

left. The body was supported by trucks with five wheels, something like small railroad-trucks. These wheels never touched the ground, but ran upon steel rails. In the ordinary tractor about seven feet of belt and rails were on the ground at one time. The machines could bridge any trench that was not wider than the length of track they could lay on the ground at one time.

Bridgeport claimed the honor of having first furnished the British and French Governments with the idea of transforming the huge tractors into a new and terrible engine of war. The Bridgeport design, however, was called an "alligator," rather than a "caterpillar" type. Norman Leeds of Bridgeport had submitted to the British Government plans drawn by himself, in the hope of securing a market for tractor-motors manufactured by his company. He contended that the caterpillar-tractors sold in Peoria were too small for hurdling trenches and could be used only for hauling supplies. His design called for twenty-five feet long tractors, instead of only twelve, and for six guns and armor heavy enough to resist three-inch shells, with a speed of eight miles an hour.

The machine had been used in America to knock down trees before the British thought of making a war chariot of it. When narrow lumber roads through Florida woods had to be widened for the passage of a tractor, instead of having men go ahead to cut down trees on either side of the road, the caterpillars themselves had been run against trees that stood in the way. The ordinary frame of the tractor was easily run through a brick wall. Some machines weighed 25,000 pounds; with armor and armament one would probably come to about 31,000. A machine of this weight driven with a motor of not less than 129-horse-power could easily break through a wall. As late as October, Berlin was insisting that the armored cars were failures. One of them had become "hopelessly entangled in barbed wire," another was disabled by a shell while advancing at a point north of Flers, the ammunition it contained exploding, and the car burning up. Of two others utilized in an attack on the Guillemont-Combles road, one had been blown up with a hand-grenade when it was approaching to within forty yards of the German trenches, and this was annihilated by a shell on the road to Ligny-Thilloy. Berlin added that the British fleet of "tanks" would soon be composed of nothing but wrecks.[28]

As a new experiment, the "tanks" had done wonders, tho some of them broke down at Combles. Of twenty-four which crossed the German lines, seven came to grief early in the day; but the remaining seventeen did brilliant service, some straddling enemy trenches and clearing them by machine-gun fire, some flattening out uncut wire, others destroying machine-gun nests and redoubts or strong points like the

[28] Overseas News Agency.

sugar factory at Courcelette. But their moral effect was greater than the material damage they wrought. The sight of those impersonal fighters ruthlessly grinding down the most cherished defenses put something like panic into troops who had always prided themselves on the superior merit of their own war-machine. Beyond doubt the presence of the "tanks" added greatly to the zeal and confidence of the assaulting infantry. An element of sheer comedy had been introduced into the grim business of war, and comedy was dear to the heart of the British soldier. The crews of the "tanks" seemed to acquire some of the light-heartedness of the British sailor. Penned up in narrow and stuffy quarters, condemned to a form of motion compared with which that of the queasiest vessel was steady, and at the mercy of unknown perils, these adventurers faced their task with the zest of boys on holiday. With infinite humor they described how the enemy sometimes surrounded them when they were stuck, and tried in vain to crack their shell, while they themselves sat inside laughing.[29]

[29] Principal Sources: "Nelson's History of the War" by John Buchan, The *Daily Chronicle* (London), The *Times*, The *Tribune*, *The Literary Digest*, New York; The *Daily News* (London), The *World* (New York), Associated Press and United Press dispatches, "Bulletins" of the National Geographic Society, The *Evening Sun* (New York), The *Times* (London), The *Evening Post* (New York).

FAILURE OF A TANK TO CROSS A TRENCH

IV

FURTHER PROGRESS TOWARD BAPAUME AND PÉRONNE—THE BATTLE FOR THE ANCRE VALLEY

October 1, 1916—January 17, 1917

LONDON was described as only quietly elated over news of the capture of Combles and Thiepval. While the value of possessing them was appreciated, the achievements were regarded only as an introduction to greater things that could be gained by equally hard fighting. The casualties, meanwhile, among both French and British, were being reduced at every fresh move forward, not merely because of terrific bombardments that preceded advances, but owing to new methods that were adopted. The *Frankfurter Zeitung* conceded a "tactical gain" to the Allies. It had been a terrible time, "appallingly sanguinary for the assailants, and had resulted in a most trying situation for the defenders," but in strategy the Entente had won nothing. Hindenburg had not swerved "a hair'sbreadth from the calm course he had laid down." While the Germans had experienced the most severe period of the war they had yet known, and in it had lost stubbornly defended villages and valuable positions, the front as a whole remained firm, and the Allies found it "impossible to break through."

The British losses in September, 1915, had been at the rate of more than 3,800 a day, on all fronts—officers, 5,439; men, 114,110. Heavy as these losses were, they were lighter than in August, when they were 127,945, or a daily average of 4,127. But in July, the first month of the Somme offensive, the losses had been about half those of August or September, 1915, or only 59,675 casualties. The total for the three months on the Somme was 307,169. Since January 28, the British Government had issued no figures of total losses, but up to that time the daily average from the beginning of the war had been slightly more than 1,000. Altho the casualties in September, 1916, were about four times those

BRITISH LANCASHIRE SOLDIERS EQUIPPED WITH NEW HELMETS

III.

of the first sixteen months of the war, the increase was due, not only to the intensity of the offensive, but to the fact that Great Britain's forces in the field were then far greater than in the earlier period of the war.

Estimates of the strength of the German forces on all fronts, made by General Fonville [30] and by Ashmead-Bartlett in dispatches from the front, at this time represented what was the official judgment in Allied circles. Fonville placed the German strength at 171 divisions on June 1. Bartlett gave it as 193 divisions. Since June 1 had occurred Brusiloff's forward movement, so that the difference of twenty-two divisions would represent Germany's response to the threat in the east. The German strength in the west was believed to be 119 divisions, against 117 divisions on June 1. From these figures it would appear that upon the Somme Germany had elected to stand strictly on the defensive and even to yield when necessary, while countering against the Russians. Of her divisions in the west, forty were facing the British army, thirty were around Verdun, and fifty were strung out from the Somme to the Swiss frontier, excluding the Verdun sector. Boys of the 1916 class had been in battle on both sides.

The British on the Somme by October 1 had command of high ground from which they could look down on a landscape extending to Bapaume, a wide stretch of country dotted with bombarded villages. Here the Germans could no longer move about safely in the daylight, neither their infantry guns nor their transports, without being found by British areoplanes which were hovering like hawks over the ground, or by British observing officers who were searching through glasses from high positions. A gain of ground had been made on September 28 when the British advanced northward from the black trees of Thiepval to "Schwaben" redoubt, on the edge of a plateau. Here a large number of batteries concentrated an intense fire on German positions beyond blighted trees on the ridge where were unheaved lines of soil of white chalk and brown earth marking the next German defensive system. Heavy shells "tore up the ground, opening great chasms and raising hell-fires until

[30] In the *Revue de Paris.*

the blue of the sky was hidden behind the heavy spreading smoke, gushing up in round dense masses which mingled and thickened the overhanging pall."

The remarkable part of the offensive in the west was that it still went on. If the Allies could continue to advance at any such rate as they had maintained thus far, the time promised to come when the great defensive system of the Germans in that territory would cease to exist. That it existed on the same grand scale eastward from Combles to the German frontier was not believed possible. The twenty-mile battle-arc running from the Ancre River to the Somme had rapidly been transformed into an irregular triangular wedge in the German line, with its bases respectively in front of Thiepval and west of Péronne, the point projecting across the Béthune road into the St. Pierre-Vaast Forest. British gains included German trenches on a front of 2,000 yards north of Flers and a strong redoubt on a hill 2,000 yards northeast of Thiepval. Ten thousand prisoners had fallen into the hands of the British in a fortnight's fighting. To the south from Bouchavesnes to the southern edge of the Bois l'Abbé farm, the French had been compelled to face a violent attack by the Germans, but it was beaten off.

Driving slowly but relentlessly northward, the British were making ready for another surge toward Bapaume, moving along two lines of attack—one north of Thiepval, the other north of Combles, seeking to pocket Bapaume as Combles had been pocketed. The battle continued without pause. Haig's troops won the greater part of a redoubt 500 yards north of Thiepval, overlooking the northern bank of the Ancre. From this dominating position the ground that separated Haig's line from the Ancre could be shelled so effectively that its conquest was expected to be comparatively easy. At the end of the northern front the British were less than half a mile from Le Sars, which blocked the way along the Albert-Bapaume road. The Germans had made only feeble efforts at counter-attacks, for they were occupied chiefly in constructing new defenses to withstand the next Allied assault. Fierce fighting was certain to take place before Bapaume could be reached. The Germans held a strong line from Miraumont to that objective and thence south to Sailly. Much heavy fighting also remained before Péronne could be won. While the British were striving to flank Bapaume, the French intended to pocket Péronne before they attempted its capture.

On October 1 the left wing of the British, between the Ancre and Somme, advanced on nearly a two-mile front from east of Eaucort l'Abbaye to the Albert-Bapaume road, capturing the town of Eaucort l'Abbaye and throwing their line to within about four miles of Bapaume. The Germans having been cleared out of positions near the "Stuff" redoubt, were forced to give up all except a small

CAPTURED GERMAN CANNON AT THE INVALIDES IN PARIS

portion of the "Schwaben" redoubt. Berlin reported that attacks by the British east of Thiepval and by the French in Rancourt, Courcelette, Morval and Halle, had been repulsed. Curiously enough, naval forces had joined the Allies in this land battle on the Somme at a point seventy miles from the sea. Iron-clad monitors, utilizing the magnificent network of French canals along the Somme centering at Péronne, participated in the bombardment of Mont St. Quentin, the key to the defense of Péronne, now slowly and steadily being encircled by the French in the same manner that Combles was. The village of Mont St. Quentin had suffered the same fate as forty-eight other villages captured by the Allies; it was reduced to heaps of brickbats and protruding tree-stumps. The Germans, however, still retained strongly fortified positions, especially in cellars. French artillery, at the same time, completely encircled the hill. This was for the purpose of interrupting German communications with the rear. Occasional shells were directed at Mont St. Quentin itself to keep the Germans busy in dugouts and cellars.

A general advance was made on October 2, on a front of about three miles north of Courcelette, Martinpuich, and Flers, to the outskirts of Le Sars and to the north of Eaucort l'Abbaye. Fighting began about 3.30 in the afternoon and continued all night, with heavy German counterattacks from the north. Next day there was no progress, because the weather was against the British, the battlefield lost in mist and observation made impossible. As the rain continued, both the British and the French swung forward for local advances. Between Morval and the St. Pierre-Vaast Forest, near the junction of the two Allied fronts, Foch's troops completed the seizure of a line of German trenches, while Haig's forces contented themselves with clearing Eaucort l'Abbaye, an important position less than three miles south of Bapaume, which had been partly retaken by the Germans three days before.

With this town in the hands of the British, the line became once more straightened in this sector and the way was open for wider operations against both the Albert-Bapaume highway and the Béthune road. Because a little romance clung to it, a place like Eaucort l'Abbaye seemed of greater importance than a heap of earth and a network of ditches such as the "Schwaben" or "Hessian" redoubts. This place had a special interest because its old brick walls had been built up centuries before by French monks as an inclosure for prayer and peaceful work. Here for three days and nights in October, 1916, men were fighting and killing each other in attack, retreat, and counter-attack. Dead bodies lay thick among broken bricks or down in vaults. Men fought with bombs which loosened heavy stones, shattered great pillars and filled dark places with explosive lights.

When the fighting began at the Abbey, two monster "tanks" went crawling up to ditches which had been dug by fighting-men outside the monastery walls, breathing out smoke and fire, their sides opening with stabs of flame, killing men in ditches by rolling on them, crushing them and hurling invisible bolts at them. The ghosts of monks, if they were there, would have seen how, in the "tank," modern warfare had brought back the medieval dragon myth and made it more real and more terrible than superstition had ever done.

Severe fighting on the Western Front now became practically suspended for weeks on account of the weather. An incessant downpour made any general effective action out of the question. Aviators could not work; artillery could not find an objective; men could not move out of trenches. Pressure, however, did not let up, even tho no blows were struck. The lines advanced slightly, but the general situation did not change. The losses of the Germans and the Allies had been about the same, 450,000 men since July 1. Of these the percentage of permanent losses was believed to be greater on the part of the Germans than with the Allies, due to the fact that Germany's capture of prisoners had been negligible, while the Allies had taken a total of about 68,000 men. This was a side of the story that would tell against the Germans in the long run. There was no disputing the fact that the Allies had a superiority in men and were at least equal in supplies and organization.

On October 7 British troops took advantage of fine weather that followed heavy rains to make a new attack on a German front of 12,000 yards in which they captured a number of important positions, including the fortified village of Le Sars. The same men who had taken Eaucort l'Abbaye made their way across a tangle of trenches and shell-craters just below the village and gained a deep cutting from which they struck into the village from the right, leaving as the only way of escape for the Germans a belt of scarred and blackened tree-stumps. East of Le Sars and north of Lesbœufs the British also made progress, driving the Germans out of trenches they had hurriedly scraped up during recent weeks. The Germans here were not so richly provided with dugouts, as they had been earlier. When Allied guns concentrated fire on their new trenches, the only means of escape for the Germans from slaughter was to hold them thinly and put their main reliance for defense on machine-guns. After the British right wing advanced about a kilometer from Lesbœufs toward Le Transloy, it was linked up with French battalions pressing forward to Sailly-Sallisel.

By advances north and south of Le Transloy the French and British were beginning the envelopment of that village in the same manner that they had begun the envelopment of Combles. The French line was carried forward nearly a mile northeast of Morval, and across the Péronne-Bapaume road, connecting Le Transloy with Sailly-Sallisel. Thus direct communications between two German garrisons was cut off. The French were within a little over 200 yards of the northern entrance to Sailly and occupied valuable positions on the summit of the Sailly-Sallisel ridge. To the south of Sailly-Sallisel, an advance was made that marked the beginning of the encircling of that town. The French pushed their lines ahead to the edge of the St. Pierre-Vaast Forest, and thence over Hill 130, an important summit southeast of Bouchavesnes.

On October 12 the French, pressing forward south, and the British and French north of the Somme, made progress in their drive against the Béthune road and Chaulnes. The British made local attacks near Thiepval and along the Sar-Guedecourt lines and successful raids on German positions in other sectors. By advancing west of Sailly-Sallisel, Foch's troops repeated against that position the pocketing movement that had brought about the fall of Combles. This success opened the way for a joint operation south of Transloy aiming to drive the Germans out of their positions on the two-mile stretch of the Béthune road south of Transloy. The French also moved forward at this time from their new lines east of Vermandovillers and penetrated further into the village of Ablaincourt, two miles northeast of Chaulnes. House-to-house fighting of a desperate character took place in Ablaincourt. On October 13 British troops advanced from Guedecourt to Lesbœufs, about one and one-half miles, in severe fighting. Gains were also made northwest of Guedecourt. Fourteen British raiding parties entered

THE ALLIED DRIVE ON THE SOMME

German trenches in the regions of Ypres and Armentières during the same night, when it became known that British "tanks" had now appeared on the French front about Chaulnes. One of these entirely effaced a farm-house that had been converted into a strong fortress. It dashed upon the farm, passing through lines of defenders who vainly fired at it, crashing through walls and mangling the site. All the men who remained to stand their ground were killed outright or crunched beneath it.

The Germans on this front had withdrawn their heavy guns from one and a half to five miles behind their front, the withdrawal having been ordered in order to save the guns from capture. In recent dashes of Allied infantry into German lines many heavy guns had been taken before the Germans had an opportunity to withdraw them. The Germans now had 2,100 guns opposing the French and British on the thirty-mile Somme front, compared with the 2,500 guns they had used in the attack on Verdun. Of this number 600 were south of the Somme, facing the French, and 650 opposed the French north of the Somme. The British were opposed by 850 German pieces. Since the Allied offensive began more than 500 German guns had been captured. In one of the artillery duels on October 12, the size as well as the number of guns used set observers aghast. One of the largest British guns was a howitzer of 18-inch caliber which threw nearly a ton of metal. A mobile gun of 12-inch caliber, big beyond the imagination of soldiers, hit

A SHATTERED GERMAN TRENCH IN NORTHERN FRANCE

a target eleven miles away. Lesser monsters, especially 9.2 and 8-inch guns, crouched on the field here, there, and everywhere. In front of them other guns were set along the slope in the ground in diminishing scales, so close in places that one could scarcely have passed between them. German guns, too, had multiplied. New ones had to supply the great wastage, but the British were able to out-multiply the German multiplication. The British gun birth-rate exceeded the death-rate by large figures. The result was that, after five minutes or less of a bombardment which preceded an attack, little was visible anywhere of the battle itself. The only thing that penetrated the smoke and dust was the flame of a gun and the flash of a bursting shell.

A correspondent [31] who walked some miles over trench and shell-holes, past Bernafay Wood and Longueval to a point on the high ground to the west of Delville Wood, described what he saw when he looked down on Flers. Beyond was a terrible region, all a network of battered German trenches, winding their way through a wilderness of shell-holes and the débris of battle. This battle area had been utterly wrecked and swept clear of traces of what such a country ought to be. Hardly any green thing grew there, except where, between shell-holes, there were patches of sickly grass, studded now and again with stunted plants and ragged patches of thistle not one-half their normal size. Over all was that awful smell—sometimes only a taint in the air, sometimes sickeningly strong—which belongs to battlefields; but in patches there were other smells, chemical and very pungent, the smell of gas-shells and other abominations which had burst at one time and another in hundreds. There were acres and acres where shells had been so thick that they ran into one another. Berlin admitted that detailed reports of this fighting "showed distinctly that the attacks between October 9 and October 13 were to be reckoned among the greatest actions of the whole Somme battle."

The terrible destruction wrought on these battlefields was well described in an official communication from the Canadian War Records Office. Never had human agency controlled such engines of destruction, nor had war "so pro-

[31] Of The *Times* (London).

foundly imprest itself upon the face of nature." No plague could be more ruthless, no natural blight more devastating. After describing the peaceful scenes in the rear of the battle-line—perfectly tilled fields, farms cultivated to the last inch of their available space—and after paying tribute to the "brave, silent industry of the women, the old men, and the children, of France," the communication continued:

"The transition from this scene of beauty, peace, and ancient prosperity is infinitely distressing. Fields are given over to the trampling rows of tethered horses, and are disfigured by a variety of encampments, from ordered white tents to huts of rusted biscuit tins and low, discolored shacks of nondescript material. This area of active occupation gradually thins and abuts a region of more sinister appearance. Here trees have broken bodies and the houses seem in pain, for their roofs are rent, their windows gone, their walls scarred and pierced. But the full view of the land of war is reached with the crossing of the bleak, grassy slopes east of Albert, with their chalky scars cut by the long lines of trenches.

"Of La Boisselle there is more upon the map than on the ground. A few shattered trunks, here and there a splintered beam, perhaps a corner-stone or two, some cellars roofed with wreckage. Otherwise only the upheaval of tortured earth, mine craters, heaps of rotting white sand-bags, half-choked trenches, and a dreary litter of old wire, cans, and human rubbish remain. Pozières shares the fate of La Boisselle. No land could trace the outlines of a single house or garden plot. There are no bricks or beams which could be used in restoration. As a village Pozières has disappeared. Just beyond Pozières is the acme of destruction. No grain of surface remains undisturbed. There is no room for a fresh shell-hole. Nowhere is the power of modern artillery or the thoroughness of preparation better exemplified. We have literally blasted our way forward. Ruin appears not only in the devastated earth and the crusht houses, but also in the sadder waste of human life."

More than three and one-half months of battle on the Somme, with the heaviest concentration of artillery, infantry, and every type of war material, and the most skilful and desperate fighting the world has ever known, had resulted in a marked development of British fighting efficiency. Here, where every village was found to be a fortress which had to be besieged and stormed, the British, by October 23, had driven back the Germans on a front of eleven miles to a depth of four to eight miles. When the next spring came peasants would be able to plow and seed behind ground which for two years had lain fallow under shell-storms. In Fricourt and Mametz, taken on July 1, trees, with their trunks torn and their foliage blasted by shells, by October had thrown out fresh roots, while new crops of grass were hiding shell-craters in neighboring fields and carpeting earth that had been trodden by the British in their early charges. Former citizens of captured villages were requesting that they be allowed to return and build new homes .on the ruins of their old ones.

A correspondent [32] who, near the end of September, passed through "the tumbled ruins of Fricourt," described how twisted tree-trunks in the Mametz Wood stood out naked against a sky-line, stript of branches and foliage, with bark gashed and showing many gaping wounds, the white hearts "bared to the fierce sun's glare." Along the roads leading south great dust columns "rose in spirals heavenward, hiding slow-moving horse-transports." Further on "broad eddies of dust rode on passing heat-currents and scattered across the field like spent smoke." The landscape was of a leaden gray, buried under a heavy mantle of dust. Ashen gray were tunics, rifle-barrels, and even the faces of men who came in from first-line trenches, their eyes "staring out of deepened sockets, rimmed round with dust." Steel helmets of darkened green had taken on the dull-hued patina of a Greek bronze. Water-carts, field-kitchens, heavy batteries, which were being moved forward, great lorries in long, serpent lines extending upon miles, all wore this pall of dust. As far as the eye could see, were "low rolling hills, bare and treeless save for small patches of woodland, the fields thick grown with thistle, bettles, and lusty weeds, waist high."

Could this be "the pleasant land of France?" asked this correspondent. Could these fields be the same which, two years before, "had stood rich with golden grain?" The bad lands of the Dakotas, the wastes of the Sahara, the dust-swept desert of Gobi, seemed fair to him in comparison

[32] Of The *Times* (New York).

with that region of the Somme. His throat was parched, his eyes almost bleeding after walking only half an hour, "picking a way through shell-craters and upturned soil, jumping across abandoned German trenches, through a terrain littered with unexploded shells of all calibers and kinds." One might come across an innocent-looking little "Mills" bomb, not much larger than a duck's egg, the man who threw it having forgotten to pull out the cotter-pin, so that it did not go off. So there it lay, apparently harmless, and yet it had a potential strength sufficient to blow half a platoon into "Kingdom come." Next to it might be what looked like a giant's dumb-bell, the great iron balls at either end larger than a man's head, a mighty engine of war which could wipe out a company. Overhead, strung out like monster snub-nosed whales on a line, were the captive balloons of observation officers, hanging limply. Twenty-two such craft were counted within one short sector. To the left of him the correspondent saw a great mound of brass and empty shell-cartridge cases, fifteen feet high and forty feet long, and it was only one of many such.

KING GEORGE IN A DEVASTATED FIELD

On the Somme the British attacked late in October under weather conditions such as only tragic heroism could endure. Units would go into trenches under a soft, soaking rain only to encounter before morning seven degrees of frost, with a clammy mist to follow. In the afternoon when they were to attack rain had melted the country to a loathy yellow paste, half-gummy, half-filth of superposed black grease, "the terrain a moon-like landscape of craters." Trenches were crumbling like sugar in the wet. Here and there men were so bogged and mud-clogged that a word to "get out and get over" found them floundering almost to their waists.

French artillery-fighting on the Somme had brought barrage- and curtain-fire to a wonderful degree of perfection. When French soldiers dashed to an assault on German positions, they were under the protection of a sheet of artillery-fire that often preceded them by not more than 200 feet. A curtain of exploding shells moved steadily forward, not only screening them completely from the fire of the Germans, but wiping out every remaining obstacle and every remaining German that might be in its path. When finally they reached and captured a position, the curtain-fire kept just in front of them, offering protection from counter-attacks until new positions could be thoroughly organized. Early in the war, when the French first began to develop curtain-fire, a distance of 600 to 700 feet in front of advancing infantry was considered absolutely necessary to make certain that the troops might not, by a sudden dash forward, run into their own fire. But French aeroplane observers had since so improved their methods and artillery-men had become so skilful that the distance was reduced by two-thirds. Every time French infantry now moved to an attack a score of observation aeroplanes hovered over them and with their wireless apparatus told the artillerymen where to place the curtain of bursting shells.

Weather conditions early in November almost entirely precluded military operations. In order that two arms of the service might work in coordination, the weather had to be such as to make effective flying possible, and at the same time the atmosphere had to be fairly clear, so that signals from air scouts could reach artillery commanders, and the latter could see and follow the results of their fire. Ground had to be dry and easily passed over, so that when infantry . left the trenches they would be able to move rapidly and so minimize the time during which they would be subjected to fire without cover or protection. It was coordination that made the work of the French effective on this front. In particular was this true of their artillery and infantry. French artillery had always stood preeminently above that of other nations. Napoleon was an artillery officer and developed artillery more than any other branch of the service. The supremacy which the French artillery achieved in his day has survived and so now it was due in large part to the skill with which the French handled their guns, that they

GIANT SEARCHLIGHT USED IN THE DEFENSE OF PARIS
With these the coming of hostile aircraft was detected.
The French called them "eyes"

were able to make sensational advances against German positions.

There was no indication that the French had been bled white. Their losses had been heavy, the rate of wastage had been greater than the rate of supply, but this condition was by no means peculiar to the French. The same thing held true in a larger sense of the Germans, as elsewhere it was true in still greater degree of the Austrians. France was weakened, but she was still relatively stronger than Germany. No more eloquent proof of this could be asked than the actions that took place in October. During the fiercest of the Somme fighting, the casualties in one week probably exceeded the total losses in the entire Franco-Prussian War, but the Allies considered that the price they paid for gains was reasonable. Against their losses they balanced their territorial gains, their capture of prisoners, guns and ammunition, and the German casualties. Had the Allies decided to push on to the Bapaume-Péronne road in the first three weeks of the Somme offensive, they probably could have done so, but nothing would have pleased the German general staff more, because the cost of the success would have been enormous even compared with present standards. Americans often exprest surprize that the Allies did not advance faster, asking why, if the Allies were so much stronger than the Germans, they did not throw in enough men to push through. The answer was that the gains would not have offset the losses.

And yet confident expectations of the final triumph of the German arms breathed in every sentence of an interview with Hindenburg printed in an Austrian newspaper early in November,[33] its obvious purpose being to reassure Austria of ultimate victory by the Teutonic powers. A reference to rumors that he contemplated a shortening of his lines on the Western Front drew from him an emphatic denial. "It is nonsense," said he, "I never thought of it. Why should I do it? The front in the west stands as firm as a rock, and if our enemies, by gigantic use of artillery, here and there gain a little terrain, they shall never break through. In order to do this they would have to attack for thirty years, provided they had enough men." Five months after this interview (in March, 1917) Hindenburg was making his great retreat eastward, by which he not only shortened his line, but gave up some thousands of square miles of territory, including scores of cities and villages which the Germans had occupied for four years, and which they had fought several major battles, including Ypres, Arras and the Somme, to retain.

Questioned as to the duration of the war, he said it was possible that the year 1917 would bring battles which would decide the war, but he knew the Germans "would fight this war to a final decision." At the time when Hindenburg was

[33] The Vienna *Neue Freie Presse.*

saying these boastful things there was a renewal in German newspapers of agitation for peace, even on the basis of a draw.[34] A dispatch to the New York *Evening Journal,* from Berlin by way of Paris, quoted Edward Bernstein, a German socialist deputy, as admitting in the Reichstag that "we started the war, but we are unable to finish it." The Berlin *Vorwärts* also sounded a warning note in its assertion that "if we are going to drag this war on indefinitely, then the whole of Europe will bleed to death, and American and the colored races will be our heirs." A few days later the French gave an eloquent reply to the statement by Hindenburg as to their waning power. Altho for some days they had been fighting desperately on the Somme front, and in addition had fully finished up their work of restoring the solidity of their Verdun defensive positions, there was enough vigor in the French army and sufficient resources to strike, and strike hard, at a third section of the front—that of Chaulnes, which had been practically neglected. As for the British, it was not until the battle of the Somme that there existed a British army in the modern sense, or in the sense that there had been a French, or a German, army. This army of 1,500,000 had been created in almost every detail, not out of the accumulated resources and experience of many years or centuries, but out of nothing except British citizens. In this way British democracy had answered German autocracy, British individualism had met German collectivism.

After a long period of activity, the British now launched a major attack in an entirely new section of the Somme line, and against positions which three months before had been practically impregnable. Apparently the Germans had suffered so much that they were able no longer to defend more than a comparatively short section of their line. This might not mean any real insufficiency in German numbers, but if it meant anything else the meaning was not apparent. Certainly the German reserve seemed to be sufficient to feed men and munitions into the firing-line at a rate

[34] From this period, October 30th, dates a notable but ineffectual German movement for a peace conference with the Entente Allies, as officially proposed in December in the Reichstag by Chancellor Bethmann-Hollweg.

equal to the wastage. Consequently, such reinforcements as were thrown into the firing-line had to come from other sections in order that the threatened point might not give way. This spread of the British attack north of the Ancre seemed significant. If the British could advance up this valley, important objects could be achieved. First a double salient would be created. South of the Ancre the Germans would be taken in the rear and almost surrounded, while north of it a similar situation would arise, altho in a form not so exaggerated. German positions south of the brook, which had been giving the British a good deal of trouble, would be taken from the rear, and would have to be evacuated as the British north of the brook pushed forward.

After the severe blows driven home on the Ancre, the Germans, on November 15, turned savagely against the French south of the Somme. They struck toward the heel of the new French line at its junction with the original position before the offensive began, and hurled their attack against the Ablaincourt-Pressoire line, where the French had approached uncomfortably near Chaulnes. Asphyxiating gas, lachrymose gas and liquid flame were used in a desperate effort to unseat the French. Gray-green German hordes swept toward the French lines, but only to be blasted and withered by French fire. After a dozen waves of the assault had been shattered, the surviving Germans managed to assemble in a group of shell-swept houses between Pressoire and Comiecourt, across the road from a cemetery. Elsewhere the French had held their positions, making prisoners of Germans who escaped the machine-guns and entered their lines. This German attempt, from the standpoint of artillery preparation and the number of men used and sacrificed, was regarded as the heaviest counter-attack yet directed toward the French on the Somme.

By the middle of December, warfare on the Somme had become stationary. While there might be another movement at any moment, it seemed natural to say that the battle of the Somme had ended. Whatever came later would belong to a second battle. Yet there was no point at which the battle entirely ceased. Guns were never silent, night or day. Guns blotted out communication-trenches through which supplies came to German lines and made their repair impossible. Prisoners and documents told how everything had to be brought up over-night, how, often under the barrage, things of immediate urgency failed to arrive. Among thousands of captured German letters, written to men at the front by people at home, the feeling of rebellion

FRONTIER TRENCHES IN WINTER

against the war was shown to be growing bitter and the longing for peace more acute.

How much this was a machine-war one realized more as winter covered the earth with ice, mud, and snow. The purely human element was balked but the machines kept the war grinding on. Infantry could not march but auto-busses could shunt men back and forth. Land scouts were almost paralyzed, but aeroplanes could defy the elements. Soldiers could not pass over mud-holes between their line and the Germans and so stuck to trench-work and trench-mortars.

When a *communiqué* read "there is nothing to report," it did not mean the front was silent, because machine-fighting never ceased. By the middle of December one of the wettest, dreariest snowfalls on record seemed to have ushered in a soggy winter. Huge flakes of snow, "resembling monstrous goose feathers," and at times completely arresting aerial operations, limited one's vision to scarcely a hundred yards. But artillery- and trench-warfare went on. Even when snow, rain, and fog prevented all attempts at observation there were always charted points against which artillery could hammer. Freezing weather and thaws damaged trenches, which had a tendency to crumble and cave in.

A German attack on Lassigny, that part of the front nearest to Paris, was made in great force on December 14. It appeared to have been planned to coincide with Bethmann-Hollweg's proposed peace,[35] probably with a view to impressing the French by a local success. The Germans brought together about 40,000 men and concentrated corresponding quantities of artillery. The attack was preceded by a bombardment lasting for hours. The French were not taken by surprize, and received the assaulting waves with a fire from three-inch guns and machine-guns. Germans reached the French trenches over a frontage of 300 yards. A counter-attack enabled the French to regain the trenches. Only a few survivors of the attacking columns escaped. Most of them were killed after stubborn resistance. The Germans renewed the assault without success, French heavy artillery dispersing the reserves as they came up.

While the French in December were also holding back the German Crown Prince's army before Verdun, the British army was nowhere entirely idle. Through swirling snow and driving rain, with a cold tang in the air reminiscent of Christmas, they plugged away in accord with the French defenders of Verdun. That the British did not intend that the Germans should have any rest until the end of the war became apparent. Visits of correspondents to back areas

---

[35] Of this famous proposal and the diplomatic exchanges that ensued, including President Wilson's appeal to the belligerent powers, details are given in a later chapter of this work—Volume IV, Part XV, Chapter I.

gave this impression as distinctly as visits to the front lines.

By January 11 the British army was holding ninety miles of the Western Front. This included a strip taken over from the French at Christmas time. While doing this they were withstanding a force of Germans equal to those who were spread along the French line still 230 miles in extent. The Germans for some reason had massed their troops in stronger array against the British front than against the French, except around Verdun. Through rain, mist, fog, and deep mud the British army continued day by day to pound the German line. Altho there was no distinctly spectacular action, daily and nightly trench-raids and the drumming of artillery continued. These operations yielded a constant inflow of prisoners and kept the casualty list growing. According to stories by prisoners, the British tactics harassed the German troops "almost beyond endurance." British troops hit German lines hard at two places on January 17. Northeast of Cité Calonne the Canadians carried out a brilliant raid on a front of 700 yards and penetrated positions to a depth of 300 yards. German dugouts were completely wrecked and 100 men made prisoners. At Beaucourt-sur-Ancre another drive by the British gave them German positions over a front of 600 yards, which they held despite a counter-attack in which the Germans lost heavily under British barrage-fire.

Before July 1, 1916, Verdun had been the greatest continuous battle in the world's history; but the Somme surpassed it both in numbers of men engaged, in tactical difficulties of the objectives, and in importance in the strategical scheme of the campaign. It was the fashion in Germany to describe it as a futile attack upon an unshakable fortress, an attack which might be disregarded by public opinion at home while Germany continued her business of conquest in the East. But the fact remained that the great bulk of German troops, and by far the best of them, had still to be kept in this area. In November Germany had 127 divisions on the Western Front, and no more than seventy-five in the East. Tannenburg had been a victory for Germany, the Marne one for France, and the first battle of Ypres one for Great Britain. The battle of the Somme was no less a victory, since it achieved the purpose of the Allies. In the first place, it relieved Verdun, and enabled Nivelle to advance to conspicuous victories. In the second place, it detained the main German forces on the Western Front and in the third drew into the battle, and gravely depleted, the surplus man-power of the enemy, and struck a shattering blow at his morale. The battle of the Somme had, therefore, fulfilled the Allied purpose in taxing to the uttermost the German war-machine. It tried the British command, it tried the nation at home, and it tried to the last limit of endurance the men in the line. The place became a name of terror. Altho belittled in German *communiqués,* and rarely mentioned in the German press, it was a word of ill-omen to the whole German people, a "blood-bath" to which many journeyed and from which few returned. No great thing is achieved without a price, however. On the Somme fell the very flower of the British race, young men who died almost before they had fully gazed upon the world of action, who had been possible makers and doers of real things, but who left their tasks unfinished.

In the larger sense, the summer campaign was unfavorable to Germany. It saw her loss of the offensive, saw a steady pounding upon all her fronts redoubled, saw a new strain on her resources, gave to her enemies new assurances of victory and disclosed them at last cooperating and coordinating superior resources in men and in money. The summer had been the worst period of the war for the Germans, because it saw a gradual rise in the strength and efficiency of her enemies, who were always bound to defeat Germany, because of superior numbers, wealth and resources—that is, provided the war could be prolonged into a test of endurance. The certainty of German defeat to neutral observers was no longer questioned. In the United States this conviction had become well-nigh universal. Men who had the Civil War as an illuminating parallel always before their eyes knew how inevitable must be the outcome of any war which was fought under conditions similar to Civil War conditions.

The objects of the Somme advance had been three: First, to relieve Verdun; second, to prevent the Germans from transferring masses of troops to the east against Russia;

third, to wear down German strength. Haig had declared that the accomplishment of any one of these aims would nave justified the Somme battle, but all three aims had been accomplished. When the battle began, the Germans still calculated on taking Verdun, and had begun to dispatch troops to the east. Then they failed to take Verdun, stopt their eastward movement and abandoned the offensive against Russia. Thereafter the only German troops sent eastward were such as had been exhausted in the Somme battle. Haig declared it beyond doubt that the German losses in men and material were "very considerably higher" than those of the Allies, while morally the balance of advantage on the Allies' side was still greater. As the battle continued through several months, the German resistance had grown "decidedly feebler," and toward the end of the operations, when the weather unfortunately broke, there was

GEN. COUNT SIXT VON ARNIM

no doubt that "his power of resistance had been very seriously diminished." As victory consists in the attainment of an object, the battle of the Somme was regarded by Haig as a victory for the Allies. A decisive victory it was not, but, according to him, no decisive victory was expected.

After Hindenburg and Ludendorff, the most conspicuous German commander in the Somme battle was Count Sixt von Arnim. In his report on the battle of the Somme Arnim declared that all the tactically important German positions "were methodically bombarded by English artillery, as well as all known infantry and battery positions."

Extremely heavy fire was continuously directed on villages situated immediately behind the firing-line, as well as on all natural cover afforded by the ground "while registration and fire-control were assisted by well-organized aerial observation." He admitted the numerical superiority of the British airmen, while the fact that their machines were better "was made disagreeably apparent to us, particularly in the direction of the artillery-fire and bomb-dropping." Germany's battle-planes, he said, were too few in number, and British airmen "were often able to fire successfully on our troops with machine-guns, by descending to a height of a few hundred meters." The anti-aircraft guns of the Germans could not continue firing at that height "without exposing their own troops to serious danger from fragments of shell."

Arnim, as already stated in an earlier volume, met an ignominious fate in March, 1919, when he was beaten to death by peasants on his own estate at Asch in Bohemia, after he had fired on these peasants while they were gathering firewood on his property. Having killed him the peasants then proceeded to pillage his château. Arnim had been in the war from the beginning. He led the first German corps into Belgium in 1914, and after the Belgian army left Brussels, was sent to the front where he became known as having the clearest common-sense of all the generals in the German army. He looked upon war as Napoleon did, merely as a scientific game; had no concern with the causes of the war, or its outcome, no hostility toward Haig, or anybody serving under Haig; he was simply a machine, carrying out orders. His reports were among the most illuminating things published. He never depreciated his enemies and praise of them was characteristic of him, dealing it out in the same calm way in which he dealt out praise for his own troops. A royalist and an imperialist, an able soldier, not in the least disposed to withhold credit from his enemy, he was now beaten to death with clubs on a Bohemian farm.

The British had at last secured that artillery preponderance for which they had been striving with all their might during the previous year. Their guns both outclassed and outnumbered those of the Germans, and the preponderance was increasing. They had made good the leeway lost in the first year of the war, owing to want of foresight and failure to realize the deciding rôle heavy artillery plays on the modern field of battle. The lessons of Neuve Chapelle and Loos had been taken to heart. No more was heard of rash rushes into enemy lines before troops were ready to support the attack. No more, even among Germans, was heard of the invincibility of German armies.

France was now able to supply to Belgians, Russians, Italians, Serbians, and Roumanians, quantities of arms and munitions which she manufactured herself, and she also apportioned to her Allies a considerable part of what she bought abroad. Up to October 16, 1916, France had supplied Russia with more than 600,000 rifles and more than 300,000,000 cartridges; had sent to her several hundred pieces of heavy artillery, millions of projectiles, millions of hand-grenades, and thousands of aeroplane motors. She had also sent technical experts and specialists to intensify the Russian home production. In December, 1916, twenty-two officers and 236 subaltern officers and soldiers of the French army were occupying important posts in Russian munition factories. The most important French mission sent to Russia was headed by Colonel Pyot, who transferred into munition factories a great many establishments that had not previously worked for national defense. Raw materials and coal were sent from France to Italy, together with a number of batteries of heavy artillery with a supply of shells. Besides keeping up the Russian supply of projectiles for heavy guns, France furnished Italy with a considerable quantity of charged three-inch shells and engaged to supply regularly several thousand empty shells a day. Helmets, 500,000; trench-shields, 40,000; more than 100 trench-mortars, hundreds of tons of aluminum and chemical products, were among the other things furnished to Italy, while a French Flying Corps constituted the defense of Venice against Austrian air attacks.

England produced war material at a rate that was almost inconceivable. Neutral markets shipped enormous quantities to the Allies. Japan was turned into a mighty arsenal, manufacturing for Russia. The result had been conspicuously shown in the fighting in the west in 1916 where the Germans were unable to match the Allied artillery-fire, either in the number of guns used, the volume of metal thrown, or the effectiveness of the individual shell. German artillery-fire at Verdun was far inferior to that of the Allies on the Somme, and German artillery-fire on the Somme was

FRENCH MOTOR BATTERY GOING TO THE FRONT

inferior to what it had been at Verdun. On the whole there was a steady decline in the Teutonic fighting resources during 1916 and an equally steady rise of that of the Allies. From Kitchener's little army, the "first hundred thousand," there had sprung up in England probably 2,000,000 men under arms. These had been an unknown quantity until the battle of the Somme when they received their baptism of fire. Once he had learned the game, there was no better fighting man in Europe than the British "Tommy," and he knew the game now, having learned it on the battlefield.

There was said to be plenty of money in Germany, but there had to be, since Germany was living on herself. Her condition was compared to that of a bear which, during the period of hibernation, lives on its own fat. But the time would come—if the war lasted long enough—when a day's wages would buy nothing, or somewhat the same situation would come that existed in the South during the last days of our Civil War when the purchasing power of Confederate money fell to a point where hundreds of dollars were needed to buy a pair of boots.[36] This was the condi-

[36] A frock coat made in Richmond for Jefferson Davis in the last year of the war cost $700.

tion Germany was facing. Late in 1916 there were certain kinds of commodities which promised eventually to disappear from Germany, and they were absolutely necessary to her. Among these things were cotton, rubber, copper, and fats, in all of which there was a serious shortage.

Figures revealed the futility of demonstrating by exact arithmetic that this or that belligerent was on his last legs in the matter of fighting men. Estimates had been a favorite game on both sides. There were Allied war-experts who had no difficulty in showing early in 1916 that Germany was virtually down to her last man. But when the Austrians, in 1916, collapsed before Brusiloff's attack and lost nearly half a million troops, Germany managed to scrape up enough men to fill the gap in the Austrian line

RESPIRATION DRILL AT THE FRONT

and later managed to bring up an army sufficient for the conquest of Roumania. The Germans themselves early in 1916 had France bled white; and that was before Verdun and the Somme. Nearly at the same time they had proved in precise German fashion that Russia's human supplies were exhausted, after which came the Russian conquest of

Armenia and Brusiloff's advance upon Lemberg. By the end of 1916, however, it was plain in Europe that, in spite of all schemes for efficiency organization, in spite of civic, industrial and agricultural mobilizations, the economic life of the nations was approaching exhaustion. The earth's fruitfulness was wearing out. The fact that 1916 had been a bad crop-year all over the world did not entirely account for fear of famine. You can not take away millions of laborers from the fields and starve the soil for want of nutriment without undermining the food-supply. The railroads, too, were wearing out. Train economies were being practised in Germany, France, and England. The shifting of hundreds of thousands of men from front to front, by which Germany had astonished the world, had imposed an enormous strain on trackage and rolling-stock. Her food dictator announced that the food-shortage was due in large measure to difficulties of transportation. Grain from Roumania, which was expected to relieve the food situation in the empire—to an altogether exaggerated degree, as matters turned out—had not been brought up for lack of railroad facilities. Factory machinery was wearing out under the strain of day- and night-work on munitions. German efficiency even was wearing out. Food regulations had been practised in Germany for more than two years, and there was greater complaint than ever of mismanagement in distribution. The nations might not be running short of men for trenches, military machines might still function efficiently, but the machinery of Europe's economic civilization was creaking and groaning under lack of fuel, lubricants, and labor.[38]

[38] Principal Sources: The *Times* (New York), The *Times* (London), The *Tribune* (New York), Associated Press dispatches, The *Evening Post* (New York), *The Fortnightly Review,* "Nelson's History of the War" by John Buchan.

ON THE WESTERN FRONT

Part XI

THE GERMAN RETREAT IN THE WEST, AND THE NEW ARRAS AND AISNE BATTLES

THE DESTROYED CASTLE OF COUCY

In the upper picture the Castle is shown after the Germans had destroyed it during their retreat; in the lower one, its previous appearance is shown, with its great donjon 200 feet high

I

BAPAUME, NOYON AND PÉRONNE ABANDONED— A LAND OF UTTER DESOLATION

February 1, 1917—March 21, 1917

OBSERVERS realized during the winter that the advance made on the Somme in 1916 was successful as an operation, but that it had been begun too late in the season for the more complete success hoped for. Moreover, it was halted by rains in September, and finally stopt altogether by a deluge in November. Until bad weather intervened, the Germans had been pushed steadily back, their resistance becoming feebler with each new attack until the advance lost itself in the mud. Haig, however, had become almost convinced that he and the French might have decided the war, provided their success could have been kept up that year without interference from the weather.

Early in the following year the British made advances on the Ancre but these attracted little attention. If they had come in a single rush instead of in driblets, they might have been understood as powerful British operations. In three weeks ending February 21, the British had carried the villages of Beaucourt, Beaumont, Baillescourt, Grandcourt, and the outskirts of Serre, and had occupied several square miles of territory wrested from the Germans. They had not suffered the loss of any position once it was taken. These gains were a late development of the Somme offensive of the previous summer; an amplification of earlier gains that made them possible and were carried out against the same forces by the same means. They lasted longer than the German Verdun operation, or the Russian Galician drive, or the British campaign in Gallipoli. More ground was gained than in any other undertaking by either side on the Western Front since the beginning of trench-warfare.

Finally, on February 24, under cover of a mist which had been particularly heavy for forty-eight hours, the Germans began the greatest retirement they had made on the Western Front in two years, or since the battle of the Marne, and the British swept into possession of Pys, Serre, Miraumont and Petit Miraumont, including the Butte de Warlencourt, which had been the scene of some of the fiercest fighting of the war and in places was strewn deep with the bodies of dead men. It was thought that the British might soon be in a position to force the evacuation of Bapaume, which had been the key to the German position since the battle of the Somme began. They continued to move forward all along the line from just south of Gommecourt to Le Transloy, the latter apparently the pivot from which the German retreat swung backward. The line by February 26 was carried well to the northeast of Serre, with Pys, Warlencourt, Miraumont and Irles in British possession. Like other points in the Somme battlefield, such as Pozières, Courcelette and Contalmaison, these places long since had ceased to have any form as villages. Artillery-fire continued for months had pulverized them to bits of stone and brick, remnants of which were now used by the British in restoring roads.

On February 28 the German troops abandoned Gommecourt and the British took possession. It was here that, on July 1, 1916, waves of London men had assaulted an almost impregnable position, had broken it and held the lines until forced back by massed gunfire which threatened them with annihilation. Many British dead still lay there. When the gates were opened on February 27 it was found that the German troops had stolen away in the dusk, leaving behind nothing but the refuse of trench-life and a litter of trench-tools. Strong posts of Germans with machine-guns still held out in the wedge just south of Rossignol Wood and another wood, west of Bucquoy. These rear-guard posts, with an officer or two and from fifty to sixty men with machine-guns, and telephones keeping them in touch with the main army, had stayed behind with orders to hold on until the last possible moment. The Germans in retreat had destroyed the Irles church-tower, the church of Achiet-le-Petit, and the famous clock-tower of Bapaume, in order to get rid of observation posts that might be useful to the British in their advance. Gommecourt had been the "nose" of a salient jutting into the British lines for months. Its occupation marked the giving way of what was regarded as the northern hinge of the German line, which now swinging back lent further color to the theory that this was only the first step toward shortening the German line in the Arras-Somme region. Meantime the British had approached to within a mile of Bapaume, in which town further explosions were heard. Hindenburg, in spite of all he had said, was to shorten his line.

The task of connecting new positions and building roads through the former "no-man's land" was proving an enormous one for the British. All the Somme and Ancre area presented an aspect more or less of liquid mud, resulting from thaw. The Germans had timed their retirement to coincide with this condition. They got started when the ground was in good condition, knowing that the British would have to pursue them when it was at its worst. Whatever might be the ultimate strategy lying behind the German retirement between Gommecourt and Le Transloy, even a casual inspection of some of the evacuated lines near Bapaume revealed an immediate reason for their abandonment. They had been smashed to pieces by incessant and ever increasing British artillery-fire. Communication-trenches, built for the purpose of bringing up food and ammunition, had been flattened almost beyond recognition and long since had ceased to serve their purpose. The wide belt area back of the German lines had been lasht by bursting shells until it had become practically impassable. For hours at a time, often for days, the drum-fire of British guns made it impossible for any man to reach or leave a trench. Abandoned ground was found covered with hundreds of German dead.

The next problem before the British was to discover whether the Germans intended to defend this line with great resistance, or whether they would go further back until they were quite clear of the salient and so shorten their line by something like thirty miles. It was still doubtful whether they would challenge the British with what chess-players call the *"grand jeu,"* the really strategical game, or whether they were merely saving pawns. The British by March held the entire Somme front. In the gradual replacing of French troops by British on the Somme that had been going on for upward of two months, the British had extended the section of the front in France which they covered by twenty-five miles. They now had almost exactly 100 of the 300-mile front in France and Belgium, while the French held 175 miles and the Belgians 26. French troops whom the British relieved went into the reserves or went to strengthen other parts of the line. The new move was highly significant of the greater part that the British army was to play in the war.

While the withdrawal was the most considerable change in the German line without immediate pressure since the battle of the Marne, it was as yet scarcely a significant or decisive incident. The retirements had only a local value because the Germans had had time to complete a system of trench-lines and fortified villages far behind the line for which the British had fought gallantly in the summer and fall of 1916. Even if the Germans should be, forced from the Arras-Bapaume-Péronne line, they would have a perfectly organized line running from Lens, through Cambrai and St. Quentin, to the Oise at La Fère. The idea that the Germans were worn out, unable to attack, lacking men or munitions, was misleading, if not fallacious. The morale of the Germans had apparently declined, but this decline was due in the main to the constant superiority of British and French artillery, and to the steady, if inconsiderable, advances made. The retirement was to some extent a consequence of British progress, but it had chief importance as adding to British confidence. Both British and French now became serenely confident of their ability to check and repel a new German offensive, as they had repelled every German effort in the west since the Marne, but neither the French nor the British imagined that the German had said his last word in the west or that a new German attack would be a small affair.

Early in March news came of a far greater movement by the Germans. A general retirement set in along the great salient from Lille and Arras to Reims. In a few days the

Germans gave up some two hundred and fifty towns and many hundred square miles of French soil. Early in the operations, Bapaume and Péronne, which had been the objectives of the Allied attacks, were evacuated. The distance which the Allied forces were able to advance varied from a few yards at the end of the line to fifteen miles or more in the middle. For the first time on this front in more than two years troops now fought in the open, and cavalry was used on a large scale. For many weeks it had been evident that the German trenches had become untenable. The artillery-fire had been so terrific that subterranean defenses were destroyed, and even those which proved able to withstand shell-fire were in many cases cut off from supplies by the curtain of high explosives.

Whatever the German motive, the retirement went steadily on. By March 14 it was understood that Bapaume, toward which British eyes had looked longingly since July of the previous year, might soon swarm with Haig's soldiers. Under pressure from British advances, the Germans were at last retreating from that stronghold. Further advances, west of Bapaume, were made on a front of more than one and one-half miles. Haig was exerting pressure at all points along the southern line of the Bapaume-Arras salient. Operations were sometimes carried out with a heavy rain beating in the faces of British troops, unable to see more than a few yards. Correspondents declared that some of the positions abandoned by the Germans were not abandoned voluntarily, but that they were pounded out of them by British guns. From the Loupart Ridge they ran away, leaving intact dugouts which British artillery had spared. They sacrificed ammunition and supplies. Some of the abandoned dugouts contained quantities of champagne and cigars.

No army enjoys retreating, and Hindenburg apparently was shortening his lines, not because he wanted to, but because he had to. That was the Entente, and generally it was the neutral, opinion. At points where the battle of the Somme had left off in consequence of bad weather, Germans were being forced back. While they were making the terrain over which the British had to advance as difficult as possible, that was not the object of their retreat; the object was to abandon lines that were no longer defensible and go back to lines which might be defended. What had been accomplished so far was disproof of the theory that trench-warfare must of necessity end in a stalemate. Trench-de-defenses were supposed to be indestructible, but history has shown that the ingenuity of man has never been permanently baffled by any new methods of warfare. The British had found a way to break trench-defenses by making the trenches indefensible. With airplanes to tell them where to attack, they blasted trenches to pieces before infantry advanced.

On March 17 British and French troops were forcing a retirement in three separate places on a total front of forty-five miles. As Bapaume fell to the British, so Roye and Lassigny fell to the French. Fourteen villages around which there had been much fighting were also occupied. Bapaume fell after stiff fighting with the German guard. Haig's report said the town had been systematically pillaged by the Germans before they departed. All private houses and public buildings were destroyed and everything of value carried off or burned. In reprisal for this a French airplane bombarded Frankfort-on-the-Main.

Next day the Germans continued their withdrawal, yielding between 400 and 600 square miles along a front of nearly seventy miles, extending from the Arras sector to the Oise. Pressing close on the heels of the retreating enemy, French and British troops occupied mile after mile of open ground. The retirement reached its greatest proportions within the Arras and Noyon salients, which had now been nearly eliminated. At points in the former, the British advanced to a depth of ten miles, while the French forward movement reached a depth of twelve. About seventy villages and towns fell into the hands of the Allied forces during that day. Péronne, Chaulnes, and Nesle were occupied by the British, while the French took Noyon, the largest strategic center to fall. In the Noyon sector the British and French joined hands in the advance, their lines temporarily overlapping for a distance of several miles. Together they entered Nesle. At almost every point along the whole front they were now out of the trenches, and for the first time in months the cavalry of both armies were operating extensively in wide-open territory. In every direction mounted troops were sent forward ahead of the main forces.

Encounters between German rear-guards and Allied units were rare, so rapid was the German retreat and so cautious the French and British commanders in preventing soldiers from falling into a possible trap. The Germans were burning, destroying, and looting all the way, leaving a trail of devastation over the rolling countryside. Hardly a house in all these villages and towns was left standing; scarcely a field failed to show the inroads of the retreating army. Amid the smoking ruins of Roye and Lassigny 800 inhabitants were discovered still alive when the French entered. They were almost crazed with joy at the sight of the tricolor and the horizon-blue uniforms. To gain the best idea of the extent of the French territory evacuated in three weeks, it was only necessary to state that it amounted to more than three times the area of ground won on the Somme front during eight months.[2]

It would have been difficult enough to guess at the purpose of the German retreat provided it had come as an isolated phenomenon; but at the further end of the intercontinental battle-line, in Mesopotamia and Armenia, significant events had been working themselves out until the face of things was altered completely, and afterward the Russian upheaval had come to upset all military calculations, all existing states of mind, in every one of the belligerent capitals. Russia was no longer the Russia the world had known. Berlin, by reactions to events in Petrograd, had also been changed from the Berlin of two weeks before. At Verdun and on the Somme men had measured advances and retreats by hundreds of feet; now they were talking in dozens of miles. War in the trenches along nearly one-half of the Western Front had ended and cavalry were in motion. It was no longer coal-heaps and factories that were being occupied, but towns and cities. The movement might have been absolutely forced by fear of an approaching grand attack by the Allies, or it might have been a voluntary movement with a strategic purpose, such as to draw the Allies out of trenches into open warfare, leading them to make hot

[2] Cable dispatch from Arthur S. Draper to The New York *Tribune.*

pursuits, to a dislocation of the Allied line—to something, in fact, like the fatal German error in their rush to the Marne in 1914. Or the retirement might have been partly forced and partly voluntary, with the purpose of economizing men and munitions for use elsewhere. Whatever the impelling cause, whether necessity or design, it gave a heavy blow to German prestige and an enormous acceleration to Allied confidence.

On February 23 the German retirement on the Ancre had begun; on February 24 the British captured Kut-el-Amara; on February 27 the Russian Duma reassembled at Petrograd. We may establish a connection between these three dates by assuming that there was foreknowledge at Berlin of what was going to happen on the Tigris and in Petrograd. So complete had been the Turkish defeat in Mesopotamia, so immediate was the follow-up by the British on the Tigris, and by the Russians from Persia and Armenia, that men were warranted in assuming that Hindenburg had knowledge of the parlous state of the Turkish forces. Of conditions in Russia, men in Berlin unquestionably had foreknowledge, and what the British feared might come the German government hoped to see; namely, a revolution with possible civil war, and certain confusion leading to paralysis.

A "retreat to victory" and "another von Hindenburg master-stroke" were terms used by the German War Office to describe the withdrawal from a hundred miles of elaborately entrenched and supposedly impregnable positions, with the surrender of more than a thousand square miles of French territory which had been held by the Germans almost since the beginning of the war. They claimed that it took the German army back to a shorter, stronger, and more scientifically prepared line, and put into confusion all the elaborate preparations of the Allies for a spring offensive. A high German military authority exulted in the fact that "we are now getting the enemy out of their trenches." An American editor ironically remarked that repetitions of this master-stroke would take the German armies back to Berlin. The New York *World* noted that, while the French and English were certainly coming out of their trenches, it was "on the side facing away from Paris." Altogether the attempt of the Germans to call their retirement a victory rather than a defeat was to the New York *Times* "forlorn whistling in a graveyard."

The evacuation of Bapaume, Roye, Noyon, and Péronne was in general represented in Berlin as "part of a great strategic undertaking which promised to revolutionize warfare on the Western Front and would constitute one of the most decisive efforts in the war." Just as a month before the Germans had evacuated an important sector on the Ancre, but kept the fact secret for a week while the British bombarded empty trenches, so these later movements were declared to be the most important development of 1917 on any front. The Germans, in giving up this portion of the front, were said to have "put an end to all the finely laid Allied spring offensive plans." Ever since November, hundreds of thousands of men had been at work building trenches, munition depots, railroads, and cable lines to prepare for the biggest spring offensive of the war, but now, at one blow, all that had gone for nothing. Work representing millions upon millions of dollars had been rendered valueless. Meanwhile the Allies "were left at the mercy of our plans." "It is important to remember," added this semi-official statement, "that the new positions we are taking up back of the old front are built with the aid of every possible device developed by two and a half years of warfare." The old positions "were the result of the breaking off of the unfinished offensive toward Paris, but the new

PÉRONNE AFTER ITS EVACUATION BY THE GERMANS
The placard (in English) says: "Do not be vexed; do not be astonished"

had been laid out in the best possible locations, with the finest observation points and deep concrete shelters for the battery positions." While the Allies were coming up to them, they would be "in the greatest possible difficulties in devastated battlefields." Again it was declared that the Germans were not moving back because of enemy pressure, but were remaking the western lines, so that they would have an aggressive initiative.

Such was the German explanation of their retreat—composed, as outside readers believed, largely to comfort readers at home. The British plan had been to recapture, by costly fighting, the very area which the Germans were evacuating. When the Germans gave it up without a fight, of course they disarranged that plan, but they disarranged it by giving the British what they had planned to fight for. Naturally the British would now have to plan for a new fight, but if it was a great military feat to disarrange an enemy's plans, the Germans might have further disarranged Allied plans by retiring again. What the Berlin writers of these statements had done was to take a successful military operation, view it by itself, and then to spin from it a dream of victory. As a retreat the German retirement had unquestionably been skilfully carried out. In a sense it was voluntary, since where the Germans chose to go back, they went back, and where they chose to hold fast, as on their right wing at Arras, they held fast. But that was all. While the retreat was probably voluntary at the time, this did not make it clear that it had not been forced upon the Germans in a larger sense. They themselves admitted as much when they spoke of the clever way in which Hindenburg had frustrated the Allied preparations. When Berlin writers rejoiced over Allied preparations that had gone to waste, they proved altogether too much; they virtually admitted that the Allies had a very good chance of breaking through, and that the retreat was, after all, forced upon the Germans.

The German front, however, had been shortened by some forty miles, which would be a saving of not less than 150,000 troops for the Germans, but one of at least twice as many for the Allies, who held their lines much more strongly. In the second place, all the preparations made by the Allies for a spring drive on the front between Arras and Soissons had been rendered useless. There was now between the front on which the preparations for attack were made and the new front a devastated area varying from five to twenty-five miles in depth, which was destitute of roads and railroads and had been turned into a blackened waste. This was the immediate gain for the Germans in their retreat, and it was necessary to recognize its meaning, both negatively and positively. But the Germans by this act declined to fight another battle on ground they had defended in 1916. They

A STREET IN NOYON FLOODED BY THE GERMANS

had conceded Allied success in the battle of the Somme by retreating from positions they occupied at the close of that battle, and they had thoroughly confirmed the British claim that, had the weather remained favorable for another month in 1916, the results of the battle of the Somme might have been very great, if not actually decisive. The German retreat was a retreat that had been forced by Allied cannon and Allied operations, quite as much as was the retreat from the Marne, and clearly established the battle of the Somme as an Allied victory. It also demonstrated the enormous progress made by the British in the art of trench-warfare and of British artillery in mastering German defense, but the Germans had made a remarkably successful retreat.

Bapaume, fallen at last after nearly a year's offensive in which it had been only one of the Allied objectives, was a village of some three thousand souls, the center of a flourishing agricultural trade, and had been a community of some note for nearly a thousand years. In 1871 one of the bloodiest engagements of the Franco-Prussian war took place here. That earlier battle of Bapaume between French and Germans comprised one of the few successes won by the Army of the North while Paris lay besieged; but, as a French chronicler sadly recorded, it was a success "without a morrow." Philip Gibbs [3] went into the town and felt something of the old thrill that came to him in 1914 when the Germans fell back from the Marne and retreated to the Aisne. Bapaume was still standing, but broken and burned. Unlike many villages on the Somme battlefield, its houses had not quite disappeared off the face of the earth; many were old brick houses two stories high with gray-slated roofs, but the walls had been pierced with shell and the roofs were gaping. The only living inhabitant was a kitten, which ran across the square and was captured by British patrols.

Two days later Mr. Gibbs had an extraordinary experience in going through an abandoned country from which the Germans had fled. He tramped through the district around Péronne and went into that deserted and destroyed town; went down into "a wild chaos and ruin of trenches and through barbed wire still uncut so that he was tangled and caught in it." He managed to get into Péronne by a wide curve through the Faubourg de Paris, over piled stones of a broken bridge, with planks across the gaps, put there by British soldiers so that the Germans could be followed in pursuit. In the Faubourg de Paris all trees had been cut down and had fallen across the street, making a great barricade. Fire-brands had been set to all houses not previously smashed by shell-fire. Of many enough was still standing to show they had once been houses, but there was hardly one that had escaped the wrath of war. Mr. Gibbs went into many

[3] Correspondent of The *Daily Chronicle* (London) in The New York *Times*.

houses that were littered with muck, with here and there scraps of broken furniture. Péronne was a dead town, like Ypres, like Bapaume, like many villages in the wake of the German retreat. Over its old fortifications built by Vauban and over its marshes wild duck were flying.

William P. Simms [4] gave as one reason why the Germans retreated from the Ancre. the fact that they were "fast becoming a garrison of gibbering lunatics." Mud that was bottomless in places and the ceaseless pounding of British guns had turned their positions into pits too horrible for human nerves to stand. He saw ground compared with which Mme. Tussaud's [4a] chamber of horrors "was as cheerful as a May day," zigzagged as it was around stagnant cesspools and interlocking shell-craters. He found himself stepping on German bodies which littered the region in all imaginable conditions and positions—sometimes piled several deep, arms sticking full length out of mud that concealed all else of the bodies of which they were parts. Legs, feet, and half bodies, or hands alone, were protruding, some face downward, some on their backs, as if asleep. On a pile several deep lay a boyish officer, fair as a girl, with his arms thrown back and his blue eyes staring to the sky, his sandy hair brushed back modishly by rain. Scenes like these covered miles of ground from which every trace of vegetation had long since been blasted away and where earth-powder had been stained and churned up from ten to sixty feet in depth. The mud was so bottomless that German prisoners claimed that men had frequently been swallowed up whole in attempting to cross it after dark. Such was the territory the Germans had left. It was too horrible for human nerves to stand longer, and made Mr. Simms believe stories of soldiers who had becoming raving maniacs.

The deliberate character of the destruction wrought by the Germans before their withdrawal from Péronne was painfully evident in the condition of the once beautiful avenue of trees leading to the Péronne railway-station. These trees had been untouched by shell-fire, but each had now been hacked in two with axes. The gashes and chips showed

[4] Correspondent of the United Press.
[4a] A wax-work exhibition in London.

that the work had been done within a few days. The railway-station was completely wrecked, including tracks and bridges. German signs had been substituted for French in the station. On a bulletin-board was a time-table of trains for Lille, Munich, and other points within German lines. Many rifles left behind showed German occupancy of French barracks, in some of which Christmas trees, decorated with tinsel, were still standing. It was strange to find in shattered and partly burned houses remnants of children's toys, including doll-carriages and bits of dolls which had been left behind with other household belongings when the French inhabitants first fled before the German invaders in 1914. In some of the finer residences libraries had now been wrecked, books torn in pieces and scattered in streets. Traveling on the thirteen-mile front around Roye, Chaulnes, and the Oise, one found roads everywhere blown up, trees and fences cut down, houses and other buildings razed, and the very land itself damaged to as great an extent as possible. The city of Roye looked as if it had been stricken by an earthquake. The Germans before they left mined street corners in such manner as not only to cause a great crater when explosives were touched off, thus blocking the streets, but the collapse of buildings on the four corners. The whole city of Roye had been mined to impede the French advance.

With other correspondents in the first week of March, Mr. Simms "explored the new Sahara, that hideous band of country abandoned by the Germans lest their troops go mad." It was the British who gave it the name of Sahara. Crown Prince Rupprecht's men had called it "the Graveyard." Mr. Simms suggested another still—"the field of a thousand shudders, the place where nightmares are made." From Bapaume west and south lay this new Sahara. Before the war it was covered with hamlets, villages, and towns. Now all these were gone. As one stood in that blighted country no sprig of grass, no sign of a tree, no weed, flower, or shrub met the vision as far as eyes could see. There was only "a greenish black soil, freshly churned up and be-cratered by explosives ranging in depth from five to sixty or more feet." "Look out for the bayonet!" was a common cry of warning as you stumbled through mud, for hundreds and

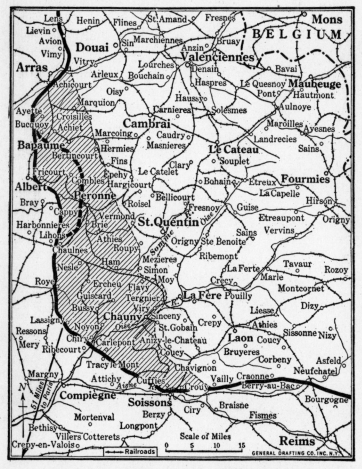

THE SOMME GAINS AND THE GERMAN RETREAT

The area in the above map crossed by diagonal lines shows the ground out of which the Germans retreated between July 1, 1916, and March 22, 1917. The smaller part of the area (enclosed in heavy lines, including the broken heavy lines) represents the gains made in the battle of the Somme. The larger territory is that from which Hindenburg made his "victorious retreat" in March, 1917, and is the country which the Germans devastated so terribly as they went along thousands of rifles were buried in the ground, and frequently only the blades of bayonets were sticking out. The great waste of war was everywhere evident. Wrought and twisted rifle-barrels, splintered stocks, cartridge-clips full of cartridges in uncountable number, unexploded shells of all sizes, hand-grenades of every size and shape, trench-mortar bombs, aerial torpedoes, brass shell-cases, abandoned stores of live shells, knapsacks, cartridge-belts, articles of clothing, steel helmets, fatigue-caps and what-not littered the surface of the new Sahara, and one could only imagine the amazing quantity of stuff which must lie beneath it.

Toward the butte of Warlencourt, Ligny-Thilley and thereabouts, "one reached hell's own acres." The water covering the slime in the crater beds "had become grue-somely red—exactly like blood, for some uncanny reason—and to the noisome smell of miles of muck was added an unmistakable stench." Intuition would tell you the cause of it, even were not the bodies lying about plainly to be seen. They lay singly in all kinds of attitudes, or in groups, or piles. They were "on mounds, or at the bottom of shell-holes in fragments, or so entire as to resemble merely a very tired and muddy soldier gone to sleep regardless of time or place."

Here ran the German lines during December and January following the battle of the Somme. There were no com-municating trenches leading back—the British smashed them as fast as dug—and to get into or out of the foremost posi-tions the soldiers had to traverse the open ground at night. Food and ammunition had to be brought up in the same way, and as shells never ceased falling in this area and every now and then the darkness was swept by machine-guns, those holding the line often went hungry and spent weary days and nights waiting for relief parties which never came. When a German fell in the open he lay where he fell. When he fell in the trenches he was buried in the side of the trench, provided the walls were firm enough; if not, his body was thrown outside. The bodies of soldiers who fell in this sector during November were only now being buried, and buried by the English—the Germans had been unable to get at them.

GERMAN RETREAT; ARRAS AND THE AISNE

This new Sahara was the work of British artillery. People asked why the Germans retired. Should they wonder why they left? Here was an inkling, "but only an inkling, of what the British guns were doing—making new Saharas along the German front." Similar, if not more horrible, accounts were given by other observers—for example the writer of the following,[5] under date of March 28, or more than a month after the retreat began:

"Five miles of slogging along the old German lines in the vicinity of Bapaume to-day revealed a picture of ghastliness which may never be seen again in this war or any other war. The front line was a long, open, dilapidated, crumbling grave, which disappeared in the mud at times, but could be picked up further on by means of the bodies that marked the way. One realized with a shudder how the men doomed to live in these trenches had been plagued by their own dead. Such a ceremony as decent burial had been wholly out of the question, and there was no means of conveying the bodies to the rear. It had been like passing through a fiery rain from hades to bring up food and water to the living. So the dead had simply been tossed out of the trenches, only to be blown back again by an exploding shell. Sometimes they came back in fragments, for there were arms and legs, feet and hands everywhere. Occasionally graves had been dug in the sides of the trench itself, but the dead could not even rest there. At frequent intervals the inevitable skeleton hands and feet protruded from the trench walls—grim sights this war has had for the men who passed up and down those trenches during the long and bitter nights of winter. It has been an enthralling thing to stand by the British guns in the last three or four months and wonder what was the meaning of all their continuous roar. There was no set battle in progress, and the gunners said it was merely the 'daily hate' going on to keep Fritz unhappy. The hideous revelations of the German trenches, however, give the gruesome answer to what the guns were doing. In some places there were veritable mangled masses of what were once human beings. Neither by day nor by night had the Germans rest. Their trusted barbed wire, in which they always placed such great reliance, had been swept completely away over thousands of yards, and they dared not venture out to repair it. Pathways over the fields of death were also strewn with fragments of human bodies. Some of the dead had the look of mummies. One of the fallen soldiers had his right arm thrown over his rifle as if his last impulse was to protect

[5] An Associated Press correspondent.

333

this weapon of defense. But there was no defense against the constant shelling. Some pieces of metal thrown about by the high-explosive shells must have weighed at least ten pounds."

Between Albert and Bapaume lay the battlefield of the greatest martial struggle of all history thus far, called the battle of the Somme, but which more correctly might be termed the battle of the Bapaume road. It had been a long ten miles, but at last Bapaume had been taken, and the British khaki line extended well beyond it in all directions. The defensive works about Bapaume were all that the Germans claimed for them, splendid trenches which formed a network about the place with veritable forests of barbed wire. Nothing approaching the amount of wire employed about Bapaume had been encountered elsewhere on this front. Acres upon acres of rusted strands were stretched on iron posts well screwed in the ground. Between fixt barriers were countless balls of wire—"gooseberries," as the British called them. There were also widespread reels of wire and various other tangled designs scattered everywhere to make progress difficult. Old redoubts and other fortified points about the town had ben transformed into modern defenses. In the town itself were numberless underground galleries that must have housed at times thousands of German troops. British heavy shells had penetrated some of these shelters, leaving a toll of dead behind.

There was not the slightest glimmering of moral restraint in the manner of the retreat. Not content with having long before ruined much of the country, the Germans left new ruins in their wake. They maintained their worst traditions. G. H. Perris [6] tramped over some fifteen miles in an afternoon among villages between Lassigny and the Roye-Noyon highroad. He found Lassigny completely destroyed, including the fine church built of great blocks of white sandstone. The population had long before evacuated it. At La Potière and Plessis-Cacheleux no civilians remained to welcome the French troops, but in the larger village of Lagny were nearly 200 women, children and old men—the remnants of a once prosperous community, now broken, scattered

[6] Correspondent of The *Daily Chronicle* (London) and of The *Times* (New York).

and impoverished. Barns had been blown up from sheer spite, and without a shadow of good reason. On the northern horizon columns of smoke were rising from three burning villages. No church-services and no school-work had been allowed here during the war. The people had been compelled, so far as able, to work in fields and otherwise for the garrison. At the beginning of the war the curé and three leading villagers had been shot, while others were taken into captivity, nominally as hostages. When the French entered this village and others in the region, the pathos of their welcome may be imagined. If one could have multiplied that simple scene and imagined all France, after two years of entrenched lines, looking on breathlessly at this vast territory of ruin, one would have had some idea of what its moral effects on the nation would be.

Philip Gibbs for several days went with the advancing troops into other towns, villages, and open country that had been abandoned by the Germans. Germans had ruined all the roads, opening vast craters in them, and had broken all bridges, but the British were wonderfully quick in making their way over these gaps. After passing an area of shell-fire, with its field of shell-craters, smashed barns, houses, and churches, tattered tree-trunks, great belts of barbed wire, he came to a country where grass grew again, where fields were smooth and rolling, and where the woods would be clothed with foliage when spring returned. German sentry-boxes still stood at cross-roads. German notices on boards stared at one from cottage walls or at points where villages began. Scattered about fields were crosses on German graves. Thousands of coils of barbed wire lay about in heaps, for the Germans relied a great deal on this means of defense. In many places were piles of shells which the Germans had not removed, with gun-pits, machine-gun emplacements and screens to hide the view. Observation-posts built in tall trees remained as signs of military life a mile or two back from the front lines.

The Germans spared nothing along the way of their retreat. They destroyed every village with systematic and detailed destruction. Not only in Bapaume and Péronne had they blown up or burned all the houses which were untouched by shell-fire, but in scores of villages they laid waste the cottages of poor peasants, their little farms and their orchards. In Bapaume and Péronne, in Roye, Nesle, and Lianecourt, in all places over a wide area, they not only blew out the fronts of houses, but with picks and axes smashed mirrors, furniture, and picture-frames. There was nothing but ruin and filth in Bapaume or Péronne. Family portraits had been kicked into gutters. Black bonnets belonging to old women who had lived in those houses lay about on rubbish heaps, almost the only signs left of inhabitants who had lived here before the Germans wrecked their homes.

That Germany intended to bleed northern France to the ruination point was the conclusion of Mr. Simms. Not only was every person capable of working driven back, and children, the aged and infirm left behind, but property, even that of the poorest civilians, was confiscated without promise to pay. One wrinkled-faced old woman told him she was forced to leave her home with nothing but the clothing she had on. The Germans had taken all her remaining garments. Other peasants told him the same thing. Fruit trees throughout the whole zone—those which were not wholly cut down—were so mutilated, the bark so cut, that they would perish. Agricultural implements which could not be removed were broken up with sledge-hammers or burned. Spokes of cart-wheels and other vehicles were sawed off. At the Château of Goyencourt the family chapel was violated. Metal was removed from coffins. One coffin was open exposing the foot of a corpse.

Another correspondent[7] said that in one place he visited more than three hundred women, children and aged men were known to have succumbed to exposure or starvation. In Chauny alone the victims numbered 150. They were buried, coffinless, in a corner of the village. Every one of the refugees with whom he talked declared that the greatest mortality resulted from a barbarous system of inspection which the Germans employed. Having been concentrated in great camps all the civilians were ordered to present themselves at a fixt date for final identification. Altho the

[7] Henry Wood of the United Press.

temperature ranged from zero to nine degrees below, every one was forced to enter an open square, the sick carried on stretchers, the exhausted and helpless borne by their less helpless friends. From six o'clock in the morning, the hour set for the inspection, these ill-clad, ill-nourished refugees were forced to wait in this freezing cold, without shelter, without food, for five or six hours before the German officers arrived. At Chauny, where 6,000 women, children, and aged men underwent such an ordeal, three died before the inspection was ended, and thirty the following night from pneumonia, lung-congestion, or pleurisy. On succeeding days the resulting deaths reached 150. This was true, not only of Chauny, but of other concentration centers—the number of deaths depending on the degree of cold and the length of exposure.

In larger towns in the path of the German retreat, such as Ham, Chauny and Tergnier, refugees said the destruction of houses and property had been going on for three weeks before the retreat actually began. Meantime the population was massed in the poorest districts. Often twenty or thirty persons were forced to occupy a single room, without heat and almost without food. Regular squads of soldiers systematically burned and dynamited houses in various parts of these towns. Moving vans carried off to Germany furniture and valuables. Ham, like Roye, was blown up during the night. The explosions and shocks terrified the civilians. They did not know that a wholesale destruction had been planned. When the detonations shook the town, they were huddled together and a panic ensued. They had been strictly forbidden to leave before morning the houses in which they were packed. When the dawn came and they emerged, they found the Germans gone. The mining of Roye, Ham, and other towns had been effected three weeks before the fuses were touched off. The miners worked only at night in order to avoid observation from Allied aviators.

Nothing made a greater impression along the devastated path of the retreat than the absolute lack of animal life. During a twenty-mile walk one could not see a cow, a horse, a pig, a chicken, or a rabbit. Every living animal had been killed, eaten or carried off by the Germans. Even in forests, denuded by the Germans, and in orchards, where they had ruined all the trees, one could not see a bird. All had apparently been forced to migrate elsewhere in search of food. Augmenting this impression of a stricken and scourged country were endless miles in the valleys of the Oise and Ailette, where the waters of canals had been used to flood the land, and so create great desolate areas, waveless and dead. Since the first German invasion no atrocity produced greater anger among French soldiers, who are 60 per cent. peasants and small farmers, than the hewing down of orchards by the Germans. Orchards require from twenty to fifty years to grow, so that it would take that long for this work of destruction to be replaced.

Mme. Alexis Carrel, wife of Dr. Carrel of the Rockefeller Institute, who was doing splendid service in French hospitals, reached Noyon twenty-four hours after the Germans left. She found that every woman between the ages of fourteen and thirty had been carried off nine days before the retreat began. People whom she saw crowded in cellars had hideous tales to tell. None of the French civil population had had any meat of any kind for seventeen months. They had lived on black bread and rice, and many had died in their struggle to keep alive. The mortality among children had been terrible. Bodies of those who had died had been kept for as many as five days unburied in the midst of the living. In an orphan asylum beds were kept so close together that they touched. Children had slept without mattresses, pillows or covering since December, all in their clothes, unwashed, unkempt and uncared for. No words could describe the filth of their condition. Wounded French were still in a hospital uncared for and reduced to the last gasp.

All over this country by roadside and in fields were graves of German dead. Here and there was to be seen one of their cemeteries, strong-walled with heavy blocks of stone, each grave with its big wooden headpiece, with a stone chapel built for burial service, and a monument in the center of all these dead. It was a memorial put up by Hessian troops in July, 1915, to men who had fallen on the field. In this graveyard one saw the deep respect paid by Germans to the dead—to the French dead as well as the German dead; but just a hundred yards away was another graveyard, the ancient cemetery of a little church within the grounds of the château, full of vaults and tombs where lay the dust of French citizens, men, women, and children, who died long before the horrors of this war. Here vaults had been opened by pickaxes, tombstones split across, graves exposed. Into these little houses of the dead rubbish had been flung. From one vault a coffin had been taken away. The church had

AFTER THE BLIGHT OF WAR HAD PASSED

been a little gem, with a tall pointed spire. It had been destroyed, not by shell-fire, but by an explosive charge placed there the day before the Germans went away. The spire had been flung down, one end of the church blown away, the sanctuary opened and reliquaries smashed. Statues of saints had been overturned and vestments of priests trampled and torn. In the village of Cremery, not far away, graves again had been opened in a churchyard. In the church relics of saints had been looted, in the sacristy fine old books of prayer and music lay torn and soiled on the floor.

Edith Wharton visited this devastated region in March

and described [8] how the havoc began soon after the Germans turned north from Compiègne. She found that the cruelties of the German retreat surpassed even those of the German invasion of 1914, "as greatly as the subtle tortures of Nero surpassed the cruelties of primitive warfare." Humble villages and isolated farmhouses had been destroyed for the mere joy of destroying. She had seen Ypres, Gerbevillers, Sermaize, Badonviller—all the towns from the North Sea to the Vosges whose extermination men shuddered over in the early days of the war, but those earlier ruins, senseless altho they were, were less dreadful. Many of the farm-houses had been blown up; not burned. Among fallen beams, splintered tiles, and twisted pipes, one searched in vain for any trace of furniture or domestic utensils. There was "not a fragment of a chair or bed, not a torn scrap of blanket, or sheet, or clothing," because, for a month beforehand the Germans had been busy systematically packing up and carrying away every movable article which these poor peasants possest.

Mrs. Wharton visited Appilly, Chauny, Villequier, Cuts, Roye, Lassigny and many villages, but in only one house did she see a fragment of a bed, and that was dangling through a gutted floor. Everywhere in the fields was the same systematic ruin. Near each destroyed house were ruined farming utensils, choked up wells and orchards with prostrate fruit trees. When there was no time to cut down trees the bark had been stript off, or a deep ring was hacked into the trunks. In one of the doomed valleys where were blackened farms, ruined orchards, and flooded fields, she came on a carefully tended German graveyard, above which was inscribed in conspicuous lettering, "I am the resurrection and the life." Elsewhere she saw similar German graveyards still untouched, significant in their showing of "the abyss in ideals that exists between the two races," since at Château Goyencourt the Germans had broken open and defiled a French family vault, at Nesle had torn up gravestones from the cemetery to build a platform for a heavy gun, in another village had uncovered all the graves and flung broken slabs in a heap among filth and refuse. Nowhere did Mrs. Whar-

[8] In The *Sun* (New York).

ton see a shrub uprooted or a stone displaced by the French in any of the garden-like German cemeteries. French reverence for the dead had extended "even to the dead of such an enemy."

The Germans asserted that their devastations were due to military necessity, that they had to destroy everything behind them to secure their retreat. Mrs. Wharton thought it did not take a military expert to see that the best way of securing the retreat would have been to blow up roads and bridges, instead of giving far more time to wrecking farmhouses, smashing plows, and hacking down fruit-trees. Aimless and vindictive cruelty was proclaimed in every slaughtered orchard, in every stack of shattered agricultural implements. The idea that cutting down fruit-trees and breaking up plows could check the progress of an advancing army was senseless so long as roads remained over which supplies could be pushed forward.

EDITH WHARTON

The damage to roads in the region she saw was "not a hundredth part of what it might have been, if the well-poisoners, tree-hackers and furniture-robbers had all been concentrated on the job."

By the end of March the French had taken Coucy-le-Château, about half-way between Soissons and Le Fère. Here the Germans committed their greatest piece of ruthless vandalism in the retreat. Coucy Castle, one of the most splendid surviving relics of the thirteenth century, was "utterly blasted from the face of the earth." [9] Nothing was left but a great pile of broken masonry and pulverized rock. Before they left the Germans had boasted to French inhabitants that thirty tons of explosives had been used to

[9] Henry Wood, United Press correspondent.

destroy the castle. Pieces of its ancient masonry were spread over 10,000 square yards. Not a vestige remained of the great tower. Coucy Castle long since had been set aside as a historical museum. One German gave as an explanation for its destruction "that it was not worth more than the life of a single German soldier" and that "there were plenty of such castles in southern Germany."

Coucy-le-Château was a village visited annually before the war by thousands of tourists, attracted by the castle. The great pile was dominated by a massive donjon 210 feet high and 100 feet in diameter, with walls 34 feet thick, a giant among feudal towers. Dating from the early part of the thirteenth century, it had been dismantled by order of Mazarin in 1652, and for some years it had been state property, open to visitors.

In announcing an evacuation of the Somme front and the Noyon angle, Germany, as if to forestall neutral criticism, sent an explanation of the proposed vandalism to America by wireless. It was issued as from some "higher German military authority," who described the vandalism as a war measure which Germany was compelled to take in order to carry out a military plan to meet the big offensive the Entente had planned. Nothing was destroyed "except out of military necessity." There was no wish to destroy homes, or other structures which offered no military advantage to the enemy. Germany had to make a battlefield out of the territory given up and "could leave nothing in the hands of the enemy." Hence the Germans "were forced to destroy roads, railroads, wells, buildings of value for military purposes, depots, even whole cities." The writer knew Germany "would be accused again of barbarism, but we are fighting for our existence."

On the last day of March the French Senate received an official report on the devastations in northern France, and adopted a resolution denouncing to the civilized world the acts of the Germans, demanding that the authors be punished and declaring for a continuance of the war until German imperialism and militarism were crusht. Germany, as a signatory of The Hague Conventions, had given a "guaranty against abuse of person or property," but this had been treated as a "scrap of paper." A member of the committee making the report said the committee had visited a number of cities and about fifty villages. Everywhere were pillage and systematic devastation. In a cemetery where was seen a German statue of Peace, a tomb had been violated, a coffin opened, emptied of its remains and filled with filth. The report accused the Germans of having committed "crimes against private property, public edifices, honor, liberty, and life." Acts of violence had been perpetrated "without any excuse of military necessity and with systematic disregard of the international convention of October 18, 1907, ratified by the representatives of the German Empire." So barbarous were these acts that the Senate doomed their authors to "a universal curse." [10]

[10] Principal Sources: The *Daily Chronicle* (London), The *Times*, The the National Geographic Society, The *Evening Sun*, The *Evening Post*, The *Tribune*, The *Sun*, New York; Associated Press dispatches, "Bulletins" of *Outlook*, New York; "Nelson's History of the War" by John Buchan.

II

THE BATTLE OF ARRAS, WITH VIMY RIDGE, AND LENS AS THE FIRST PHASE— CLANCY AND GENET

April 7, 1917—April 26, 1917

THE new German front, christened "the Hindenburg line," and along which in the autumn of 1918 was to be fought the decisive battle of the whole war, extended almost straight from Arras, before Cambrai and Le Catelet and east of St. Quentin, to the Oise, and thence to La Fère, and through the Forest of St. Gobain to the suburbs of Soissons. On this line the Germans expected to meet an attack, having reached positions on which they could make a stand. Allied strategy at once had to conform itself to the new situation created by the Germans. Before the German retreat began Haig and Nivelle had planned to strike on the old line, but now they could not attack there at least for several months. For an immediate offensive they had to attack either north or south of the two extremities of the new line. They chose for this attack the two pivots of the retiring German movement, which were the Vimy Ridge, north of Arras and the Craonne Plateau, east of Soissons, terrain over which the Germans had not yet spread the blight of devastation.

Operations of the character to be undertaken required very special transport preparations. Construction work, both of standard- and narrow-gage railways, had to be carried on to make the service adequate to army needs. Roads had to be improved or changed, and preparations made to carry them further forward as the troops advanced. In this work much use was made of plank roads, built chiefly of heavy beech slabs, laid side by side and capable of rapid construction over any kind of ground. Owing to these efforts accumulations of vast stocks of munitions and stores of all kinds, and their distribution to troops were made possible. Numberless other measures that had been resorted to the year before for the Somme offensive were revived with such improvements and additions as experience dictated. Nine months had elapsed since the battle of the Somme began. In

GENERAL MAUD'HUY IN A FIRST-LINE WESTERN TRENCH

the interval German artillerymen had made every effort which experience could suggest to render the wide barrier between the British and the plains of the Scheldt impregnable. Naval guns—the 24 c.m. with a range of 29,000 yards (or nearly 16 miles), had been brought up with a view to impeding by long-range fire the concentration of British troops. The range of field-guns had been increased to 9,000 yards. An improved machine-gun—the 08/15—had been served out lavishly, and an anti-tank gun, resembling a short-barreled 77 c.m. field-gun, mounted on two wheels with a narrow track, had been introduced.

In modern battles infantry frontal attacks were no longer possible against entrenchments. Every advance had become an affair of superior artillery, infantry being employed against demoralized garrisons after the guns had prepared the way. Guns, in numbers which, before the war, would have seemed fantastic, had been accumulated by the Allies—howitzers and field-guns, with bomb-proof cover trenches, wire-entanglements, trench-mortars hundreds in number, and liquid-fire shells. Thanks to ingenious ''camouflage'' and the courage of airmen, who kept off German aviators, the positions of the pieces were mostly hidden from observation. Vimy heights and the neighborhood had been reproduced for the British command on a plasticine model, where ridges, spurs, gullies, plateaux, trenches, roads, tracks, redoubts, craters, and wire-entanglements were shown in detail.

The Arras neighborhood had seen some of the bloodiest fighting of the war. There, in October, 1914, Maud'huy, through a desperate month, had beaten back Bülow's attempt to hew a way to the Channel. There, in May and June, 1915, D'Urbal and the French Tenth Army had battled in vain for the Vimy Heights. There, in September of the same year, during the battle of Loos, while a portion of the heights was won, the true crest was never gained, and during the succeeding month the British were forced back to the boggy valley of Souchez. The key to all this area was the Vimy Ridge, which dominated the British Souchez lines as the Messines Ridge dominated the southern part of the Ypres salient.

The city of Arras, situated as it was less than a mile inside the British lines, was destined to share the fate of Ypres. It was, like Ypres, the neck of the bottle, and through it and its environs went all the transport for the front between the Scarpe and the Cojeul. For two years it had been a place of comparative peace. It had been badly shelled, but mainly in the autumn and winter of 1914. The cathedral, a poor rococo edifice in the Palladian manner, had been wholly destroyed, and looked far nobler in its ruin than it had ever done in its integrity. The beautiful old Hôtel de Ville had been wrecked, and much damage had been done among exquisite Spanish houses in the Grande Place. Few buildings had altogether escaped. The place was now almost a desert. It was still a habitable, altho a desolated, city.

Entering it by the Baudimont Gate on a summer's day, the stranger saw a long white street running intact toward the railway station. It was not till he looked closer that he noted shell-marks, broken windows and other signs of war. Some hundreds of civilians were still living there, and occasionally children could be seen playing on the pavement. Visitors came often, for it was the easiest place in all France from which to enter the first lines. Across the railway in short walk in communication trenches, or even on the open road, a visitor could see the actual battle-front west of Blangy or in the faubourg of St. Sauveur. One inn at least was still open, where men could dine in comfort, and then proceed to their posts in the line. But the place had the air of a tomb, or a city stricken by a plague, whole yet tenantless. Especially eery did it seem in the winter twilight, when in long echoing streets the only sign of life was an occasional British soldier or a hurrying peasant woman. The rumble of guns beyond Vimy alone broke the silence. The gaunt ruins of the cathedral rose like a splendid headstone in a graveyard.

In two and a half years there had been fought in this war land-battles on a scale far outdistancing those of any other of the world's wars in numbers of men employed, use made of guns and ammunition, and territory covered, but now it could be said that there never had been such a battle in the air as one fought on April 7. Large squadrons of British airplanes were sent up over the German lines for the purpose of photographing new German positions and bombarding strategic points behind the front. These formations were flanked by other squadrons of fighting airplanes. Numerous battles took place. The British reported twenty-eight of their machines as missing, the greater part of which were shot down in combat behind the German line, while Berlin reported that forty-four Allied machines had been destroyed. The Germans lost fifteen airplanes and ten balloons. The British also drove to the ground thirty-one additional machines, a large proportion of which Haig reported "must have been totally destroyed." That the British accomplished their purpose—that of photographing and mapping the new German positions and the country behind the lines—was indicated by Haig's statement that large tracts of the enemy's country for many miles in the rear had been photographed, over 1,700 negatives being taken.

The bombing air squadrons were also successful in their regular day's work. Seventeen raids were carried out on German airdromes, ammunition depots and railways, over eight tons of bombs being dropt. Stupendous things were done in this battle. Two short years before, when aeroplanes were still in the experimental stage, no one but an imaginative inventor would have believed that squadrons of light airships, flying at speed exceeding 100 miles an hour, would scout in front of armies and meet in the shock of battle, disabling or destroying each other with guns mounted on their fabrics. As usual, British and German estimates of losses in the air did not agree, but the raid seemed beyond question to have been an Entente success. Eight tons of bombs were dropt by the raiders, who were well informed concerning the points to be attacked. As the negatives were developed and printed without loss of time, the British staff soon had a clear idea of the German defenses for miles back. Without this knowledge offensive operations would have been somewhat futile and there must have been a reversion to the trench deadlock.

The spring offensive of the Allies had begun; in fact, the great battle on the Arras-Lens front dated from this air-engagement. When Haig was ready with guns and men in position, before making an advance, he had learned from photographs exactly what was going on in the German rear. When British airmen came back to their lines with their 1,700 photographs, victory was assured. Artillery already in position opened fire, infantry moved forward on a ten-mile front, and war on the western front broke out once more in full swing. Artillery prepared a path for the attack by clearing away barbed-wire entanglements and smashing in concrete caissons. The curtain of fire was lifted just as the troops advanced. Steel-clad "tanks" lumbered out from Arras on radiating lines, pushed through barbed-wire barricades, scrambled over trenches and craters and wandered through village streets heedless of shrapnel and rifle-ball. Here the trenches were held by Bavarians, with Prussians kept in reserve, but the British guns placed a curtain of fire behind the front lines, so that, when the Bavarians sent up green rockets as signals of distress, no help could reach them from the rear, and when the Canadians reached them they surrendered with docility, begging first for their lives and next for bread. At the end of the first day the Canadians had captured three lines of entrenchments and 3,000 prisoners.

Widening the attacks on the retreating Germans, the British struck north, and in a series of assaults on a broad front, with Arras more or less the pivotal point, drove the Germans from important positions, and penetrated their lines. The number of prisoners taken in twelve hours exceeded 5,000. The heaviest fighting developed along a line a few miles southeast of Arras and in a direction northerly from the neighborhood of Lens, but the action extended far in the direction of St. Quentin. In the territory captured was Vimy Ridge. Back of the northern end of the ridge lie the principal coal-fields of France, which were still in the hands of the Germans.

A considerable part of the fighting here was done by Canadians, who had retained a footing on the ridge all winter, altho higher up on the ridge the Germans had been in possession. On either side of the Canadians were English and Scottish battalions. One position captured to the northeast of Arras was a sort of labyrinth of trenches enmeshed in multiple bands of wire called "the harp," because of its shape. Prisoners had declared this strong point to be practically unassailable, but the British took it and with it nearly a thousand prisoners. They also captured three German battalion commanders, who compared in rank with colonels in the British army. In only a few instances did the Germans put up a strong fight. The tanks were of great assistance to the infantry. At the same time aviators remained active and brought down seventeen German airplanes and two kite balloons with a loss of ten British machines.

The first day's success was far greater than what the British gained in the first day of the Somme offensive. They had penetrated two or three miles into the enemy's territory and everywhere had crumpled up German defenses. The fate of the German line was sealed when the Vimy Ridge fell before the Canadians; its whole right flank in this region then gave way. Telegraph Hill, Observation Ridge, Neuville Vitasse, the Harp, La Folie Farm, St. Laurent-Blangy— names familiar in the war news for two years—succumbed in quick succession as the British troops advanced behind the fire of the tanks. For mile after mile the offensive spread, until the German armies were in retreat along a twelve-mile stretch and were deserting their guns and surrendering. Before the week was over, the British had taken some 15,000 prisoners, 200 guns, and large stores of ammunition. Among the guns were eight of the 8-inch howitzers and twenty-eight of the 5.9-inch howitzers. Besides these, 250 machine-guns were taken. Many guns were still in working order and the shells stacked beside them were at once used against the retiring Germans. As soon as Vimy Ridge was taken, the British troops were able to overlook Lens and the coal-fields and factories that lie round about it.

The speed and power of the British assault, in what may probably be known in history as the battle of Arras, surprized the Germans so much that their usual retaliatory artillery-fire was neglible for two days. This was partly due to the number of guns captured, to which had to be added the number knocked out by British artillery before the assault began. It was also due to the fact that the Germans had been too busy getting their guns away from immediate danger to think about firing them at the enemy. In a German artillery position east of Arras, known as Battery Valley, could be seen the remains of twenty-four field-pieces.

Philip Gibbs [11] saw the beginning of this offensive, when "all the sky was on fire with it, the most tragic and

---

[11] Correspondent of The *Daily Chronicle* (London) and of The *Times* (New York).

© UNDERWOOD & UNDERWOOD. BRITISH OFFICIAL PHOTO.

AFTER VIMY RIDGE WAS TAKEN

After the Canadians had completed their victory on April 9, 1917, this
picture of a part of the field was taken

351

frightful sight that men have ever seen, with infernal splendor beyond words." The bombardment before the infantry assault lasted several days, and when it finally reached a great height men smiled with a kind of tragic irony because it was Easter Sunday. In little villages behind the battle-lines the bells of French churches were ringing gladly. On the altar-steps priests were reciting splendid words of faith such as *"Resurrexi et adhuc tecum sum, Alleluia!"* For the first time since the autumn before the sun now had a touch of warmth in it, altho patches of snow still remained. The sky was blue and the light glinted on wet tree-trunks and in furrows of new plowed earth. From the British side went out a great bombardment all along the Vimy Ridge, above Neuville-St. Vaast, sweeping around St. Nicholas and Blagny, two suburbs of Arras, and then southwest of the city on the ridge about the road to Cambrai. It was "one continuous roar of death." There was one figure in the landscape which made officers smile. A French plowman was upholding the tradition of war in his locality. As Zola saw such a man in the War of 1870, so Mr. Gibbs saw one on the edge of this battlefield, driving a pair of sturdy brown horses with plow across a sloping field, "not a furlough from a village where German shells were raising a rosy cloud of brick-dust."

Behind the front of battle there was great traffic. All that modern warfare means in organization and in preparation for an enormous operation was in movement. Mr. Gibbs had just come from British outpost-lines further south, "from the silence of that great desert which the enemy had left in the wake of his retreat east of Bapaume and Péronne." Round about Arras he saw concentration for the old form of battle, attacks upon entrenched positions, fortified hills, and great natural fortresses defended by masses as in the battles on the Somme. For miles along the way were great camps and stores, and restless activity. Supply-columns of food for men and guns were going forward in an endless tide with transport mules in long trails. Field-batteries were going up to add to the mass of metal poured on German lines. It was "a vast circus of the world's great war" in which everything that belongs to the machinery of killing streamed on and on. In ambulances were seen army-nurses to whom men, marching on the roads, waved their hands, and who laughed and waved back greetings "which made one's heart go soft awhile." In fields by the roadside men were lying on the earth between spells of long marching, or were encamped, clean-shaven, gray-eyed, young and splendid to see. Some of them sat between stacked rifles and were writing letters home, but the tide of traffic "passed them by and flowed on to the edge of the battlefield."

Vimy Ridge was important because, on that part of the line, it was the last high ground between the rolling country of western France and the open plain of Artois and Flanders. From its crest is a clear view with no natural obstacle, not only of Lens with its surrounding coal-mines, but of Douai and open country as far as Lille, Cambrai, and the Low Countries. Foch had tried to take it in September, 1915, simultaneously with the British attack north of Lens and the French blow in Champagne, and had succeeded in carrying Souchez, Vimy Ridge, the village of Thélus and Telegraph Hill, but at such terrific cost—it was reported that the French suffered 100,000 casualties—that they could not hold them. Successive German counterattacks drove them from the ridge and back nearly two miles to Neuville-St. Vaast. It was this ridge, 450 feet high at its highest point, that the British now stormed, successfully. In September, 1915, the French attacked on a front of about five miles; in the present offensive the British advanced on a twelve-mile front, taking more territory in a single day than Foch had been able to secure two years before in two months.

During the night of April 6-7, British troops gained a number of points between Selency and Jeancourt, two and six miles respectively northwest of St. Quentin and nearer to Arras. During the following night they made progress on a front of 3,000 yards north of Louveral on the Bapaume-Cambrai road. The result of these operations showed Haig that there was no likelihood of disturbance from any counterattack by Hindenburg over the devastated region, and they served to divert the attention of the latter from the real point of attack. For a brief interval the bombardment by the British guns ceased; there was some speculation as to what was going to happen. Suddenly all doubts were set at rest.

The amphitheater of hills and fields behind Arras, the chalky heights captured by the French in the battle of Artois and Vimy, burst into flames. Myriads of shells swept overhead, and some seconds later the ears of the onlookers were deafened by the wave of sound set up by the discharge of guns from behind and the explosions of shells descending on the German lines. To all this was added the explosion of mines, mingled with huge spurts of blood-red flame, which hurled upward tons of earth and masonry into the air. So violent was the uproar that the rattle of the field-guns and the ceaseless rat-a-tat of the machine-guns were scarcely audible. The reports of the heavy guns shook the walls of the tunnels and caves below Arras from which troops were pouring to the assault. Above the flashing turmoil of bursting shells and mines, German rockets shot up, discharging red, white, green, and orange colored stars, telling those in the rear that the long-expected attack had been begun and asking for supports to meet it and for the protecting barrage. To add to the deadliness of shell-fire, the British were hurling their latest death-dealing invention—cylinders of liquid fire—into the German trenches.

The condition of the heights, at 5.30 A.M. on Easter Monday, when the Canadian Corps and British troops on their left and right advanced to storm them, was a striking example of the devastation of war. The woods had been reduced to splinters, the barbed-wire entanglements had been torn to pieces, and the thin covering of soil on which they stood churned up and blended with the chalk below it. Buildings had been obliterated, dugouts battered in, while the ground resembled frozen earth-waves rather than its once even surface. Nowhere was progress possible in a straight line so cut up was the earth with shell-holes and mine-craters filled to the brim with chalky water.

By April 13 the Vimy Ridge, with its western, northern, eastern and southern slopes, was securely within British lines. The Canadians had had one of the hardest bits of the front to contend with and yet they obtained complete occupation of the ridge, whence they now looked down over the plain of Douai. With Vimy Ridge gone the whole German line covering French towns and industrial districts to the north became a wavering one, and any leisurely retreat the Germans may have planned was rendered uncertain and precarious. With the capture of the ridge, the British made a considerable stride along the road to Douai, and at the same time by the capture of high ground northwest of St. Quentin, tightened the chain which they and the French were drawing around that town. Some 150 officers were among the German prisoners taken, these including five battalion-commanders. The weather was bitterly cold, with snow flurries, but the British were clad in sheepskins and were well fed. It was under blinding snow-squalls, with intermittent flashes of sunshine, that they pushed on. Snow was blowing gustily across the battlefield and powdering caps and helmets when the troops rode or marched forward to the front. But presently the sunlight broke through the clouds and flooded all the countryside by Neuville-St. Vaast, Thélus, and La Folíe Farm up to the crest of the ridge where the Canadians had just fought their way. The British batteries were firing from many hiding-places, revealed by short, sharp flashes of light. Few answering shells came back. The ridge itself, patched with snowdrifts, was quiet. Not a single German stayed on the ridge out of all those who had so long held it.

The Canadian attack was carried out by the victors of

CAPTURED BRITISH TANK SHOWN IN BERLIN

Courcelette in the battle of the Somme. They went out at dawn, cheering and laughing, through mud and rain, and followed close and warily to the barrage of the British guns, the most stupendous line of fire ever seen. By 6.30 they had taken their first goals, which included the whole front line system of German trenches above Neuville-St. Vaast, by La Folie Farm and La Folie Wood, and up by Thélus, where they met with fierce resistance. The German garrisons were for the most part in long, deep tunnels pierced through the hill. There were hundreds of ditches in Prinz Arnault Tunnel and hundreds more in the great Volker Tunnel, but as the Canadians surged up to them with wave after wave of bayonets, the Germans came forward with hands up.

Every American felt a thrill of admiration at the achievement of the Canadian troops. Nor could they forget that some thousands of citizens of the United States, serving under the flag of a nation now for seven days allied to them in the struggle against a common enemy, shared in the exploit. It was just a week before the taking of the ridge that the resolution of Congress declaring war on Germany was signed by President Wilson. The Canadian fight at the Ypres salient, almost exactly two years before, had been too little appreciated. Rarely in history had volunteer troops, suddenly exposed to a flank attack through no fault of their own, but by the collapse of their neighbors, borne a more terrific blow than that which followed the first gas-attack at Ypres. Yet, in the midst of confusion, assailed by poison, Canadian volunteers stood and died as the British regulars had stood and died in the greater battle of Ypres, in 1914. And now the Canadians had swept up the same Vimy Ridge, which in 1915 had halted the French veterans of Foch, proving itself too great an obstacle even for the finest offensive fighting genius France produced in the war. So it was that in 1917, after long months of waiting, the Canadians had their "crowded hour of glorious life."

Once more in this episode was dissipated a German dream. Early in the war Germans had promised the downfall of the British Empire. Their spies had labored in South

Africa, in Australia and New Zealand, in Canada, and in India, and the Bernhardis had forecast the collapse of the great empire under attacks from German armies and fleets and a secession of British colonies. The answer of India came early in the war, when an Indian corps was arrayed with the British Expeditionary Force in Flanders; New Zealand seized Samoa, August 29, 1914; Canada spoke at Ypres in the spring of 1915, Australia at Gallipoli in the summer, South Africa, first in German Southwest Africa in the con-

BRITISH OFFICIAL PHOTO.

DISTRIBUTING CIGARETS AT THE FRONT

quest of that German colony in July, 1915, and then in German East Africa, where the last fragment of German colonial power finally collapsed under the pressure of South African and Indian troops December 1, 1917. Bagdad, captured in March, 1917, was an achievement of Indian troops. In seeking to destroy an empire the Germans had only consolidated one.

Nearly three-quarters of a million of Canadian and Australian troops had responded to the call of the British Empire, more than half of them wearing the Canadian maple leaf. Praise of the Canadians and Australians was written even in home letters of German soldiers captured at the front, and found its way into the official reports of German officers. Among the Canadians a considerable contingent of citizens of the United States were an unofficial vanguard of that American army which, in the fulness of time, was to take its place along the French front. Canada had sent across the ocean an army greater than Napoleon ever commanded on any battlefield; her volunteer regiments had shown that stubborn and tenacious quality which was the inheritance of the British army; they had revealed also a dash and fury of attack, an initiative and resourcefulness, which recalled the armies which fought in our Civil War. A democratic army, an army of citizens going voluntarily to the battle-front beyond the seas, waiting neither for the appeal nor the demand of the mother country, had thrust a wedge into the defenses of autocracy and won for liberty, not merely a few square miles of French territory, but a victory which made answer to the German idea that the world could be reconstructed by material forces alone.

The Stars and Stripes went into battle for the first time during this war, at the storming of Vimy Ridge, when to a young man from Texas came the honor of carrying the first American flag into the fight. When, in April, 1917, the United States declared war, his regiment was chosen to form part of the first wave of men that were to storm Vimy Ridge. As the regiment started he took out his flag and tied it to his bayonet. In this way the Germans had a first view of their newest enemy a few days after our declaration of "a state of war." The Texas boy carried his flag to the very front, but in the assault on Thélus, near the southern end of the ridge, he fell with a bullet through his body and was sent to a hospital. William Clancy was his name. Clancy was born in Boston, and lived when young with his grandmother in Ipswich, but he had lived for some time in Texas working on a railroad at Hearne. Of this exploit Clancy wrote in a letter home:[12]

"There were some awful sights. One young fellow got hit with a

[12] Printed in The Houston *Post* (Texas).

piece of shell. He asked me to remember him to all his people in Newark, New Jersey. The last words he said were: 'Bill Clancy, I am glad I gave my life for the freedom of the world.' He died in my arms. So I let him lie, but just before he died he kissed my flag. 'Old Glory,' he said. And I told him: 'Yes, Old Glory, and new glory, too.' Poor chap, I did not see him any more for when I went forward again under heavy fire I met my accident. Old Fritz sent a shell over and it struck near me, blowing up some of the ammunition. Of course, I can only remember now that I was being dug out from a trench where I was buried alive. Now I am in England and have about recovered from the effects. I am waiting to be transferred to the American army."

Clancy was in Paris when the war started in 1914 and immediately started for England, where at Liverpool he enlisted in the Royal Field Artillery. After spending the winter in an English training cantonment he proceeded to France with his regiment in March, 1915, and was soon in action for the first time. At Neuve Chapelle he was wounded in the head by shrapnel splinters. He was in the hospital six weeks, but was back in action in time to have a part in the taking of the Hohenzollern redoubt. He also fought in the battle of the Somme where he was again wounded, this time in the head, hands, and shoulders. In September following he was with his company, and while going to the relief of the hard-prest Cornwalls for a third time fell a victim to German marksmanship.

Another American, Edmont Charles Clinton Genet, an aviator at the front in France, was killed on April 17. Genet was the first American to die in France fighting under the American flag. He was killed near Ham, while escorting Sergeant Raoul Lufberry over the German lines, the two being attacked by German aircraft. Lufberry escaped, but Genet's machine was riddled and he was killed. His body was recovered in a French advance. As soon as Genet learned that the United States had entered the war he had raised the Stars and Stripes over his plane. He had been known as a daring flier and was popular on account of a cheery and optimistic nature. He had fought in the French Foreign Legion for two years, had been wounded in the Champagne in October, 1915. Genet was a great-great-grandson of Governor George Clinton of New York, and a great-grandson of the once famous Citizen Genet, minister from France to the United States in 1793, who was recalled afterward by France at the request of Washington. A month before his death Genet had been wounded when making a reconnaissance over the Somme line with another member of the corps, James R. McConnell. Flying high, he was guarding McConnell, who was flying low to make observations, when the pair were attacked by two German aviators. Genet was slightly wounded in the face and the blood in his eyes forced him to come down, altho he managed to land inside the French lines; but McConnell was never heard from again.

With the fall of Vimy Ridge the German line south seemed to crumple up and fall back. The pressure from several directions was more than the Germans could stand. One place after another fell into British hands, the bulge in the line growing deeper and deeper. The Germans were even unable to get their horse-artillery away, somewhat more than 150 guns, varying from three inches to nine inches, being taken. This in itself was sufficient indication of the speed and the effectiveness with which the British went forward.

A heavy snow that was falling all the next day greatly impeded operations by rendering observations by the air-service impossible. Notwithstanding these conditions, the British captured the village and heights of Monchy-le-Preux, five miles east of Arras, and the hamlet of La Bergère near by. Later in the same day the Germans made two strong counter-attacks in the neighborhood of Monchy, but were driven off. On the southern leg of this new salient they met strong forces of Germans and were compelled to fall back on their own lines. The storm, accompanied by snow, rain and sleet and a gale which seldom fell below forty miles an hour, continued for days, with occasional bits of sunshine lasting less than half an hour. Night temperatures were well below freezing. It was not until large numbers of British field-batteries were brought into play that the Germans were definitely beaten off. During the fighting British airplanes hovered above Monchy and cavalry helped, splendid bodies of men riding at a gallop in a snowstorm

© UNDERWOOD & UNDERWOOD, N. Y. GERMAN PRISONERS CAPTURED ON THE WESTERN FRONT

III.

which covered them with white mantles and crowned their steel hats. Many cavalrymen were afterward carried back wounded and many gallant horses lay dead. Horses that came back were caked with mud and walked with drooping heads, exhausted in every limb. After the cavalry had ridden into Monchy and captured the north side of the village, the enemy fled. Few Germans were seen, as they had retreated to the southern side in order to escape that way. The Germans had many machine-guns and some few defended themselves from the windows and roofs of houses, firing down upon the British. It was a house-to-house hunt. About 200 prisoners were taken, others having fled.

The taking of Monchy-le-Preux was aided by a tank. When the British infantry reached the village, German machine-guns posted there needed special attention before an attack could be made. So, digging themselves in, the "Tommies" watched through the night, and early the next day artillery was turned against the machine-gun emplacements, while a tank circled the town, scattering terror and death. When its work was completed infantry sprang forward from shallow trenches and charged in a sort of circling movement, meeting with little opposition. The tanks did splendidly all through the attack. German guns intended especially as "anti-tank" weapons were captured. One cavalry corps charged two big German howitzers in the open, sabered or captured the crews, and took the guns. A German motor-transport column was captured intact.

The tanks were regarded as on the whole a success in the battle of Arras. Germans claimed to have destroyed nine of them, and it was true that a few of them lay stranded about the battlefield, but they saved hundreds, perhaps thousands, of lives and won strong places. Their successes vastly outweighed their failures. The critical point of the whole Arras battle was Monchy-le-Preux, which lies five miles southeast of Arras. Further north, along the Vimy Ridge, the British, having secured commanding positions overlooking Lens and the plain of Douai, consolidated their gains, but in the new and narrow salient created in the German line by the British capture of Monchy-le-Preux, the British gave a threat to the flank of the whole German line to the southeast, facing the British advance on the front as far as St. Quentin in the general direction of Cambrai.

When Hindenburg retreated from the Somme and from Arras, he perhaps intended to strike at Russia. He conducted the retreat successfully, but just as it came to an end the British struck him at Arras. The retreat, as Germans said, was made for the purpose of "disarranging the enemy's plans," but the British attack at Arras was made for the purpose of disarranging Hindenburg's plan. Of these two

GERMAN DUGOUTS THIRTY FEET DEEP

ways of disarranging an adversary's plans—one by retiring and the other by attacking—the retreating method employed by the Germans had not been successful, while the attacking method employed by the British meanwhile had filled all Great Britain with joy. Hindenburg had drawn back one fist, as if intending to lunge at his adversary with the other, but before he could do that, the British hit him square in the face. The blow at Arras was not wholly a surprize to the Germans. They had expected it for some time, but it came too soon for them to repel it and it sent them staggering.

GERMAN RETREAT; ARRAS AND THE AISNE

The Germans thus far had conducted no real "strategic retreat to victory." The Kaiser could send no congratulations to Hindenburg for a victorious retirement. In one day's fight the British had taken 9,000 prisoners and more than forty guns, a figure which later was increased to more than 11,000 prisoners and over 100 guns, and later still to a total of 13,000. The Germans could not fight now as well as the British. A deterioration in their morale had been noted toward the close of the four months' Somme battle.

GERMAN TRENCHES UNDER SHELL-FIRE

The battle of Arras offered further proof of the futility of militarism in the long run. Instead of proceeding cautiously, the French when the Noyon salient was broken, had dashed on and the British had forged steadily ahead from Arras. The German argument that the plans for a spring offensive by the enemy had been "knocked into a cocked hat" by the strategic withdrawal of the Germans from the Somme seemed by this time to have collapsed completely.

The Franco-British army had become a machine that was unexcelled even by that of those German legions who poured into France in the first month of the war. In fact, German efficiency had been outdone. The secret was that the superior initiative of the units composing the Allied armies, when brought under rigid discipline and sedulously trained, produced a more formidable fighting force than the Germans had ever put into the field since the war began. The French and British were also better rationed at this time and probably better equipped in material, including artillery and high-power shells. It was doubted whether the world had ever seen finer infantry than the citizen soldiers of France and the British Empire who were now driving the Germans back.

The German prisoners were of all sizes, ages, and types, "elderly bewhiskered men with big spectacles belonging to the professor tribe, and young lads who ought to have been in the German high-schools." Some of their faces "looked very wizened and small beneath their great shrapnel helmets." Many looked ill and starved, but others were tall, stout, hefty fellows. Some had been without food for four days, because the British gun-fire had boxed them in. "When do you think the war will end?" asked one of them. "When the British are in Berlin," was the answer. "What about America?" the German was asked. He shrugged his shoulders and said: "America can't send an army across the ocean." At this the Canadian soldiers laughed loudly and answered: "Don't you believe it. We came across the ocean to fight you and the Yankees will do the same."[13]

Crowded cages holding prisoners at corps and divisional headquarters became a source of great interest to the "Tommies," when waiting for their turn at the front. Gathering around a circle of barbed wire, they would converse with such Germans as were able to speak English. Among the number might be waiters who had been employed in English hotels, and who would anxiously inquire how things were going in London, or ask seriously if the Zeppelins had left "any visible signs remaining of the city." Loud laughter would follow some of these queries. Many prisoners tossed out empty water-bottles, which the British refilled and flung back to them. There were also exchanges of souvenirs.

[13] Philip Gibbs in The *Daily Chronicle* (London) and in The *Times* (New York).

With the retirement—only temporary, as later events so memorably showed, and perhaps not an actual retirement so much as a release from command at the front to do pressing service in Italy and elsewhere—of Foch from active service early in April, seemed to go the last of outstanding figures to whom France and the world owed the victory of the Marne and the frustration of German hopes. It would long continue to be debated whether the principal credit for the Marne, after Joffre, should go to Foch, who broke the German center in the marshes of St. Gond; to Maunoury, who threw himself on the German right flank on the Ourcq and so forced the dislocation in the enemy line and gave Foch his opportunity; or to Castlenau, who had beaten off the Kaiser's armies from Nancy and, by holding the line of eastern fortifications, gave Joffre the necessary breathing spell. Joffre, Maunoury, and Foch were now all in retirement, and Castlenau's activities seemed restricted to a military and diplomatic mission which had taken him to Petrograd on the eve of the revolution. Joffre was soon to make his memorable visit to the United States.

One of the most striking incidents of this fighting was the rout of the Germans at Langnicourt on April 19 after what they had believed would be a successful attack. Running for their own trenches, which were part of the Hindenburg line, they were trapt by barbed-wire entanglements which had been built with great strength and thickness in front of them. The strength of the Hindenburg line had been its belts of protective wire. Caught now within the meshes of this wire, the German guardsmen screamed madly for help and guidance. Some, like trapt rabbits, scurried up and down the outer barrier, searching in vain for openings. The British meantime had their greatest opportunity for open field rifle-shooting since the battle of the Marne. Lying flat upon the ground they poured bullets into the panic-stricken gray-coated Germans until each man had fired a full 100 rounds. While this was going on, British field-guns came into play with a shrapnel barrage, which completed the demolition of the entrapt enemy and 1,500 German dead lay on the ground while 400 guardsmen with hands up surrendered with emotional cries of *"Kamerad."*

In six months on the Somme the British and French together took at least 75,000 prisoners and upward of 150 square miles of territory, the harvest of half a year, won at a price that was staggering. In the battle of Arras, in the first week, the British advanced an average of four miles on a front of twelve, and in the center at least six miles in six days, as contrasted with six miles in six months on the Somme. That was the real measure of the German disaster in 1917, and the British had taken not less than 15,000 prisoners. Above all, they had shown complete superiority over the Germans in artillery, in organization, and in the semi-open warfare that followed the first dash. Any considerable further British advance beyond Douai, for example, which was only ten miles from the British front, would have meant that the Germans would have had to retire on their whole front from the North Sea to the Meuse River, and retire under pressure rapidly when exposed to all the perils of a forced retreat. The battle of Arras almost seemed at one time as if it might prove the decisive battle of the war—the battle which liberated France. It had unmistakably disclosed weakness in the German morale and difficulty in German organization hitherto believed to be impossible. One success after another followed the device of working round the north and south of a town and shelling it furiously until nothing remained for the Germans but a precipitate retreat to the next defensive position. The German morale suffered with every experience of this sort, and the faith of British infantry in their own superiority rose in proportion until they considered themselves invincible, which was 90 per cent. of victory.

A trip over the newly taken lines revealed a condition of trenches closely approximating those evacuated by the Germans on the Somme. Many dugouts still had damaged portals, but the trenches themselves, including all communication lines, had been unmercifully battered. So successful was the artillery barrier set up by the British that prisoners reported they had been without food for four days. Barbed-wire entanglements were obliterated. Only stray strands could be seen here and there on the first line. The zest of offensive warfare could be felt in all parts of the British front. Troops were swinging forward with bands playing. Scotch troops, behind their pipers, were particularly picturesque, for not even the vicissitudes of nearly three years of war had caused them to discard their kilts. Out over newly won ground airplanes were scouting, while below were tanks at rest. Two and a half years after initial defeats the British had now won, unaided, their greatest victory in the war, and purely as a result of success in training new armies and making new guns. The whole aspect of the western war had changed. Arras was the finishing stroke of the Somme.

The battle of Arras, in the opinion of the German press, was an event of only local importance—lamentable, it was true, but already brought to a standstill and not affecting in any degree the strategic situation. It was interpreted by general consent as part of the plan of the Anglo-French command already foiled in its intentions of delivering a shattering blow on the Somme front, and now aiming to roll up the new "Hindenburg line" by assaults on both flanks—at Soissons and Arras. Both attempts were described as failures despite regrettable German losses in men and probably guns. An interview with Hindenburg by a Spanish war-correspondent, featured by the German press, shared in headline rank a place with the battle of Arras. Hindenburg avowed his confidence in the strength of the German fronts on the west and east and exprest a conviction that the submarine campaign would not fail. The interview had an effect on German public opinion and was intended to do so, now that another German loan was seeking subscribers. The field-marshal still bulked large as a confidence-inspiring hero. The interview was obviously intended to counteract any feeling of discouragement at home at the growing dimensions of what *Vorwärts* termed "a world league for the destruction of Germany."

After Péronne was taken, Cambrai became one of the important objectives in the Allied line of advance. This town is 121 miles by rail northeast of Paris, twenty miles southeast of Arras and about the same distance north of St. Quentin. Cambrai had a population approaching 30,000 before the war, and was one of the most interesting towns in northern France. Situated on the right bank of the Scheldt at its juncture with the St. Quentin Canal, it enjoyed considerable commercial prosperity on account of its soap-works, sugar-mills, and textile factories. Its importance to France now was sentimental rather than strategic. The event connected with Cambrai which commended it to womankind throughout the Western World was the invention here, in the fifteenth century, of the fine linen fabric which takes its name from the town—cambric, originally spelled "cameryk" from Kameryk, the Flemish name of Cambrai.

Meanwhile the French on the Aisne and east of Reims were carrying out an offensive almost identical with that of the British about Lens and Arras. In purpose the two operations aimed to break down the German defense at a point where the permanent German trench-lines merged into the "Hindenburg line." British and French each applied their maximum artillery and infantry pressure on a wide front. The British went forward against Vimy Ridge and trenches east of Arras on April 9, but the French did not storm the heights about Craonne and the lines near Reims until the 16th. The operations, however, were considered a single great offensive. They were directed against both wings of the German position. An offensive at the same time was maintained along the intervening front, so that the Allies were conducting a general offensive from Loos in the northwest to Auberive, on a front of at least 130 miles. This battle was waged with the greatest intensity which war preparations permitted along sections aggregating over forty miles.

By April 18 the Germans were apparently hemmed in, almost beyond further defense, in Lens and St. Quentin. They had been driven out of their trench-front to a depth of two miles or more along some forty miles of front, with a loss of about 30,000 prisoners and proportionate casualties in killed and wounded. They had been thwarted in each and every one of several attempts to retake ground and their artillery-munition supplies had shown signs of giving out in one or two places. It was now necessary for them either to fight with weakened forces and exhausted reserves in unfavorable positions, or to prolong the retirement of March and extend it greatly on either flank.

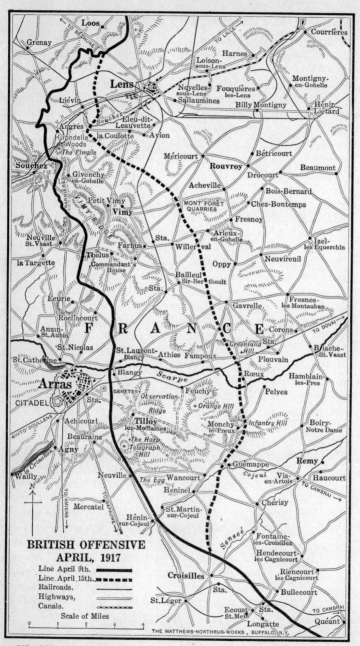

**BRITISH OFFENSIVE
APRIL, 1917**

Line April 9th.
Line April 15th.
Railroads,
Highways,
Canals.

Scale of Miles

0   1   2   3   4

THE MATTHEWS-NORTHRUP WORKS, BUFFALO, N.Y.

GERMAN RETREAT; ARRAS AND THE AISNE

By April 23 British preparation for another blow at the "Hindenburg line" and Lens neared a climax, just as the French offensive was temporarily dying down. Toward the western and northwestern outskirts of the big coal city Haig's troops pushed forward, capturing prisoners and machine-guns. Later in the day they engaged in a sharp fight with the Germans southeast of Loos, pushed down a wedge to the rear of the city, gained ground and captured more prisoners. The artillery fighting increased to "extreme violence" in the Arras and Lens region. British troops

BRITISH OFFICIAL·PHOTO.

RUINS OF A VILLAGE IN ARTOIS

were observed to be moving behind their lines and British aviators were active again, the weather having improved. They brought down eleven German machines in one day, losing four, after much fighting. Ineffectual German counter-attacks were made. Over a wide front on both sides of the river Haig resumed the drive. "We attacked at dawn this morning on both banks of the Scarpe and made satisfactory progress," he reported. "South of the Bapaume-Cambrai road we captured the remainder of the village of Trescault and at night gained the greater part of the Havrincourt Wood." While the French were making a terrific assault on the Soissons-Auberive front, the British seized the time to consolidate positions they had won in the first drive and during the week more or less confined their offensive to smashing drives suddenly executed at scattered points.

On April 23 the British Royal Flying Corps established a new record by bringing down forty German machines, fifteen of which were actually seen to crash, while twenty-five collapsed or fell in spinning nose-dives, completely out of control. The fights took place 15,000 feet, or nearly three miles up, from which distance it is barely possible to see the ground, and wholly impossible to see an adversary crash unless the pilot deliberately follows an adversary down. Such a course was not feasible where the fighting had taken on the character of a general *mêlée*. A remarkable part of the performance of April 23 was that after it only two British machines were missing. For two days the British airmen had been revelling in weather they had long desired. Hardly a cloud, behind which a German could find shelter, was in the sky. Deprived of that means of "digging themselves in," German fliers were scarcer than usual and difficult to find. Everywhere along the battle-front British machines were able to go far behind the German lines. Bombing raids were carried back forty-five miles, machines deliberately flying over ground where battles were raging with the greatest fury. German trains rushing reinforcements to the front were attacked from planes, and transport columns on the roads bombed and disorganized. In several instances British machines, descending low over the fighting lines, poured machine-gun fire into the German ranks.

The greatest fight was a drawn battle. For a full hour the two maneuvered in a marvelous manner without either being able to bring his gun to bear on the other. They rolled, looped, twisted, deliberately stalled their engines and, standing the machines on their tails, slid backward through the air, but all to no avail. It was described as probably the most wonderful air-duel the war had seen. The British pilot reported that several times he felt sure he would get his adversary between his sights, but the latter invariably wriggled out of the line of fire. The British flier himself was kept busy avoiding the German, and once had to dive almost perpendicularly. The combat did not break off until both planes had fairly exhausted themselves and their petrol.

At the close of two days' fighting, which observers asserted were the fiercest yet seen in the war, the British on the Arras front not only held against counter-attacks every important position gained, but had advanced at various points on a four-mile front south of the Scarpe. Simultaneously south of the Arras front a separate night attack turned the Germans out of their trenches on a wide front, giving the British worth-while places, one of them being the village of Beaucamp, and reaching the western bank of the St. Quentin Canal. In the two days' fighting more than 2,000 prisoners were known to have been captured and there were more uncounted. The fighting placed the British only a few hundred yards from the villages of Fountaine-les-Croisilles and Chérisy, outer defenses of the "Wotan line," at the point of its junction with the main "Hindenburg line" near Quéant. More ground beyond the Monchy ridge was gained, and near Rœux, on the Scarpe, the British made progress. Two violent German efforts to recapture Gavrelle, north of the Scarpe, were frustrated by artillery, machine-guns and rifle-fire. Haig's troops reached the St. Quentin Canal near Vendhuille, only two miles west of the railroad junction of Le Catelet, the midpoint between St. Quentin and Cambrai.

Part of the Allied strategy had been those alternating attacks that had been conducted by the British and French. It was when Haig stopt to take breath after the conquest of Vimy that the French began the battle of the Aisne. When Nivelle was slowing down on the Aisne, Haig began the fight again in the north, and in three days between Hulluch and Lens was seen the most gigantic infantry effort ever made by the British. All accounts agreed that the battle had become a slaughter and that thousands of German and British dead covered the field. The great British effort had not been in vain, for the British total of prisoners was now 3,029, of whom fifty-six were officers. Two field-guns besides many machine-guns had been captured. In an attack toward Cambrai the British took the little hamlet of Bithem, near

Havrincourt Wood. Hindenburg's new tactics of throwing his troops forward in unceasing counter-attacks regardless of life had been extremely costly. The British, however, suffered more heavily than an attacking force ordinarily suffers. In twenty-four hours the Germans threw eight separate counter-attacks against Gavrelle, in some of which 5,000 or 6,000 men were employed. Some were broken up by the British guns almost before they began; others, in which the slaughter was more terrible, crossed a considerable space of open ground before coming under artillery-fire, when whole battalions would seem to be blown to bits. The slaughter was so terrible that it amounted almost to a massacre, but the Germans had not abandoned hope of retaking lost ground and to that end were bringing up fresh battalions. Some of the best troops from other parts of the German lines in the west were being unloaded from crowded troop-trains in the area between Douai and Cambrai. Among these were the Württemburgers and the Fourth Division of the Prussian Guards.

Monchy-les-Preux, five miles east of Arras, will stand out in history as one of the bloodiest spots in the world-war. The fighting north, east, and south of this little Artois village, perched upon a high knoll, had exceeded in intensity any of the individual struggles of the Somme. The ground around Monchy, as far as the eye could reach, was covered with dead, the Germans at times having employed their old tactics of attacking in mass formation. Letters taken from German prisoners, written in front of Monchy, said they regarded the situation as worse than it was on the Somme, while the casualties were mounting up as at Verdun. Finding Monchy too difficult, the Germans directed a counter-attack on Gavrelle. Four thousand men formed for attack at a distance of 4,000 yards. British field-guns, massed in great number, were trained on the Germans, but their fire was held until the advancing enemy was about 2,000 yards away. Then a perfect hurricane of fire was opened and shrapnel shells played about the advancing column like fire-flies in a summer thicket. The oncoming waves trembled for a time and then broke, their path strewn with dead and wounded. On April 26 Haig was able to announce a "complete repulse of a violent massed counter-attack by German forces against new British positions around Gavrelle."

Germany was now suffering probably her most appalling losses of the war in desperate endeavors to stop the British drive by sheer weight of human masses. North of the Scarpe River, where the British fought ahead almost inch by inch in the face of great masses of men, the carnage was greater than ever before suffered by Germans since the war started. The Germans, realizing no trench-works could stand against the leveling fire of the British artillery, were seeking to make a wall of living human beings against the advance. The British and Germans agreed on one point—that the world had never seen so great a battle as that which began on April 6 and was still raging on April 24 all along the 125-mile line from Lens to Reims. The objective still was Lens. The civilian population of Lens had evacuated the town on April 13. Great fires showed that the Germans were destroying stores preparatory to their departure. British troops were then on the outskirts of the town.

The battle of Arras went on unabated without an issue in sight. What was coming to be regarded as the fiercest battle of the war ended in a virtual deadlock. All the British could do, with terrific and accurate artillery-fire, repeated and persistent attacks, was to storm here and there a fragment of trench, a few yards of a position. Once captured positions were almost always held, but the German reserves were too many and their courage too desperate to permit of anything like a sweeping victory. The deadly nature of the struggle and its tremendous importance resulted in a strict censorship. Both sides issued only brief official announcements telling little of the progress of events. Correspondents were permitted to tell almost nothing of the struggle in which the two armies were locked.[14]

[14] Principal Sources: The London *Times'* "History of the War," "Nelson's History of the War" by John Buchan, The *Evening Sun* (New York), Associated Press and United Press dispatches, The *Daily Telegraph* (London), The *World,* The *Evening Post,* New York; the "Military Expert" of The New York *Times;* The *Evening Sun,* The *Tribune,* New York.

III

GERMANS UNDER FIRE ABANDON THE AISNE
COUNTRY—ON THE HEIGHTS OF
MORONVILLIERS

March, 1917—May 6, 1917

THE whole Western Front had developed into one great
battle area in which the most important success was
won by the French. Inspired to new determination by the
wanton acts of destruction which the Germans had committed in their retreat, Nivelle's troops south of the Oise
pushed ahead in March almost unchecked, until they were
seriously threatening the country around Courcy and seemed
by April 1 to have reached the "Hindenburg line." Nivelle,
the hero of the later French successes at Verdun, was here
expected to achieve great results. In one sense he did that,
but in another he failed, as the sequel of the Aisne-Moron-
villiers battle, lasting more than a month, was to show.

The French by April 1 had driven the Germans from the
southern suburbs of St. Quentin and were only a mile from
the city itself, so that the fall of Hindenburg's stronghold
seemed possible. Charging with irresistible dash on a front
of six miles, the poilus scored the most brilliant success
since the German retreat began. Advancing through squalls
of snow and over ground deep in mud, they captured a position officially described as "very important," since it
dominated St. Quentin itself. Three villages through which
German lines ran were taken. As the gray-blue figures
swept down upon them, the Germans jumped from the
trenches and fled. Within a fortnight French troops under
Nivelle had delivered violent artillery attacks against the
Germans over a front of twenty-five miles, made important
gains of terrain, captured more than 10,000 prisoners and
large quantities of war material, all between Soissons and
Reims. From Soissons to Craonne, German first-line posi-

374

tions fell into their hands, while east of Craonne second-line positions were captured. Vigorous counter-attacks delivered by the Germans on several sectors were repulsed. Artillery for several days violently shelled the entire region. On April 9, when British activity along the front from Lens to St. Quentin almost ceased, owing to a heavy rainfall, the French launched their infantry in an endeavor to break through or press back the Germans from a point which was one of great strategic value. To the east, in the Champagne, violent artillery activity continued at the same time.

FRENCH OFFICIAL PHOTO.

GUNS SCREENED BEHIND AN UNDERGROWTH
These guns, forming a battery, are heavy 120 mm. French guns

By the end of the first week of April the French had cleared the enemy out of most of the devastated area in the angle made by the confluence of the Oise and Aisne. They had crossed at places the Ailette, a tributary of the Oise, and were entering the densely wooded region—Basse Forêt de Coucy and the Forêt de Gobain—which lay between the Ailette and the important railway centers of Laon to the east and La Fère on the Oise to the north. If the French could expel the Germans from the Craonne heights north of the Aisne and hold them, their position would threaten

the communications of the enemy in rear of the entrenchments between the eastern outskirts of Reims and the western outskirts of Verdun. The French attack, therefore,
formed an important part of the general advance, since it
might hold the Germans there as the main line of attack
and so divert attention from the left of the Allied line.
The British attack had, therefore, been in the first instance
preparatory to a more decisive operation by the French.

Berlin, admitting the ferocity of the French attacks, said
"a bitter fight was proceeding around our foremost positions." The French were thrusting at the Craonne plateau,
a position even more formidable than the Vimy Ridge, the
other end of the far-flung battle-line being already in the
hands of the British. Craonne was the lower hinge of the
Hindenburg line, or the pier, upon which Hindenburg
had hung a suspension-bridge during his great retirement.
The French were now trying to sweep northeastward, past
and around it, so that they could bring their guns to bear
upon its gentler slope. The vast cooperating drive of
the Allies was over a front that, in sky-line alone, covered
more than a hundred miles from the slag-heaps of Lens to
the rolling uplands and canal country through which the
French were smashing. Hindenburg faced a critical week.
Berlin referred to the operation as "a great French attempt
to break through with a far-distant object."

The mass-fire of guns, which never cleared for ten days,
rose steadily on the first day to a nerve-shattering pitch, and
then suddenly, all along the line, as by a stop-watch, the
continuous clangor ceased, and Nivelle's soldiers, thousands
and thousands of them, mile after mile of them, went over
the trenches and were seen trotting in the open. Black
patches of bursting German shell rained over them, but still
they pushed on, dropping here and there until their gray-
blue uniforms became part of the grayness of the day. In
churned-up trenches, the fighting, once the first lines were
massed, became a matter of man to man and of the most
savage nature. In a short time German prisoners, singly and
in groups, began to stagger back to the French positions,
caked with mud and trench-filth, and many of them blood-
soaked. The assault was long and carefully planned. For

a month French artillery had been pounding German positions.

Battle opened on the left of the line shortly after 8 o'clock on the morning of April 16 when the French infantry swept forward in an irresistible wave. In spite of stiff resistance, the Germans were driven back and inside of half an hour prisoners began streaming toward the rear by hundreds. The struggle was hottest east of Loivre, in the sector of Berry-au-Bac, and to the east of Craonnelle, but before noon the whole first line was won. On the right the action began a little later in the morning. Here the French met with a determined resistance and the fighting was terrible. After several hours of Homeric struggle the French infanry, thanks to the support of several hundred heavy quick-firing guns, forced their way into the German first line. It was a fine success, as the terrain was difficult and the positions were formidable. In the afternoon the Germans counter-attacked with extreme violence almost everywhere along the front. The majority of their reserves were engaged south and east of the Brimont Ridge. It was from the Brimont fort, built on a crest which dominates all the plain around, that the Germans had for two years periodically bombarded the city of Reims. The French were now very close to this ridge. In capturing Loivre they had drawn nearer Brémericourt and so gone far beyond the famous position which they lost in the first weeks of the war and failed to win back at the battle of the Marne. If the purpose of the "strategic retreat" of the Germans from the Noyon angle was to delay an expected attack by the Allies in the west, the failure of that strategy had now been signally demonstrated.

The Germans did not expect to give up the positions the British and French had taken; they had counted on the delaying power of the "strategic retreat," but it was now seen that this did not delay Haig and Nivelle at all. Strong positions which the Germans had been preparing for months, and even years, to defend, they were giving up, and had to stand on new positions, less advantageous in themselves and taken up after only slight preparations. Now was the time when Germany had been expected to attack Russia, march on Petrograd and excite a rebellion, but Germany was having all she could do to hold her Western Line, and she was not holding that. The entry simultaneously of the Belgians into Dixmude appealed to the American imagination as much as the great battles going on further down the line. It was the first earnest return of the Belgians to their own

ON THE YSER

Here once more in 1917 fighting occurred. Along the stream at Dixmude in October, 1914, took place a part of the great Battle of Flanders

country which they had been longing to see for two years. It was not much in itself, but the effect on the minds and morale of King Albert's sorely tried little army, when they found themselves going forward at last on their own soil, was incalculable. It stirred the American heart even more. Once more the Yser came into this history.

A German official report now referred to the losses of the "French, British, and Americans," in air-battles in Artois, the Aisne, the Champagne, and the Vosges regions, which could mean nothing except that a permission accorded by the French Government had been acted on and that Americans, who for two years had been fighting under the French flag, were going into action under their own banner. The Stars and Stripes were therefore now flying in battle for the redemption of France. The British in giving out casualty lists also mentioned "Americans," with their names and addresses, and the names of Americans killed and wounded were recorded at Ottawa. Two were killed and two lieutenants and seven enlisted men were wounded. It was significant that, on the casualty list of eleven Americans shot down in the taking of the long-embattled ridge, six were names of men from the Middle West, one from the Pacific Coast, one from the Mountain States, and three from the East.

With war raging along the entire Western Front, it was known that each detail of the offensive had been worked out at prolonged conferences between Nivelle, Haig, and the war councils of France and England. The part to be played by each belligerent had been definitely agreed upon, and a schedule arranged as for one great cohesive force. Various tasks were allotted along the wide-reaching battle-lines, and results thus far led to a conclusion that the supreme military test of the war was near at hand. It was planned that the British should strike from Arras while the French were still engaged at their artillery preparation for infantry hostilities along a wide front further south. The successes gained in the first stages of the British advance gave the French great confidence in their own enterprises. Indeed the whole struggle in the western theater promised to be titanic. The Allies were prepared as never before both in material and personnel and were cooperating with a smoothness which came from complete understanding and thorough appreciation of the work at hand. In fact, from this experience at Arras and on the Aisne was to come, in the next year, the appointment of a generalissimo in the person of Foch.

The great offensive of the French went on next day and resulted in further important gains, a continuation of which promised to menace the German front from Lens to Soissons. The fighting had made an extension of the line well into the Champagne, where evidence of its coming had been presaged by days of violent bombardment. The attack of the French was irresistible, despite snow and rain. South of Moron-villiers first-line positions over a front of nine and one-half miles were taken, and to the east and southeast a strongly organized line on a front of nearly eight miles was captured. German counter-attacks at several points were without result. Near Mont Carnillet, southwest of Moronvilliers, an especially violent one was broken up by French guns. On this sector more than 2,500 Germans were made prisoners. Midway between Soissons and Reims another counter-attack was repulsed, while still another, launched by the Germans near Courcy, north of Reims, was put down by Russians who guarded this part of the line. Thirteen thousand five hundred Germans had been made prisoners in two days' fighting, according to Paris, 11,000 having been taken in one day's attack between Reims and Soissons.

Official communications from Berlin said the French efforts to break through on the Aisne had failed and that there had been no renewal of the attack. A previous communication which described the battle as one of the greatest in the war, admitted that under terrific bombardment between the Oise and Condé-sur-Aisne, French shells "leveled

A FRENCH CHAPEL WITH ALTAR IN A WINE-VAULT AT REIMS
Champagne cases have been arranged for seats

the German positions and produced wide, deep craters, rendering an obstinate defense no longer possible." Two places, one of them Chivy, were captured by the French on the eighteenth and three desperate counter-attacks by the Germans in the Champagne were checked. France in fact had made gains in the greatest offensive movement yet undertaken, against an army that expected the blow and had massed gigantic reserves to stop it. For this reason the magnitude of the French achievement was the more notable. Probably four million men were now engaged in the Allied offensive in the west, making the combined attack the biggest battle of the war since the Marne. No previous conflict had seen that number of men engaged, nor had any conflict been marked by such a tremendous concentration of artillery.

It became a struggle between Hindenburg and the master strategists of the Franco-British staffs. Millions of shells were hurled over the lines daily. French marksmanship was so deadly that the first German prisoners caught in the infantry-sweep declared that of companies of 250 men, the average that survived was only eighty. From Soissons eastward into the Champagne the offense was continued unabated. Numerous new points of vantage were taken, prisoners and guns captured and violent counter-attacks put down. In three days' fighting more than 17,000 unwounded prisoners fell into the hands of the French, together with seventy-five cannon. On April 18, in the forest of Ville-au-Bois, where an enveloping movement was carried out, 1,300 threw down their arms and surrendered and 180 machine-guns were captured. Between Soissons and Reims the villages of Ostel and Braye-en-Laonnois were captured. The Germans left behind much war material and nineteen cannon. Between Juvincourt and the Aisne the Germans threw a counter-attack against the French line with about 40,000 men, but artillery repulsed the attack. South of St. Quentin the Germans also made attacks which failed. At the close of the third day of battle from Soissons to Auberive, the Germans for the first time in more than two years found themselves completely driven north of the Aisne. The last German hold on the south bank of the river, east of Soissons, forming the nearest point in their line to Paris, fell into the hands of the French on April 18.

This battle and the battle of Arras, as fought in conjunction with the battle between Soissons and Reims, was logically a return to the Allied autumn offensive of a year and a half before, when the French attacked in the Champagne while the British struck out for Lens and fought the sanguinary battle of Loos. At two points more than 100 miles apart, the Allies had attempted to cut through the German lines, with an idea that success would mean the collapse of the entire intervening section. Neither attempt, Champagne nor Loos, was successful. The French failure was due to the inherent difficulties of the task, but the British was due to

poor workmanship in war. It was probably recognition of
the fact that the British at that time were not expert enough in
modern methods to operate alone and unaided, that brought
about the plan of the Somme, in which French and English
armies fought together shoulder to shoulder. In 1917 the
main effort of the British and French was directed once
more at points separated by nearly one hundred miles, but
by this time the British had learned their trade and could
be trusted to shift for themselves. The plan of the offensive
offered, as one great advantage, that the enemy could not
concentrate his attention along a single front as he had done
at the Somme. He had now to watch his line in Flanders
and Belgium simultaneously with his line on the Aisne and
in Champagne.

Along the French offensive line alone, Nivelle's troops were
now opposed by eighteen divisions of reserves—285,000
men—but the French were believed to number twice that force
themselves. "One of the greatest battles of the war, and,
therefore, also in the history of the world, was in progress
on the Aisne," said Hindenburg's report, which spoke of
French gun-fire along the whole line as being "unprecedented in duration, volume, and intensity," and admitted
that the German positions were leveled, "rendering an
obstinate defense no longer possible." An admission that a
victory at arms was now necessary for the maintenance of
the German monarchy was made by Count zu Reventlow, the
uncompromising military Junker, writing in the Berlin
Tagezeitung, where he declared that "without a German
victory the German monarchy will soon cease to exist."
Maximilian Harden, noted since about the end of the first
year of the war as the frankest of German critics of German
aims and methods, declared that the general outlook was
"as black as could be, unless Germany could be saved by
conversion to Democracy." In a striking passage Harden
went on to say that, with Bagdad now English, with advanced British and Russian troops in contact on the frontier of Persia, with wide areas of the soil of France once
more in possession of the republic, with China in revolt
from Germany, with success for the British at Arras, and
with a new belligerent in 100,000,000 Americans who de-

sired for themselves neither land nor money nor even re-payment for the cost of the war, and who, with their idealistic solution, working upon the nerves of mankind, including other nations in Central America and South America—in these circumstances, Harden asked how it was "possible for any sober man who did not want to blush before Germany's warriors, to say in his madness that the results of these three months had at last wearied our enemies and set them whimpering for a feeble peace?"

On both wings of the fifty-mile front, from north of Soissons to Auberive in the Champagne, the French on April 19 scored further gains. On the right they stormed a powerful German position north of Auberive, over a mile long, and pushed up to the outskirts of Vaudesincourt, a mile beyond Auberive. Altho the Germans had thrown eighteen new divisions into the fight, they were unable to stop the French, who in the night stormed Mont Haut and other strong points above the Moronvilliers Ridge, and beat back a number of furious counter-attacks; eighteen German divisions would represent between 252,000 and 300,000 men, the number depending on whether they were two-brigade or three-brigade divisions. Since the beginning of the French offensive more than 19,000 Germans had been taken prisoners. The guns captured in five days exceeded one hundred, not including machine-guns. Abandonment of the Aisne be-tween Condé and Soupir was admitted by Berlin, which de-clared that this action completed their occupation of what they called the "Siegfried positions." Berlin said the French had "followed hesitantly."

Signs that Hindenburg had almost met his match in Nivelle and that the attack was stronger than the German defense were given in these and later operations. On April 20 a series of terrific German counter-attacks failed to take back one of the trenches the French had gained. Time after time the Germans tried to take them but they could not reach the French lines. The first phase of the French offensive had practically ended with some success. The Germans had been driven from old lines, held for more than two years, to new positions. Berlin admitted this, but said noth-ing of the cost—19,000 prisoners and 100 guns in five days' fighting, the greatest record of any trench-offensive by any army since the war began. On a considerable extent of the front from Soissons to Craonne, the Germans were retiring to their new line, the old line having been definitely broken. That the French had out-Hindenburged Hindenburg in this offensive was commonly held. French cleverness had been the same here as when they forced the Germans to accept ground previously chosen by them for the battle of the Marne. Hindenburg's "strategic retreat" for the purpose of forcing the French to accept battle on ground which the German Staff might choose, had failed. The French chose their own field.

The ability of the .French command to bombard without limit any point at any time had now seemed to give absolute certainty to an advance. Such a concentration of fire as the French poured in, just where they wanted it, completely wiped out every defensive device known to German genius or constructed by German labor since 1914. There was everywhere visible a titanic concentration of men, munitions and material. Valleys, woods and ravines were filled with cavalry, infantry, hitched batteries, munition-trains, automobiles, trucks, cannon—all either advancing or awaiting the word to dash to the front.[15] The failure of the Germans to resist this steady and methodical pressure of the French was the outstanding feature of the operations. It was clear that Nivelle's armies were in no danger of losing the initiative, and that gradually, but surely, all the salients along the Soissons-Auberive front would be crusht. The principal salient to which the Germans had clung formed an angle where the front, running south from St. Quentin, hinged to the line running eastward toward Reims. Caught as in a vise by the troops advancing northeast from Laffaux and northwest from Vailly and Chavonne, the angle collapsed when Fort Condé was captured. Substantial progress was also made in the center, ground being won east and west of Craonne, which was gradually being enveloped. The primary object of Allied strategy was not to pierce German lines, but to break German resistance on any line on which Hindenburg elected to stand and

15 Dispatch from Henry Wood, United Press correspondent.

fight. Possessing superior numbers, superior artillery and an enormous advantage in ammunition, the Allies proposed to use these deliberately and methodically, to break down both the physical and the moral strength of the Germans.

The simple question had become whether the Germans could long endure such constant pounding. In ten days they had lost nearly 35,000 prisoners and more than 300 guns. They had been driven from some of the strongest

A LOOKOUT EAST OF REIMS

This lookout was held for four years by the Germans and was not captured from them until October, 1918. It commanded a wide sweep of country

positions on their front and they had been unable, despite desperate efforts, to regain any of the lost territory. The testimony of figures as well as of eye-witnesses was available to show an unmistakable lowering of German morale. The conviction of the German soldier that the German machine was invincible, that his generals could not make mistakes, and that his enemy was beneath contempt—these ideas were passing away. The world was seeing a final test of endurance. It might be a long test or a short test, as German morale yielded quickly or slowly to superior numbers and guns. For the present the measure of Allied progress was primarily the number of guns captured, and, secondly, the number of men captured. The surrender of more than 200 guns at Arras, many of them large pieces, was a disaster the like of which no German army had suffered since Napoleonic times. It demonstrated a breakdown in morale and in organization which, however local it might prove to be, would have seemed incredible a year before and beyond conception before the battle of the Marne.

No man could say whether the modern German would endure defeat as the French endured it for many long months after Sedan, when all hopes of victory had vanished, but it was recalled that, after Napoleon's victory at Jena and Auerstadt, the Prussian army had melted away in a wild flight; that a single blow had destroyed the military structure of Frederick II. It was possible that such a collapse might come again. Many who knew Germany predicted that the first defeats would be followed by a complete breakdown—as was proved in 1918 after the second battle of the Marne. Germany had still some millions of soldiers, enormous reserves of munitions and of guns, and there was no military reason why she should not hold out through another year. After the North had established a complete superiority over the South at Gettysburg and Vicksburg, the South, altho beaten, resisted for two years longer. About a year separated the Wilderness from Appomatox.

The French fought with a ferocity they had never exhibited before. There was burning in them a desire to wreak vengeance on the despoilers of their land, the enslavers of their civilian men and women. They were fighting an enemy in every sense their inferior, man for man, an enemy who saw the only hope of victory in the grim task of trying to hold on, and when retreat became necessary to fall back as slowly as possible. There was all the difference in the world in the morale of the two forces, that intangible thing which spells the difference between victory and defeat. The Germans were feeling the pressure as they had never felt it before. Periodic lapses in the fighting occurred, in order that the French artillery might adjust itself to the advance and that stores of ammunition might be brought up over roads which had also to be improved to allow the passage of the transports. But Germans in the trenches knew that these lapses were only temporary breathing-spaces, and that in a short time they would have to face that hurricane of shell which blasted their strongest earthworks.

After five days of progress there had to be a drawing together of forces, leading to a pause. In the work of any of the armies taken as a whole there was no pause whatever, but all parts could not proceed at the same rate. When the French paused on the Aisne, the British, after a respite, resumed their advance from Arras. Thus to the Germans was left no respite. The time came when each Ally had to get its formidable fighting-machine forward for a distance of five miles into new positions and in such trim that a fresh bound could be made. Big guns presented only one of a hundred problems which the transport service had to solve. It was no doubt to minimize any possibility of the enemy's taking advantage of these intervals that the advance of the Allies went as it were by spasms, striking now here, now there, so that, while some part of the extreme front was always in violent activity, the solid organization of the movement as a whole was never lost.

By April 23 Germany had gone through her most disastrous period in the war. Nivelle's forces had captured more than 100 guns, taken 20,000 prisoners, occupied twenty relatively large villages—not including hamlets—or about fifty square miles of French territory, and inflicted losses in killed, wounded and missing estimated at 100,000. The estimate of the German losses was based on the number of prisoners taken and special information obtained by the French Staff, and were for the French drive alone. They did not include the achievements of the British. Nivelle had definitely wrested from Hindenburg the initiative. He had forced him to fight from trenches which the French commander-in-chief had himself previously chosen and had also forced him to throw into the Aisne battle his much-vaunted "strategic reserve army." [16] The usual formula among mili-

[16] Henry Wood, United Press correspondent.

tary experts is to estimate the casualties at five times the number of prisoners, but this five-to-one ratio did not hold good in the present case owing to the sanguinary character of the fighting. All reports showed that in some cases whole regiments were destroyed. Around Moronvilliers the French in terrific struggles had taken surrounding hills. Here in command was Anthoine, a Lorrainer, who had been chief of staff to Castelnau at Nancy. Degoutte also was here with his prized Legionaries from Morocco. Tunnels, quarries and grottoes were fought for in these hills.

On April 29 Pétain, who had commanded the French army defending Verdun during the critical stages of the battle in February and March, 1916, was appointed chief of staff. The new post conferred was one which at that time had not existed. On the first day of mobilization, in August, 1914, there had been a Chief of the General Staff who went to the front with the Commander-in-Chief. Meanwhile at the Ministry of War only a few officers and departments remained to keep up connections between the front and rear. The entire direction of army affairs, in short, had been taken to the front under Joffre. Matters remained pretty much in that condition until the spring of 1917, when it was felt that there should be in Paris, close to the Council of Ministers and the Council of War, a powerful organization capable of co-ordinating efforts at the front and at the rear, English and French efforts, French and Italian efforts. This new organization had now been created and Pétain was made its head. Nivelle was and still remained Commander-in-Chief of troops fighting at the front—that is, he directed and executed the operations of the war on the Somme and Aisne, in the Champagne and in Lorraine and Alsace. But his authority did not extend to the armies in preparation, or those being formed in the interior, nor did it extend to the English or the Italian army. Nivelle was, in a word, the great executive chief of war operations; but he was not the great directing chief. The latter was now Pétain. It was he who would prepare for great operations and coordinate them with English, Italian, and Russian operations.

When a great offensive was to be launched at a given moment on the Western Front, it would be Pétain's task to decide exactly when this offensive was to be carried out, at what point it was to be especially driven forward, what part in it was to be played by the French army, the Belgian army, and the coming American army. Once the place, the time, and the conditions were determined upon, Nivelle would assume the chief command in executing these operations, so far as the French forces were concerned. He would work out the details and have full power to put the offensive through. Pétain as French Chief of Staff, in short, was to be the motive power which, without hampering the freedom of movement of the immense machine of war, would assure coordination in its movements.[17]

In the French attack the objective was now Laon, the corner-stone of the new German line and one of the strongest military positions in northern France, which had been fortified since the days of Roman invasion. Laon stands on high ground protected by hills on the west and south, but on the east the land is lower and more level. It was from the east that the French planned to approach it. The Germans on May 6 hurled counter-attack after counter-attack against the French in their newly acquired positions northeast of Soissons, but their efforts were futile. Nivelle's men clung tenaciously to them and inflicted heavy casualties on the Germans. The greater portion of the eighteen-mile front had now been consolidated, and, as a result of two days' fighting, 6,100 prisoners were taken. Berlin's official communications declared that the French attempt to break through the line was unavailing, that the gigantic thrust had been entirely repulsed. It admitted, however, that the intense fire of the French guns had destroyed completely German positions at Winterburg and that this eminence and several adjacent sectors were occupied by the French. For the second time the French War Office announced the storming of trenches which were part of the "Hindenburg line" and behind the old line that the Germans had held for two years. A corps that took 1,800 prisoners captured almost an entire front of two-and-a-half miles of the "Siegfried" trenches.

As an expert axman, cutting down a tree, chops first on

[17] Stephen Lausanne in The *Times* (New York).

one side and then on the other. So the British and French were driving home alternate but increasing blows against the Germans. There were already two gashes in the Hindenburg line—one between Lens and Arras, the other between Soissons and the Champagne—and they grew deeper and deeper as the Allied steel cleaved toward the heart. Nearly the entire length of the Chemin-des-Dames, running along the ridge from Laffaux to Craonne, was now held by the French, whose guns dominated the Ailette Valley, beyond which there was no natural obstacle before Laon. Emphasis was laid upon the lightness of the French losses. Altho Paris was a potential hospital city, its thousands of cots were empty and very few wounded were arriving. So far the base-hospitals, usually swamped to overflowing during offensive actions, were accommodating all cases.

Now occurred another change in the French command. Pétain was appointed commander-in-chief of the armies operating on the Western Front, and Nivelle placed in command of "a group of armies," while Foch was called from his retirement, or from Italy to succeed Pétain as Chief-of-Staff at the Ministry of War. It had been understood that when Joffre's retirement was decided upon, the Marshal chose Pétain as his successor, but that Pétain was unwilling to accept the post unless he could have extraordinary powers. According to some reports, he desired to have command over the British forces in France as well as over the French. One month before his appointment to his new place, Foch had been detached from active service. The change as to Pétain was believed to be due to the fact that Nivelle, having had his chance, had measurably failed; that the lack of decisive results in the offensive on the French side had compelled a complete revision—not merely of commanders, but of methods. The return of Pétain may rather have meant the abandonment by the French of any general policy of attack, with a return to the policy of Joffre, which was one of defending rather than attacking, except in limited fields.

In any case the unlooked for return of Foch to active work in France, reopened a career which in many respects had been the most brilliant on the Allied side during the war. When the war opened, Foch and Pétain alike were colonels, serving as professors in military colleges. The restoration of Pétain was accepted among friends of France as strengthening, rather than weakening, the French army. Nivelle had been a brilliant experiment. Pétain was a tried and proved commander and Foch, who now stood with him,

"THE DRAGON'S CAVE"

The picture shows the entrance to a vast grotto under the Chemin des Dames. It was long occupied by Germans, who until 1917 kept a machine-gun active at the entrance

had been more successful than any other French general on the offensive. In that sense he was the greatest general the war had produced on any side.

The second battle of the Aisne lasted a little more than a month. It represented, in its main intention, a departure from the policy of the Somme—a departure which after the first day or two was not persisted in. It did not achieve the aim of the French High Command, which was the dislocation of the southern pivot of the "Siegfried line," and to that extent might be written down a failure. It did not even, as at Arras, gravely endanger any vital enemy center, and thereby put out of gear his whole plans for the summer. But it was far from being barren of results. It engaged and destroyed a large number of German divisions; it used up a quantity of the best German "shock-troops"; and it cost the enemy positions which were essential to his comfort, and, ultimately, to his security. Nivelle's reach had been heroic, but it had exceeded his grasp. Only by a succession of miracles could Nivelle have succeeded, and miracles, when they happen in war, come singly and not in battalions. He fell into the error of endeavoring to reap the fruits of victory before beating the enemy. It was the error of a gifted and generous and courageous spirit, but it was none the less an error. With Pétain, the French strategy returned to the patient, laborious, and deadly methods of the Somme.[18]

[18] Principal Sources: "Nelson's History of the War" by John Buchan, The *Evening Post*, The *Tribune*, New York; the "Military Expert" of The New York *Times*, Associated Press and United Press dispatches, "Bulletins" of the National Geographical Society.

FRENCH SCOUT IN A SHELL-TORN AREA

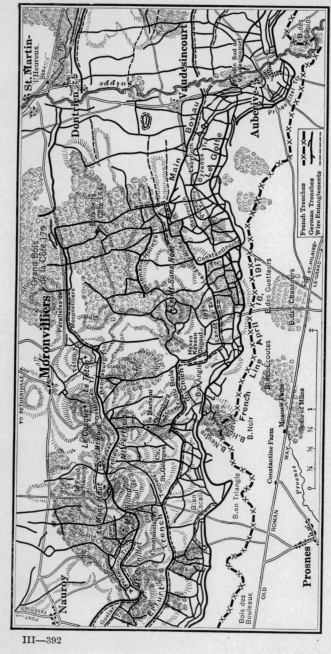

MORONVILLIERS HEIGHTS, EAST OF REIMS

Here on several occasions during the war, as was now the case in the autumn French offensive, fierce fighting occurred. The hilly country south and west of Moronvilliers is shown, but more remarkable than all that was the system of trenches also shown. It was from Moronvilliers that Gouraud in July, 1918, withdrew his forces south where, having effected a concentration, he was able to hold up the German advance, before Mangin struck south of Soissons.

THE BATTLE OF ARRAS—WITH FRESNOY AND BULLECOURT AS THE SECOND PHASE

May 1, 1917—May 29, 1917

THE Entente Allies, since the battle of the Marne, had liberated more than 50 per cent. of the territory in France invaded by the Germans in August, 1914. With advances east of Roisel and Croisilles, the department of the Somme had been entirely liberated, and the occupied territory in the Pas-de-Calais reduced to 10 per cent. In the department of the Aisne occupied territory had been reduced from 100 per cent. to 55 per cent. The entire territory invaded in August and September, 1914, comprised 8 4-10 per cent. of all France. The Germans at the beginning of 1917 held only 3 7-10 per cent of the whole of France, but since March 15 they had relinquished of that amount more than 10 per cent.

In proportion as the occupied territory was liberated the magnitude of the damage the Germans had done became apparent. A technical commission, basing its figures on inventories, estimated the probable total damage in the north of France at 15,000,000,000 francs ($3,000,000,000). The complete devastation wrought between the Oise and the Aisne showed that these figures were not excessive. Not only had buildings been destroyed, but the land had been rendered inept for cultivation over a great surface. Years of labor would be required to restore its producing capacity. The official appraisal of the property in this region for purposes of taxation placed the value of the land at 4,000,000,000 francs, the buildings at 4,800,000,000. The intrinsic value had been estimated at from 14,000,000,000 to 20,000,000,000 for land and buildings, both figures being under the actual, provided an appraisal were to take their producing capacity into account. People who had seen the ruins of Messina, and the havoc wrought in parts of San Francisco after the earthquake and fire, said that Messina, San Francisco, and Valparaiso, thrown in, with what one could conceive of Pompeii and Herculaneum, would scarcely enable the most vivid imagination to arrive at a conception of the realities seen in France.

By May 1, another period of intensive fighting, a second phase of the battle of Arras, was in progress over a front of about twelve miles from east of Vimy to west of Quéant. Using guns of all caliber, the British along the entire front surged forward in the early hours of the morning and throughout the day in glorious spring sunshine. Nightfall found them well in possession of several points of vantage which they had captured in face of stubborn resistance and held against counter-attacks. Berlin asserted that the British attempt to break through the German line had failed under heavy casualties. The British had made no claim that Haig had pierced the German front, but did assert that west of Quéant and near Chérisy goodly salients had been driven into the line and that the village of Fresnoy and positions north and south of the village, on a front of two miles, and a trench system north of Oppy, had been captured and held. The taking of Fresnoy fell to the lot of Canadians, who had pushed back the German line four miles since their capture of the Vimy Ridge, and now had the added honor of having cut their way through the "Hindenburg line." Altho the battle was fiercest and, for the British, most successful on its flanks, the fighting was intense over the whole front. The Germans used heavy reserves of men and guns and repeatedly attacked at points as far north as Loos. The Germans fought with desperate obstinacy. Several new divisions identified on different parts of the front, showed that they were still using their strategic reserves.

The second attack on the Arras front began twenty-three days after the opening of the first. The advance made measured five and a half miles in the direction of Douai, six and a half toward Chérisy, and nearly ten miles toward Bullecourt in the direction of Cambrai. Bullecourt is halfway between Arras and Cambrai, while Fresnoy is about half-way between Arras and Douai. While this rate of progress was not like the progress achieved in open battles in other days, it was immeasurably removed from the snail's pace of trench-fighting. More significant than the total amount of ground gained was the fact that half of it was won after the first rush. The attack of April 9 brought the British close to Vimy, but they had since advanced a greater distance, through Farbus and Arleux to Fresnoy. In other words, the offensive was a sustained instead of a spasmodic one. The British on May 1 were two weeks ahead of their attacking schedule. Not only had the advance been much faster than expected, but the losses were smaller; the losses were only one-half as large proportionately as those on the Somme offensive in 1916. This was attributed to better.artillery preparation and to the fact that the men were not allowed to outrun the guns.

One secret of British and French advances lay in the volume and accuracy of their artillery-fire. Correspondents told of the "chromatic accuracy" of French fire. Even seconds of time were vital, because a difference of a quarter of a minute between the watch of a battery-commander and that of an infantry officer might mean death to the soldier at the hand of his own gunners. For this reason all important watches were compared and set to the second. A time-table was prepared governing every gun and each group of infantry involved. Every shot, both as to distance and second of firing, advance of men, moment of movement and the ground to be covered in a certain period of time, was governed inexorably by it. Accuracy of fire and perfect co-ordination between gunners and infantry became vital factors in keeping down the casualty list, because, a heavy percentage of killed and wounded in all battles has been due to their own artillery-fire.[19]

Hurling wave after wave of field-gray clad soldiers against the British in Fresnoy, the Germans on May 9 recovered part of the town, then lost it, and finally recaptured it. Stubborn hand-to-hand fighting continued, but the Germans kept possession of the village. Fresnoy had been taken by the Canadians on May 3. At no point was fighting more des-

[19] James Keeley in The Chicago *Herald*.

perate. Fresnoy lay beyond Vimy Ridge, five miles southeast of Lens and seven miles northeast of Arras. In retaking it, the Germans evidently paid a heavy price. Preceded by artillery fire, in which asphyxiating-gas shells were used in large numbers, their counter-attack had been launched in the early morning. Machine-guns and rifle-fire from the defenders met them as they threw themselves forward, and finally penetrated trenches northeast of the village and entered the outskirts of the village itself. Their tenure of the position, however, was short-lived, for the Canadians returned to the fray and drove out the Germans. Reforming later and reinforced by two fresh divisions, the Germans made another bid for victory before the village wood. The right wing of the defenders held stedfastly, but the left, despite stubborn resistance, was compelled to give ground and evacuate the village. Berlin reported that 200 prisoners and six machine-guns fell into German hands. The recapture of Fresnoy nullified to a large extent one of the greatest successes of the Canadians in the battle of Arras. Its capture had paved the way for an advance of the British on the Drocourt-Quéant line, which alone stood between them and the Douai-Cambrai defensive system. Fresnoy stood on the Oppy switch-line, the second German defensive front, near its northern pivot. Its loss had ruptured this for the time being.

In a month's fighting British and French had captured more than 50,000 prisoners, nearly 500 cannon and almost a hundred square miles of territory, the largest achievement in any month since trench-warfare began, and the largest advance since the battle of the Marne. The Germans had also lost the initiative which they had sought to regain by their "victorious retreat" in March and a greater number of prisoners than in any other month in the war; moreover, they had lost a greater amount of artillery than ever before in a single month in the history of the German empire or of the Prussian monarchy. Their tactical defeat at Arras was greater than it had been at any point during the Marne fight. They were outnumbered at least two to one, and the reserves of British and French man-power were now far greater than theirs.

GERMAN RETREAT; ARRAS AND THE AISNE

As matters stood in Russia, the British and French now had to bear the brunt of fighting against the great bulk of the German army, with no possibility that parts of that army could be diverted to any other quarter. The Germans were free to throw into the western fighting their strength and their reserves, and to drain to a great extent the trenches on other fronts. In consequence, the western offensive slackened and after the middle of May was practically checked. It was not a question of Germany having more men than formerly. Statements by German authorities that she had more men under arms than at any previous time were mere talk and boasting. The point was that her forces had acquired greater mobility because of safety in other quarters and notably on the Russian front.

After days of intensive fighting in which positions changed hands many times, British troops recaptured a greater portion of the village of Bullecourt and repulsed violent counter-attacks east of the village. Along the Scarpe to the east of Arras the advantage rested with Haig's forces. The village of Rœux was also taken by the British, and another step forward made on the western slopes of Greenland Hill. The Germans made strong attacks on the plateau of Craonne, north of Reims, but the French put down three attacks with artillery and rifles.

The Germans received a heavy check north of the Scarpe on May 15 when, in massed formation, they stormed a position recently won by the British. British artillery "made the hillside look like a mushroom-farm," bulbs of shell-smoke sprouting up thickly over an entire field. Sheer weight and momentum had carried the Germans beyond the British outposts, but, like a rubber-ball, the rebound was instantaneous. Swiftly the defenders struck and after a short and hard fight, the Germans were thrown back with heavy losses, leaving the British established more securely than ever. In the meantime, the British strengthened their positions eastward toward Rœux and drew closer to Lens, where the Germans continued their work of wrecking. Buildings were blown up and machinery destroyed, in order that the great mining center should not be of use to the Allies after they had been forced to go.

Rainy weather now turned the battlefield into a mass of mud, practically precluding infantry attacks and affording the Germans an oportunity to retire to previously prepared defense-lines. A German withdrawal would have meant the evacuation of Lens, where fires had been burning for weeks. The destruction of the town was practically complete. All through this sector fires had sprung up, suggesting the same campaign of devastation which preceded the Hindenburg retreat. The "Siegfried line," on which Hindenburg had intended to stand before the battle of Arras began, was much stronger than the "Wotan system," which had been only a few months in building. The "Wotan line" was all that protected Douai, the British objective.

A greater army than that which Napoleon took to Moscow, measured numerically, had been put to fighting in the first month of this Western offensive—such was the magnitude of German losses. Not less than 600,000 casualties measured the cost of the battles of Arras and the Aisne. At Gettysburg, 160,000 men fought for three days with a casualty of but 45,000. At Waterloo the British lost only 14,000. In the greatest battle of the Franco-Prussian War not as many men were engaged on both sides as were killed, wounded and captured in six weeks at the battle of Arras. These great losses showed what attrition meant, and this was what the war had come to—an obliterating of the able-bodied manhood of Western Europe. In these four weeks the world had seen a supreme effort by the German military establishment. That effort had not yet been terminated, but it had caused a loss which sufficed to stagger a world already accustomed to horrors in three years of war.

So completely did the British artillery do its work on May 20 before an attack betwen Croisilles and Bullecourt, that 3,000 yards of the "Hindenburg line" were obliterated—that segment completely wiped out. While airplane photographs taken on May 1 had showed beautifully symmetrical zigzags, later pictures contained no trace of trenches. Of the supporting line some 6,000 yards were in British hands, leaving the Germans holding 2,000 yards. The prisoners taken from the Germans came mostly from the Forty-ninth Reserve Division, which had been recruited in the region of

Posen and Breslau and had come to the west from Roumania. All that remained of captured portions of the "Hindenburg line" were cement and concrete machine-gun emplacements. There was an underground corridor that ran
parallel to the support-trench thirty-five feet below surface.

By May 24 Allied general staffs considered operations for
the present closed. They were now to concentrate the energies of two armies for another offensive further north.
The lull in the fighting had no effect on the British aerial
offensive. Nightly British flyers dropt tons of bombs on
military establishments back of the German lines. Some of
the most desperate air-battles of the war took place. One
of these was at a height of 19,000 feet, or more than three
and one-half miles above the earth. In one duel a British
pilot, having run out of ammunition for his machine-gun,
got close enough to his antagonist to shoot him with his
revolver. One pilot said that when he first went to the war
in 1914 he flew a machine which took an hour and a quarter
to mount 6,000 feet, but an airplane which could not now rise
10,000 feet in well under ten minutes would be scrapped.
The toll of German planes destroyed in May mounted into
the hundreds. In one day's fighting thirty were accounted
for. Fifteen were seen to crash to the ground, fourteen were
driven down and got completely out of control and one was
shot down by artillery. One of the *mêlées* that occurred between six British and eight German machines was as thrilling as any aerial battle ever fought. It was waged at close
quarters throughout; so close, in fact, that wings scraped
against wings and fighting pilots could look each other
squarely in the eye. No sooner would a British pilot soar
up to the tail of a German machine than another German
was on his tail. This German in turn would almost immediately have another British pilot pouring bursts of
machine-gun bullets at him. At one time seven machines
were following each other in headlong fashion toward the
earth.

The battle of Arras was regarded with some truth as an
action complete in itself. It was a limited victory—that is
to say, it attained its immediate objectives; but, owing to
events outside the control of the British Command, it did

not as a whole produce the strategical result upon the Western Front that had been its ultimate design. It was, therefore, an action on the Somme model, a stage in the process
of attrition, the value of which had to be measured in terms
of its effect upon the enemy's morale and the efficiency of
his military machine. Judged by such standards it compared brilliantly with every previous British advance.

Meanwhile, across great waters, another empire, an un-
warlike empire of democracy, was gathering up its fighting
loins, and under tutelage from Balfour, Viviani and Joffre,
closeted day by day with Wilson in Washington, was sending to Europe sailors under Sims and soldiers under
Pershing, who within eighteen months were to render powerful aid in defeating submarines in the North Sea, and land
forces at Château-Thierry and St. Mihiel, in Picardy and
Flanders, and along the Meuse-Argonne battle-front, where,
when the armistice was signed, several divisions had fought
their way to Sedan.[20]

[20] Principal Sources: "Nelson's History of the War" by John Buchan, The
Sun (New York), The Chicago *Herald*, The *Tribune* (New York), Associated
Press and United Press dispatches.

A ZEPPELIN DESCENDING WHEN ON FIRE